# Rave reviews from fellow industry professionals

"High-net-worth clients unfamiliar with the techniques advisors must use to protect their clients' wealth will find this book an excellent education, as will advisors who aspire to this market. From collars and calls to estate taxes and charitable giving, True Wealth will guide those adept at making a fortune through the processes used to keep and maintain it. Explanations of complex subjects are lucid and liberally illustrated with examples that high-net-worth clients will take to heart."

**Marlene Y. Satter** – SENIOR EDITOR, *Investment Advisor* magazine

"True Wealth should find a large and receptive audience as the number of individuals with over $1 Million of investable financial assets grew rapidly throughout the 1990's and is expected to continue to grow at a rapid pace in the coming decade. Good advice is a very valuable commodity and this book provides lots of sound advice and insight for the increasing number of people fortunate enough to have achieved the 'magic million' status."

**Colin Deane** – PRINCIPAL, Global Financial Services Cap Gemini Ernst & Young, Toronto

"So you want to know how the wealthy think and invest? Then read the book written by the man who has been dealing with high-net-worth investors since the days they were just called rich people! Thane Stenner examines the many unique problems, opportunities and needs of this growing group of investors, drawing on a wealth of experience spanning more than a decade."

**Rob Bell** – VICE-PRESIDENT, Morningstar

"This is a unique book for anyone interested in the subject of wealth. It focuses on the financial challenges, problems and opportunities of the wealthy. The author shares his extensive experience in helping high-net-worth individuals deal with their assets. The parts of the book describing how the wealthy think about their wealth – and the common mistakes made by their respective personality types – makes for particularly interesting reading since it holds a mirror up to us all. The book's scope is wide and comprehensive with sections on topics such as business divestiture, stock options, and how to make charitable donations for the best effect. A fascinating and penetrating study."

**J. Mark Mobius, PhD** – MANAGING DIRECTOR, Franklin-Templeton Asset Management Ltd., PORTFOLIO MANAGER, Franklin-Templeton Emerging Markets Fund

"As a lawyer with 15 years of experience in assisting with the purchase and sale of entrepreneur-owned businesses, I've acted for many business owners who, having sold their business, suddenly realize they have a serious new responsibility – how to preserve their new-found wealth. Thane Stenner's book True Wealth answers this need. I strongly recommend that all business owners read this book – but especially business owners who are thinking of selling their business. True Wealth goes a long way to helping these new multi-millionaires preserve their hard earned fortune!"

**Don C. Sihota** – BUSINESS LAW PARTNER, Clark, Wilson, Lawyers, Vancouver, Canada

"Thane's experience gives him a unique insight into the challenges facing the wealthy. His thoughts and ideals concerning the responsibilities of the wealthy are especially important. This is a "must-read" book for everyone, but especially for the wealthy for "...to whom much is given, from him much will be required." (Luke 12:48)"

**Tim Collings** – PROFESSOR, Tech BC, V-Chip Inventor

"*Thane Stenner is a highly regarded private wealth advisor. His book,* True Wealth, *offers practical solutions to the unique challenges faced by the wealthy and the super-wealthy: how to protect and continue to grow their wealth amid uncertain markets, how to deal with the tax man, how to maximize the effectiveness of charitable giving, and how to simplify their financial affairs.* True Wealth *provides common sense and uncommon insight on these issues and more, backed by solid research and by case studies drawn from Thane's extensive experience. Whether you have $1-Million, $10-Million or $100-Million or more – or whether you simply aspire to be wealthy – you should benefit from reading* True Wealth *and applying some of its practical advice to your own financial affairs.*"

**Bill Sterling, PhD** – CHIEF INVESTMENT OFFICER, CI Global Advisors, FORMER GLOBAL CHIEF ECONOMIST, Merrill Lynch and BESTSELLING CO-AUTHOR, *Boomernomics*

"*Here it is at last. A book that is long overdue! Few individuals need as much guidance in their financial affairs as the wealthy, and even fewer advisors understand the plight of the wealthy as Thane Stenner does. If you're a high-net-worth individual, or expect to be one day, you need to read this book!*"

**Tim Cestnick, CA, CFP, TRUST AND ESTATE PRACTITIONER (TEP)** – AUTHOR, *Winning the Tax Game* and *Winning the Estate Planning Game*, MANAGING DIRECTOR, National Tax Services, AIC Group of Funds

"*True Wealth articulately addresses and provides solutions to the issues topical in the mind of the ultra-high-net-worth individual. It is an excellent educational and reference tool for advisors and their clients. Congratulations Thane, you certainly nailed it.*"

**Michael A. Lee-Chin** – CHAIRMAN AND CHIEF EXECUTIVE OFFICER, AIC Group of Funds

"*Essential reading for investors with substantial wealth.* True Wealth *explores the broad financial issues that wealthy investors need to understand and translates them into specific guidance and advice. Of critical importance, it goes beyond generalities and gets into the specifics required to make informed decisions – and does so in an engaging fashion which is easy to read and understand.*"

**Dan Richards** – PRESIDENT, Richards Buitenhuis Associates

"*Becoming a millionaire is just the first step. It's keeping your money and enjoying it that's the real challenge. Thane Stenner reveals the secrets of everlasting wealth in this highly readable and immensely useful book. A must-read for anyone who has achieved financial success.*"

**Gordon Pape** – BESTSELLING AUTHOR, *6 Steps to $1-Million* and *Buyers Guide to Mutual Funds*

"*My experience in discussing wealth management with more than 50,000 investors over the past ten years has me convinced that Thane has hit the nail on the head – the thing that wealthy people fear most is not being wealthy. This is one of the most encompassing and compelling treatments of the subject of managing money for high-net-worth individuals that I have ever seen – and from someone who knows whereof they speak.*"

**George Hartman** – BESTSELLING AUTHOR, *Risk is STILL a Four Letter Word*, COLUMNIST, *Investment Executive*

"*Taking on the life and financial challenges of the wealthy is a uniquely courageous thing, especially in a country that likes to skewer its rich and famous. Stenner, no stranger to this world, offers up an immensely readable abundance of personal and technical wisdom...the kind those with serious cash should not even remotely consider living without.*"

**Joanne Thomas Yaccato** – FOUNDER AND PRESIDENT, Women and Money Inc., Educating Women About Money, Educating Companies About Women, AUTHOR, *Balancing Act*

"Having known Thane on both a personal and a professional level for over ten years, I'm in a unique position to judge his talent. And I can say without hesitation that no one else I know is more capable of either talking about or solving the unique challenges facing wealthy people today. What makes Thane stand out is his understanding of not only the financial challenges of wealth, but the personal challenges — Thane understands the mindset of the high-net-worth investor as much as he does the financial strategies. Quite simply, True Wealth is a world-class resource written by an exceptional and trusted financial professional who works for a top-notch firm. A great addition to the library of every wealthy investor."

**Bill Holland** — PRESIDENT AND CEO, CI Group

"A must read for those who have accumulated wealth and for those who aspire to do so. It will provide you with a fascinating insight into how to maintain and grow your wealth for your own benefit. But just as importantly, it will also show you ways in which to steward your wealth for your loved ones and society at large as you define it. True Wealth will clearly help you define your 'True Self' when it comes to principled wealth accumulation."

**David R. Temple, TEP** — Insurance & Estate Planning Specialist

"Thane's track record speaks for itself. His expert insights on all aspects of wealth management will help make the road travelled by high-net-worth Investors smooth and profitable."

**Donald F. Reed** — PRESIDENT & CHIEF EXECUTIVE OFFICER, Franklin-Templeton Investments Corp.

"True Wealth is a must read for high-net-worth individuals and their advisors. Wealth accumulation, wealth utilization and wealth preservation are discussed with an insight never before put to paper. High-net-worth individuals will use True Wealth as a confirmation, or challenge, of their tax minimization strategies, balanced with the advancement of family, community and charitable objectives."

**Tom R. Kirstein, CA** — Kirstein, Neidig & Vance Chartered Accountants

"Stenner's book on wealth management is one of the most comprehensive books produced to date on the topic in North America. A powerful reference tool for the high-net-worth individual. An essential educational tool for the high-net-worth financial advisor."

**Kurt Rosentreter, CA, CFP, CIMA, TEP** — BESTSELLING AUTHOR AND RENOWNED WEALTH MANAGEMENT STRATEGIST, VICE-PRESIDENT, Private Client Services, AIC Limited

"While conventional wisdom says that wealth makes life easy, experience shows that achieving high-net-worth status actually creates many new challenges. But, as Thane Stenner shows in True Wealth, dependable wealth management solutions are at hand for anyone prepared to follow his logical and truly co-ordinated approach. Highly recommended!"

**Phil Cunningham** — PRESIDENT, Mackenzie Financial Services Inc.

"Thane Stenner has created a blueprint for keeping, building, and managing wealth. More importantly, this book addresses broader wealth management issues including taxes, estate planning, trusts and foundations. True Wealth is a comprehensive and cogent analysis of the key issues facing the wealthy and those who advise them."

**Robert Parnell** — PRESIDENT, Tremont Investment Management, Inc.
(WELL-KNOWN AND RESPECTED HEDGE FUND MANAGER)

"I have known Thane Stenner personally for over eight years and have watched him invest more time and resources into making his advisory practice one of the top in Canada, and become an expert on the high-net-worth investor. You do not achieve that without hard work and satisfied clients. Certainly wealthy people (and those aspiring to wealth) can benefit from reading this book. More importantly, serious financial advisors MUST read AND follow this book. Why? Because, those high-net-worth clients will become increasing dependent on your advice — advice that is best done with a true understanding of their life situation and the complex needs of the wealthy."

**Stephen J. Kangas, CA, CFA** — MANAGING EDITOR, Fundlibrary.com

"You won't 'get' this book unless you've already got real wealth. For those who do, the book offers something I've never seen from any guide to money: enduring perspective. Thane knows what you're going through. His perspective is enhanced by the years of work he's done with families that have real wealth. This fabulous book is the one important read you need this year. Share it with your family and friends."

**Duff Young, CFA** — CEO, FundMonitor.com Corp., BESTSELLING AUTHOR AND COLUMNIST, *The Globe And Mail*

"Believe it or not, the simple thing is making money...most everybody with a bit of entrepreneurial spirit has that chance once or even several times in their working life. The tough part is keeping it and making it grow...Thane's book is a simple guide that gives you the building blocks to keep and grow your fortune. A great and easy read."

**Michael Levy** — FINANCIAL ANALYST, CKNW Radio, Vancouver Canada, SENIOR EXECUTIVE VICE-PRESIDENT, Custom House Currency Exchange

"Busy executives in fast growing companies (private or publicly traded) have little or no time to spend on managing their personal financial affairs. Very few financial advisors understand the many challenges and risks that face today's business owner and corporate executive as well as Thane Stenner does. Thane understands the value of time and his new book offers many insights and recommendations that will help "wired" executives regain their family balance, control their financial futures and reduce the risks of having all their eggs in one business basket. The sections on selling businesses and dealing with concentration risk are worth the cost of entry alone. True Wealth is a blueprint for showing busy executives how to protect their hard earned assets and enjoy life by knowing that they have secured their wealth."

**Christopher Hanna, PhD** — PRESIDENT AND CEO, TeraMEDICA Inc., Milwaukee, WI, USA

# true
# wealth™

An expert guide for high-net-worth individuals
*(and their advisors)*

## Thane Stenner

with James Dolan

True Wealth Enterprises, Inc.
123 – 1600 West 6th Avenue
Vancouver, British Columbia
Canada V6J 1R3
www.truewealth.ca

**National Library of Canada Cataloguing in Publication Data**
Stenner, Thane, 1964–
  True wealth

ISBN 0-9689544-0-5

1. Rich people--Finance, Personal. 2. Wealth 3. Finance, Personal
I. Dolan, James, 1971–  II. Title.
HG179.S539 2001     332.024'0621     C2001-911538-5

Note: True Wealth contains the opinions, thoughts, and ideas of the authors. It is sold with the understanding that the publisher is not engaged in rendering professional services. If professional advice or other expert assistance is required, the services of a competent professional person should be sought.

Readers should be aware that the opinions and interpretations expressed herein are of the authors and do not necessarily reflect the current opinions or attitudes of CIBC Inc. or its affiliates worldwide.

Production Credits:
Cover, text design, and electronic formatting: Natalie Clark, The Newsletter Factory
Book jacket photography: Sommerfield Photography, Vancouver, Canada
Printer: Friesens, Manitoba, Canada
Printed and bound in Canada

*I dedicate this book*
*to my love, Darci Stenner,*
*my beautiful family, and God.*

# Contents

# List of charts/graphs/tables

# Acknowledgements

Writing a book is a monumental task – something you can't do by yourself. If not for the help and ongoing assistance of the following, *True Wealth* wouldn't exist.

There have been a number of industry professionals who have provided valuable feedback throughout this project. You'll see many of them listed on the first few pages of this book. In particular, I'd like to thank Bill Sterling for his gracious preface, Bill Holland of C.I. for providing some valuable insight into recent fund industry developments, and David Temple, who proved himself a reputable authority when it came to tax and estate planning information. Rob Bell and Stephen Burnie from Morningstar provided a number of excellent charts, graphs, and other data, while Rob Parnell of Tremont helped give me an insider's perspective on hedge funds and alternative investments.

A number of people have offered valuable insight with proofing, editing, and layout suggestions. I'd like to extend my thanks to my colleague Barbara Podor, my father-in-law David Steffins, my good friends Tim Collings and Eric Vanderham, and of course, my wife Darci for all their help throughout the writing of this book. I'd also like to thank my personal assistant, Lisa Cindrich, whose organizational talents have been greatly appreciated over the past year. At head office, I'd like to mention Gary Mayzes, Sophie Fillios, Frank Tucci, and Steve Darley for their comments and suggestions regarding content and structure.

Last but not least, I'd like to thank the people who have helped put *True Wealth* together: Natalie Clark, Cindy Sommerfield, Jeff Thorsteinson, and in particular, James Dolan. This project has certainly been a long haul, but working with you made it a real pleasure.

Thank you.

# Foreward

**Bill Sterling** – Chief Investment Officer, CI Global Advisors, LLP

T hane Stenner is a leader among a new breed of financial professionals. As an Investment Advisor for CIBC World Markets, he focuses on providing a wide range of financial services to high-net-worth individuals (HNWIs), or those with more than $1 million to invest. Thanks to the tremendous wealth creation of the last decade, the ranks of wealthy investors have expanded rapidly. That has created the need for highly specialized wealth advisors who can help wealthy investors face the unique challenges of protecting and growing their wealth.

There have always been private wealth advisors serving wealthy investors. But the profession has evolved rapidly in recent years from cottage industry status, where untrained advisors played a jack-of-all-trades role, to an increasingly technical profession requiring highly specialized training and access to research, sophisticated products, and other resources that typically are available only at large, well-capitalized financial institutions with a global presence. That explains Thane's affiliation with CIBC World Markets, which is among the leading providers of financial advisory services to wealthy individuals in North America – and which has exacting standards for the training and accreditation process of its advisors.

Through my association with CI Funds, I have known Thane since the mid-1990s, when I began managing mutual funds for some of his clients. Thane and I shared a common view about the growing importance of the wave of aging baby boomers to financial markets, and about the extraordinary opportunities for wealth creation that were being created by the technology revolution and the globalization of the world economy. A logical extension of some of these themes is that we are likely to see a growing number of wealthy individuals who will be in need of what Thane calls "personal CFOs" – i.e., personal chief financial officers.

Just as corporations have had to employ chief financial officers with increasingly specialized training in complex areas like financial derivatives and currency hedging, wealthy individuals now need highly trained advisors who are capable of providing integrated services touching on all aspects of their financial lives. In *True Wealth*, Thane provides facts and figures about the wealthy and super wealthy that document the growing importance of this class of investors and highlights the role of a private wealth advisor – or personal CFO – in prudently managing their wealth.

Who are the high–net–worth individuals this book seeks as readers? The group obviously includes wealthy celebrities including sports stars, entertainers, and corporate moguls. But as Thane documents, the ranks of high- and ultra-high-net-worth individuals also include an increasing number of not-so-famous "millionaires next door" who may be retired corporate executives, successful entrepreneurs, IPO insiders, hard-working people who have invested successfully, or those who simply chose their parents well. While the individual circumstances of these individuals can vary widely, they all share certain common problems when it comes to protecting and growing their wealth.

What should corporate executives do if too much of their wealth is tied up in their company's stock? Are there efficient ways to diversify their exposure without paying too much in taxes? How can individuals best deal with the complications associated with selling a private business or commercial property? How can estate plans be set up to minimize estate taxes and also deal with the particular personal and tax circumstances facing the heirs? How should individuals deal with windfall inheritance or business gains? Should they invest the proceeds immediately or on a dollar-cost-averaging timetable? How can donations to charity be structured to be efficient from a tax perspective? Most of *True Wealth* is devoted to addressing these types of practical issues facing wealthy investors, and is based on case studies resulting from Thane's extensive experience.

One of the most interesting sections of the book is on the "psychographics" of wealthy individuals, which deals with sensitive issues surrounding how people's personalities can get in the way of prudent and efficient management of their financial affairs. Thane describes an entire spectrum of personalities ranging from prudent financial stewards, who are easy to work with, to investment phobics who are afraid to make decisions, to controlling corporate moguls who have trouble delegating responsibility for their financial affairs even when they might be better off to do so. I have long felt that one of the most important roles of financial advisors is to help people deal rationally with the complex emotions associated with managing money, and Thane provides an excellent account of the human side of investment management.

Whether you have $1-million, $10-million, or $100-million or more – or whether you simply aspire to be wealthy – you should benefit from reading *True Wealth* and applying some of its practical advice to your own financial affairs. Thane begins *True Wealth* with a simple statement: "Congratulations, you're rich." I will end this preface by congratulating Thane on producing an excellent guide that will show wealthy investors, and their advisors, how to handle their riches.

Happy total returns!

**Bill Sterling,** PhD
Chief Investment Officer
CI Global Advisors, LLP

---

*William Sterling, Chief Investment Officer of CI Global Advisors LLP, has 17 years of Wall Street experience. He has worked on the staff of General Motors as Senior Economist with the Competitive Analysis Group, and at Merrill Lynch as Chief Strategist. He was Global Strategist and Portfolio Manager for BEA/Credit Suisse Asset Management before founding CI Global Advisors. He is co-author of **Boomernomics**, a book advising how to integrate demographics and investing.*

*Mr. Sterling has earned an MA and PhD in economics from Harvard University and studied at the University of Tokyo as a Fulbright Scholar.*

# **Welcome** to wealth

*"It requires a great deal of boldness and a great deal of caution to make a great fortune; and when you have got it, it requires ten times as much wit to keep it."*

**Meyer A. Rothschild**

# **C**ongratulations. You're rich.

I don't know exactly how you managed to get here. Maybe you came into your wealth suddenly – perhaps through an inheritance, or some other unexpected event. Maybe you built your wealth over time – perhaps by slowly building a business from the ground up. Maybe you are an executive for a large corporation – one that granted you a generous stock option package. Or maybe you are a working professional – one whose profession commands an enviable salary. You could be an actor or an entertainer – someone who has turned sport or acting talent into fame and fortune. Or maybe, just maybe, you became wealthy the old fashioned way – by regular and judicious investing.

Whatever route you took to acquire it, your wealth probably came at a price. Whether you had to sacrifice your time, your privacy, or some of the routine consumer goods that other people were busy enjoying while you were busy saving, I'm sure it took a significant effort in order for you to become wealthy. Just in case no one's given you a pat on the back yet, let me be the first to congratulate you on overcoming these challenges and achieving a significant financial goal.

## *So what's next?*

It's an important question. And in my experience, it's a question far too few wealthy people ever ask themselves. I suppose that's only understandable. To a large extent, our society is more interested in the accumulation of wealth than in the safekeeping of it. And that's too bad. Just because you've reached a certain level of wealth doesn't mean the financial challenges are over. There's no denying wealth can bring great freedom – the freedom to enjoy luxuries and advantages most people never have a chance to enjoy. But along with that freedom comes an entire range of new responsibilities, new challenges, and yes, new problems.

None of this would matter too much if wealthy people had resources that could teach them how to handle these new issues. But as a quick scan of your local bookstore will tell you, there are precious few books that aim to show wealthy people how to navigate through the many financial and lifestyle challenges that accompany wealth. All this at a time when the need for those resources is critical: after nearly a decade of tremendous growth, there are more wealthy people today than at any other time in history. All of which has made the simple question of *what's next?* a very important question indeed.

## The concept of true wealth

This book is built around a simple concept of what wealth really is – and what it isn't. No matter what the dictionary may tell you, wealth is more than just money. Wealth is the capital – intellectual, emotional, financial, or otherwise – which an individual uses to achieve a given quality of life. Those who are wealthy have *secured* this capital. They have achieved an intellectual, emotional, and financial balance that allows them to lead a fulfilling, complete life, and to make a positive impact on the people and the causes they care about. *This I what I mean when I talk about "true" wealth.* Because at the end of the day, it simply doesn't matter how much money you have – if you don't have the ability to lead the life you want to lead, *you're not wealthy.*

Given this definition, the end goal of wealth management becomes clear. Contrary to popular belief, wealth management is not about accumulating more money, but rather about securing a high quality of life. Investments and strategies that lead the individual toward this security – these should be followed. Investments and strategies that distract or mislead the individual from this goal – these should be ignored. The purpose of this book is to show you how to tell the difference between the two.

## The $1-million mark

So what does my definition of *true wealth* mean in practical terms? Well, among other things, it means there is a significant difference between those who have the financial means to secure their quality of life *right now*, and those who aren't quite there yet. Speaking from the experience I've had in managing wealth — an experience that stretches back nearly fifteen years now — individuals reach that point once their investment accounts hit the $1-million mark. It is at that point that you have the ability to secure a high quality of life without ever having to work again. It is at that point that you become what we financial professionals call a "high-net-worth individual." It is at that point that you need to read this book.

I'm not just picking that number out of a hat. I've seen it happen to many clients: once you have investable assets of $1-million, things start to change. At this level of wealth, new financial challenges will arise. So will new opportunities — opportunities that simply didn't exist before. What's more, at this level of wealth, you'll begin to experience a number of changes to your everyday life — some of which you will welcome, some of which you won't. The decisions you make about how to react to these financial and life changes can have a profound effect on your financial security — and by extension, your quality of life. The purpose of *True Wealth* is to teach you how to prepare for these changes, and how to make the right decisions when it comes time to react to them.

Don't get me wrong here: I have met some wealthy people who are exceptions to the general rule. Such people often have few personal or family relationships, and deliberately choose to keep their financial matters as simple as possible, often at the expense of a larger net worth. I have also met people in the opposite situation — people whose investment account falls shy of the $1-million mark but whose financial situation is complex enough to demand extra attention. Both groups are in the minority. On average, the change starts to happen once people accumulate $1-million in investable assets. It is at this significant milestone that most people understand they are playing in a different league.

## What this book will teach you . . .

*True Wealth* is the most extensive, most comprehensive guide on the subject of wealth management written in quite some time. To my knowledge, it is also the only one written exclusively for wealthy people. Simply put, if you or someone you know is wealthy, this book will show you how to successfully navigate through the financial and the lifestyle challenges brought on by your wealth.

A complicated subject, to be sure. But I think you'll find *True Wealth* somewhat easier to digest than your typical financial handbook. For one, I've tried to stick to a crisp, conversational tone, and have kept the jargon to a minimum. Yes, some of the chapters do get a little complicated. But for the most part, I've tried to structure our discussion as if we were talking in person, in an everyday language everyone can understand. Sprinkled throughout the chapters are graphs, charts, and diagrams that I regularly use to clarify strategies and concepts with my high-net-worth clients. I've also tried to tie down the more theoretical portions of the book with examples taken from real life – this should help to make the more complicated parts a little easier to understand. Finally, at the end of every chapter, I've presented a brief point-form summary of the important concepts we've covered, making it easier for you to digest the information *True Wealth* presents. The end result should be a clear, direct explanation of complicated financial topics, presented in a language that won't put you to sleep.

The content of *True Wealth* follows a logical sequence, a sequence that roughly corresponds to the approach I take with my clients. The first section establishes the parameters for our discussion of wealth. In this section, we'll define our terms, explain who the wealthy are, and talk about how wealthy people actually *think* about their money. I'll also give you a "code of conduct": some rules that should guide your relationship with your wealth. We'll also take a close look at some case studies that illustrate some of the more common wealth scenarios – situations in which wealthy people like you have had to overcome financial or lifestyle challenges. All this should give us a solid foundation for understanding the specific wealth management products and strategies we discuss throughout the book.

In the second section, we'll take a close look at some of the issues that surround the ongoing management of wealth. I'll start by explaining some of the principles that guide my own investment decisions, and the decisions I make for clients. I'll then move on to an examination of some of the specific challenges and risks facing wealthy investors, as well as some of the possible strategies that will help you overcome them. As you read, you may find a chapter or two that's not really relevant to your individual financial situation. Fair enough – feel free to skip ahead to one that's more important to you. That said, understand that I've tried to organize the content in *True Wealth* around wealth management *concepts* rather than specific strategy suggestions. Which means you should find at least *something* of value in nearly every chapter.

We'll talk about passing on wealth in **section three**. In my experience, this is an area of wealth management many wealthy people are a little reluctant to talk about. Yet it remains one of the most important ways to secure wealth for the long term. We'll take a close look at some of the most important issues surrounding estate planning – taxation, trust structures, charitable giving – and back that discussion up with illustrations and case studies drawn from real life. At the end of the day, you'll be in a better position to ensure your wealth keeps on doing what you want it to do long after you're gone.

In section four, we won't talk about money at all – at least not directly. Rather, we'll discuss some of the life changes that wealth forces an individual to confront, and provide some general advice on how to deal with them. Strangely enough, these are the topics that have largely gone ignored by writers and other experts when considering wealth. I say strange because as I'll reiterate throughout *True Wealth*, wealth management is about more than just managing your money – it's about managing your life as well. For those looking to not only secure their wealth, but secure their *quality of life*, section four will be the most valuable part of this book.

## . . . **and** what it won't

As extensive as it is, there are a number of things this book won't teach you. It won't tell you what will be the next "hot" market sector. It won't discuss cutting-edge strategies and new investment approaches that will turn you into a billionaire overnight. And it definitely won't tell you how to bend the tax laws to your advantage, or how to set up a secret bank account to hide assets. All these topics might make for interesting headlines, but they have little to do with making *true wealth*.

Perhaps most importantly, this book will not teach you how to *make* a million dollars. There are plenty of books that can help you do that – I'm sure some of them are even worth the money. Instead, *True Wealth* will focus on what to do once you already have wealth. That's not to say those who are still striving toward $1-million won't find this book valuable. In fact, if you're expecting to join the ranks of the wealthy in the near future, this book may be the most important one on your shelf. Many of the concepts I discuss and the strategies I illustrate will become very important to you before too long. Many of the case studies I provide demonstrate financial problems other wealthy people had to learn from the hard way. By learning about them now, you may well be saving yourself a good deal of financial hardship in the future.

## **Who I am,** what I do, and what I think about wealth

Before we begin, I think it's important to tell you something about who I am, what I do, and what I think about wealth. As an Investment Advisor and First Vice-President with CIBC World Markets, a firm that provides wealth management services for a good many high-net-worth individuals in North America and around the world, wealthy people hire me to be their advisor, their confidant, and their financial coach. In other words, they look to me to be their their personal Chief Financial Officer. An important job, to say the least. I oversee money decisions, make appropriate recommendations, and ensure my clients do whatever needs to be done in order to secure their wealth and build upon it. This, in a nutshell, is what I do for every high-net-worth client that comes through my door.

Working with these people has given me a unique insight into the needs and desires of the wealthy – and a unique perspective on what difference wealth makes to one's life. If I could boil down what I have learned from these many experiences into a single piece of wisdom, it would be this: *it is more difficult to stay wealthy than it is to become wealthy*. Those who have attained a certain level of wealth – enough to allow them to enjoy life without worrying about the day-to-day financial obligations most people face – they have different needs than those still busy acquiring it. The simple fact of the matter is, wealth does not solve all problems – either financial or personal. If you're wealthy, some of the most difficult, most complex financial (and life!) challenges may still be ahead of you. If you wish to *stay* wealthy, you'll need to be fully aware of what those challenges are, and what options you have available to solve them. It is for this select group of people that *True Wealth* is written.

## **Housekeeping** issues

Now that I've given you a general understanding of what this book is all about – and what I'm all about – it's time to teach you more about wealth. Before we start, however, there are a number of "housekeeping" issues I need to address.

### Client **confidentiality**

As I mentioned a little earlier, I'll be using case studies to illustrate how specific wealth management strategies work in the real world. At the same time, as a practicing wealth advisor, it's my duty to protect the confidentiality of my clients – and that's a responsibility I take very seriously. These two positions have demanded a compromise when it comes to some of the finer details in the case studies. A lot of these cases come from my own experiences with real-life clients. Others come from within my firm. Some of them come by way of conversations with colleagues. Still others I've read about in various industry publications. No matter where they come from, I've tried to preserve the confidentiality of the people involved by modifying names, dates, and certain non-essential details of each case study. But while I admit to having shifted some of these details around, I have by no means *distorted* the underlying circumstances. The essential elements of each case study remain the same, and serve to illustrate some of the most important points of wealth management. They remain essential reading for everyone with a significant net worth.

## Global **scope**

I live in Canada, and I work in Canada. But like most Canadians, I've always been aware that I live in a "global village." To that end, I've tried hard to write about concepts applicable to high-net-worth individuals all over the world. While the rules and regulations that give shape to the following strategies may be slightly different where you live, *the concepts that form the underlying framework of the entire book are universal.* It simply doesn't matter what corner of the globe you're from: the challenges of wealth know no boundaries.

But while wealthy people live all over the world, there are only a few places in the world keeping statistics on them. Which brings up a problem: how does one write a book on wealth management with a global perspective using regional or country-specific data? A compromise seems appropriate. Throughout *True Wealth*, I cite global data whenever I can. But instead of excluding country-specific statistics altogether, I've included them where they occur, and tried to avoid making global conclusions based on regional data. The result is a mixture of statistics focused primarily on North America, but with significant global scope. At the end of the day, I feel this mixture does do justice to the international character of the high-net-worth population, and is a fair reflection of the opportunities and challenges wealthy people face, whether they face them in New York, Toronto, or London.

## Resources

No single book on wealth management can cover every conceivable topic. Which is why I've included suggestions for further reading at the end of every chapter. A good many of these suggestions have a space reserved on my personal bookshelf; those that don't come with hearty recommendations from close colleagues and U/HNWI clients. In addition, I've included a number of on-line resources. At the time of writing, these links were operational, but considering how fast the Internet changes, some of them could well be out of date at the time you read this. And remember, some of the information may not be relevant to your personal situation – or, even worse, it could be inaccurate. Make sure to doublecheck with a qualified professional before acting on any advice given over the Internet.

## Website

While I've tried hard to ensure the content of *True Wealth* is timeless, it is possible the passage of time will make the strategies and issues I raise somewhat obsolete. Not to worry. I've constructed a website that will provide ongoing coverage of a variety of wealth and lifestyle related topics, meaning U/HNWIs will always have a current source of information on the strategies and other issues raised in *True Wealth*. The next time you're online, surf on over to *www.truewealth.ca* and take a look around. You'll find case studies, articles of interest, and a variety of additional resources for U/HNWIs looking to supplement their knowledge of wealth topics. And if you'd like to order another copy of *True Wealth* for a friend, a family member, or a colleague, you can do that too. All in all, a pretty useful site to visit.

## Credit **and acknowledgements**

Throughout *True Wealth*, I've relied on numerous examples, statistics, charts, and other data, all compiled from a wide variety of sources. I have made every effort to give these sources their just due by crediting them where applicable. If an error or omission has been made somewhere, please write to me care of the publisher. Alternatively, please email me at thane.stenner@cibc.ca.

By now, I hope I've peaked your interest – and maybe raised a few questions too. I'll try to answer them as best I can in the pages that follow. In the meantime, I'd like to once more congratulate you for making it this far – not only in this book, but in your life as well. You've successfully completed what I consider to be the first step toward achieving *true wealth*.

Here's what to do next.

# section 1

## Considering wealth

What is wealth? Who are the wealthy?
And what do they think about their
money? Before we talk about wealth, we
have to know what we're talking about.

# The rich *are* different

chapter

1

*"Let me tell you something about the very rich. They are different from you and me."*

**F. Scott Fitzgerald**

*"Yes, they have more money."*

**Ernest Hemingway, in reply to Fitzgerald**

Yes, the wealthy are different from the rest of the population. They face different challenges. And they have access to different opportunities. But what — or rather, who — do we mean when we use the word wealthy?

Rich, wealthy, affluent — there are many different words that describe those with a high-net-worth. And these words mean different things to different people. For the purposes of this book, however, I will keep my definition of "wealthy" rather strict: when I talk about the wealthy, I mean those people who have at least $1-million in investable assets. I will refer to these people as *high-net-worth individuals*, or HNWIs for short. Those who have more than $10-million in investable assets I will call *ultra-high-net-worth individuals* (UHNWIs). Those who have more than $100-million in investable assets I will call the *Superwealthy*.

These are the definitions I'll be using throughout this book. To make things easier on both of us, though, I'll be using the acronym U/HNWI to indicate all three groups collectively. Understand, however, that when I use the term, I'm not trying to eliminate the differences between these groups. As I'll explain, each of these groups is slightly different than the others — different in the way they became wealthy, different in the way they manage their wealth, different in the way they *think* about wealth. They will face slightly different challenges when it comes to securing their wealth, and they will be able to access slightly different opportunities when it comes to enlarging their wealth.

To understand what wealth is all about, we need to take a closer look at each of these groups, and try to understand the relationship each of them has to their wealth. That, in a nutshell, is the purpose of this chapter. By the end of this chapter, you should have a good idea of who the wealthy actually are, how they acquired their wealth, and what wealth means to them. This will help give us a solid starting point for our examination of the central issue of this entire book: that is, what these people should be doing to ensure they *stay* wealthy.

Before we start, I'd like to return to my basic definition of a high-net-worth individual, and draw your attention to two key words that communicate a couple of essential concepts behind my definition.

## The importance of *investable* assets (rather than just assets)

The first of these is the word "investable." As in, *investable* assets of at least $1-million. By that I mean readily available for placement in capital markets, separate from money tied up in a property (either residential or commercial) or an ongoing business concern. Yes, such illiquid assets certainly represent wealth, and the people who hold them do deserve to be called wealthy in their own right. But for the purposes of this book, they are not the people I mean when I speak about high-net-worth individuals.

Let me clarify my position by way of an example. I live in the Vancouver area of British Columbia, Canada, a region that has experienced one of the greatest real estate booms in North America. The reasons for this boom are complicated, but suffice it to say that over the past thirty years, the once sleepy, laid-back town of Vancouver has blossomed into a world-class city – a city everyone wants to visit and where many want to live. The people who lived here before the boom have seen the value of their homes rise exponentially – in some cases at a rate far exceeding market returns. In 1980, a modest home on the west side of the city cost something like $170,000. That same home is now worth anywhere from $600,000 to $1,000,000. Couple that with the other assets people typically accumulate over a lifetime – a small investment account, a retirement account, a life insurance policy – and it's relatively easy for many of these people to accumulate $1-million.

Again, I'm not saying these people aren't wealthy. And I'm not dismissing the financial challenges they face. *But these challenges are very different from the ones experienced by those who have liquid assets.* Those who have the bulk of their assets tied up in a piece of property (what I call the "real-estate-rich") don't have to make the same day-to-day decisions about their wealth as U/HNWIs do. Sure, they may have to paint the house once in awhile, but they don't have to monitor its growth, redistribute or reallocate it every quarter, or hire a professional manager to supervise its performance. More importantly, it is quite possible for the real-estate-rich to deal with most of their financial challenges with standardized financial products and traditional financial strategies. For those with investment accounts of moderate size, the benefits of these products and strategies (their cost; the ease of their implementation) are self-evident. Of course, once these people are ready to divest themselves of their properties, their businesses, their farms, or whatever it is that forms the bulk of their wealth, then it's another story. When that time comes, *True Wealth* will show these people what to expect, and what changes they can expect in their lives.

## The importance of assets (rather than income)

The second important word in my definition of a high-net-worth individual is the word "assets" – as opposed to income. Let me be blunt: when it comes to wealth, it's what's in the investment account that counts, not what's on the paycheck. Quite frankly, there are a lot of people out there who *look* wealthy – they drive fancy cars, live in big houses, attend important social functions, work in high-profile jobs, whatever. Take a closer look at their investment account, however, and it's quite a different story.

Doctors Thomas J. Stanley and William D. Danko published a seminal work on this very subject back in 1996. *The Millionaire Next Door* takes a good look at many of the widely-held myths and misconceptions about how the wealthy in America actually live. Number one on the list of these misconceptions is that the "high life" is indicative of a high-net-worth. Through hundreds of personal interviews with real-life millionaires, Stanley and Danko found that the average American millionaire wasn't cruising Rodeo Drive, shopping on Park Avenue, or wintering on the Riviera. In fact, the vast bulk of the millionaires in America live and work in the towns and neighborhoods they've known all their lives, and live rather frugally. What's more, they are generally happy doing so. They are not the people gracing the nation's society pages – they are people who build small, community-based businesses, live in reasonably priced neighborhoods, and drive F-150 pick-ups. In other words, they are the people who live next door. They acquired their wealth not by earning an enviable income (although many do), but rather by living *below* their means.

I imagine for those who don't know many wealthy people, this is a groundbreaking idea. But for those who actually work with the affluent — those who actually understand how the wealthy become wealthy, and what money actually means to them — the revelations contained in *The Millionaire Next Door* are simply a confirmation of what we have always known. It should be common sense that those who draw six-figure salaries but have little to show for it aren't truly wealthy, no matter how high they may be living today. The opposite is also true: those who drive domestic cars and live in "average" suburban homes are often more wealthy than you would ever imagine. The simple fact of the matter is, through prudent management of one's wealth, it is quite possible for a person with an average income to accumulate an above-average net-worth. It is for these people that *True Wealth* is written.

## Who are the wealthy?

Now that we know exactly what we mean when we talk about wealth, we're ready to take a closer look at the people who actually hold this wealth. I've classified my personal observations and comments into the three general sub-segments of the wealthy population, and included a fair bit of data on these groups.

### The high-net-worth individual (HNWI)

Much of what I'll say about the first of these groups, the HNWIs, applies to the other two, so my comments will be a little more extensive here than elsewhere in the chapter.

#### HNWIs around the world

Let's start with a simple question: how many HNWIs are there in the world? In the past decade, consulting firm Cap Gemini/Ernst & Young estimates more people have joined the ranks of the HNWIs than in any other time in history. In fact, in the 2001 edition of their annual *World Wealth Report*, issued in conjunction with Merrill Lynch, the firm estimates more than 180,000 people became HNWIs over the past twelve months. Worldwide, that brings the total to 7.2 million people with at least $1-million in investable assets. These people have a combined net worth of about $27-trillion. That growth was well below the numbers posted for 1999, when over one million people attained high-net-worth status for the first time. This wealth is expected to grow at an average rate of 8% a year, for a total of $39.7-trillion by the year 2005. This rate is much more moderate than estimated in previous years, and reflects the uncertainty of the equity markets in 2001 and beyond.

HNWIs are concentrated in three major regions of the world: North America, Europe, and Asia. North America accounts for more than 35% of the world's HNWIs, or just over 2.5 million in total. Altogether, North American HNWIs control almost $8.8-trillion in wealth, up 9% from the year before.

graph 1.1: **Millions of U/HNWIs by region**

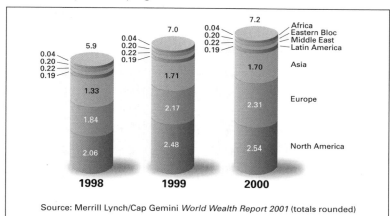

Source: Merrill Lynch/Cap Gemini *World Wealth Report 2001* (totals rounded)

graph 1.2: **Wealth by region ($tr)**

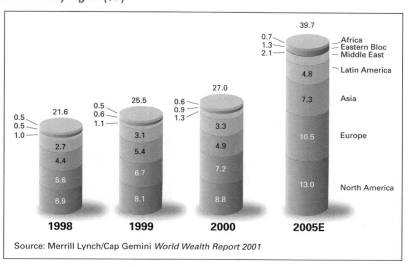

Source: Merrill Lynch/Cap Gemini *World Wealth Report 2001*

There are approximately 2.3 million HNWIs who call Europe their home; that figure accounts for 26% of global HNWI wealth, or $7.2-trillion. Asia comes in third with 1.7 million HNWIs, accounting for $4.9-trillion, or about 18% of the total. And although only about 190,000 HNWIs live in Latin America (only 2.6% of all U/HNWIs in the world), they control a remarkable concentration of wealth – almost $3.3-trillion, or 12% of the world's HNWI wealth.

### Profile of the high-net-worth individual: Canada

Merrill Lynch Canada estimates there were a total of 252,000 HNW households in Canada as of November of 2000. Collectively, these households enjoyed a net worth of about $629-billion CDN. A good many of these (47,000 in total, although that number does include some UHNWIs) have incomes of over $200,000 per year. As could be expected, the bulk of Canadian HNWIs reside in Central Canada. In the year 2000 edition of its annual survey of the Canadian wealth market Cap Gemini/Ernst & Young found 40% of those Canadians with over $1-million in investment products live in Ontario, and 23% live in Quebec. But the West is gaining – BC accounts for 16% of Canadians with over $1-million in investment products, and Alberta a further 12%. The population of the wealthy tends to be older than the general population: the same Cap Gemini study found 79% of Canadians with over $250,000 in investable assets were over the age of 50. I understand that's considerably lower than the high-net-worth threshold, but the general trend holds true of the HNWI population as well.

Much like in the rest of the world, the HNWI population is growing rapidly in Canada. The Cap Gemini report mentioned above projects the number of HNWIs with between $1-million and $2-million of investment products is expected to grow by 8.0% between 1999 and 2010. (By way of comparison, the same report estimates the overall number of Canadians owning investment products is expected to grow at a rate of 1.5%.) The number of HNWIs with $2-million to $5-million is expected to grow at a rate of 9.9%. Between $5-million and $10-million, the growth rate is expected to be 20.2%. By the year 2010, Cap Gemini estimates there will be over 915,000 Canadians who will have total investable assets over $1-million.

### How HNWIs became wealthy

By and large, most HNWIs don't live off the wealth of a previous generation – most have created their fortunes themselves. In one installment of its ongoing series of surveys of the wealthiest 1% of Americans (a group that would include U/HNWIs as well as the Superwealthy), U.S. Trust found fully 46% of respondents acquired their wealth with earnings from a business they owned. 33% became wealthy from corporate employment, while 29% from earnings from a professional practice (law, medicine, dentistry are typical examples). Only 10% owe their wealth to inheritance. Of course, these numbers have fluctuated in the past few years, according to the fortunes of many of the technology-related start ups that have made HNWIs wealthy. But my own experience suggests these general figures are representative of a good many HNWIs.

### How HNWIs manage their wealth

How do HNWIs manage their wealth? In my experience, the personality of the individual has as much to do with how wealth is managed as any other factor. That said, I have noticed there are considerable similarities in the way many HNWIs handle their money. My personal observations are supported by the conclusions of a number of important studies of the HNWI population, including the annual Merrill Lynch/Cap Gemini *World Wealth Report* as well as the ongoing *Survey of Affluent Americans* series conducted by U.S. Trust.

In general, I have found most HNWIs are more concerned with maintaining their income level and standard of living than they are with increasing their already substantial fortunes. This general observation is backed up by a large body of research. 75% of respondents to one U.S. Trust survey indicated providing for retirement income was a top investment goal. And while HNWIs certainly enjoy a high standard of living, a significant portion of their income is directed toward saving and investing. U.S. Trust noted affluent Americans typically spend 27% of their after-tax dollars on savings and investment. And this rate of savings seems to be growing: when a 1998 survey by U.S. Trust asked respondents to compare their savings habits today with those five years previous, 37% of survey respondents admitted they save more than they had in the past, while only 7% responded they saved more in 1993 (this in the middle of the longest period of affluence in U.S.

history). Speaking from my own experience, this commitment to saving and investing is a significant difference between HNWIs and the rest of the population.

## The HNWI portfolio

The HNWI portfolio varies widely with the individual. Generally speaking, however, the HNWI portfolio is less "exotic" than stereotypes might suggest.

chart 1.3: **The typical UHNWI portfolio**

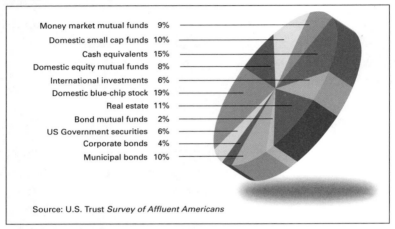

| | |
|---|---|
| Money market mutual funds | 9% |
| Domestic small cap funds | 10% |
| Cash equivalents | 15% |
| Domestic equity mutual funds | 8% |
| International investments | 6% |
| Domestic blue-chip stock | 19% |
| Real estate | 11% |
| Bond mutual funds | 2% |
| US Government securities | 6% |
| Corporate bonds | 4% |
| Municipal bonds | 10% |

Source: U.S. Trust *Survey of Affluent Americans*

In fact, many HNWIs continue to invest in the same investment vehicles that are popular among non-HNWIs: mutual funds, common stock, investment-quality bonds, and certificates of deposit. A U.S. Trust survey revealed that the bulk of the typical affluent portfolio is composed of the tried-and-true investments known to most everyone (see graph 1.3).

The same survey found that relatively few HNWIs have utilized the more sophisticated strategies and financial products available to them. Only 23% said they have invested in venture capital, and only 6% responded that they had invested in hedge funds. These allocations mirror the rather conservative mindset of the HNWI: only 30% of U.S. Trust survey respondents considered themselves more willing to accept risk than the average investor. These data support my own observations: while the acceptance of more sophisticated investments is certainly growing (a good thing), the majority of HNWIs stick to the same products and strategies most everyone uses when it comes to investing their wealth.

**Challenges facing the HNWI**

Wealth is an intensely personal experience – no two people will experience it in quite the same way. Still, there are financial and lifestyle challenges common to many HNWIs. In addition to the obvious financial challenges of wealth – dealing with more sophisticated investments, tackling a complicated estate plan, or executing a complex business sale – many HNWIs face a number of *life* challenges. At this level, wealth is often new, making the acceptance of wealth a number one challenge. For most HNWIs, recognizing their status as HNWIs and accepting the changing demands wealth has put on them is the first challenge they will face. Fittingly, it is also the most dangerous. Failing to recognize how your new financial situation requires a new way of thinking can be the bigger threat to your wealth.

Among financial challenges, the question of how to diversify an excessively concentrated portfolio is a common one among this sub-section of the wealthy population. The failure to properly diversify after a business sale or options exercise can pose a significant threat to wealth, and, in extreme cases, may even threaten a HNWI's ability to secure a high quality of life. Dealing with this challenge should be a primary goal for all HNWIs who hold concentrated positions. This is a central principle of my personal investment philosophy, and a subject I'll be taking up in more detail later on.

Finally, the need for a comprehensive approach to wealth management is another challenge I've noticed among HNWIs. It takes some time before some HNWIs understand that *wealth* management is much more than simply *investment* management. Such a narrow definition of their financial responsibilities can lead them into trouble. By failing to organize their estates, for instance, or properly considering the tax implications of their wealth, these people can actually cripple the long-term security of their family. Again, these are topics I'll be taking up at various points of the book.

## The next **level of wealth**

Those with over $10-million in investable assets are on a different level. The size of their fortunes creates distinct challenges, and opens distinct possibilities unavailable to other HNWIs. Let's take a look at each of these groups.

## Ultra high-net-worth **individuals**

Those with over $10-million in investable assets are what financial professionals call ultra-high-net-worth individuals. According to Merrill Lynch Canada, at least 4,800 of the world's UHNWIs reside in Canada, and they enjoy a total net worth of about $192-billion CDN. As with other segments of the wealth population, this group is growing strongly: in Canada, research firm Cap Gemini estimates the annual growth of the number of those with over $10-million in investable assets between now and 2010 will be 12.8%.

### Sources of U/HNWI wealth

Like the overall wealthy population, the makeup of the U/HNWI group is changing rapidly. As the Merrill Lynch/Cap Gemini *World Wealth Report 2000* explains, the source of wealth for the typical UHNWI is no longer oil, real estate, and inherited money. Rather, the ranks of the UHNWIs are increasingly full of young, smart, entrepreneurs who have transformed a unique idea into an enviable net worth. For evidence of this trend, Cap Gemini looks at the changing nature of *Forbes* magazine's annual list of the 400 wealthiest Americans. Back in 1984, fully 32% of the individuals on the list had inherited their wealth, with real estate accounting for 10% and oil for 8%. Collectively, that accounts for fully half the list. Over the past fifteen years, this has changed dramatically. Today, only 22% of those gracing the Forbes 400 owe their wealth to a previous generation, while only 3% have become wealthy from real estate and only 2% from oil. Collectively, they comprise a quarter of the Forbes 400.

### Challenges facing the UHNWI

While UHNWIs have much in common with HNWIs, their financial affairs are more complex, and involve many different elements of financial planning. Where the HNWI may have one or two significant financial challenges facing them (selling the family business, for example, or organizing their estate in a tax-efficient manner), the UHNWI typically faces many, and usually all at the same time. This multiplication of challenges is a primary hurdle for UHNWIs. Typically, estate and retirement planning, asset and income protection, business divestiture, and the assistance of other family members all must be considered in a well co-ordinated wealth management plan for the UHNWI to achieve *true wealth*.

chart 1.4: **Sources of wealth**

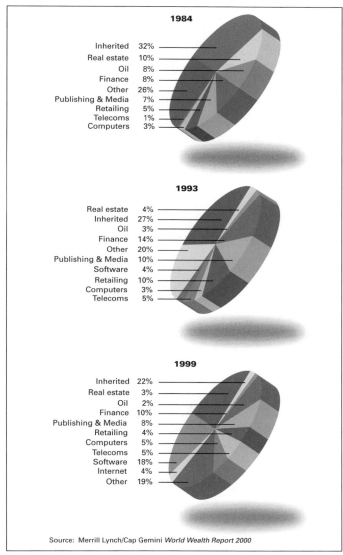

**1984**

| | |
|---|---|
| Inherited | 32% |
| Real estate | 10% |
| Oil | 8% |
| Finance | 8% |
| Other | 26% |
| Publishing & Media | 7% |
| Retailing | 5% |
| Telecoms | 1% |
| Computers | 3% |

**1993**

| | |
|---|---|
| Real estate | 4% |
| Inherited | 27% |
| Oil | 3% |
| Finance | 14% |
| Other | 20% |
| Publishing & Media | 10% |
| Software | 4% |
| Retailing | 10% |
| Computers | 3% |
| Telecoms | 5% |

**1999**

| | |
|---|---|
| Inherited | 22% |
| Real estate | 3% |
| Oil | 2% |
| Finance | 10% |
| Publishing & Media | 8% |
| Retailing | 4% |
| Computers | 5% |
| Telecoms | 5% |
| Software | 18% |
| Internet | 4% |
| Other | 19% |

Source: Merrill Lynch/Cap Gemini *World Wealth Report 2000*

The sheer number of opportunities available to UHNWIs can further complicate these issues. With liquid assets over $10-million, opportunities for sophisticated, alternative investment products and services abound. As such, the portfolio of the UHNWI tends to be a little more complicated than that of the HNWI: hedge funds, private equity, and special monetization strategies are all part of the plan for UHNWIs. Assessing these complicated products and forming effective strategies for putting them into place should be an important priority for every UHNWI. The same can be said for finding a specially-trained wealth advisor well-versed in co-ordinating the UHNWI portfolio.

## The **Superwealthy**

This is the upper echelon of wealth – those with $100-million or more in investable assets. Their ranks read like a "who's who" of the rich and famous: many of the world's best-known entertainers, sports stars, and business billionaires all count themselves among this exclusive group.

graph 1.5: **Number of billionaires by region**

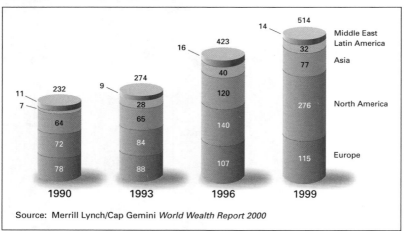

Source: Merrill Lynch/Cap Gemini *World Wealth Report 2000*

At this level of wealth, the quest for confidentiality and discretion are top priorities, making it difficult to obtain precise figures and statistics on this exclusive group. But while they may be hard to come by, some statistics do exist. The 2000 edition of Cap Gemini's *World Wealth Report* confirms that this segment is growing as fast as the overall wealthy population – if not faster. Once again drawing on information from *Forbes* magazine, Cap Gemini presents the number of billionaires as proof of how the upper end of the wealthy population is growing.

The number of billionaires in the world has increased dramatically over the past decade or so. In 1990, there were 232 billionaires in the world. By 1999, there were

514. By and large, North America is the region that has been responsible for this growth: by 1999, the USA accounted for 54% of the world's billionaires. That's up from only 31% in 1990. Beyond the billionaires, it seems America is where most of the Superwealthy reside. In an industry report released last year, MFS Investment Management looked back at the growth of the wealthy in America, and found a startling growth in the number of the Superwealthy. In 1990, there were 3,133 households in America with $100,000,000 in total net worth. As of 1997, there were 5,635. I understand that's not a very recent figure, but it does indicate how quickly wealth is being created. I'm sure the explosion in technology-related wealth over the past few years has only increased that number – even after the recent tech stock meltdown is taken into account.

### Challenges facing the Superwealthy

As could be expected, the Superwealthy face challenges that make them distinct from other segments of the wealthy population. In addition to the "usual" investments (stocks, bonds, and the like), the Superwealthy are uniquely able to capitalize on high-profile alternative investments: upper-level hedge funds, private equity placements, or outright purchase of entire companies. The complexity of such opportunities demands careful attention from the Superwealthy, and requires special abilities from the professionals who work with them. What's more, participation in these higher-risk investments is very exclusive, and is often reserved for the privileged clients of a given firm. For this reason, it is even more important for the Superwealthy to consider not only the knowledge and the experience of the individual wealth advisor, but the depth and global presence of the firm for which that advisor works.

## It all starts here . . .

This general understanding is the start of our consideration of wealth. This basic understanding of who the wealthy are, and how they approach the subject of wealth, will serve as a general foundation for the more specific discussion of specific financial topics and wealth strategies. Before we get to that, however, we need to understand one crucial element of the equation: how U/HNWIs think about wealth. We'll talk about that in the next chapter.

## Key concepts: Chapter one

- High-net-worth individuals (HNWIs) are those who have at least $1-million in investable assets; ultra-high-net-worth individuals (UHNWIs) are those who have $10-million or more in investable assets; the Superwealthy are those who have $100-million or more in investable assets.

- Those who have illiquid, non-investable assets may be wealthy, but their needs and experiences are different from HNWIs.

- Those who have a high income may look wealthy, but their balance sheet may suggest otherwise.

- There are over 7.2 million HNWIs in the world. Their combined wealth is about $27.0-trillion. By 2005, this wealth is projected to total $39.7-trillion.

- In Canada, there are 252,000 HNWI households; collectively they hold $629-billion in wealth.

- Most HNWIs earned their wealth by owning their own businesses.

- A large portion of HNWIs consider maintaining current wealth and income more important than building it.

- Many HNWIs continue to invest in the same investments non-HNWIs invest in.

- HNWIs face a number of challenges when it comes to managing their wealth. Three general challenges are:

    (a) recognizing their status and accepting the new responsibilities of wealth

    (b) having an overly concentrated portfolio

    (c) understanding that wealth management means more than investing

- The financial affairs of UHNWIs are more complex; they face different challenges.

- Two general challenges facing U/HNWI are:

    (a) ensuring they have a comprehensive financial plan

    (b) matching sophisticated investments with their unique needs

- The ranks of the Superwealthy are growing as quickly as other segments of the U/HNWI population.

## Resources

Most of the statistics I've cited throughout this chapter come from research papers and articles published in industry reports. That said, I have found a number of other books and other materials on the wealthy. Here's a brief list of some of the most interesting resources I've come across.

***How to Be a Billionaire*** by Martin S. Fridson

Cynthia Crossen's ***The Rich and How They Got that Way***

Michael Kleeper and Robert Gunther ***The Wealthy 100***

***The Rich Are Different*** by Jon Winokur

## Websites

Forbes magazine *www.forbes.com* – the world's premiere magazine for U/HNWIs

Fortune magazine *www.fortune.com* – another excellent magazine for the wealthy

# It takes all types

- *Understanding your U/HNWI profile*
- *The importance of psychographics*
- *What psychographics can tell you (and what it can't)*
- *The nine personalities of the wealthy*

*"No man can tell whether he is rich or poor by turning to his ledger — it is the heart that makes a man rich — he is rich, according to what he is, not according to what he has."*

**Henry Ward Beecher**

The financial services industry spends a lot of time talking numbers. Quite frankly, that's always surprised me. Sure, numbers are an important part of what we do as financial professionals, but at the end of the day, our business is about *people*. In my experience, all the performance figures, betas, and price-to-earnings ratios aren't worth the paper they're printed on if you don't understand the *person* behind the portfolio.

As I've explained, I believe wealth isn't just a number on your quarterly investment statement — it's a state of mind. And while money certainly can't buy happiness, when one accumulates a certain amount of it, it can certainly change the way that person thinks, and the way that person lives life. It seems to me that any book hoping to provide instruction on how the wealthy should manage their money needs to demonstrate the connection between how the wealthy actually think about their wealth and what they actually do with their wealth.

The general name for the study of such connections is "psychographics." And in the last few years, it's become an important tool for those looking to match specific strategies with specific U/HNWIs. While there have been many books written on the general subject, there has been only one that comes close to reflecting how U/HNWIs actually think: *High-Net-Worth Psychology* by Russ Alan Prince and Karen Maru File. The book's system of U/HNWI personality types is one I've found very workable — with a few changes, that is.

What follows in this chapter is an overview of Prince and File's basic findings, modified to more accurately reflect what goes on in the U/HNWI mind. I've also supplemented their insights with a good number of my own observations from the personal experiences I've had with U/HNWI clients through the years. By the end of this chapter, you should have a good idea of how the personality of a given U/HNWI can shape that individual's approach to managing that wealth.

## What psychographics can tell you (and what it can't!)

Let me be very clear about something: the primary purpose of psychographics isn't to slot individuals into pre-fabricated portfolios. Rather, it's to answer two important questions:

(a) **What does money mean to you?**

What kind of emotions do you experience when thinking about (or managing) your money? What patterns of behavior do these emotions lead to?

(b) **What do you want from your money?**

What goals are you pursuing when you manage your wealth? What impact will having more wealth (or less) make to your lifestyle?

Answering these two basic questions is an important first step when formulating effective strategies for the ongoing management of your wealth. These questions allow you to zero in on the emotions that dominate your thinking about wealth. Understand these emotions, and you'll be a long way toward understanding appropriate solutions to the particular wealth challenges that face you. After that, it should be clear what you have to do with your wealth to ensure you never lose it.

Understand, though, that psychographics is by its very nature only a *general* survey of common personality types. No matter how comprehensive, psychographics can't reproduce the subtleties and nuances of an individual mind. And while it can certainly highlight potential challenges and possible courses of action, psychographics can never replace a detailed, one-on-one analysis of an individual's financial situation. In other words, psychographics should only be considered a *starting point* for understanding how an individual relates to wealth. It is not a set-in-stone system that dictates how all individuals will behave in all situations.

# **The nine** U/HNWI personality types

In my experience, most U/HNWIs fall into one of about nine personality "profiles." Such a system makes it easier to identify attitudes surrounding key wealth behaviors, and identify opportunities and challenges facing a U/HNWI. This in turn makes it easier to formulate customized wealth management solutions and avoid potential pitfalls before they turn into real problems.

chart 2.1: **Percentage of U/HNWIs in each personality**

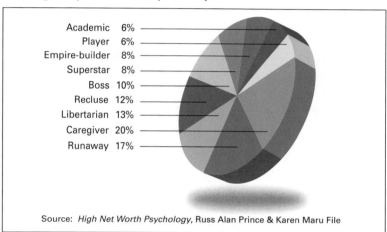

| | |
|---|---|
| Academic | 6% |
| Player | 6% |
| Empire-builder | 8% |
| Superstar | 8% |
| Boss | 10% |
| Recluse | 12% |
| Libertarian | 13% |
| Caregiver | 20% |
| Runaway | 17% |

Source: *High Net Worth Psychology*, Russ Alan Prince & Karen Maru File

The descriptions below provide summaries of these nine basic profiles, and how each profile perceives wealth. I've also outlined some of the specific opportunities the given personality can easily capitalize on, as well as some of the financial challenges they will likely face. Finally, I've included a brief note on what I consider to be the "next step" for each of the profiles – the specific actions the U/HNWI can take that will make it easier to achieve *true wealth*.

It's very rare that a U/HNWI fits neatly into a single profile. In fact, most U/HNWI's I've met exhibit primary and secondary traits from two or more profiles. So understand, what follows isn't meant to be the final word on how U/HNWIs think about money. Rather, these profiles are simply meant to suggest a plausible "starting point" for considering the topic of U/HNWI psychology.

## "I'm taking care of my own": **The Caregiver**

Caregivers are U/HNWIs motivated by a selfless goal: the financial well-being of their families. These people tend to approach wealth in a very humble way – as something they've worked hard to accumulate. Their primary financial goal is to leave behind enough of it to liberate their families from having to work as hard as they did themselves. Does this personality sound familiar? It should. According to Prince and File, caregivers account for about 20% of all U/HNWIs, the largest single portion of the U/HNWI population.

The caregiver is probably the most well-balanced of all U/HNWI personality types. They typically have a healthy, level-headed vision of what life is all about, a vision in which wealth certainly plays a significant role, but by no means is it the be-all, end-all of existence. Typically caregivers are focused more on goals than returns, which makes them less susceptible to market panic – definitely a positive trait. It also makes them less willing to put their money into high-risk "pie-in-the-sky" investments that other U/HNWIs often find hard to pass up. Quite the opposite: I have found some caregivers to be so biased toward the "slow-and-steady" approach that they forego higher-return opportunities – often to the detriment of their long-term financial health. By and large, however, this security-minded approach to investing demonstrates a maturity about wealth, and a willingness to keep the big picture in mind. I think this maturity is echoed in the nobility of the caregiver's goal: the desire to manage wealth on behalf of family and heirs demonstrates a sense of duty and responsibility I admire.

The primary challenges facing caregivers have more to do with their families than their finances. The desire to provide for one's family is surely a noble goal, but there is such thing as too much of a good thing. An endless stream of handouts can actually undermine a child's financial security, making the child incapable of securing wealth (I call this syndrome "affluenza" – I'll discuss it further a little later). It can also lead to bitter squabbles as relatives fight over pieces of a substantial pie.

## The Caregiver

| | |
|---|---|
| **Characteristics:** | • strong desire to provide for family; |
| | • often generous and charitable with money; |
| **Opportunities:** | • less prone to high-risk investments; |
| | • well-balanced mindset allows them to focus on the big picture; |
| **The next step:** | • eliminate bias toward secure or "safe" investments; |
| | • consider: is your generosity leading to conflict or laziness among family members? |

## "Don't talk to me about money": **The Runaway**

When the subject of wealth management comes up, runaways do what their name suggests: they "run away," avoiding or deflecting the topic in a number of subtle and not-so-subtle ways. That's not to say runaways don't appreciate the finer things wealth can bring, or understand what kind of difference wealth can make in life. They just don't want to be involved in the day-to-day details of its management. Theirs is the second most numerous group among the wealthy, accounting for about 17% of all U/HNWIs.

You might assume this "stick-your-head-in-the-sand" attitude to be a liability. Most of the time it isn't. Because of their innate anxiety about wealth (often a result of an event that left them financially "scarred" and unwilling to take responsibility for their money), the runaway often turns to a financial professional for help. That's often the best move any U/HNWI can make. By delegating the wealth management duties to a professional, runaways not only avoid dealing with their wealth, they avoid many of the common problems that face other U/HNWIs.

That said, there is a fine line between delegation and abdication. Because of the tremendous trust runaways place in the professionals they work with, shifty sales people and other con artists often find the runaway to be relatively easy prey. And if the runaway fails to find a skilled professional, the consequences of their financial inaction can often be disastrous. In the absence of professional help, I've seen some runaways "turtle" and ignore even the most basic financial responsibilities. That can leave them without even the most basic of estate, tax, or retirement plans.

## The Runaway

| | |
|---|---|
| **Characteristics:** | • discussion of money causes anxiety, impatience, or disinterest; |
| | • strong desire to avoid, defer, or delegate financial decisions; |
| **Opportunities:** | • trusting in professional management helps avoid bad investment decisions, ensures proper asset allocation, etc. ; |
| **The next step:** | • exercise care in choosing a professional; |
| | • examine all parts of your financial plan – don't ignore important financial issues |

## "Give me freedom!": **The Libertarian**

A good many U/HNWIs dream about the day they won't have to work anymore. For the libertarian, this dream is an obsession, and underlies the majority of wealth management decisions. Wealth is the means by which libertarians plan their escape from the prison of bills, mortgages, and the dull drudgery of work. Now that they have attained a comfortable level of wealth, these U/HNWIs are looking to secure the freedom they've gained. They account for about 13% of all U/HNWIs.

As people who value financial independence above all else, the libertarian is often a highly motivated investor, with very clear goals in mind. This is a good thing. They have a keen interest in financial planning and investment management, and are willing to work with a skilled professional. Most libertarians are more interested in security than they are in absolute performance, and usually understand when enough wealth is enough. In my experience, libertarians seem to implicitly understand the value of strategic asset allocation and the benefits of professional money management – most likely because they take more interest in the results of wealth management rather than the process.

That's not to say there aren't specific challenges libertarians face. Probably the most significant of these is their impatience – their willingness to declare financial independence before their investment account can truly support it. Many libertarians lack a wide financial vision. All too often, their intense focus on the one goal that matters to them can force equally important goals to the back burner – goals such as securing their family's well-being, organizing their estate, or reducing the taxes they pay. Finally, even though the financial goals of the libertarian may be well-defined, that doesn't mean the libertarian's portfolio is. Often, the libertarian's intense focus on financial independence comes at the expense of examining the methods used to achieve that independence. The result is a cluttered mish-mash of a portfolio full of unsuitable investments.

## The Libertarian

| | |
|---|---|
| **Characteristics:** | • highly motivated, intensely focused individual; |
| | • concerned with one goal: financial freedom; |
| **Opportunities:** | • ability to delegate financial responsibilities; |
| | • understanding of complicated financial strategies; |
| **The next step:** | • develop patience: building wealth takes time; |
| | • don't let your focus on independence distract you from other financial responsibilities |

## "It's my business": **The Recluse**

Wealth brings many things: privilege, freedom, responsibility. It can also bring the envy of others. The recluse is a U/HNWIs who is acutely aware of this envy, and values privacy above all else. For this reason, the recluse insists on a high degree of financial discretion and absolute privacy – privacy from strangers, privacy from the government, and often privacy from family members too. They account for about 12% of the total U/HNWI population.

Unlike some of the other U/HNWI profiles, the recluse is keenly aware of the need to manage wealth. Whether the recluse chooses someone else to help with that management is another question. More often than not, a desire for privacy has made the recluse reluctant to discuss financial affairs with strangers; this in turn has led many of these people to manage their own wealth. Personally, I have known recluses to be capable, independent-minded people, with a strong understanding of what it takes to manage a high-net-worth portfolio. Most appreciate the value of tax and estate planning (if only to ensure the ongoing privacy of their financial affairs), although this doesn't necessarily mean they have taken action in either of these areas.

When it comes to managing wealth, the recluse faces considerable challenges. As mentioned, the recluse often finds it difficult to work with a wealth advisor. And even if the recluse does find a trustworthy professional, the recluse can often withhold key information from that professional, or spread wealth among several professionals to prevent any one from knowing too much. Either way, this can make it difficult for a wealth advisor to formulate a personalized financial strategy for the recluse. In some cases, this reluctance to discuss financial matters can extend to members of the recluse's family. Such a tight-lipped approach can make estate planning extremely difficult. In extreme cases, it could breed considerable stress and conflict among family members.

## The Recluse

| | |
|---|---|
| **Characteristics:** | • anxious about privacy; |
| | • most money decisions made with privacy in mind; |
| **Opportunities:** | • often knowledgeable about investments/wealth management; |
| | • aware of the importance of estate, tax planning; |
| **The next step:** | • develop working relationships with trustworthy professionals; |
| | • don't let your desire for privacy lead to family conflicts; |

The above four profiles describe the U/HNWIs who will find it relatively easy to secure their wealth. Certainly, some of these profiles have considerable challenges ahead of them. But most of these challenges can be overcome with the help of a qualified professional who understands the specialized needs of wealthy people. It goes without saying the above profiles are the U/HNWIs whom I can best help.

As for the remaining profiles . . . well, let's just say their personalities make it a challenge for them (and their advisors) to manage wealth in a responsible manner. Don't get me wrong: I'm not saying there aren't unique opportunities available to these personalities. Nor am I saying there aren't skilled professionals capable of handling wealth for these personalities. What I am saying, however, is that U/HNWIs who belong to the following profiles can be their own worst enemy – their personalities can actually interfere with their ability to secure their wealth, and in some cases, actually *prohibit* it.

## "Do what I say. Now!": **The Boss**

With the boss, wealth means power: the power to shape the world and influence others. As the vehicle that makes this power possible, wealth is something the boss needs – and relishes – but it is never an end in itself. More often than not, the boss is a significant figure in the local business community. Such an environment is a natural fit with the ambition and drive this personality type commonly exhibits. But I have also met bosses who exhibit their need for control primarily through relationships with family and friends. Bosses account for about 10% of the U/HNWI population.

In extreme cases, the boss can be a pushy, domineering bully. But most cases aren't that extreme. In fact, there are elements of this personality type that are very positive. In a business context the desire to control and influence can be indicative of a strong, visionary leader, someone who has a clear idea of what he or she wishes to accomplish and is confident in his or her ability to transform that vision into reality. When it comes to personal finance, the boss' aggressive personality can make for a highly motivated U/HNWI who's driven to achieve both financial and life goals and more than willing to accept risk. As long as the boss can temper this ambition with a disciplined, long-term approach and keep his or her personality in check, many professionals (myself included) find the boss to be a focused, agreeable participant in the wealth management process.

Most of the time, however, the desire for power is quite disruptive. Bosses are often impatient people, with busy, hectic lives that lead them to require the services of a financial professional. But the boss' willingness to seek professional advice can be misleading – the boss is usually more concerned with getting someone to do what the boss *wants* rather than hearing about what the boss actually *needs*. What's more, the domineering personality of the boss can be difficult to work with: bosses can become very entrenched in their opinions, and can take offense to alternative suggestions. In extreme cases, this conflict can force bosses to manage their own portfolios. Ironically, this can leave them with less control over their wealth than before.

## The Boss

| | |
|---|---|
| **Characteristics:** | • strong, aggressive personality;<br>• desire to control financial decisions |
| **Opportunities:** | • strong vision; determination to meet financial and life goals;<br>• willingness to accept risk; |
| **The next step:** | • appreciate the value of professional advice;<br>• consider (and accept) other views and differing financial strategies |

## "I'm an important person": The Superstar

These are the U/HNWIs whose primary goal is to see themselves on *Lifestyles of the Rich and Famous*. For superstars, preserving wealth is ultimately an exercise in preserving not only money, but prestige and self-worth. For these people, wealth is an infinitely important part of identity – a tangible symbol of their status in the community. Approximately 8% of all U/HNWIs are superstars.

Not all the traits of the superstar are negative, however. For one, superstars usually don't mind delegating important financial decisions to a skilled professional. In the hands of someone who can keep their spending habits in check, superstars are often able to maintain the wealth they take such pride in. Personally, I have found superstars to be open to those investments with a ring of exclusivity to them (i.e., private equity, or collectibles), although the reason for investing in these vehicles usually has more to do with prestige than it does with any wealth management strategy. The same can be said of the desire to make charitable contributions. Sometimes such donations are intended not only to make a difference, but to build prestige.

On balance though, it's tough to be a superstar. Obviously, the desire to sustain a high profile can quickly whittle down even the largest investment accounts. Superstars can also be highly susceptible to charm: high-pressure sales people can flatter them into inappropriate investments with relative ease. In addition, I've found superstars usually don't care too much about what happens to their wealth – as long as they have enough of it to spend. Again, that doesn't have to be a bad thing (if they can find a qualified professional who can secure their wealth for them), but it can result in a poorly-constructed financial plan and a lazy, come-what-may attitude to wealth preservation.

## The Superstar

| | |
|---|---|
| **Characteristics :** | • status–oriented individuals with big spending habits; |
| | • money is a symbol of status and the source of identity; |
| **Opportunities:** | • willingness to delegate financial responsibilities; |
| | • open to charitable giving and estate planning; |
| **The next step:** | • be cautious with spending; |
| | • be on guard against high–pressure, high–flattery sales; |
| | • learn to take an active interest in financial matters |

## "I want more": **The Empire-builder**

For the empire-builder, money isn't a means to an end. It's an end in itself – a kind of scorecard by which to track one's success. Most of the time you can spot an empire-builder fairly easily: when an empire-builder talks about finances, the talk is about *performance*, not about meeting life goals. Other times, an empire-building personality will come out in more subtle ways. An intense focus on getting ahead at work or building a business, a powerful longing for the status symbols of wealth, or constant comparisons to the wealth of other individuals are all signs of an empire-builder. Empire-builders comprise about 8% of the U/HNWI population.

Of course, I don't think the desire to build wealth is always a bad thing. Because they are driven more by the investment returns rather than the means through which they achieve them, most empire-builders are open-minded when it comes to selecting assets for their investment portfolios, as long as the returns are attractive. That flexibility makes it relatively easy for a wealth advisor to construct a well-diversified (if perhaps more aggressive) portfolio for the empire-builder. Empire builders also tend to be genuinely interested in investing, and are usually active participants in the wealth management process. Again, this active interest can make it easier for a financial professional to coordinate effective strategies and construct viable financial solutions for the individual.

At the same time, it's not always easy for an empire-builder to acquire *true wealth*. Because they place more value on *building* wealth than they do on *securing* wealth, empire-builders can easily become distracted by some of the most dangerous elements of the wealth management business – short-term market movements, "hot tips" and other current news, and performance figures. This can make them financial "nomads" – wandering from investment to investment (and often from advisor to advisor) in search of higher returns. That's rarely a good way to build *or* secure wealth. Because of their intense focus, the portfolios of most empire-builders are often rather unbalanced, chock full of aggressive or speculative investments. This can expose them to excessive risks that put their wealth in jeopardy. Finally, the empire-builder's concentration on the bottom line often translates into a lack of interest for what they consider to be the "boring" side of wealth management: estate and tax planning, for example. Ironically, these elements of a financial plan are often the most important determinants of an individual's net worth.

## The Empire-builder

| | |
|---|---|
| **Characteristics:** | • focused, performance-driven investors; |
| | • money is a measure of success; |
| **Opportunities:** | • focused; driven; highly motivated investors; |
| | • open to a wide variety of investments; |
| | • little or no fear of risk; |
| **The next step:** | • diversify the portfolio; |
| | • stick to an investment plan; avoid "stock-hopping;" |
| | • focus on "big-picture" goals, not short-term events |

## "Let it ride . . .": The Player

There's no denying it: investing can be exciting. Players seek out that excitement, and look to intensify the thrills they get from the market. For the player, building wealth is a kind of game, a game where the stakes are high and the payoffs equally so. About 6% of the U/HNWI population belong to this profile.

You'd think this kind of personality would be a recipe for financial disaster. In extreme cases, it is, but there are also many players who manage to hold their own in the market. Players will often utilize a financial professional as an information source, drawing upon the professional's research and other resources to confirm their own investment ideas. The end goal of such a relationship is rarely to construct a cohesive financial plan or to achieve tangible investment goals, however. Rather, it's to find a kind of playmate, someone who shares the player's passion for risk and finds investing just as exciting. Even so, the relationship a player develops with a professional often results in a more balanced portfolio than would otherwise be possible. I have known many U/HNWIs who are *partial* players. These people enjoy the risk of investing, and assign large portions of "play money" to ultra-speculative ventures. At the same time, they leave their "serious money" in the hands of a trusted professional, one who can construct a well-balanced portfolio to compensate for their more speculative ventures. That's not what I consider an ideal approach to wealth management, but it doesn't have to be a disaster, either.

The danger, of course, is when players fail to understand how to keep their passion for risk in check. As I'll explain a little later on, deliberately seeking out risk is one of the quickest, most certain ways to destroy wealth. And it is exactly the multiplication of risk that the player craves. Often this behavior leads to bungled strategies and hodge-podge portfolios — collections of investments that lack any clear purpose and fail to fit any long-term strategy. Of course, players are often overly concerned with short-term performance (how else to judge whether they've "won" or not?), and often ignore the need for comprehensive, long-term planning. For obvious reasons, the player's behavior can be an incredibly disruptive force within a U/HNWI family, breeding anxiety and conflict among those who don't share the player's passion for "the game."

## The Player

| | |
|---|---|
| **Characteristics:** | • high-risk individuals who see investing as a game; |
| **Opportunities:** | • ability to accept risk; |
| | • working with a professional — albeit for the wrong reasons; |
| **The next step:** | • focus on planning, not stock picking; |
| | • learn to reduce rather than multiply risk |

## "I'm in the know": **The Academic**

Academics are highly knowledgeable investors, and comprise the final 6% of the U/HNWI population. When academics think about wealth, they think about their mastery of it. They pride themselves on being on the "cutting edge" of the financial world — the first to understand economic news, the first to utilize new financial strategies, the first to invest in the "next best thing." It's not so much performance these people are after (although that's important). Rather, it is the pride that comes with being "in the know."

No doubt the academic's knowledge of the complicated strategies and investment products can be a substantial benefit in the effort to secure wealth. They are committed to learning all they can about investing, and will devour new ideas and investment information with relish. If they choose to work with a professional, they usually follow that professional's advice — although they are quite demanding to work with. Their intense interest in what's new makes them slightly more aggressive than other U/HNWI profiles. And that's not necessarily a bad thing.

But the academic often has some challenges to overcome. In my experience, most academics are biased toward whatever is "new" in the financial world, and have an inherent love of complicated financial strategies. This can lead them to ignore the tried and true strategies that are almost certain to build wealth over time. Often an academic's pride in his or her own knowledge can lead to assumptions about being more competent than a financial professional, making academics less prone to work with a wealth advisor. Their constant attention to the numbers of financial planning – the statistics, the calculations, the performance figures – makes it easy for them to forget the big picture, and spend more time talking about the latest economic news than the realization of tangible financial goals. Many academics are also market timers, comparing statistics and hopping from investment to investment in search of the newest and the best.

## The Academic

| | |
|---|---|
| **Characteristics:** | • strong desire to be innovative and invest in new products; |
| | • being wealthy means being knowledgeable and well-informed; |
| **Opportunities:** | • no problem participating in sophisticated investment strategies; |
| | • willingness to learn more about wealth management; |
| **The next step:** | • manage pride; |
| | • don't ignore simple, tried-and-true methods of building wealth; |
| | • avoid shuffling the portfolio in search of the "best" investment; |

# Making use of your U/HNWI profile

As I said at the start of this chapter, it's very rare that a U/HNWI belongs to only one psychographic profile. If you're like most U/HNWIs I've worked with, you have a "primary" and a "secondary" profile. The former is your dominant profile, the one that best describes your general feelings about wealth. But your secondary profile plays an equally important role, qualifying (and sometimes contradicting) the features of the first. To my mind, this vision of complementary yet competing profiles accurately reflects the complex, sometimes confusing attitudes many people have about wealth.

So, we come to the important question: how does one actually put this information to good use? I recommend a simple, three-step process. First, find the profile with which you best identify (and a second, or third), and review some of the challenges your profile is likely to face. Second, assess how you feel about those challenges.

Take your time on this one: you'll probably be thinking about some of these challenges for the first time in your life, so you'll need to let them roll around in your mind for a day or two. Finally (and most importantly), make sure to meet with a qualified wealth manager – one experienced in dealing with U/HNWIs – and discuss your findings. By talking about some of the specific challenges that you'll likely be facing in the future, you'll be giving your financial professional advance notice of what you need to become *truly wealthy*. The end result: you're a long way ahead on the road to securing wealth.

And really, that's all you need to do. Because no matter what profile you fall under, the *wrong* thing to do is to fight your personality. If you recognize some bad habits in these profiles, be gentle with yourself. It's OK to be who you are.

## A final word on high-net-worth personalities

The end goal of wealth management is to develop a healthy, balanced attitude toward wealth – an attitude that makes it easier for us to secure wealth. But developing such balance doesn't happen overnight. So give yourself time to make the change. Like most things that are actually worth having, it will be worth it in the end.

## Key concepts: Chapter two

- Wealth isn't just a number. It's a state of mind.
- Once you accumulate a certain level of wealth, it changes the way you *think*.
- Most HNWIs fall into one of nine basic personality profiles:

    1. Caregivers (20% of the U/HNWI population)

    2. Runaways (17%)

    3. Libertarians (13%)

    4. The recluse (12%)

    5. Bosses (10%)

    6. Superstars (8%)

    7. Empire-builders (8%)

    8. Players (6%)

    9. Academics (6%)

- Finding what profile you fall into can help answer two questions:

    1. What does money mean to you?

    2. What do you want from your money?

- These profiles are rarely a "neat fit": most U/HNWIs have a "primary" and a "secondary" profile.
- Answering these questions will help you understand what you need to do to secure your wealth.
- How do you use these profiles?

    1. review the challenges your profile is likely to face

    2. conduct an honest assessment of how you feel about those challenges

    3. tell a qualified professional about your profile

- Don't try to fight your personality profile – at least not right away. It takes time to eliminate bad habits.

## Resources

Investor psychology is still a developing field, making useful resources rather hard to come by. Here are some of the few resources available that can help U/HNWIs understand themselves – and people like them – a little better.

*High-Net-Worth Psychology* by Russ Alan Prince and Karen Maru File

*The Prime Movers* by Edwin A. Locke

*World Wealth Report* by Merrill Lynch and Cap Gemini (various years)

## Websites

The Encyclopedia of Psychology *www.psychology.org/links* - everything you wanted to know about psychology (click on "environment behavior relationships," then click on "economics")

# Five rules of wealth

- *You're in a different league now*
- *Five rules all U/HNWIs should follow*

*"For many men, the acquisition of wealth does not end their troubles. It only changes them."*

*Seneca*

Welcome to the big leagues. You're playing a different game now. A game where the stakes are higher, and the rules are different. A *lot* different. Feeling a little overwhelmed? That's understandable. But not to worry. All you need to know are the rules of the game. It's with this idea in mind that I present to you the five rules of wealth for U/HNWIs.

What follows in this chapter is the *essence* of wealth management for U/HNWIs. For the most part these rules are universal: no matter how you came to be wealthy, you need to follow them. They are also *elemental*: they are simple, easy to understand concepts that cannot be broken down any further. In other words, if you learn nothing else from this book, these five simple rules will help you do more to secure your wealth than anything you will likely ever read in a long-winded economics textbook.

These rules have an additional benefit: they don't come from a book. Rather, they all come from my direct experience from working with U/HNWIs. Over the years, I've made a number of observations concerning how U/HNWIs regard their wealth, and what steps they're likely to take to secure it. I've seen many of the approaches U/HNWIs take to managing their wealth — both good and bad. The results of these observations can be boiled down to the following five rules.

Before I tell you what they are, however, I want be perfectly clear about something. When I talk about "rules," I am *not* talking about particular investment strategies or specific investment products. Rather, I'm speaking about a general code of conduct that helps maintain a healthy mental attitude and balanced perspective of what we're doing when we go about managing wealth. Ultimately, that perspective involves understanding the real goal of wealth management: that wealth management is not about accumulating more wealth, rather it's about enriching one's life. Of course, this vision of wealth management naturally steers us toward certain investment strategies and away from others, but that's not really the point — at least not yet. Right now, it's important we discuss the *concepts* behind wealth management for U/HNWIs. We'll get to the *details* later. It's in this spirit that I present these five rules.

## Rule #1: You must be personally responsible for your wealth

All U/HNWIs need to establish a *personal responsibility* for their wealth. No matter how capable, no matter how knowledgeable, no matter how brilliant the advisors who supervise their portfolios happen to be, U/HNWIs must accept personal responsibility for securing their wealth. Making *yourself* accountable for your own financial success or failure — not the analysts, not the media, not the market — is the best defense against ill-considered decisions and silly mistakes. It is the best way to ensure continued, steady progress toward your life goals. In other words, it is the best way to *stay* wealthy.

In practical terms, this means U/HNWIs must commit to a minimum involvement in the management of their wealth. For most U/HNWIs, this rule isn't a problem — by far the majority I've worked with take a semi-active interest in their financial situation. But that's not always the case. Some U/HNWIs just aren't interested in their money. Instead of learning more about it, or participating in wealth management decisions, they abdicate financial responsibility, leaving someone else in charge. That's not a position I support.

The exact form of required involvement is by and large up to the individual. For some U/HNWIs, participation will mean daily tracking of portfolio holdings in the newspaper or on the Internet, researching potential investment opportunities, and reviewing their financial situation with a professional on a regular basis. For other U/HNWIs, participation will mean little more than quarterly meetings and keeping abreast of decisions made by qualified professionals. Either one can be perfectly workable, but at a bare minimum, all U/HNWIs should be ready and able to discuss opportunities and challenges with their wealth advisor as the need arises, and have a clear vision of what they want to accomplish with their wealth at all times.

Along with this minimum level of participation should come a minimum level of financial knowledge, and a commitment to expanding that knowledge over time. But when I say knowledge, I'm talking about a general awareness about financial products and services, and a basic understanding of your personal financial situation. Eventually, most U/HNWIs will want to expand that knowledge to an understanding of the specific challenges that are facing them now, and may face in the future. But I am not suggesting U/HNWIs spend every spare minute poring over financial textbooks cramming for some kind of "wealth exam."

At the end of the day, responsibility means balance. In many ways, it makes sense for U/HNWIs to keep a certain distance from their wealth, and leave the day-to-day management of their financial affairs to someone who knows a lot more about it than they do – clearly delegating authority to such a person is the *responsible* thing to do. Carry that too far, however, and you can run into danger.

## Rule #2: You need to consider wealth in a different way

Wealth means different things to different people. But the one thing that's constant is the change wealth brings. U/HNWIs need to accept this change, and consider their wealth – and their lives – from a different perspective.

At the core of this consideration is viewing wealth from a lifestyle perspective rather than a financial perspective. Instead of seeing wealth for the toys it can buy, U/HNWIs need to see it for the difference it can make to the way they live their lives. If you see your wealth as an ocean-going yacht, a mansion in the hills, or the five cars you have in the garage, you're more likely to devalue it: it is simply the tool to satisfy your desires. As such, you're more likely to spend it without much thought, and take risks to ensure you always have enough of it to satisfy your desires. If, on the other hand, you see wealth as a way to secure *freedom* – the freedom to do what you want for the rest of your life – you're more likely to treat the management of your wealth a little more seriously. You're more likely to think before you spend it, and you're more likely to make conservative decisions about what to do with it. In the end, this life-oriented attitude toward wealth is actually a level of protection for U/HNWIs.

Considering wealth in a different way also means being comfortable with your status as a U/HNWI. Again, I'm not talking about being comfortable with your cars and yachts. I'm talking about a level of comfort when looking at your investment account – an ability to look at performance figures without cringing in horror at how much the statement dropped in one month. I'm talking about an ability to delegate important financial responsibilities to strong, capable professionals without worrying about what they're doing to your net worth, and without poking your nose into each and every detail of what they're doing. Most of all, I'm talking about a calm, confident approach to making financial decisions for the betterment of you and your family without getting caught up in some of the emotional difficulties wealth can bring. In other words, I'm talking about considering how you *behave* around wealth, and changing bad behaviors that threaten that wealth.

Finally, and most importantly, considering wealth in a new way also means understanding that with wealth comes responsibility. U/HNWIs need to accept the responsibility they have to both their families and their communities, a responsibility to manage their wealth capably, and pass that wealth on to both their family and their community in an easy and efficient manner. This is a responsibility the rest of the population doesn't always share. Quite frankly, it doesn't need to. U/HNWIs must be *stewards* of wealth, protecting and nurturing that wealth so that it can continue to do good in the next generation – and beyond. In the end, that's what makes having wealth worthwhile.

## Rule #3: Secure wealth first; build wealth second

If you're like many U/HNWIs, chances are building wealth was a central concern for many years of your life. Now that you've attained it, it's time to think differently. U/HNWIs need to stop thinking about *building* their wealth, and start thinking about *securing* their wealth. This is a fundamental principle of responsible wealth management – an idea that governs the advice I give to all my U/HNWI clients.

Such caution may sound a little strange coming from someone in the investment world. And I admit, to many aggressively-minded U/HNWIs, my "secure wealth first; build wealth second" approach sounds downright foreign. *But it is fundamentally more important for U/HNWIs to keep the money they have than to accumulate more.*

This is the way I explain it to my U/HNWI clients. After all is said and done, most people would agree that the primary purpose of wealth – and the only reason for acquiring it – is to give you the ability to enjoy a high quality of life. Chances are, if you have a million or more in investable assets, you're already beginning to reach this point – *you already have "enough."* So ask yourself: would another zero at the end of your net worth statement really make that much of a difference to how you enjoy your life? Probably not. Then why would you risk giving up your comfortable lifestyle by pursuing aggressive investments? What would you have to gain – *what practical difference would more money make to the way you live your life?* Sure, it might be nice to leave behind a little more to your heirs or the community, and that's reason enough to pursue some growth positions in your portfolio. But by constantly investing in high-risk investments you could be threatening the lifestyle you've built for yourself. One wrong turn and you could be faced with having to cut back on spending, sell some of your assets, or go back to work. So why risk it?

For many U/HNWIs, the moment they understand there is such a thing as "enough" – and the fact that they already have it – is a life-changing one. It has far-reaching implications not only about one's investment strategy, but on how one spends one's time. Once you realize that you have enough, then you start to think about the dangers of a given investment before you get excited about the potential reward. You're less susceptible to the high-pressure investment salespeople who often target the U/HNWI population. And you're more able to take a calm, steady approach to your life, without having to worry, fret, or fuss over whether your investments returned 12% or 13% a year. After all, isn't this the kind of freedom that wealth is supposed to give you in the first place?

## Rule #4: You need to investigate new options

Contrary to popular belief, wealth doesn't solve all financial challenges. In fact, it often multiplies them. In order to meet these new challenges, U/HNWIs need to investigate new investment options and consider new financial strategies.

It really doesn't matter what your individual goals for your wealth or your life may be. If you're wealthy, you need to become familiar with how wealthy people like you invest. You need to understand what challenges wealthy people like you have faced. You need to understand what solutions wealthy people like you have used to overcome these challenges. You need to understand what life changes wealthy people like you have had to go through. Because like it or not, you may well be going through these things yourself in the near future. Without at least a basic understanding of what U/HNWIs have done before, it can be difficult to make informed decisions about how you should manage your wealth or your life.

Keep in mind, though, the rule is to *investigate* these options – not necessarily to pursue them. Not all U/HNWIs need to utilize all of the financial options they have available to them. And just because you're wealthy doesn't mean you should forget about the standard investment products and the tried-and-true strategies that helped you become wealthy in the first place. But everyone needs to at least take a look at these options before they determine what works best for them.

## Rule #5: Work with a professional

An absolutely imperative rule for U/HNWIs to understand. If you have accumulated a significant amount of wealth – enough wealth to satisfy most of your lifestyle goals – you need to work with a financial professional at some point in your life. Period.

A decade ago, this rule would be taken as a given. But with the rise of internet trading and online brokerages, many investors have been duped into believing the myth that they can manage wealth on their own. For those with a more modest net worth, the consequences of believing this myth are less serious – it may very well be possible for these people to muddle their way through the markets for years without making a truly catastrophic error. That's not the case with U/HNWIs. The complexity of a U/HNWIs financial situation demands professional attention at all times. Solving complicated financial challenges, assessing alternative investment opportunities, and compiling a comprehensive financial plan – a plan that includes a detailed strategy for organizing a U/HNWI's estate, managing a U/HNWI's ongoing tax liability, and divesting a U/HNWI's business – leaving all that to an amateur can be a recipe for disaster.

It would be easy for me to illustrate my point with stories of U/HNWIs who have squandered their wealth by trying to manage their own financial affairs. But the purpose of this book isn't to scare you. So allow me to make my point with common sense. You may consider yourself an astute investor, capable of assessing investments and managing risks. Are you good enough to be paid for it? Would a reasonably-minded U/HNWI hire you to manage their investment account? No?

Then ask yourself this: *why would a wise, successful U/HNWI such as yourself hire someone like that?* Knowing that so much is riding on your decisions, why would you be comfortable trusting your wealth to someone in which you had less than absolute, 100% confidence?

And what about the other areas of wealth management? While it might be easy for some U/HNWIs to convince themselves of their ability to pick stocks, U/HNWIs need much more than a stock picker. They need someone with a wide range of financial experience, someone with a basic grounding in estate planning, tax planning, and alternative investments – someone who can analyze a private equity deal, divest a significant stock position, and establish a charitable remainder trust all in one week. They need someone who is backed up by a team of financial specialists, and is skilled at playing the role of "personal CFO" for the U/HNWI – the professional who co-ordinates this team and oversees its performance. At the end of the day, I doubt many U/HNWIs would be willing to say they have even a fraction of these skills.

Most of the U/HNWIs I've ever met understand that working with a qualified professional helps them secure their wealth. More often than not, I've found this mindset to be a natural extension of the route many of them took to became wealthy in the first place. Many of the U/HNWIs I know have achieved their wealth through building their own businesses. In the course of building these businesses, most entrepreneurs come to realize how difficult it is to do anything right if one tries to do everything oneself. Sooner or later, they have to hire others – other specialists – to do the kind of work they can't do well themselves. Working with a professional wealth advisor is simply another example of what they've had to do for as long as they can remember.

For those who have become wealthy suddenly, it can take some time to reach this conclusion. Until they do, their wealth is at great risk. In many cases, such individuals have managed their own wealth for some time with relative ease. All of a sudden, a wealth "event" elevates their net worth to a new level, and they assume they can continue to manage their wealth in the way they always have. While it's certainly possible for U/HNWIs to be able to survive without a financial professional, sooner or later there comes a point in time where they will face an important financial challenge, a decision they realize they can't solve on their own. Without an established relationship already in place with a financial professional they know and trust, it will be difficult to act in an appropriate and timely manner. If that's not a question of security, I don't know what is.

## A final word on the rules

There's no denying that wealth can be a complicated subject. But the foundation of wealth is pure simplicity. If you ever find yourself bogged down by the complexity of wealth management, just come back to the rules above. A refresher will give you perspective on what you *really* need to know.

# Key concepts: Chapter three

- Wealth can be an overwhelming subject. Sticking to five basic rules can help you navigate through these complexities.

- These rules aren't meant to suggest specific investment strategies. Rather, they indicate a certain mindset that should guide wealth strategies and financial decision-making.

    #1: U/HNWIs must be personally responsible for their wealth. This means accepting a minimum level of participation in the management of their wealth.

    #2: U/HNWIs need to consider wealth in a different way. This means seeing wealth from a lifestyle perspective – for the practical difference it makes in their life.

    #3: U/HNWIs need to secure wealth first, build wealth second. Now that they have enough wealth to guarantee a high quality of life, they need to be more concerned with securing what they have rather than building more.

    #4: U/HNWIs need to investigate new wealth management options, because the challenges they face are different from any they've faced before.

    #5: U/HNWIs need to work with a financial professional. This is the most important rule. U/HNWIs need a highly skilled "personal CFO" who is well-versed in a variety of financial areas, someone who can co-ordinate effective wealth strategies among multiple specialists.

## Resources

"The rules" of wealth come from my personal experiences with U/HNWIs I've known over the years. That said, there are a few resources that should help you understand some of the general concepts behind these rules a little better.

***Wealth: An Owner's Manual*** by Michael Stolper

***The Wright Exit Strategy*** by Bruce R. Wright

# New money, old money

chapter

- *New money vs. old money*
- *Different ways of achieving rapid wealth*
- *Process for handling rapid wealth*

**4**

*"Remember, that money is of a prolific generating nature. Money can beget money, and its offspring can beget more."*

**Benjamin Franklin**

Until very recently, the surest way to become a U/HNWI was to be born into the right family. Consider the list of the wealthiest people in America, published annually by *Forbes* magazine. Back in 1980, some 60% of Forbes 400 households reported their wealth was inherited. By 1997, only 20% of reporting households in the Forbes 400 reported inheritance as the primary source of their wealth. This general trend holds true of the larger U/HNWI population.

Over the past ten years, a number of factors – the rise of entrepreneurship, the increasing use of stock options in executive compensation, increasing mergers and acquisitions by corporations – have resulted in more U/HNWIs who have created their wealth (rather than having received it) than in any other time in history.

These "new money" families often face a tough transition into their wealth. The sudden and sometimes shocking accumulation of wealth brings a whole host of problems which are often not present in a family who has been wealthy for a generation or two. Often an "old money" family is somewhat "seasoned" when it comes to handling their wealth. An old money family is generally more aware of the financial and life challenges the affluent must face. Members of old money families tend to be more comfortable with their identity as wealthy people, and generally more willing to accept the responsibilities that wealth can bring. That's not to say old money families are without their problems. But when they face these problems, an old money family often has a support network of financial professionals already in place. That help can make all the difference in the struggle to stay wealthy.

In contrast, new money families often have little time to prepare before they must confront the issues and challenges that accompany wealth. Such events often leave people in a state of shock – not only because of the financial implications of the wealth event, but because of the ongoing emotional or psychological effect wealth can have on a family's way of life. Without the skills or the resources to manage wealth effectively, these families face stress, conflict, and hardships. In extreme cases, a new money family can buckle under these pressures, and squander their hard-won wealth.

This chapter details some of the common scenarios that lead one to become wealthy rapidly, and lists some of the inherent challenges of new wealth. It also provides a simplified method of handling some of those challenges. It will be immensely valuable to those who have attained wealth in a short period of time – or expect to at some time in the future. But even if you've been wealthy for awhile, you'll want to read the following pages. Understanding what responsibilities new money families have to face may make it easier to accept your own. Perhaps more importantly, even if you are accustomed to your wealth, your children (or grandchildren) may not be. Understanding the difficulties faced by those not accustomed to wealth will help you understand some of the emotions your heirs will likely face, and teach you about what you can do to ensure they don't stumble on their way to becoming U/HNWIs themselves.

## New wealth events

There are many, many ways to become wealthy; what follows is by no means an exhaustive list, but rather some of the most common I've encountered while working with U/HNWI clients. Along with a basic description of the circumstances the truly wealthy may find themselves in, I've included a brief list of some of the challenges these people face, as well as possible solutions to those challenges. You'll notice that in many cases, they are as much *psychological* as they are *financial*. Again, I believe anyone providing guidance to the wealthy must understand the psychological component of wealth – how wealth changes a person's perception of the world – and account for it when formulating any personalized strategy to secure that wealth.

New wealth event #1: **the business owner**

A business is usually the product of a life's work. Little wonder, then, that when the time comes to finally sell, that work can command a hefty price. So hefty, in fact, that business owners can transform themselves into U/HNWIs almost overnight.

Such a transformation is rarely easy for the business owner. The sale of a long-standing business is often fraught with emotions. While some business owners find it easy to separate their emotions from the decision to sell, for most owners, selling is a difficult experience. Usually, a long-standing business is more than an asset for the owner — it is a part of an identity. If the sale of that identity is sudden, or the result of financial or personal pressures rather than a genuine desire to sell, a business owner can suffer restlessness, anxiety, or even depression. Those U/HNWIs thinking about selling their businesses must be prepared for such emotions, and should have a well-considered succession plan in place — including an idea of what they'd like to do after they leave the business — long before finalizing the sale.

In addition to these emotional challenges, business-owner U/HNWIs face a number of financial challenges when it comes to dealing with their new wealth. Most of the time, a business sale to a publicly-traded company results in a highly concentrated portfolio — a portfolio that lacks any meaningful diversification and exposes the new U/HNWI to significant concentration risk. "Lock in" provisions that prevent the former business owner from selling that stake (a common feature of many sales to public companies) further complicate the problem. Establishing an income replacement plan is another financial challenge that many business owners must confront. In many cases, the proceeds from a business sale results in a large pool of capital — more than large enough for the business owner to live on. But that capital must be structured and managed properly to ensure a secure income. Business owners can also face a number of challenges when it comes to estate planning. Most businesses are sold in the later stages of the owner's life (high-tech firms are a recent and notable exception), making estate planning almost an immediate concern as soon as the business is sold.

Preparation is the key to success for business-owner U/HNWIs. As mentioned, business owners must have a clear understanding of what they want to do after the business is sold. Financially, the U/HNWI should investigate financing options prior to the sale — including stock collars, if applicable — with an eye to minimizing taxes.

If a post-sale "lock up" or other restriction is an issue, the U/HNWI will need to explore specialized divestiture strategies, preferably with a trained professional. It's also a good idea for U/HNWIs to review their estate plans: selling a business is a dramatic financial change, and typically makes an existing plan obsolete.

## New wealth event #2: **the executive**

Over the past decade or so, there has been a significant change in the way executives, upper-level management, and senior employees are paid. More and more of the corporate elite are sidestepping rich salaries in favor of options and bonus packages. As a result, more and more of them are joining the ranks of the wealthy.

While options can bring wealth, they also bring a barrage of financial and psychological challenges. Often, an options package can initiate a profound shift in the personality of the individual. Personally, I have seen otherwise frugal executives begin reckless spending sprees after receiving options. I have seen otherwise rational, long-term investors become slaves to the stock ticker after their options vest. And I have seen otherwise well-grounded individuals suffer bouts of financial euphoria, making reckless financial decisions without proper consideration of issues such as goals, taxes, or lifestyle planning. All because they were granted a generous options package. It should be obvious how damaging such a mindset can be.

The financial challenges facing the executive U/HNWI can be equally complicated. Among the most important of these challenges: deciding when to exercise options. Answering the question requires detailed planning, and careful consideration of a number of variables (such as tax planning and estate planning issues). The need for diversification is another significant challenge. Typically, options leave the executive with a massive position in company stock – a potentially dangerous situation. While there can be sound financial reasons for hanging on to that stock (the desire to delay a large tax bill, for example), in most cases the risks of an excessively concentrated portfolio significantly outweigh these benefits. Making matters more complicated is the fierce loyalty many long-serving executives and senior employees feel toward their employer. In other cases, the executive is reluctant to sell a position because of the message it might send to the market. Such considerations often prevent an executive from selling company stock, even when it makes considerable financial sense.

To overcome these challenges, executives must first control their own behavior. Despite any opinion to the contrary, options aren't wealth – they are the *potential* for wealth – so making significant lifestyle changes based on their estimated future worth isn't a wise idea. Beyond that, executives must learn about their options package, and understand how decisions regarding it can affect their future wealth. Finally, the executive must understand what to do after exercising an options package.

## New wealth event #3: **the heir**

Inheritance has certainly become a less common method of becoming a U/HNWI. But that may be about to change. In its annual *Survey of Affluent Americans*, U.S. Trust estimates that over $5-trillion will change hands over the next 15-20 years. No doubt that will create a good number of new U/HNWIs.

Receiving any inheritance can be a challenging experience, both financially and emotionally. If the inheritance is significant – significant enough to propel a recipient of otherwise modest means into U/HNWI status – these challenges are magnified. Even when death is an inevitable end to a long-running illness, a large inheritance can result in grief and remorse. If relations with that parent were strained, the heir can feel reluctant or even guilty about receiving wealth, and can make unwise financial decisions as a way of "getting back" at the deceased. Even if the relationship was healthy and the death expected, grief can cloud sound investment judgement, and result in decisions which jeopardize the new U/HNWI's financial security.

The financial challenges of an inheritance are usually just as difficult as the emotional challenges. If children or grandchildren are unprepared for the responsibilities of wealth, a large inheritance can be a real burden. A common financial challenge faced by heirs is the inheritance of an unsuitable portfolio. Assets held by an aging parent or grandparent are rarely appropriate for children in their working years, meaning many U/HNWI heirs have to spend considerable time and energy reorganizing and reallocating the portfolios they inherit. Emotional attachments to particular assets (the family cottage, for example) can make these decisions more difficult. Finally, if the organization of the parent's estate was less than perfect, heirs can inherit a legacy of legal and financial headaches as well as wealth. I've personally seen estates so poorly organized that heirs were forced to sell significant portions of the estate simply to pay taxes and fees.

Solutions to these challenges involve two people: the heir and the parent. The parent can prevent some of these challenges by taking time to educate heirs about the responsibilities that come with wealth. Letting heirs know about their eventual inheritance ahead of time can also make the transition to wealth smoother. Preparation is also crucial for heirs. Learning more about wealth before receiving an inheritance is an obvious first step, as is approaching parents and learning about their estate planning intentions. In an ideal situation, both the heir and the parent would communicate fully throughout the wealth transfer process, and put specialized financial structures and strategies in place to make that transfer as smooth as possible. That usually requires the services of a skilled professional.

## New wealth event #4: **the athlete and the entertainer**

Salaries continue to balloon in both professional sports and in the entertainment industry. Sports heroes, rock stars, and other celebrities can transform themselves from starving artists into multi-millionaires overnight.

As could be expected, this kind of windfall brings a number of unique financial and emotional challenges. One significant challenge is the publicity this kind of wealth often brings. It's become standard practice for the press to report large sports contracts immediately after they're signed. The resulting debate (and sometimes criticism) can often be difficult for the new athlete to face, raising feelings of resentment or even guilt. Another issue is the loss of privacy these U/HNWIs face. Unless prepared for it, the instant fame of a large sports contract or hit album can be unsettling and disruptive. Yet another emotional challenge is the feeling of exploitation: a new fortune can create a number of "long-lost" friends and family members who want nothing more than to cash in on the individual's success.

In terms of financial challenges, athletes and entertainers must face the issue of financial maturity: having rocketed from obscurity to the forefront of the public eye (most of the time at an extremely young age), athletes and entertainers are often ill-equipped to handle the responsibility their massive contracts bring. Instead of carefully managing their wealth, they can quickly give in to a number of temptations, and squander it rapidly. Managing an unsecure income is another financial challenge facing these U/HNWIs. Often an initially generous contract can be followed up with something much less generous, as the market value for the U/HNWIs talents or skills dries up.

To navigate through these challenges, athletes and entertainers need to move quickly – both in terms of their life and in terms of their wealth. Once the euphoria of "making it big" wears off, they need to become comfortable with the idea of being wealthy. They need to develop resistance to the temptation to spend wildly, and need to see their wealth as something that will give them long-term financial security rather than short-term fun. Financially, these U/HNWIs need to learn how to allocate their wealth wisely, and become familiar with specialized financial structures that will turn short-term contracts into lasting wealth. Professional help will almost always play a key role here. The speed at which these U/HNWIs acquire wealth will almost always demand it.

## New wealth event #5: **the divorcee**

Of all the ways to acquire wealth, divorce is perhaps the most challenging. For both partners, a divorce usually means the rebuilding of almost every element of one's finances. On top of it all, there are the complex, often volatile emotions spawned by a divorce – emotions that can often derail efforts to secure and build wealth.

The distribution of assets in a divorce can be an enormous emotional challenge. Depending on the level of hostility during the proceedings, it's common for divorcees to feel contradictory emotions – anxiety and relief, fear and freedom, depression and euphoria – often in rapid succession. Such emotions can make it difficult to make timely financial decisions, or can drive a divorcing spouse to agree to unfair settlements simply to resolve a prolonged conflict. On a longer term basis, divorced U/HNWIs often discover wealth acquired through a divorce comes with emotional strings: managing that wealth can bring up bad memories, or feelings of regret or rage, even after several years. Such emotions can interfere with prudent wealth management, and may lead the divorcee to be apathetic or even hostile to their wealth.

The financial challenges can be equally enormous. In many cases, basic income needs will be met through alimony or ongoing maintenance settlements, but in many others, settlements only approximate the lifestyle the divorcee enjoyed while married.

For the spouse transferring wealth to the other, settlements and ongoing payments may be a tremendous obstacle to rebuilding wealth. In most cases, the estate plans of ex-spouses will need a complete redrafting, and securing appropriate insurance will be a top priority, as will renaming beneficiaries.

Divorcees need to attack both the emotional and the financial challenges of wealth at the same time. Divorcees need to separate the emotional consequences of divorce from the financial decisions that need to be made. In some cases, all that will be required is heightened self-awareness. In others, a qualified counselor might be required. Divorcees also need to be ready for a complete financial reconstruction after their divorce – everything from income to estate planning must be examined closely, and new strategies devised for new life circumstances. Often, working with a trusted financial professional will be necessary, to ensure new wealth is being managed properly and appropriate decisions are made at the right time.

## New wealth: a practical management guide

I've outlined some of the specific challenges facing some of the more common new wealth scenarios. Now I'd like to provide a practical guide that will help any new U/HNWI navigate through the critical first few months of their wealth. Here are five essential steps you can take that will help you turn new money into old money.

### Step #1: Take time; develop perspective

Most people who become wealthy rapidly go through a period of shock. Sometimes that shock will come out in subtle ways – perhaps in an occasional moment of euphoria or disbelief. In other cases the shock will be drastic and obvious: a complete withdrawal from friends and family, feelings of extreme guilt, or sudden, uncharacteristic behavior. These emotions can be incredibly disruptive, and can actually hinder efforts to manage wealth. For this reason, the first thing any new U/HNWI should do after their "wealth event" is to do nothing – at least for awhile. By taking a "time out" and gaining some perspective on the changes your wealth will bring, you'll be giving yourself time to grow accustomed to your new status. More importantly, you'll be protecting your new wealth from ill-considered financial decisions.

Of course, we all need money to live, so this time out has to be enacted in the right way. Here's how. First, determine how much money you'll need to meet ongoing expenses for a specified period of time (say, three to six months). Be generous here, just to be on the safe side. Whatever that sum is, put it aside in a simple savings or money market account. Then, put the rest of your wealth in a short-term investment – an investment that pays a guaranteed rate of interest and locks in your money for a given length of time. It doesn't matter all that much what vehicle you choose. The goal isn't to maximize your investment return, but to prevent you from doing something stupid. That said, don't think you can just walk into the bank and buy a standard CD or GIC. For U/HNWIs like you, there are better options available – so you should speak to a professional and find out what works for you.

How long should that "time out" be? It's difficult to come up with any hard and fast answer – it really depends on the personality involved, and his or her ability to manage the emotions that accompany new wealth. At a bare minimum, I recommend three months. Three months is the minimum amount of time new U/HNWIs will need to grow comfortable with the idea of being wealthy. Three months is also adequate time to find a qualified investment professional – someone specially trained and capable of helping new U/HNWIs manage the specific challenges their wealth has created.

## Step #2: **Construct a wish list**

After securing your wealth for the short term, it's time to construct a "wish list." Ideally, this should be more than a list of things. Rather, it should be a detailed list of lifestyle choices your money can make possible. Ask yourself: what would you like to do with your life now that you don't have to worry about money? What do you see yourself doing in five, ten, twenty years? Where would you like to live? What causes would you like to support? Some of the items on your list will be immediately obvious – they are the things you've waited your entire life for. Others will only become clear in time.

Once you have this list, you'll be able to assign each goal a priority. It's perfectly acceptable to have multiple priorities here, but at the very least, you'll want to classify priorities in terms of short-term, mid-term and long-term goals as in table 4.1 below. The more specific you are, the better able you'll be to formulate strategies to make these wishes a reality. At this point in time, don't try to limit your imagination with ideas of what you can actually afford. Instead let your thoughts run, and think about the person you'd like to be if money were no object. It's one of the best ways to understand what wealth means to you, and to answer the age-old question, "how much is enough?"

table 4.1: **Sample wish list**

| Goal | How Much | When | Amount Allocated |
|---|---|---|---|
| **Short Term** | | | |
| A new home | $750,000 | Now | $750,000 |
| A vacation home | $300,000 | Now | $300,000 |
| A boat | $100,000 | Now | $100,000 |
| Gifts for children | $250,000 | Now | $250,000 |
| **Long Term** | | | |
| Annual income from investments | $250,000 per year after tax | For 45 years at 3% inflation | $5,950,000 |
| Income for parents | $50,000 year after tax | For 20 years at 3% inflation | $660,000 |

## Step #3: **Re-visit goals**

Now that you've constructed your list, you can think about what you can actually afford. This can be the most difficult part of the new money experience: those who have come into their wealth rapidly often have a hard time believing there is any limit to wealth.

For most new U/HNWIs, determining the cost of wish-list items isn't easy. Sure, the cost of one-time, immediate wishes (a new house, a new car, etc.) is easy to determine. But the cost of ongoing or future wishes usually requires a few calculations. Start with the current cost of your wish – as if you were paying for it today. Be generous with your estimate, just to play it safe. Next, determine how many years you have before you pay for it. Factor in inflation – the gradual increase in the cost of everything – and assume a basic return on your wealth while you wait to make your purchase. You should now have a rough estimate of how much your future goals will cost you in today's dollars.

Table 4.2 should help you. It projects the rise in the price of an imaginary $100,000 purchase through the years, assuming a variety of inflation rates. Using this basic table, you should be able to estimate how many future dollars you'll have to save for a purchase you'd like to make in several years. An example will make my point clear. Let's say you want to purchase a $700,000 vacation property within five years. At an inflation rate of about 3%, the future cost will be $115,933 per $100,000 of property value; so $115,933 multiplied by seven will equal $811,531.

table 4.2: **Future cost of a $100,000 purchase**

| Inflation Rate | Time Period (in years) | | | | | | |
|---|---|---|---|---|---|---|---|
| | 5 | 10 | 15 | 20 | 25 | 30 | 35 |
| 3% | $115,933 | $134,403 | $155,815 | $180,638 | $209,414 | $242,774 | $281,447 |
| 4% | $121,671 | $148,036 | $180,114 | $219,142 | $266,625 | $324,396 | $394,683 |
| 5% | $127,634 | $162,902 | $207,914 | $265,363 | $338,683 | $432,261 | $551,692 |

Understand, however, this procedure will only amount to the most rudimentary estimation of future costs. While it's a good place to start your wealth planning, you'll want to follow it up with some more sophisticated simulations which will project how your capital will perform given a wide range of investment and lifestyle assumptions.

## Step #4: **Segregate wealth**

Now comes the time to divide your wealth into two distinct pools. The first is your pool of "safe" money – the wealth that maintains your current standard of living, the wealth you can't afford to lose. Again, you'll want to discuss your options with a qualified professional. Your wealth advisor should be able to help you find a suitable investment that will provide safety and tax-preferred performance at the same time.

The second pool is your "play" money. This is the wealth you can use to make positive changes, purchase luxury goods, or do whatever it is you want. Whatever you do with it, don't feel sorry about spending it. It will provide you with some enjoyment after a difficult transition from your old life to your new.

Step #5: **seek professional help**

There's only one more task to complete before you start on the road to *true wealth*. And it's the most important. For the vast majority of new U/HNWIs, seeking professional help is an absolute must. The sooner you start working with a professional, the sooner new wealth can be made secure.

Understand that not just any financial professional will do, however. Now that you're wealthy, you need to understand that your finances require more care, more attention, and more knowledge from the financial professionals you work with. When you go looking for a professional, you'll want to find one who has been specially trained in some of the common scenarios facing the newly wealthy, and preferably someone who has had direct experience in helping them manage their new wealth. You can read a little more about some of the qualities that person should have in the appendix at the back of this book.

## A final word on new money

Managing wealth is always a very personal experience – and the experience is usually more complicated than these short pages can really do justice. For that reason, you'll need to find a financial professional, and find one now. There is simply no better way to ensure your specific wealth challenges are solved than by working with someone who's had experience in solving them before.

# Key concepts: Chapter four

- There are currently more U/HNWIs who have created their wealth (rather than having received it) than at any other time in history.

- Those who become wealthy suddenly face significant challenges when it comes to managing that wealth on an ongoing basis.

### The business owner

- Business-owner U/HNWIs need to prepare for wealth well in advance of the sale of their business. They should investigate divestiture options, and explore appropriate diversification strategies well before the sale is finalized.

### The executive

- Executives need to control their own behavior about their new wealth. They need to learn what they can about their options, and understand what to do after exercising those options.

### The heir

- Both the parent and the heir can help make the transition to wealth smoother. Parents can help by preparing heirs for their inheritance and educating them about wealth. Heirs can help themselves by learning more about wealth and approaching parents about their intentions. Ideally, both parent and heir should work together to formulate specialized financial structures to make a transfer of wealth as smooth as possible.

### The athlete/entertainer

- Athletes and entertainers need to move quickly to secure wealth. They need to grow comfortable with wealth, and resist some of the easy temptations wealth offers. They also need to see wealth from a long-term perspective, and take action to secure it so that it lasts for many years.

### The divorcee

- The emotional challenges of a divorce are particularly trying. Divorcees need to separate the emotional consequences of divorce from their financial decision-making. Divorcees also need to prepare for a complete overhaul of their financial plan, and work with a trusted professional to ensure appropriate decisions are made at the appropriate time.

- There are four steps the newly wealthy can take to manage the challenges presented by their rapid wealth:

  **Step 1: Take a time out.** Establish a period of time when you defer important financial decisions. The length of time will vary according to the individual.

  **Step 2: Construct a "wish list".** Determine what kinds of positive changes you'd like to make to your life now that you have wealth.

**Step 3: Re-visit goals.** Determine what wishes you can actually afford. Remember to take inflation into account.

**Step 4: Segregate your wealth.** Put it into two piles: safe money and play money. The first is the money you require to fund a generous lifestyle. The latter is the money you can use to purchase whatever you want.

**Step 5: Work with a professional.** The most important step. Working with a qualified wealth advisor will ensure you have a chance to turn your new money into old money.

## Resources

There are many resources available for those looking to learn more about old money — most of them provide an interesting look at how the wealthy families of the past built their fortunes. When it comes to the subject of new money, however, the information is a little sparse. Here are the best resources I could find.

***Sudden Money*** by Susan Bradley and Mary Martin

***Old Money: the Mythology of Wealth in America*** by Nelson Aldrich

## Websites

Sudden Money Institute *www.suddenmoney.com* — good advice for the newly wealthy

National Association of Family Wealth Counselors *www.nafwc.org* — information on wealth management from a family perspective

# **Money** in motion

• *Five case studies*

*"Rich or poor, it's nice to have money."*

**Dorothy Parker**

N ow that we've discussed wealth from a statistical, emotional, and even psychological perspective, it's time to get down to business. It's time to take a look at how wealth works in the real world.

As I've explained, managing wealth means more than just managing money – it means managing one's *life*. Because the financial challenges facing any individual are inevitably connected with that individual's life circumstances, any examination of wealth management must involve an equally detailed examination of the individual's life goals. This simple principle explains my life-centered approach to managing a client's finances: if you don't know anything about the *person*, how can you construct the right *portfolio*?

It also explains why I think it's important to back up the more conceptual sections of this book with examples from real life. To that end, here are five case studies – some of them taken from my own client files, some of them from the files of colleagues within my firm – that describe the typical interaction between a wealth advisor and a U/HNWI. To my mind, case studies are the most effective, most interesting method of presenting complicated financial details – part of the reason why I've included them whenever possible throughout *True Wealth*. By taking a look at real-life examples, we're more "connected" with the wealth management process – we're better able to understand its potential value to our lives. They are also a good way to show how the various elements of wealth planning co-ordinate with each other, and how any consideration of wealth must include a consideration of life context. In other words, they are an immensely powerful learning tool.

These case studies follow a natural progression. You'll notice the first two cover fairly common financial challenges – the need for retirement planning and an example of asset allocation in action. My point in presenting them is not to present standard information, but rather to demonstrate how wealth can make even routine financial challenges more complicated. After that, I'll present an example of managing an options exercise and establishing a charitable foundation. Both of them demonstrate what I mean when I say wealth can sometimes create new challenges, challenges that simply didn't exist before. I'll end the chapter by taking a look at a complex business sale that involved a multitude of financial professionals working together. It should give you a good indication of how complicated wealth management can be for U/HNWIs.

You may find some portions of the following studies a little confusing – after all, we haven't yet discussed some of the more complex challenges and solutions that I'll be presenting here. So much the better. By giving you a brief taste of some common wealth management topics at the start of the book, you'll be more familiar with them when we take them up in more detail later on. At the very least, you'll be better able to appreciate the *life context* behind the various wealth management strategies I describe.

## Money in motion: the challenges of wealth

Of course, there were many challenges I could have chosen. But I've selected these case studies with an important idea in mind. You'll notice I've titled this chapter "Money in motion." I did that for a reason. The examples that follow describe scenarios in which wealth is in a state of flux or unsettled change. While the individual wealth solutions that lie behind these case studies are vastly different, they all have one thing in common: *they all constitute an attempt to move wealth out of that state of flux and into a more secure environment.* The assistance of a skilled wealth advisor (and the assistance of a number of other professionals) is crucial in such situations for making sure that wealth comes to *rest*, to a point where the U/HNWI can depend on it, and enjoy it. In a lot of ways, this is the central goal of wealth management: to build a secure financial foundation for an individual. Such a foundation will allow U/HNWIs to secure a high quality of life and to pursue whatever life goals are important to them.

Another point I'd like to make about these studies is my involvement with the various clients. As you'll notice through reading the examples in this chapter, I meet clients in a variety of ways. Many times, the people I work with are longstanding clients. In other cases, I'm introduced to clients as a financial problem-solver – as a specialist who can help a given U/HNWI overcome a specific wealth challenge. It's relatively common that I receive phone calls from an accountant, or a lawyer looking for specialized financial planning advice for one of their clients. I often return the favor with clients of mine who require particularly complex tax or legal arrangements. Sometimes I even receive a call from another financial professional – someone who doesn't necessarily have all the resources to handle a particularly complicated situation with a U/HNWI client. That may sound a little different from the way most people do business, but I've noticed that it's becoming standard practice within the financial services industry (at least at the U/HNWI level). Personally, I think it's a good thing. By fostering a climate of "co-opetition," financial professionals can spend less time competing with each other, and more time on what we're supposed to be doing: helping our clients.

Finally, you should understand that I've changed the names, modified some of the numbers and "tweaked" the personal details in many of the case studies in this chapter – and indeed, throughout *True Wealth*. This, of course, is to better protect my clients' confidentiality. And given space constraints, I've had to keep the cases as simple as possible, without sacrificing the context of the problem. The result should be a more enjoyable read, one that still does justice to the original circumstances.

## Case study #1: securing wealth for retirement

Many times, the challenges facing the U/HNWI are quite similar to the financial challenges facing the general population. But as we'll see, wealth can complicate even the most common financial challenges.

Perry was a former professional hockey player, who had come to see me a few years ago. As a former professional athlete, he was in a comfortable financial position. Of course, hockey didn't pay quite as well when he was playing as it does now, but Perry's frugal nature, coupled with additional jobs (he had been an assistant coach on a junior team after his playing career was over, and had lately been a sports commentator on a local radio program) had allowed Perry to live off his income and keep his principal largely intact. Even though it had been several years since he had been making an athlete's salary, Perry had built a reasonable net worth – just under $5-million, in fact.

As much as he loved the game of hockey, Perry was ready for a change. Essentially, he wanted to retire and spend more time on other activities. A fairly common goal, I admit, and by no means exclusive to U/HNWIs. But while the basic problem might be the same, Perry's status as a U/HNWI demanded we look at more sophisticated wealth management options.

### General approach

Perry's financial goals were similar to most retirees: to provide a long-term source of tax-preferred income, to build a conservative growth portfolio (in order to stay ahead of inflation and taxes, and provide for future needs and unexpected expenses), and to leave an estate large enough to provide for his family. Such goals suggested we divide Perry's portfolio into two components: the first to provide income, the second to provide growth.

### Solution

For the income component of the portfolio, we decided to allocate money to two separate portions. The first was a large investment in a laddered bond portfolio. Laddering would provide maximum flexibility and reduce the risk of interest rate fluctuations affecting Perry's income. The second portion was a substantial investment assigned to two *managed yield mutual funds*. As I'll describe a little later, these are funds that provide ongoing income, excellent liquidity, and significant tax advantages all at the same time.

The second component of Perry's portfolio would be allocated to growth-oriented investments. For this component, we decided on a large investment in a diversified portfolio of *I-class and F-class mutual funds*. Again, I'll discuss these in detail a little later, but in a nutshell, these would provide all the benefits of a mutual fund at a substantial cost savings. At this stage, we decided against a hedge fund or other specialized investment products – Perry just wasn't comfortable with them. That said, we did allocate a portion of the growth portfolio (5%) to more aggressive holdings, including some investments in individual growth stocks. The result would be a well-diversified portfolio that offered Perry security *and* growth.

As I said, it wasn't the challenge that Perry faced that made his situation unique – rather, it was the solution. Because of the size of their portfolios, U/HNWIs are able to access opportunities unavailable to the general population. It's my belief that U/HNWIs have a responsibility to explore these opportunities. As Perry's case shows, they can make the difference in the effort to ensure wealth isn't lost.

# Case study #2: allocating wealth after a business sale

Contrary to what some may believe, it is easier to become wealthy than it is to stay wealthy. In many cases, an individual will accumulate wealth suddenly, not fully understanding the ongoing challenges that wealth will present. This was the situation facing an entrepreneur I met some years ago.

David had been a farmer all his life. And a successful one, too: after inheriting his family's business and property some years ago, he had transformed it into a top-quality supplier of meat to the gourmet market. As much as David enjoyed his life's work, when he was approached by a processing company looking to consolidate in the area, he leapt at the chance to sell. As these things go, the sale was a fairly simple one: David would receive half of the purchase price of about $30-million in a large lump sum payment, with the remainder to be transferred in a series of cash payments over the next five years.

In this case, I wasn't involved in the actual sale of the business – that was arranged through the business broker who had approached David in the first place. But when David asked the broker about what to do with the wealth, the broker mentioned my name. At our initial meeting, I took David through what I call the "discovery" process – that is, looking at his exact needs and goals for the next several years. That's standard procedure for financial professionals, but the complexities of David's situation demanded a little more than the usual questions. Specifically, we needed to isolate David's immediate needs, and come up with a detailed wealth management plan for the rest.

### General approach

Barring any unforeseen difficulties, David's income would be more than taken care of for the next five years by the ongoing payments from the business sale. That simplified matters from an asset allocation perspective, and allowed us to divide his lump sum payment into two portions. David determined he would need about $2.5-million to satisfy immediate tax needs and provide the funds for some special purchases he had his eye on. That left approximately $12.5-million to place into a well-diversified long-term growth portfolio.

## Solution

We decided to divide David's portfolio into "core" and "satellite" positions. The former would comprise the bulk of the portfolio, and would provide consistent, conservative, tax-preferred cash flow over the long term. The latter would be reserved for more aggressive holdings – hedge funds, individual growth stocks, special situations, etc. – where the goal would be to maximize growth.

After reviewing a number of options, we decided to build the portfolio around separately managed accounts. The majority of the money (about $7-million) would be placed with a world-renowned global value manager. This particular manager is a value style specialist, with an outstanding track record of building very secure portfolios that consistently outperform benchmark indices. This manager also happens to manage a fund in which David had invested for many years. In other words, it was a natural fit. We split a further $4-million between two other managers who offered complementary styles and investment mandates with little correlation to the first manager. This allocation would provide balanced growth in most market conditions.

For the aggressive portion of the portfolio, we decided to make a placement of about $1.5-million into a multi-manager, multi-strategy hedge fund. This would boost performance, and provide David with additional protection in the event of a market downturn. After reviewing a number of options, we selected a "fund-of-funds" structure. The diversification offered by such an option appeals to me when it comes to aggressive investments. The remainder of the funds (about $500,000) we kept in cash, in part to take advantage of any special opportunities that might come along, in part to construct a "just in case" fund for unforeseen emergencies.

Throughout the process, we consulted with a tax specialist I know, someone who could help David formulate strategies to minimize taxes on the payments he could expect over the next several years. By taking the time now to plan for the coming tax hit, David would be much better off in the future. We also constructed a personal estate plan, something that would keep David's wealth secure for the next generation.

David's case demonstrates the necessity of careful planning after a rapid wealth event. By notifying me of his exact situation right away, David was able to formulate strategies across a spectrum of wealth management areas. That should help him stay wealthy in the years ahead.

# Case study #3: executive options

More and more executives and senior-level employees are acquiring wealth by way of options. But as familiar as they are becoming, options are complicated financial instruments, demanding great care and skillful management. Let me give you an example.

My client Diana works for a pharmaceutical company here in the Vancouver area. For more than a decade, this company has been researching various treatments for certain age-related illnesses; a few years ago one of its products had become the product of choice in the treatment of a particular ailment. In a matter of months, income from this product had transformed the company from a small, unknown start-up to an industry leader. The result had been a dramatic increase in the company's stock price. For employees, this development was the payoff for years of hard work. As the share price soared, so too did the value of options and other incentive packages. This was the situation Diana found herself in when a colleague suggested she contact me.

As one of the company's senior executives, Diana had amassed a considerable stockpile of options – the value of which had passed the $15-million mark. This had turned out to be something of a mixed blessing. While Diana was certainly ecstatic about the value of her options, she also noticed she was becoming more and more anxious about her financial position. She found herself tracking the movements of company stock frequently, (several times a day in fact) and she was more concerned about the company's future prospects. She had also found it difficult to make any decision about when to exercise her options. She needed to know what to do.

### General approach

Like many options holders, the challenge facing Diana was as much mental as it was financial. Before she considered what to do with her options, Diana needed to develop a strong mental attitude, and learn to minimize the role of emotions in her investment decisions. The first step was to clarify Diana's financial position, and find out exactly where she stood. We reviewed the exact terms of her options package together, and determined an approximate value for her holdings. This helped Diana to put her options into perspective, and concentrate on the most important issue at hand: minimizing the risk presented by holding over 98% of her net worth in a single stock position.

**Solution**

The first step in dealing with this risk was to establish an appropriate exercise schedule for the options. After discussing a number of Diana's lifestyle goals, we decided on a systematic option exercise schedule. By exercising the oldest, cheapest options at pre-set times throughout the year, we could eliminate the guesswork that often plagues options planning, and reduce the temptation to try to co-ordinate an exercise with market events. I brought in an accountant colleague of mine who's had considerable experience in dealing with exercise strategies; the three of us discussed the tax implications of the proposed schedule. I wanted to ensure Diana took full advantage of tax opportunities regarding her options, and ensure she wasn't surprised by anything come tax-time.

Next, we constructed a plan to deal with the proceeds of the ongoing exercises. Personally, I believe options holders compound risk by hanging on to their stock for too long after exercise. So I recommended an asset allocation program that would help shift Diana's wealth to a more diversified portfolio as stock was sold. Yes, given the company's future prospects, this quick transfer might mean cutting gains short. But by taking some of her wealth off the table, Diana could secure her quality of life, and her peace of mind. That's ultimately more important than taking a chance on the big score.

Diana's case is a classic study in the complexity of an options package. By working with a team of qualified financial professionals, Diana was able to overcome the financial and emotional challenges of her options position and secure her wealth for many years to come. That's a lesson every U/HNWI needs to learn.

# Case study #4: setting up a foundation

With wealth comes responsibility. Most U/HNWIs believe they have an obligation to protect their wealth for the next generation – and that includes not only their family, but the community-at-large. It's a position I support, as we'll see in the next study.

The Hendersons are what you would call an "old money" family. In a previous generation, the family had made a considerable fortune owning and operating a chain of grocery outlets throughout Vancouver and its suburbs. Over the course of years, most of these stores had been sold, and the bulk of the family's wealth was invested in property. A colleague in another firm had been working with a younger branch of the Henderson family for some time when he approached me about the elderly Hendersons wanting to add something to their estate plan. As longtime residents in the Vancouver area, the Hendersons were looking to give something back to the community that had been good to them. My colleague was just starting to become involved with estate planning in his own practice, and realized the Hendersons needed something more than he could provide at this time. We agreed to meet with the family together, and discuss the possibility of restructuring their current estate plan to include generous charitable donations to a variety of local and regional causes.

### General approach

The first order of business was to establish the family's charitable goals. After a detailed discussion, the Hendersons identified three: (a) they wanted to donate to a wide variety of causes; (b) they wanted their charitable effort to last for as long as possible; (c) they were looking to make a considerable donation, having set aside about $25-million out of their estate for giving. That said, it became clear through my questioning that the Hendersons remained concerned about giving that kind of money immediately. What was needed was a structure that would allow the Hendersons to maintain control over their assets until such time as they were certain their needs could be met.

### Solutions

After discussing a number of options, my colleague and I decided that a charitable foundation made the most sense. First and foremost, a foundation would give the Hendersons the ability to target smaller, local causes, and still have control over how those donations would be distributed. It would also give them an opportunity to involve their family in the charitable effort, and the chance to have those efforts extend well into the future. Finally, a foundation would allow the Hendersons to make ongoing gifts while keeping the bulk of their capital in reserve for other needs.

I introduced the Hendersons to a tax advisor, in order to secure specialized advice on the exact structure of the proposed foundation. Together, we decided to establish the Henderson's foundation with a $5-million cash bequest – enough to give the foundation a significant pool of capital. The donation would result in a large tax credit. On the advice of the tax advisor, the Hendersons held a good portion of the credit for subsequent years. This would be a more efficient use of the credit, as the Hendersons would be able to use it to draw down their annual income to a lower level for several years.

I then reviewed some of the financial features of the foundation with the family. The Hendersons established an initial target bequest level of 10-12% a year – a little higher than normal, perhaps, but the family felt it important to see the results of their bequest in their community while they were still alive. Besides, the Hendersons fully intended to donate more in the future – if all goes according to plan, the Hendersons will make an additional bequest through their estate, which will help to offset taxes on their real estate portfolio, ensuring their heirs won't have to sell the properties to cover taxes. We drew up an allocation plan that would allow foundation assets to keep up with the drawdown, and provide for additional growth. That plan would help ensure the Henderson's generosity will be felt in the community for many years to come.

The Hendersons' case demonstrates the benefit of the team approach when it comes to making a charitable bequest. By considering a variety of options and consulting a number of professionals, the Hendersons were able to ensure their charitable goals were met – and that their charitable dollars were put to the greatest use possible.

## Case study #5: business divestiture

As I'll explain throughout this book, wealth management is not a one-time event. Most of the time, the complexities of wealth demand ongoing attention and co-ordinated financial strategies. This is demonstrated in our final case study, a situation that involved many elements of wealth management and was enacted over a number of years.

Tom was the majority owner of a large manufacturing business that provided parts and equipment to the automotive industry. By most standards, the company was successful, with sales of about $40 million a year. One day as we were sitting down for a "working lunch," Tom mentioned that he was looking forward to retirement. This in turn led to a discussion of his "exit strategy" from the business. It was clear Tom's decision was very much in the preliminary stages – he certainly wasn't *mentally* ready to leave his business yet. Even so, I suggested he meet with our firm's exclusive sales and divestitures division – a team of professionals who specialize in helping entrepreneurs co-ordinate a business sale. A meeting could help him determine what his options were, and perhaps give him a rough estimate of what his business would be worth.

### General approach

After a number of fact-finding conference calls with Tom and myself, the sales and divestitures team flew out to meet with Tom and examine his business. They then conducted a preliminary valuation. The team calculated that given company profit margins and other considerations, Tom's business was worth a little more than $25-million. That's certainly nothing to be ashamed about, but it was clear that Tom was disappointed. But all was not lost. Along with its evaluation, the divestiture team provided a list of initiatives Tom could implement over the next several years, changes that could dramatically increase the value of the business. This suited Tom's situation perfectly. He was more than willing to put in a little more elbow grease to ensure maximum value for his business. Besides, as I mentioned above, he wasn't ready to leave the business just yet anyway.

### Solution

The solutions to Tom's situation took place in two phases. First of all, Tom and I identified a credible date for his exit from the business. Two to three years seemed a reasonable target. This would give Tom the time he needed to increase the value of his business. The second phase of the strategy would come when Tom actually sold. At that time, we'd have to develop a feasible strategy for securing and allocating his new wealth.

#### Phase 1

Over the next several years, Tom enacted most of the recommendations the sales and divestitures team had made, including hiring outside management, introducing strict quality controls, and updating plant facilities. When the time came to sell, I contacted the sales and divestitures team again, and this time, the situation was much different. Over the course of three years, the business had boosted sales dramatically – to over $160 million a year. The divestiture team estimated the business to now be worth anywhere between $85-and $110-million.

Tom was now ready to put the team to use. In exchange for a percentage of the sale price, the divestiture team agreed to market the business worldwide, screen potential buyers, and assist in securing financing. In a little over three months, the team identified 87 potential buyers, split almost evenly between firms operating within the industry and private-equity interests. The team whittled this list down to five interested parties, with offers between $90-million and $125-million. In the end, Tom opted for a combined cash and stock purchase by an industry leader. This would leave him with a cash payment of a little under $15-million, and an equity position of about $100-million.

### Phase 2

Tom's business had brought him considerable wealth. But now that he had sold, the goal shifted to *securing* that wealth. While Tom was certainly confident in the prospects of the company that had bought his business, a $100-million position in a single stock was something we simply weren't comfortable with. Which is why we arranged for a *prepaid equity collar strategy* – a strategy that would provide Tom with downside protection without passing up further growth. After discussing the matter thoroughly, we determined that $75-million would give Tom enough money to do everything he would ever want to in life, including spending, gifts, and charitable bequests. Clearly, this was the wealth we had to secure. Tom then entered into a five-year agreement with my firm to protect $75-million of his position. The agreement would provide Tom with 90% protection against the current value of his position (that is, down to $67.5-million), with the potential for 200% upside participation. The remaining $25-million in stock would be kept in the market – a level of risk Tom was comfortable with, now that he could count on $75-million no matter what the market did.

In order to gain even more protection, Tom agreed to a *prepaid forward transaction* on the stock. The firm forwarded him $45-million in cash (60% of the value of his collared shares). The bulk of that we then invested in a well-diversified equity portfolio – something that would allow for growth and tax-efficient returns, yet help reduce the risk of holding a single stock. The remainder we invested in a laddered bond portfolio that would provide Tom with further security and a stable source of additional income. As for the $15-million in cash Tom received from the sale, we put that in a variety of short-term instruments in order to fund immediate purchases as well as the anticipated tax liability.

Understand that I'm simplifying Tom's case here, leaving out much of the heavy-duty negotiations, tax planning, and estate planning that naturally accompanies any business sale. Even so, the complexity of Tom's situation should demonstrate how wealth management for U/HNWIs should be a co-ordinated, sustained effort, involving several different professionals on several different levels. This multi-layered approach ensures U/HNWIs get to keep the wealth they worked so hard to acquire.

## A final word on money in motion

The case studies I've described here are highly personal. Inevitably, there will be differences in the scenarios that you encounter. Don't let that discourage you from using these examples as a guide. At the end of the day, the general concepts at work in these studies are applicable to nearly all U/HNWI challenges, whether they have $1-million, $10-million, $100-million or more.

# section 2

## Managing wealth

Any way you look at it, wealth is a
complicated subject. To manage it
properly, you'll need patience,
discipline, and a fair bit of knowledge.
This section will get you started.

# My investment principles

- *My guiding investment principles*
- *Why I believe them*
- *Why you should too*

*"Not a tenth of us who are in business are doing as well as we could if we merely followed the principles that were known to our grandfathers."*

**William Feather**

In a time when most investors pay more attention to performance than to principles, it seems to me it's time for financial professionals to stand up for what we believe in.

Let me be blunt: investors need to have clear guiding principles in their mind *before* they invest. This is true of all investors, but it is especially true of U/HNWIs. Without a strong sense of what you believe in, it's easy to become sidetracked, distracted, or even duped into putting your wealth where it doesn't belong. On the other hand, with a strong set of principles to guide you, it will be easier to stay focused on your financial and lifestyle goals. These principles make it easier to determine what investments belong in your portfolio, and which ones don't, making you a more capable and responsible steward of your own wealth.

To that end, I think it only fair that I explain the principles that guide the investment decisions I make for my U/HNWI clients. What follows in this chapter is a detailed explanation of the fundamental principles that are at the heart of every investment recommendation, every estate planning recommendation, and every tax planning recommendation I make. Taken together, they form a coherent system of beliefs that guides my actions as a wealth advisor. I'm not saying there aren't other ways to secure and build wealth. But in my experience, these principles have given my clients the best opportunity to secure a high-quality lifestyle for themselves and the people they care about. My guess is that they'll work for you too.

## Principle #1: Adapt a contrarian mindset

I don't believe in following the investment crowd. I often do the opposite. In fact, I actively look for opportunities to *exploit* the decisions made by the crowd. I believe most U/HNWIs should adapt a similar approach.

This is only the most general summary of a contrarian mindset – in reality, it means something more than simply doing the opposite of what the crowd does. At the core of the contrarian mindset is a philosophy of independence. To me, a contrarian is someone who is sensitive to market emotions, but disciplined enough to resist acting upon them. *To the contrarian, investment opportunities make sense not because the majority agrees they make sense, but rather because the fundamentals of the given investment make sense.* True contrarians are people who are confident in their own abilities – and in their own principles – and courageous enough to go *with* the crowd when the crowd evaluates an investment opportunity correctly, and to go *against* the crowd when the crowd doesn't seem to know what it's doing. That is the kind of investor I am for my clients.

What does all this mean on a practical level? Well, it means I align myself more with the "value" school of investing, buying investments that are of high quality, but temporarily underpriced due to their unpopularity. I say this with a number of qualifications, however. I do not think that just because a given stock has been beaten down in the market, that it should necessarily be added to the portfolio – as I said, it has to make sense because the fundamentals make sense. I also recognize that high quality sometimes demands high prices – and sometimes that price is worth paying. Finally, I also recognize that just because the price of a given investment has exceeded its "fair" value, it doesn't necessarily mean the time to sell has come. The long and the short of it is that the popularity of a given investment is only a starting point for making sensible purchase or sale decisions.

The benefits of such an investment approach are well documented: by buying what the crowd has devalued unfairly, investors can buy quality assets for less than their intrinsic value. Investing in what is unpopular at the moment also offers a degree of protection against the bad things that can happen when the crowd becomes disaffected with a popular stock. Over time, such a strategy can pay off in a big way. For proof, I turn to well-known value managers Brandes Investment Partners L.P. They recently sent me some interesting information that compares the long-term performance of the most popular investments (the top 10% of the S&P 500 index on a price/earnings basis) against the performance of the least popular investments (the bottom 10%). To me, the results are vindication of the value investing style, and proof that those investors who go against the crowd are usually handsomely rewarded over time.

graph 6.1: **Comparison of lowest decile/highest decile returns**

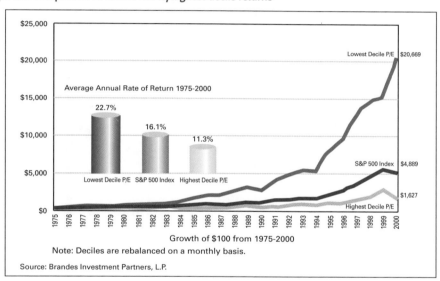

Being a contrarian also means I like to know what's going on in the market. Not to verify my own opinions of a given stock, or to see what other people think of the current economic climate, but rather to see if the crowd is ready to become emotional. I'll come out and say it: I look forward to market downturns, and I tell my U/HNWI clients to look forward to them too. They present an excellent opportunity to add low-cost investments to a portfolio.

Of course, it's become commonplace to talk about "buying the dips." But when money is on the line, it actually takes a lot of confidence – both in the general market, and in one's individual investment decisions – to follow up on the talk. Because history has always given investors plenty of reasons to stay out of the market.

table 6.2: **Cap-weighted performance**

| | **S&P 500 Cap Weighted Performance** Price to Trailing 12 Month Earnings | | |
|---|---|---|---|
| | Lowest Decile P/E % Return | Highest Decile P/E % Return | S&P 500 % Return |
| 1975 | 61.3 | 16.1 | 37.0 |
| 1976 | 55.3 | 10.4 | 24.0 |
| 1977 | 8.8 | -15.0 | -7.3 |
| 1978 | 7.2 | -3.2 | 6.5 |
| 1979 | 22.9 | 26.8 | 18.7 |
| 1980 | 49.4 | 32.5 | 32.4 |
| 1981 | 4.8 | -18.9 | -5.1 |
| 1982 | 13.0 | 61.0 | 21.7 |
| 1983 | 32.6 | 41.1 | 22.4 |
| 1984 | 32.1 | -25.9 | 6.7 |
| 1985 | 34.6 | 24.2 | 31.8 |
| 1986 | 25.1 | -3.9 | 18.3 |
| 1987 | 5.2 | 13.0 | 5.2 |
| 1988 | 29.4 | 31.8 | 16.8 |
| 1989 | 16.5 | 25.8 | 31.2 |
| 1990 | -12.1 | -30.5 | -3.1 |
| 1991 | 47.4 | 12.9 | 30.3 |
| 1992 | 21.3 | 20.7 | 7.7 |
| 1993 | 11.5 | 37.2 | 10.2 |
| 1994 | -1.6 | 2.2 | 1.4 |
| 1995 | 48.9 | 27.5 | 37.6 |
| 1996 | 22.4 | 4.2 | 23.3 |
| 1997 | 35.9 | 40.3 | 33.4 |
| 1998 | 14.7 | 31.0 | 28.8 |
| 1999 | 4.4 | 50.6 | 20.7 |
| 2000 | 36.0 | -38.4 | -8.5 |
| **Average Annual Return 1975-2000** | **22.7%** | **11.3%** | **16.1%** |

Source: Brandes Investment Partners, L.P.

To me, these charts demonstrate what being a contrarian is all about. It means having the courage to be optimistic in the face of negative news – and backing up that confidence with hard–earned money. Ultimately, that means having the courage to formulate an independent opinion of what's going on, and of what one should be doing at any given time. That's what I strive to do for my clients, and that's what U/HNWIs need to be doing for themselves.

table 6.3: **Reasons to stay out of the market**

| Year | DJIA | | Year | DJIA | |
|------|------|---|------|------|---|
| 1934 | 104 | Great Depression | 1963 | 763 | JFK assassinated |
| 1935 | 144 | Spanish Civil War | 1964 | 874 | Gulf of Tonkin Incident |
| 1938 | 155 | War imminent in Europe, Asia | 1966 | 786 | Vietnam War escalates |
| 1939 | 150 | War in Europe | 1970 | 839 | Conflict spreads to Cambodia |
| 1940 | 131 | France falls | 1971 | 890 | Wage and price freeze |
| 1941 | 111 | Pearl Harbour | 1972 | 1020 | Largest trade deficit in U.S. history |
| 1942 | 119 | Wartime price controls | 1973 | 851 | Energy crisis |
| 1945 | 193 | Post-war recession predicted | 1974 | 616 | Steepest market drop in 40 years |
| 1947 | 181 | Cold War begins | 1978 | 805 | Interest rates rise |
| 1948 | 177 | Berlin Blockade | 1979 | 839 | Oil skyrockets – 10%+ unemployment |
| 1949 | 200 | USSR explodes atomic bomb | 1980 | 964 | Interest rates hit all-time high |
| 1950 | 235 | Korean War | 1981 | 875 | Deep recession begins, Reagan shot |
| 1951 | 269 | Excess Profits Tax | 1982 | 1047 | Worst recession in 40 years – debt crisis |
| 1952 | 292 | U.S. seizes steel mills | 1984 | 1212 | Record U.S. federal deficits |
| 1953 | 281 | USSR explodes hydrogen bomb | 1987 | 1939 | The Crash – Black Monday |
| 1955 | 485 | Eisenhower has heart attack | 1989 | 2753 | Junk bond collapse |
| 1956 | 499 | Suez Canal crisis | 1990 | 2634 | Gulf War – worst market decline in 16 years |
| 1957 | 436 | USSR launches Sputnik | 1991 | 3169 | Recession |
| 1958 | 584 | Recession | 1996 | 6448 | Fear of inflation |
| 1959 | 679 | Castro takes over Cuba | 1997 | 7908 | Irrational Exuberance |
| 1960 | 616 | USSR downs U-2 spy plane | 1998 | 9374 | Asia Crisis |
| 1961 | 731 | Berlin Wall erected | 1999 | 11497 | Y2K |
| 1962 | 652 | Cuban Missile Crisis | 2000 | 10787 | Technology correction |

Source: CI Mutual Funds

# Principle #2: Believe in equities

I believe in the long-term power of equities to maintain and build wealth. For this reason, I believe equities in their various forms should comprise at least a portion of every U/HNWI portfolio, no matter what the U/HNWI's age, risk tolerance, or individual financial circumstances.

There is a vast body of proof that substantiates my belief in equities. Perhaps the most compelling example of this proof is a comparison of the long-term returns of the major asset classes. Over the past 75 years, equities have *consistently* outperformed other asset classes. It's as simple as that. In any given year, of course, some other asset could offer better performance, but over the long term, this is all the evidence I need for ensuring my clients place a good portion of their wealth in this asset class.

graph 6.4: **The power of equities: the growth of 1 dollar**

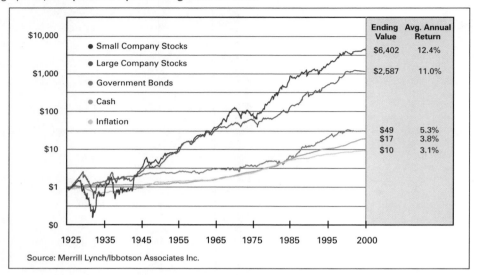

Source: Merrill Lynch/Ibbotson Associates Inc.

That said, performance isn't the only reason for investing in equities. As I practice it, equity investing is as much a *defensive* strategy as an offensive one. Let me explain. To me, the point of equity investing isn't to build a fortune – although that's certainly an intriguing side benefit. Rather, the point of equity investing for U/HNWIs should be to keep the U/HNWI portfolio far enough ahead of inflation, taxes, and spending so that one's lifestyle is never in jeopardy. The only asset class that gives one a reasonable chance of doing that is equities.

Don't get me wrong: I'm not necessarily advocating a 100% equity portfolio for U/HNWIs. Bonds, cash, and alternative investments all deserve a piece of the pie. And depending on the needs of the individual, that piece may be a substantial one. Nor am I saying all equities are created equal. When I say I believe in equities, I mean a conservative, blue-chip oriented portfolio of global companies – companies that are well managed, have healthy balance sheets, and are capable of using capital profitably. I am *not* talking about a basket of high-octane, speculative stocks. I admit, this isn't the kind of portfolio that will spark exciting conversation at cocktail parties. But at the end of the day, it's the kind of portfolio that serves the U/HNWI best. Simply put, a conservatively managed portfolio of equities offers U/HNWIs the best chance to secure a high quality of life, and never worry about the erosion of their wealth. If I didn't ensure my clients had this kind of portfolio, I'd be doing them a grave disservice.

# Principle #3: Manage risk first

The greatest risk U/HNWIs face is the risk of a reduction in their quality of life. Wealth management should seek to minimize that risk. To my mind, all else is secondary.

I put this principle into practice in two ways. First, I carefully examine the risk profile of a given investment, and ask whether the risk presented is really worth the potential reward. Secondly, I facilitate ongoing discussions with my clients about risk, and probe them about how they define risk for themselves. Such discussions are an essential part of the services my team and I perform for every U/HNWI. Because the way I see it, risk management is arguably more important to the U/HNWI than it is to the general population. For those who have the ability to live on investment income rather than employment income, investment risk has a direct relationship to the ability to maintain a comfortable lifestyle. It is my responsibility as a financial professional to identify and assess this risk, and to help U/HNWIs control this risk when it could threaten their lifestyle.

In my experience, very few U/HNWIs ever actively *seek* risk. Rather, they *forget* about it. A prime example is the technology meltdown of 2000-2001. Back in the day of pie-in-the-sky dot-com companies, it was easy to forget about risk. Performance was what mattered, and if you weren't invested in the "new economy," you weren't getting performance. Of course, what went unnoticed in all the hype was the risk investors were taking by investing in these companies. It's not as if the companies themselves were hiding anything – the information was there for anyone who cared to read about it. But most investors (including a good number of U/HNWIs) chose to look the other way. Those people are now able to appreciate the value of looking at investment opportunities from the perspective of risk rather than performance.

In practical terms, managing risk means being conservative with investments, and being vigilant about what actually makes it into the portfolio. U/HNWIs and their advisors must carefully and thoroughly analyze risk *before* making investment decisions, and maintain a watchful eye over the portfolio to make sure it stays in line with the level of risk that is appropriate for their situation. It means being highly selective about what kinds of risk one accepts, and passing up opportunities when one is in doubt about that risk. Finally, managing risk means managing expectations. Many U/HNWIs are driven toward accepting more risk than they should because they have made unreasonable assumptions about the kinds of returns they should expect from their portfolios. By clearly defining reasonable performance benchmarks, and being cautious about adding performance-enhancing investment products or strategies to their portfolios, I ensure my U/HNWI clients don't fall victim to such thinking.

## Principle #4: Construct a *diversified* portfolio

I believe U/HNWIs need to maintain a diversified portfolio of investments. That means following a disciplined asset allocation strategy, and investing in a variety of market sectors all over the world.

In my experience, diversification – or rather, the lack of it – is one of the most critical issues facing today's U/HNWIs. For a variety of reasons, U/HNWI portfolios tend to be more concentrated than those of the majority of the population. U/HNWIs who own their own business most likely have the bulk of their wealth tied up in that business. Those who have sold their business may still be sitting on a large block of company stock – and may in fact be prevented from selling it. Executives and senior-level employees who have exercised options packages may be in a similar situation. Other U/HNWIs may simply be die-hard believers in the benefits of a concentrated portfolio. Far from a good thing, such situations can be highly risky, and pose a significant threat to the U/HNWI's wealth.

There are many different ways to diversify (by asset class, by geographic market, by management style, etc.). All of these are effective methods for U/HNWIs to ensure their wealth is well protected; all of them are methods I employ in the U/HNWI portfolios I manage. Yes, at times such strategies will mean trading potential gains for security. But in my years of working with U/HNWIs, the trade-off is well worth it. By building a portfolio of complementary investments – investments that perform differently in different types of markets – I ensure my clients never have to worry about their quality of life. Ultimately, this is more important than hanging on to a concentrated position, hoping for the "big score."

That's not to say the solution to every financial problem facing U/HNWIs is a computer-generated asset allocation model. Far from it. As I practice it, the principle of diversification functions more as an ideal than as an inflexible system that all U/HNWIs must adhere to. Truth be told, it's often impossible to completely eliminate a heavily concentrated position (something that might not even be in the U/HNWI's best interests). But in almost every case I've come across, there are strategies available to minimize the potential damage such positions can cause – even when such positions are the result of "lock-in" agreements or stock restrictions surrounding the sale of a business. At the very least, U/HNWIs need to thoroughly investigate such strategies, and utilize them whenever possible.

## Principle #5: Pay attention to history

I believe in paying attention to history. The reason: studying the past is the best way to avoid the mistakes of the past. Studying how the market has performed in times of euphoria and in times of despair can provide U/HNWIs with much-needed guidance on how to overcome the specific challenges the market creates.

You'd think that this principle would be common sense. I'm sad to say it isn't. Over the past few years, history has been largely undervalued by investors and financial professionals alike. Throughout the great bull market of the late 1990s, many investors ignored history in an attempt to cash in on the boom in technology stocks. At the peak of the boom, sky-high valuations of any company even remotely connected with the Internet were simply accepted, even though history repeatedly showed such valuations were the sign of a market bubble. Instead of revising their expectations and protecting their portfolios, many investors and financial professionals chose to re-write history, rationalizing valuations in the name of a "new economy" that was going to change the world forever. This led to many U/HNWIs including unworthy investments inside their portfolios. Quite frankly, that's not the way I invest. Ever.

Doing an end-run around history may seem smart in the short term, but it often does little to provide U/HNWIs with any long-term security. As history has proven time and time again, irrational valuations are the sign of market manias, and are extremely threatening to wealth. I draw your attention to one example: at the peak of the late-80s equity boom in Japan, the Japanese market as a whole traded at an unthinkable (for that time) price-to-earnings multiple of 92 times. It has since suffered more than a decade of bad news that has shaved off some 75% of its value. Closer to our own time, the non-earnings of many of the tech market darlings drove the Nasdaq to an all-time price/earnings ratio of 350 times. As of September 2001, the Nasdaq had suffered a decline of about 70% from its peak in March of 2000.

table 6.5: **Manias of the past**

| Other examples of true manias | |
|---|---|
| **TULIP BULB MANIA** (Netherlands – 1630s) | -93% |
| **MISSISSIPPI BUBBLE** (France – 1719-1720) | -99% |
| **SOUTH SEA SHARES** (England – 1720) | -84% |
| **U.S. STOCKS** (Post 1929) | -87% |
| **SILVER** (1979-1982) | -88% |
| **JAPAN** (1989) | -60% |

Source: Merrill Lynch

History can not only serve to warn the investor of irrational euphoria, but to guide the investor out of irrational despair. The events of the recent past are a classic case in point. Almost certainly, the horrific events of September 11th, 2001 will be as infamous to the current generation as any number of earth-shattering events were to previous generations; almost certainly, the effect of that single day will be felt for many years to come. Obviously, these events will have far-reaching implications on financial markets. As I write this, investors have so far assumed that implication will be profoundly negative: on the day markets in New York re-opened after the terrorist attacks, the Dow Jones Industrial Average dropped some 685 points, its largest drop in history (although not the largest in percentage terms). Only time will tell if the long-term financial ramifications of the terrorist assault on America will be as severe as the reaction seems to suggest. Perhaps they will be, but if so, they would certainly be going against history. As history proves, market performance following a world political crisis can be quite favorable. Those wealth advisors who were able to provide historical perspective on the events were able to do their clients a great service, preventing panic and highlighting the financial opportunity presented by the crowd's overreaction. For those willing to study history – and to be courageous enough to trust it – buying right now may well end up to be the most profitable opportunity of their financial lives.

table 6.6: **Reaction of Canadian & American markets to surprise attacks**

| | 1 day | 1 wk. | 2 wks. | 1 mo. | 6 mos. | 1 year |
|---|---|---|---|---|---|---|
| **Pearl Harbor** | | | | | | |
| **December 7, 1941** | | | | | | |
| DJIA | -2.92% | -4.59% | -6.58% | -1.45% | -9.91% | -0.76% |
| **Kennedy Assassinated** | | | | | | |
| **November 22, 1963** | | | | | | |
| DJIA | -2.89% | 5.49% | 6.85% | 7.11% | 15.37% | 25.19% |
| S&P 500 | -2.81% | 5.20% | 6.31% | 6.71% | 15.97% | 23.95% |
| **Iraq invades Kuwait** | | | | | | |
| **August 2, 1990** | | | | | | |
| DJIA | -1.92% | -3.69% | -6.39% | -8.74% | -4.68% | 4.95% |
| S&P 500 | -1.14% | -3.28% | -5.43% | -8.83% | 1.43% | 10.14% |
| TSE 300 | -0.62% | -1.97% | -1.04% | -6.63% | -3.25% | -0.28% |
| **World Trade Center Bombing** | | | | | | |
| **February 26, 1993** | | | | | | |
| DJIA | -0.46% | 1.00% | 1.69% | 2.05% | 8.23% | 13.88% |
| S&P 500 | 0.24% | 0.62% | 1.45% | 0.99% | 3.87% | 5.12% |
| TSE 300 | -0.24% | 2.11% | 2.79% | 4.29% | 19.75% | 26.44% |
| **Oklahoma City Bombing** | | | | | | |
| **April 19, 1995** | | | | | | |
| DJIA | 0.55% | 2.20% | 3.94% | 3.18% | 14.14% | 31.56% |
| S&P 500 | -0.09% | 1.53% | 3.08% | 4.39% | 16.34% | 27.07% |
| TSE 300 | -0.37% | -0.01% | 0.40% | 2.10% | 4.80% | 18.20% |

Source: Franklin-Templeton Investments

I provide these examples not as a prediction of the future, but rather as a lesson in the importance of paying attention to history. Whenever considering current market events, it's imperative that U/HNWIs seek historical perspective. Such perspective helps place current events into a larger context. This larger context helps make the challenges or opportunities arising from those events more clear, and often provides a roadmap for navigating through the challenges of the present. For me, ignoring history would mean exposing my clients' wealth to extreme danger.

# Principle #6: Be a tax-wise investor

I believe in paying careful attention to taxes at all points of the wealth management process. Careful consideration of a portfolio's after–tax returns is the only real way to secure U/HNWI wealth.

For U/HNWIs, the issue of taxation is a critical one. The reason is simple: because most U/HNWIs are already in high tax brackets (if not the highest), taxes pose more of a threat to their ability to generate and secure wealth. Cultivating a general understanding of current tax legislation, and making investment decisions with the goal of providing maximum possible *real* rates of return should be the goal of every U/HNWI. It certainly is a big part of my job as a wealth advisor.

That said, I do not believe in subordinating other investment considerations just to save taxes. This is why even for the wealthiest U/HNWI clients, I remain extremely cautious about recommending true tax-shelters or specialized offshore investments. It's true, in some highly specialized cases, such solutions may be a good idea. But they need to make sense on their own merits, not simply for the tax savings they may generate. Perhaps most importantly, tax-wise investing doesn't mean forgetting about the investment needs of the individual. Even though a given strategy may make sense from a tax planning perspective, it may not make sense from the perspective of the client's lifestyle. If it doesn't, then it's of little value to my client.

With many jurisdictions clamping down on tax-advantaged investments, being a tax-wise investor often means attempting to *delay* or *defer* taxation rather than avoiding taxation altogether. On a practical level, this makes me lean toward assets that allow for such deferrals (equities, for example) when constructing U/HNWI portfolios. With regard to portfolio management, it leads me to keep portfolio turnover (that is, the percentage of a portfolio that is changed from year to year) on the low side, and to select professional managers who do the same. It also leads me to work closely with my clients' other financial professionals – their accountants, their lawyers – to construct a co-ordinated tax-saving strategy that ensures my clients retain the maximum amount of wealth possible.

## Principle #7: Be responsible to the next generation

Once an individual reaches a certain level of wealth, I believe that individual has a responsibility to manage that wealth for the next generation. Whether it's your children, your grandchildren, or the community at large, every U/HNWI needs to be a strong, capable steward of their own wealth, and manage it with the aim of passing it on to the next generation. This concept is at the very heart of what I'm talking about when I talk about *true wealth*.

A generation ago, I think this was a principle almost every U/HNWI appreciated. I still think that's generally the case, but recently, I've wondered whether the idea of *wealth stewardship* is rapidly becoming *passé*. Recently, I've run across a few articles in some well-known financial publications that seem to suggest that U/HNWIs don't owe anything to anyone – including their community. Rather, their community owes them for employing people, furthering social causes, and adding to its overall wealth. I don't support such a position. Yes, I think U/HNWIs should be recognized and applauded for the wealth they create, and the opportunities they make possible. *But I don't think that's enough.* U/HNWIs have a unique opportunity to make a practical difference in the lives of the people who live around them. U/HNWIs need to seize this opportunity, and strive to leave both their families and their communities in a better position, whether that's through ensuring children or grandchildren have a top-quality education, making a donation (or a series of donations) to a community cause, or establishing a family foundation that will serve the community for many years to come. Because they *can* help the community – something most of the population can't do, regardless of whether they want to or not – I believe U/HNWIs have an *obligation* to help.

What does all this mean in practical terms? To start with, it means every U/HNWI needs to have a well-organized, tax efficient estate plan, with clearly-defined goals that illustrate the methods by which the U/HNWI intends to help both his or her family and the community at large. An estate plan ensures the U/HNWI is acting as a *steward* of wealth – as a protector or caretaker of it until it passes on to those in the next generation. Perhaps more importantly, this principle means U/HNWIs need to think about the "larger purpose" behind their wealth: what impact they'd like to make on the world, and what causes, charities, and other goals they'd like to support. A big part of my job as a wealth advisor is to structure their financial affairs so as to make that support possible. By reviewing charitable giving structures and other opportunities, I can help my clients make a difference with their wealth.

# Principle #8: Manage wealth systematically

Wealth management is more than simply throwing a bunch of investments together and calling it a portfolio. Rather it is a detailed, step-by-step process for managing all aspects of an individual's financial well-being. Such a process allows for the co-ordination of wealth management strategies across the various elements of a U/HNWI's wealth management plan.

My process for assisting U/HNWIs is comprised of four basic parts: (1) discovery, (2) recommendation, (3) implementation, and (4) monitoring. These four parts may well go by different names, but at the end of the day, most professionals who work with U/HNWIs will follow this same method of managing wealth.

chart 6.7: **Flowchart of the U/HNWI process**

## #1 Discovery and **analysis**

The first step in the wealth management process is comprised of several parts. An analysis of what's in the existing portfolio – and its purpose for being there – is the first of these parts. Next comes an examination of the U/HNWI's estate plan, and tax minimization strategies. The purpose of such analysis is to determine whether the U/HNWI's wealth management plan is meeting its stated objectives. Of equal importance to the discovery process is an investigation of what U/HNWIs want for their lives. At the end of this step, U/HNWIs should have a general idea of the financial and lifestyle challenges that may face them in the future, as well as how to overcome those challenges.

## #2 **Recommendations**

After discovery, it's time to determine what the U/HNWI should do. Together with my team, I write a detailed *investment policy statement* (IPS) that outlines individual objectives and provides a statement of principle that will guide future investment decisions. We then look at potential solutions from a variety of different perspectives (from the perspective of tax, from the perspective of one's income needs, from the perspective of one's estate plan, etc.). Usually that means running a number of performance scenarios, and conducting a detailed analysis of the risks involved in various options the U/HNWI might choose. Only after completing these steps will I present a U/HNWI with specific recommendations. I insist on a detailed discussion of these recommendations, and encourage an ongoing dialogue regarding them. That way, I can be sure the U/HNWI understands what practical differences these recommendations will make on his or her life. Such understanding is critical to ensure the U/HNWI is committed to the plan.

## #3 **Implementation**

After determining what decisions the U/HNWI needs to make, it's time to put the plan into action. Depending on the life circumstances of the client, the first part of this process could involve the construction of a portfolio from the ground up (typically the case with the newly wealthy), or the renovation and modification of an existing portfolio. Either way, I look to maximize tax efficiency and minimize financial and lifestyle disruptions during the construction process. At the same time, I like to involve a variety of specialists to examine other elements of the U/HNWI's wealth management plan, to ensure all financial bases are covered.

## #4 Monitoring **and rebalancing**

Wealth management is not a one-time event. As the years go by, the performance of various assets needs to be assessed, and changes will inevitably need to be made. The same can be said for the U/HNWI's changing life. It's not enough for U/HNWIs to react to these changes: U/HNWIs need to *anticipate* them. To that end, I monitor my clients' wealth management strategies on an ongoing basis, and involve my clients in regular wealth reviews. These reviews ensure that we keep abreast of new financial opportunities, and solve potential challenges before they arise.

## A **final word** on my investment principles

These principles are only meant to provide you with the most basic elements of a co-ordinated investment philosophy. The rest is up to you. As you become more and more experienced with your wealth, you'll be able to refine and adjust these basic points to meet your own needs. By examining your own approach to wealth, you can ensure your wealth is managed with your individual needs in mind.

# Key concepts: Chapter six

- Investors need to be guided by strong principles when it comes to investing.

- These principles guide all the recommendations I make to my clients.

**Principle #1:** I believe in being a contrarian investor. This means following an independent mindset and tuning out the actions of the financial crowd.

**Principle #2:** I believe in the power of equities. This belief is based on the defensive power of equities – their ability to protect the U/HNWI against inflation and taxes – rather than just their ability to boost net worth.

**Principle #3:** I believe in managing risk. The primary goal of all investment strategy for U/HNWIs should be to minimize potential threats to their standard of living. All other considerations are secondary.

**Principle#4:** I believe in constructing a diversified portfolio. Diversification offers considerable financial security to U/HNWIs.

**Principle #5:** I believe in paying attention to history. U/HNWIs who ignore the history of either the markets or of other U/HNWIs are condemned to repeat the mistakes of the past.

**Principle #6:** I believe in being a tax-smart investor. A consideration of after-tax returns is the only real way to ensure long-term wealth.

**Principle #7:** I believe U/HNWIs have a responsibility to manage their wealth for the benefit of themselves, their family, and their community. From those who have much, much is expected.

**Principle #8:** I believe in a structured approach to wealth management. This approach can be described in four stages:

1. Discovery. Finding out assets and goals of the U/HNWI, including investment, estate planning, and tax minimization goals.

2. Recommendations. Options for achieving those goals.

3. Implementation. Putting the portfolio together.

4. Monitoring. Ongoing review and monitoring of objectives.

## Resources

My investment philosophy is the product of many years of experience in the real world, which makes it difficult to attribute it to a single source. A very basic selection of the many books and other materials that have influenced my thinking on wealth management for U/HNWIs is listed here.

*Simple Wealth, Inevitable Wealth* by Nick Murray

*Security Analysis* by Benjamin Graham

*Value Investing Made Easy* by Janet C. Lowe

*Learn to Earn, One Up on Wall Street* and *Beating the Street* by Peter Lynch

*Contrarian Investing* by Anthony M. Gallea, William Panalon, and Jim Rogers

*Money Logic* by Moshe Milevsky, PhD

*Smart Money Decisions* by Max H. Bazerman

# The danger of concentration risk

- *Rationale for diversification*
- *A word from the other side: the concentrationists*

*"Security depends not so much upon how much you have, as upon how much you can do without. And that is true for society as well as for the individual."*

**Joseph Wood Krutch**

Of all the risks U/HNWIs face, the most dangerous is concentration risk, in large part because it is so easy to overlook – or rather ignore. Simply put, it is easy for U/HNWIs to be seduced by the excitement, and yes, seduced by the potential gains offered by hanging on to a large concentrated position.

Don't get me wrong – most U/HNWIs don't hold concentrated positions because they're greedy. Many of the U/HNWIs who hold concentrated positions are the founders and owners of businesses. As such, they are very busy people, and have very little opportunity to think of anything other than keeping their business growing. Such people often suffer from a kind of "tunnel vision," and often let equity in their company grow into a large, concentrated position simply because they haven't really given diversification much thought. Even when they have thought about the issue, many of these same U/HNWIs are simply comfortable making big bets on the companies they own and run. Their intimate knowledge of day-to-day operations and future opportunities makes them extremely confident about their businesses. A concentrated position is a natural by-product of such confidence.

With other U/HNWIs, a concentrated portfolio is less of a personal choice than it is a matter of necessity. Years of service can result in a strong emotional attachment for a closely-held business, and can make selling extremely difficult, even when the U/HNWI logically knows better. The same situation can face a long-serving executive. Sometimes, "political" considerations within a company can prevent an executive from selling a concentrated position, regardless of whether the executive wants to or not. These people are in effect *forced* to concentrate their wealth, and that can be the cause of considerable anxiety. In fact, in the 1997 edition of its annual *Survey of Affluent Americans*, U.S. Trust found 66% of top executives reported that "too much" of their wealth being tied up in company stock was their #1 financial worry. Fully 40% felt pressured to hang on to their stock, despite knowing most financial professionals would probably advise against it.

Such anxiety over concentrated positions is well-founded. But for every U/HNWI who is worried about concentration, there is another who passionately defends concentrated positions as a viable, even a *wise* investment strategy. Those who fall into the latter group are fooling themselves. No matter how you may rationalize it, making large bets on individual securities makes you a speculator, not an investor. U/HNWIs who concentrate their portfolios are multiplying risk upon risk, and putting their portfolios – and their lifestyles – in jeopardy. And if the U/HNWI makes such bets through their company – as many did during the Internet bubble of the late 90s – then it's the lives of hundreds of employees they are putting at risk.

The simple purpose of this chapter and the next is to help U/HNWIs understand how dangerous concentration risk is to their wealth. To make things simple, I've split the argument into two parts. In this chapter, I'll explain the basic rationale for diversification, and provide some real-life examples of notable U/HNWIs who have diversified – as well as some examples of some who haven't. This should lay the groundwork for a more detailed examination of some of the practical strategies for minimizing this risk – something we'll take up in the following chapter.

## My approach to concentration risk

Let me be blunt: in the vast majority of cases, the potential risks associated with hanging on to a concentrated position far outweigh the potential benefits. Again, it comes down to the end purpose of wealth management. Most U/HNWIs shouldn't be looking for more wealth – they should be looking to secure the wealth they already have. A concentrated stock position directly contradicts that objective.

You don't have to look too far to see the danger concentration risk presents to U/HNWIs. Consider the losses suffered by some of the world's most well-known high-tech CEOs and other executives.

table 7.1: **High-tech titans count their losses**

| Biggest losses in personal wealth during 2000 | |
|---|---:|
| Bill Gates, Microsoft | $ 39.0B |
| Larry Ellison, Oracle | $ 16.0B |
| Steven Ballmer, Microsoft | $ 12.0B |
| Jefferey Bezos, Amazon.com | $ 6.5B |
| Michael Dell, Dell Computers | $ 6.0B |
| Theodore Waitt, Gateway | $ 4.7B |
| Scott McNealy, Sun Microsystems | $ 2.2B |

Source: *National Post*

Admittedly, these U/HNWIs haven't really "lost" anything until they decide to sell their positions. And yes, even if they have lost billions, they have billions more to fall back on. But not every U/HNWI is a billionaire. The technology sell-off of 2000/2001 has pushed many U/HNWIs of more modest means out of the ranks of the wealthy.

Just ask the people working at Lucent Technologies, the infamous AT&T spin-off that was caught in the telecom downdraft. Various incentive programs helped many Lucent employees pile up huge equity positions in their company. As I understand it, employees were given the opportunity to have 10% of their paycheck go to buy company stock at a 15% discount. Certainly an attractive deal for anyone working in a red-hot industry. In addition, many of these people could purchase Lucent shares through their 401(k) retirement plans, and have the company match their contributions. On top of all that, many Lucent workers received generous options packages and other stock incentives.

In my mind, this kind of scenario was a recipe for financial catastrophe. What these people faced was an extreme concentration of wealth: they placed their personal portfolios, their retirement portfolios, and even their salaries in the hands of a single company operating in a high-risk industry. The result, I'm sure, was disaster on a grand scale. If you were a Lucent executive and had a $5-million portfolio of Lucent stock (including options, your 401(k) plan, and stock you had purchased through employee purchase plans), you would have experienced a drop of some 91% of your portfolio value. Your $5-million would now be worth around $450,000. Suddenly, you're not a U/HNWI anymore – you're not even close. Lucent employees of more modest means likely had their savings obliterated. I'm sure there are many people at other telecom companies in exactly the same situation.

For a more extreme example, consider the situation facing Greg Maffei, CEO of troubled 360networks. A former Microsoft executive, Mr. Maffei was recruited by the up-and-coming company to lead its drive to build a world-wide fibre-optic network. Mr. Maffei was so confident in the company's prospects that he secured a loan for $77.5-million to buy 8% of the company's shares. Unfortunately for Mr. Maffei, the telecom bubble burst before 360networks was able to complete the ambitious project, and company shares nosedived. In the summer of 2001, the company filed for protection from its creditors, seemingly casting a death sentence on the stock. At a recent share price of 10 cents, Mr. Maffei's 62 million shares of 360networks are now worth about $6.2-million. Unless the fortunes of his company change dramatically, Mr. Maffei is looking at a liability of close to $75 million. Quite a price to pay for overconcentration.

I'm picking on the high-tech industry to make my point. But the same basic argument applies to all concentrated positions, both in publicly-traded and privately-held companies. However you acquired those positions, there comes a time when it's wise to take some of that money off the table and use it to purchase security. *All U/HNWIs need to be able to identify that time when it comes – and act on it.*

## The rationale for diversification

High-tech horror stories aside, what's the basic rationale for diversification? Can the argument be supported by hard-core facts? Yes, it can. Here are two arguments I like to draw upon whenever a U/HNWI client asks me why I believe so strongly in the need for diversification.

### Value and growth portfolios

A concentrated portfolio might make sense if all assets went up all the time. But that's simply not the case. In the real world, it's impossible to tell just what assets will outperform others in any given year. But that doesn't have to be a problem. By structuring the portfolio to hold various types of assets, U/HNWIs can smooth out their returns, and prevent a massive downturn from ruining either their portfolios or their beauty sleep.

I'll make my point first by taking a look at just two styles of stock investors – growth and value. Take a look at graph 7.2. It plots the relative performance of growth stocks and value stocks since 1975. You'll notice that when growth stocks are up, value stocks aren't doing well.

graph 7.2: **Growth/value performance**

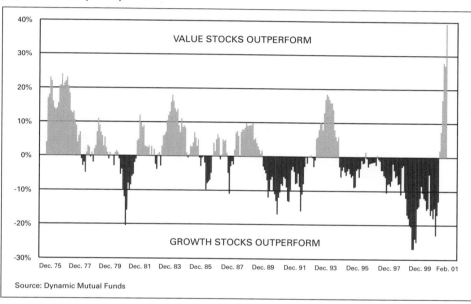

Source: Dynamic Mutual Funds

In the hands of the wise investor, this simple graph is a very important piece of information. Knowing this basic pattern, investors are faced with two choices: (a) build up concentrated positions in either growth or value stocks, and then try to guess which one will go up next, or (b) build a diversified portfolio of complementary positions that work together to minimize the effect of the market cycle on overall portfolio performance. With the former strategy, investors must spend time and energy studying the market – time and energy most U/HNWIs would rather spend on other things. And even then, they must be prepared to accept trading costs and tax liabilities, to say nothing of the anxiety of constantly worrying whether they made the right decisions.

With the second strategy, investors can minimize the time and energy they spend trying to guess the direction of the market (never an exact science anyway), cut down on fees, taxes and other costs, and ensure their portfolios grow at a steady, sure pace. Sure, that may mean giving up some performance every now and again. But it results in a better sleep and greater security. Just guess which approach I recommend.

I realize this is by no means a new idea – you've probably run across this general argument before. But it's a good argument for all U/HNWIs to keep at the top of their minds when it comes time to decide whether to diversify. Whenever you wonder about the value of diversification, remember this basic pattern of growth/value performance (that is, when one is up, the other is down). Those who balance assets against each other can smooth out the valleys and come out ahead in the long run.

## World market performance

Here's another argument that supports the value of a globally-diversified portfolio. Take a look at table 7.3 – it plots the annual performance of several asset classes and geographic markets. Notice the tremendous variance from one year to the next. No one asset or geographic market is the sure-fire winner year after year. If anything, the performance of some assets resembles the motion of a pendulum, swinging back and forth from over to under performance. Bonds are a typical example. Take a close look at the years 1981-1985. You'll notice bonds start the decade with a poor performance, losing 2.1%. Next year, they're at the top, with a 45.8% return. The year after that, they return 9.6%, which is respectable enough, but shoddy compared to other asset classes. In 1984, they're at the top of the heap again, with a 16.9% return. The next year, they post a 26.7% return. Impressive, to be sure, but not nearly as impressive as other asset classes.

table 7.3: **World asset performance**

| 1981 | 1982 | 1983 | 1984 | 1985 | 1986 | 1987 | 1988 | 1989 | 1990 |
|---|---|---|---|---|---|---|---|---|---|
| Canadian Bonds 4.2% | Bonds 35.4% | Canadian Small Caps 44.3% | Foreign Equities 15.1% | Foreign Equities 65.1% | Foreign Equities 67.8% | Foreign Equities 17.6% | Emerging Market Equities 28.7% | Emerging Market Equities 60.1% | Canadian Bonds 7.5% |
| U.S. Small Caps 1.3% | U.S. Small Caps 29.5% | Canadian Large Caps 35.5% | Canadian Bonds 14.7% | Global Equities 49.3% | Global Equities 41.0% | Global Equities 9.9% | Foreign Equities 18.0% | U.S. Large Caps 23.5% | U.S. Large Caps (6.4%) |
| Foreign Equities (1.7%) | U.S. Large Caps 19.0% | U.S. Small Caps 30.8% | Global Equities 12.9% | Canadian Small Caps 40.0% | Canadian Bonds 14.7% | Canadian Large Caps 5.9% | U.S. Small Caps 14.6% | Canadian Large Caps 21.4% | Emerging Market Equities (10.4%) |
| Global Equities (4.0%) | Global Equities 15.3% | Foreign Equities 26.2% | U.S. Large Caps 8.2% | U.S. Small Caps 38.0% | U.S. Large Caps 13.2% | Canadian Bonds 4.0% | Global Equities 13.8% | Global Equities 13.8% | Canadian Large Caps (14.8%) |
| Canadian Large Caps (10.3%) | Canadian Large Caps 5.5% | Global Equities 24.9% | U.S. Small Caps (1.1%) | U.S. Large Caps 33.1% | Canadian Small Caps 12.3% | U.S. Large Caps (4.0%) | Canadian Large Caps 11.1% | U.S. Small Caps 12.9% | Global Equities (16.3%) |
| U.S. Large Caps (10.4%) | Canadian Small Caps 4.6% | U.S. Large Caps 18.8% | Canadian Small Caps (2.3%) | Canadian Large Caps 25.1% | Canadian Large Caps 9.0% | Canadian Small Caps (5.5%) | Canadian Bonds 9.8% | Canadian Bonds 12.8% | U.S. Small Caps (19.4%) |
| Canadian Small Caps (15.1%) | Foreign Equities 2.8% | Canadian Bonds 11.5% | Canadian Large Caps (2.4%) | Canadian Bonds 21.2% | U.S. Small Caps 4.3% | U.S. Small Caps (14.1%) | U.S. Large Caps 3.2% | Foreign Equities 7.6% | Foreign Equities (23.1%) |
| NA | NA | NA | NA | NA | NA | NA | Canadian Small Caps (5.5%) | Canadian Small Caps (10.7%) | Canadian Small Caps (27.3%) |

| 1991 | 1992 | 1993 | 1994 | 1995 | 1996 | 1997 | 1998 | 1999 | 2000 |
|---|---|---|---|---|---|---|---|---|---|
| Emerging Market Equities 59.3% | U.S. Small Caps 30.5% | Emerging Market Equities 82.3% | Foreign Equities 14.6% | U.S. Large Caps 30.5% | Canadian Large Caps 28.4% | U.S. Large Caps 36.7% | U.S. Large Caps 35.7% | Emerging Market Equities 57.2% | Canadian Bonds 10.3% |
| U.S. Small Caps 45.5% | Emerging Market Equities 22.4% | Canadian Small Caps 52.3% | Global Equities 11.9% | U.S. Small Caps 25.0% | Canadian Small Caps 27.5% | U.S. Small Caps 27.7% | Global Equities 33.7% | Canadian Large Caps 31.7% | Canadian Large Caps 7.4% |
| U.S. Large Caps 25.8% | U.S. Large Caps 14.9% | Foreign Equities 38.3% | U.S. Large Caps 4.3% | Canadian Bonds 20.7% | U.S. Large Caps 20.7% | Global Equities 21.3% | Foreign Equities 28.8% | Canadian Small Caps 26.4% | U.S. Small Caps 0.7% |
| Canadian Bonds 22.1% | Canadian Small Caps 13.0% | Canadian Large Caps 32.6% | U.S. Small Caps 4.1% | Global Equities 18.1% | U.S. Small Caps 17.1% | Canadian Large Caps 15.0% | Canadian Bonds 9.2% | Foreign Equities 20.0% | Canadian Small Caps (4.3%) |
| Global Equities 18.5% | Canadian Bonds 9.4% | Global Equities 28.3% | Canadian Large Caps (0.2%) | Canadian Large Caps 14.5% | Global Equities 14.4% | Canadian Bonds 9.6% | U.S. Small Caps 4.3% | Global Equities 18.2% | U.S. Large Caps (6.6%) |
| Canadian Small Caps 18.5% | Global Equities 4.9% | U.S. Small Caps 23.7% | Emerging Market Equities (1.8%) | Canadian Small Caps 12.6% | Canadian Bonds 12.3% | Foreign Equities 6.5% | Canadian Large Caps (1.6%) | U.S. Small Caps 14.3% | Global Equities (9.5%) |
| Foreign Equities 12.1% | Canadian Large Caps (1.4%) | Canadian Bonds 22.1% | Canadian Bonds (4.3%) | Foreign Equities 8.5% | Foreign Equities 6.9% | Canadian Small Caps 2.6% | Emerging Market Equities (19.9%) | U.S. Large Caps 12.7% | Foreign Equities (10.6%) |
| Canadian Large Caps 12% | Foreign Equities (3.1%) | U.S. Large Caps 11.5% | Canadian Small Caps (9.2%) | Emerging Market Equities (7.8%) | Emerging Market Equities 6.6% | Emerging Market Equities (7.7%) | Canadian Small Caps (21.5%) | Canadian Bonds (1.1%) | Emerging Market Equities (28.2%) |

Source: Franklin-Templeton Investments

Again, this basic pattern describes a general principle behind the performance of nearly all asset classes: *no one asset class is the winner all the time.* Trying to guess which asset will be the "best" this year is usually a poor investment of one's time. Guessing only distracts you from issues that are actually important – issues such as how to leave behind a lasting legacy to your family, where to go on your next vacation, or how to improve your golf game. By including assets from a variety of classes, you don't have to guess. No matter what the markets are doing in any part of the world, there will be portions of your portfolio that will be growing. That makes for added security.

At the end of the day, the central reason behind diversification is essentially *defensive*: it's to protect what you already have rather than to give you more. If that doesn't sound exciting enough, or aggressive enough ... well, all I can say it's not my job to provide U/HNWIs with those kinds of things. Rather, it's my job to make sure my clients can do what they want to do with their lives without ever having to worry about their wealth again.

## Case study: Diversification for the family

The Bronfman family provides a shining example of a family that understands the need for diversification. The family business, Seagram Inc., once sold many of the world's best-known brands of liquor. But as the millennium drew to a close, the Bronfmans decided to move into the entertainment business. Seagram's purchase of Universal Entertainment's music and film divisions (at the time one of the largest acquisitions ever made by a Canadian company) transformed it into a major player in the industry. The transformation culminated in the buyout of Seagram by entertainment giant Vivendi of France in June of 2000, to the tune of over $49.5-billion.

The Bronfman family held a significant chunk of the newly merged company. But as an old-money family, the Bronfmans were obviously well aware of the risks of holding on to such a large position. At the end of May, 2001, the Bronfmans announced they had sold a significant portion of their Vivendi holdings. In a private transaction between the family and the company, the family sold a block of 16.9 million shares (representing about 1.5% of the company's total equity) at a price of $99 each, resulting in proceeds of $1.67-billion. Part of that block were over 2.5 million shares held by charitable entities and foundations controlled by the Bronfmans.

It's not difficult to understand the reasons for the sale. With the value of their Vivendi holdings totalling several billion dollars, the Bronfmans saw the need to diversify. While the family insists it is bullish on Vivendi's future (the former head of Seagram, Edgar Bronfman Jr., remains one of Vivendi's top-ranking executives), it saw an opportunity to take some of their money off the table. It seems Vivendi was more than willing to support such a decision. In a prepared statement released the day after the sale, Jean-Marie Messier, the chief executive for Vivendi, declared that the company understood the Bronfman family's need for greater diversification, and reiterated that the sale was not indicative of the Bronfman's lack of confidence in the direction of the company. This statement seems to reinforce statements made by the family itself. Speaking after the divestiture, Edgar Bronfman Jr. reiterated that the Bronfman family retains a large chunk of Vivendi stock (33 million shares, to be exact, making them the largest shareholders in the company, at 6.1%) and plans to keep things that way for awhile. The family has agreed not to sell or hedge any more of their position until at least the end of 2001.

The Bronfman family divestiture proves that even the largest, most wealthy families in the world are thinking about diversification. Even with a stake in one of the most powerful, most dominant companies in the world, the Bronfmans placed more value on diversification than concentration. Chalk one up for all those who believe in security.

## A word from the other side: the "concentrationists"

Not all investors concentrate their portfolios out of ignorance. In fact, there are some extremely successful investors who believe in doing exactly the opposite. Rather than adopting a co-ordinated diversification strategy, these people build large stock positions in a select few companies. Instead of a strategy that brings security, such U/HNWIs often view diversification as a strategy meant to compensate for anxiety and mediocre investment abilities.

I'm going to be honest with you: there's a strong argument to be made that in this day and age, hanging on to a significant stake in a well-managed business is one of the ways to become very wealthy. Just look at the list of the world's richest people: Bill Gates (Microsoft), Wayne Huizenga (Waste Management, Blockbuster Video), Ross Perot (EDS, Perot Systems), and Warren Buffett (Berkshire Hathaway) all became billionaires by hanging on to big chunks of equity in the companies they founded. I'm sure their stories have inspired many other U/HNWI business owners to follow the same path.

I'm not going to lie to you: concentrating wealth is a method by which you can become wealthy – fabulously wealthy. It is also a way by which you can lose everything for which you have been working. When you're just starting a business, concentrating your wealth is often something that goes with the territory – something a business owner can't necessarily avoid if the business is to grow. But as I said before, there comes a point in time when such concentration becomes unwise. A time when the risks become reckless, and aren't commensurate with the potential returns.

To me, it comes down to a question of the whole purpose of wealth. What are you working for? Have you worked hard and made sacrifices so you can risk it all in an attempt to get on the Forbes 400 list? Or have you worked hard in order to ensure you and your family won't have to? I'm sure most U/HNWIs would agree it's the latter. You can call it whatever name you choose, but to my mind, excessive concentration eventually comes down to misplaced priorities.

## The most famous concentrationist of all: **Warren Buffett**

There have always been U/HNWIs who firmly believe a concentrated portfolio is better than a diversified portfolio. Warren Buffett is one of these. Probably the most famous – and the most *successful* – investor of all time, Buffet has spoken eloquently on the merits of a concentrated portfolio in the annual reports of his company Berkshire Hathaway. As he explains with characteristic wit, "We don't believe in the Noah's Ark principle of investing, winding up with two of everything. Then you have a zoo."

I'm not going to argue with Mr. Buffett's success. From what I've read of his writings, he is one of the most sensible, most principled, and most consistent investors in the world. And his concentrated portfolios have served Berkshire shareholders very well over the years. But he is the exception to the general rule.

For a number of reasons, it is neither practical nor wise to do what Mr. Buffett has done. Number one, Buffett has demonstrated an uncanny ability to pick investments over the years. There may only be a handful of people in the world who can do what Buffett can do – and I'm being generous when I say a handful. Number two, make no mistake, Berkshire itself is a highly diversified business. The company is essentially a holding company, with dozens of enterprises under its corporate umbrella, in businesses as diverse as insurance, candy, and paint. While Mr. Buffett may make some very good points about a watered-down investment in common stock, his company conducts business in several different areas of the economy (and in some cases, several different areas of the world) all at once. While certainly risky, Mr. Buffett's investment of almost his entire net worth in the business he runs doesn't exactly present the same level of risk that other U/HNWIs may face when they do the same.

Finally, and perhaps most importantly, while Buffett may not believe in its execution, he most definitely believes in the *idea* behind diversification. That is, the idea that wealth management is first and foremost about risk management. That's not to say Buffett isn't out to make money. But at the end of the day, he manages his own portfolio conservatively, and is always concerned with *securing* the wealth of his shareholders as much as he is concerned with expanding it. He looks to make sensible, reasonable investments in companies that are fairly valued, rather than looking for all-out performance. That's the core of my own investment philosophy, and one that is in no way inconsistent with the argument for a diversified portfolio.

Perhaps the reason why investors don't hear more about concentration risk is because the story of diversification is a lot less gripping than the story of the "big score." I'm not so sure. The following case study proves it.

## Case study: Boom to bust

The story begins like a fairy tale. Small-town farmer's son leaves town for university. Ten years later, the boy's on the front page of the nation's financial newspapers, a billionaire. All before his 30th birthday.

That's the real-life story of Glenn Ballman. Ballman started life on a small family farm on the outskirts of Moose Jaw, Saskatchewan, in the heart of the Canadian prairie. Ballman left town to study at the University of Western Ontario. Soon after graduating, he landed a job in the technology industry. But after years working for someone else, Ballman decided to strike out on his own. He founded M-Depot Internet Superstore in 1997 on the eve of the Internet boom. The company had a good business plan, but it wasn't until Ballman changed the name of his growing venture to Onvia.com that things started to take off. As prospects grew, Ballman moved the young company south of the border to Seattle, where he thought it easier to secure financing for his venture. It was to be a pivotal move.

The next several months were what every Internet entrepreneur dreams of.

Onvia.com quickly secured venture capital, and went public on the technology-heavy Nasdaq exchange on February 29th, 2000 at a share price of U.S. $21.00. In what was typical fashion for the time, the share price spiked sharply, peaking at U.S. $61.50 the day after the company's IPO. Mr. Ballman's 13.5% stake was now valued at $944.2-million. By all accounts, Ballman had made it. He had turned little more than an idea into what some ranked among the brightest prospects in the so-called new economy. He had been at the forefront of one of the most successful IPOs in financial history, and had become one of the world's wealthiest people. And he had done it all before he celebrated his thirtieth birthday.

For Ballman, the road from rags to riches was a relatively short one, and indicative of the crazy times in the Internet and technology industry in the late 1990s. Unfortunately, the road back to rags was equally short, and equally indicative of the times. In response to rising losses and a business model that didn't seem to be living up to expectations, investors began to turn sour about Onvia.com. When the bottom fell out of the technology market, Onvia.com led the charge, eventually dropping to penny stock status. Ballman resigned his post as chairman (a prepared statement stated the departure was to pursue other business ventures). On the day he resigned, the stock was trading at U.S. $0.78 a share. Ballman's stake – now whittled down to 11% – was now valued at $7.3-million. What started as a fairy tale ended as a nightmare.

Ballman's case presents a dramatic study in the dangers of overconcentration. But to be fair, this concentration wasn't exactly a matter of choice. Like many founders, Mr. Ballman's shares were put in post IPO "lock up," a method of protecting other investors from a sudden landslide of early sales by corporate insiders. And let's be honest: a net worth of $7-million plus is still much more than most people can ever dream of achieving. At the same time, the decimation of 99.2% of his wealth in the space of a year must have been devastating for Mr. Ballman – both financially and psychologically. For those U/HNWIs who are business owners (particularly for those involved in the technology sector), his case serves as a shining example for the need for a sound diversification strategy.

Alright, you now have an example of what can happen when you don't diversify. What happens when you do? Here's an example of a diversification success story.

# Case study: securing hard-won wealth

If the tech-market meltdown had you licking your wounds, take comfort: the founders of many high-tech firms suffered far worse. One of those is Jeffrey Bezos, the founder and CEO of the world's leading online retailer, Amazon.com. In the wake of the high-tech meltdown, his 33% stake in his company dropped by a staggering $6.5-billion in value.

For Mr. Bezos, the road to success has not exactly been an easy one. Sure, it might be easy for an outsider to laugh off the trials and tribulations of Amazon.com as just another day at the office for Internet companies, but I'd be surprised if Mr. Bezos is able to laugh right about now. Yes, the man is still a billionaire (as I write this, his net worth is anywhere between $1.2 and $1.5-billion, depending on market sentiment). But no matter how much you've got, the loss of 84% of your wealth is surely devastating to behold. I'm sure it's not easy to be on such a ride.

The jury is still out on Amazon.com, and whether it will become a profitable enterprise remains to be seen. But it seems Mr. Bezos is a little less willing to risk his entire fortune on whether it does. Don't get me wrong: Mr. Bezos is famous for his boundless optimism – both for his company and for the Internet industry in general. And he's still willing to put his money where his mouth is, hanging on to over 117 million shares of Amazon.com. But lately, it seems he's tempering this extreme optimism. In February of 2001, Bezos sold 800,000 shares of his venture. In May, he sold 300,000 more. And in August, another 300,000. Such sales are a drop in the bucket for Mr. Bezos, representing about 1% of his total holding in Amazon.com. Even so, industry insiders say the sale is a significant one, and perhaps indicative of a gradual move to diversify his holdings.

Bezos seems to be selling at an extremely inopportune time: the Internet economy is in the dumps, and it's unclear whether some of its former stars will even survive. But the purpose behind the move obviously isn't to extract maximum value for his stock. No, I'm guessing the motivation behind the move has a lot more to do with security than with greed. No matter how confident he seems to be in the ultimate success of his company, Mr. Bezos (or at least the financial professional who works with him) seems to understand the value of taking some money off the table. By diversifying, he's making sure he gets something out of those years of hard work. Even if the bottom drops out of the new economy, Mr. Bezos has ensured a minimum level of wealth for himself – a nest egg sizable enough so that he doesn't have to curtail his lifestyle or make undue sacrifices. Even if you don't believe in the long-term fortunes of his company, you have to believe in the sense behind such a strategy.

## A final word on the philosophy of diversification

I don't mean to say diversification is the answer to all problems a U/HNWI faces. And I don't mean to be advocating diversification at all costs. But for the vast majority of U/HNWIs, there comes a point in time when a disciplined diversification strategy offers many more benefits than it takes away. Or to put it another way: concentration typically builds wealth, but diversification keeps it.

## Key concepts: Chapter seven

- Concentration risk is perhaps the most significant danger U/HNWIs face.

- The best argument for diversification goes something like this: U/HNWIs have too much to lose by concentrating their wealth. It's that simple.

- The inverse relationships between growth and value portfolios provides an example of the value of diversification. The performance of different asset classes and different markets provides another.

- While there are many examples of how concentrated portfolios can result in tremendous wealth, for most U/HNWIs, the choice is rather simple: do you want to keep on gambling with your wealth? Or do you want to seize the opportunity to take some of it off the table?

- While investors like Warren Buffett provide examples of the benefits of portfolio concentration, there are several extenuating circumstances that make his case exceptional, and unlikely to be duplicated among the majority of U/HNWIs.

- The high-tech industry is the source of many boom/bust stories of U/HNWIs who did not diversify. It is also occasionally the source of diversification success stories.

- Concentration builds wealth; diversification keeps it.

## Resources

The central idea behind both chapter 7 and 8 is relatively simple: a well-diversified portfolio makes more sense for a U/HNWI than a highly concentrated one. There are many, many books and other resources that offer an excellent explanation for why this is so. Here are some of my favourites.

George Hartman's book *Risk is a Four-Letter Word* and its appropriately-titled sequel, *Risk is Still A Four-Letter Word*

*The Intelligent Asset Allocator* by William J. Bernstein

*Seeing Tomorrow: Rewriting the Rules of Risk* by Ron S. Dembo and Andrew Freeman

## Websites

Money chimp *www.datachimp.com* — charts, graphs, articles, theory — this site has it all

# How to minimize
## concentration risk

- *Levels of risk*
- *An ounce of prevention: diversification*
- *A pound of cure: hedging*

*"The only investors who shouldn't diversify are those who are right 100% of the time."*

**Sir John Templeton**

'␣ve highlighted some of the reasons why U/HNWIs should avoid an overly concentrated portfolio. I've also illustrated what can happen when U/HNWIs don't diversify. It's time to move on to some practical advice. It's time to show you how to make a highly concentrated portfolio more secure.

This chapter will be a little more technical than the others. But it revolves around a fairly simple concept: concentration is a way to *create* wealth, but diversification is the way to *keep* wealth. Don't worry if you find some of the examples or discussion a little confusing. If you understand this one concept, you'll have understood the central point of the chapter.

Of course, any discussion about concentration risk brings up the big question: can we eliminate risk altogether? The answer to that one is simple. You can't. Despite what some hucksters and con artists may tell you, there is no such thing as a risk free investment. All investors must accept *some* risk when they put their money in the market. However, we don't have to accept *all* risks at *all* times. It all comes down to how we perceive risk.

## Levels of risk

As I like to explain to my clients, risk exists on a number of different levels, some of which are within our power to control, some of which aren't. The first of these is called *systemic* risk – the risk of simply being in the market. Broader market movements aren't something the average U/HNWI can control (or in most cases, even predict), meaning this risk simply has to be accepted as a natural part of investing. *Common* risk is the second level of risk – issues like interest rates, market capitalization, the future of the industry or market niche, and the liquidity of the stock in question. Generally, U/HNWIs can limit some of the effects of common risk with professional research and an eye to general market conditions, but again, there's only so much an individual can do. The third level of risk is *company-specific risk*. This is the risk surrounding the specific companies in which you invest. I'm speaking primarily about issues of management, debt level, revenue forecasts, future prospects, that kind of thing. To a large extent, this risk can be minimized through disciplined investment selection and reliance on professional opinion – although there will always be challenges that are completely unforeseeable. The financial fallout from the recent attack on the World Trade Center and the Pentagon is a classic example.

In my experience, by the time they become U/HNWIs, most investors are at least aware of the above levels of risk – even if they don't necessarily understand how to deal with them. But when it comes to the fourth level of risk, it's often a different story. The fourth level of risk is what I call *investor risk*: the ill-considered behavior of the individual investor.

Behavioral finance is a hot topic among financial professionals these days. But among investors themselves, it often goes ignored. It seems most investors would rather learn about efficient market theory, how to forecast interest rates, or how to value a company's future prospects, than they would about their own bad behavior. And that's too bad. Because no matter what you learn about the stock market, no matter how fully you research an investment opportunity, no matter how up-to-date you are on market events, if you're not ready to back up your knowledge with wise and prudent action, you're no further ahead. In a lot of ways, *True Wealth* is my attempt to tell U/HNWIs to stop worrying about the market (which *can't* be controlled) and start worrying about how their behavior affects their performance (which *can* be controlled). Because taking care of your own behavior can make all the difference in your effort to secure your wealth.

It's in this spirit that I like to consider concentration risk. In most cases, concentration risk doesn't just *happen*. No, the investor has to make a specific financial decision that leads to a highly concentrated portfolio (the decision to sell a business for stock, the decision to exercise a large options package, etc.). After that, the investor compounds this risk by making a decision to keep that portfolio highly concentrated (or to look at it another way, a decision *not* to diversify). All of which makes the identification of the behavior that *leads* to concentration risk an essential first step in minimizing concentration risk.

Which is all another way of saying that the first step in minimizing concentration risk is to minimize the potential for investor risk. Simply put, before U/HNWIs take any practical steps to limit concentration risk, *they need to take the step in their own minds*. It simply doesn't matter if your wealth advisor comes up with the best kind of diversification strategy possible – if you don't believe in it, it's not worth the paper it's printed on. Keep that in mind as you read through the following strategies.

## Practical measures: diversification and hedging

There are three general methods for dealing with a large, concentrated position: hold it, sell it, or hedge it. I've already told you why the first of these is an unwise idea. The second – selling – is fairly simple to understand. In such a scenario, the U/HNWI sells off a large, concentrated position (in either a publicly traded company or a closely held business) in favor of a number of smaller positions, preferably among different sectors of the economy and different geographic markets. Such a strategy shifts risk from company-specific risk (which can be unpredictable and hard to overcome) to systemic risk (which is generally easier to predict, and easier to overcome). In this way, diversification seeks to *prevent* the consequences of overconcentration from ever becoming an issue in the portfolio.

The third method is hedging. The goal of hedging isn't so much to shift risk from one category to another, but to brace the portfolio against the possible consequences of that risk. In this way, hedging is a method of *curing* concentration risk, not *preventing* it. To my mind, this is the critical difference between diversification and hedging. With the former, you've recognized that the danger of a highly concentrated portfolio outweighs the potential benefits, and you're looking to avoid getting into a mess *before* a downturn. With the latter, you're looking to limit the mess *after* the market has started to slide. Or, to put it another way, you still believe the benefits of a concentrated portfolio outweigh the risks, but you're willing to play it safe just in case you're wrong.

Personally, I believe an ounce of prevention is worth more than a pound of cure. While hedging can be an important part of the U/HNWI investment strategy, diversification is often less costly and more effective. Let's be honest here: hedging is a compromise, a solution that suits those U/HNWIs who can't diversify because of the complications in their personal financial situation, or who don't fully accept that security is more important than performance. The former I can understand (at least to some extent). The latter I cannot. As I've said throughout *True Wealth*, such a mindset is exactly the opposite of how U/HNWIs need to think about wealth.

In the real world, of course, most U/HNWIs blend these two approaches, diversifying and hedging according to their individual needs. But when push comes to shove, security is more important than growth. For that reason, I believe diversification should take priority over hedging. Only after the former has been thoroughly investigated should U/HNWIs consider the later.

## An ounce of prevention: **the diversified U/HNWI portfolio**

In practical terms, the best way to achieve portfolio diversification is by adopting a strategic asset allocation strategy. For the most part, the basic concepts of asset allocation have been well-explained in numerous other publications. Instead of rehashing what's been written before, I'm going to highlight a couple of important points about such a strategy that often go unnoticed. I'll also provide some specific guidance on how asset allocation works in the U/HNWI portfolio.

### Asset allocation: portioning of assets

Perhaps unlike other investment strategies, asset allocation is well within the grasp of even the most novice investor's understanding. By spreading the portfolio among different asset classes, investors can diversify their portfolios and minimize some of the risks inherent in concentrated positions. Simple enough. But asset allocation becomes a little more complicated when it comes to the question of which assets are appropriate for a given investor. The way it's typically explained, you'd think every investor would be served by breaking the portfolio down into three fundamental components: cash, fixed-income, and equity.

For U/HNWIs, these three asset classes are only a starting point. For my U/HNWI clients, I like to break assets into two distinct categories: core and satellite. In the first category are the central holdings that anchor your portfolio and secure your wealth. In the second are the aggressive and/or speculative positions that have greater growth potential. After that, I'll break down assets among the three basic categories, then subdivide those further into specific markets or sectors in which the U/HNWI should be investing. Ideally, every asset you have should have a place on the allocation chart, even assets that aren't exactly liquid – such as money you've invested in a closely-held business, for example, or perhaps investment real estate.

Of course, you could spend all day dividing and subdividing assets if you really wanted to, but the point of it all is to gain a full understanding of how these portions interact with one another. Such an understanding should help guide the decisions you make about future investments, and give you some kind of indication of what you should be doing in order to secure your wealth.

### Asset allocation: portioning criteria

Another important consideration with asset allocation strategy is the criteria by which assets are portioned – and the criteria by which those portions change. Most professionals base these decisions on investment objectives: if the investor is looking for growth and tax-deferred capital gains, then a high percentage of equities belong in the portfolio. If the primary objective is to secure a stable income, then it's time to add bonds, income trusts, dividend-producing products, etc.

Other professionals like to base allocation criteria on the age of the investor – older investors need more conservative portfolios, younger investors can get more aggressive, that kind of idea. Personally, I prefer to base allocation decisions on risk tolerance – specifically, the question of how much the investor can stand to lose in a given period of time without bailing out of the portfolio.

table 8.1: **Standard deviation of asset classes**

| | Average Annual Return | Risk (Standard Deviation) | Distribution of Annual Returns | | |
|---|---|---|---|---|---|
| Small Company Stocks | 12.4% | 33.4% | | | |
| Large Company Stocks | 11.0% | 20.2% | | | |
| Government Bonds | 5.3% | 9.4% | | | |
| Cash | 3.8% | 3.2% | | | |
| Inflation | 3.1% | 4.4% | | | |
| | | | -80%   -40%   0%   +40%   +80% | | |

Source: Merrill Lynch/Ibbotson Associates

Note: Assumes reinvestment of income and no transaction costs or taxes. Index sources: Small Company Stocks – represented by the fifth capitalization quintile of stocks on the NYSE for 1926-1981 and the performance of the Dimensional Fund Advisors (DFA) Small Company Fund thereafter; Large Company Stocks – Standard & Poor's 500®, Government bonds – U.S. Government Bond; Cash – 30 day U.S. Treasury Bill; Inflation – Consumer Price Index

When I make recommendations about specific investments, I like to review the standard deviations of the asset class, and understand just what an investor would be willing to put up with before pulling the plug. Obviously, if the U/HNWI can't stomach a 50% loss in a single year, then putting 10% or 15% of the portfolio into a high-risk, currency trading hedge fund wouldn't be a wise move – 1% to 3% might be appropriate.

It's impossible for me to recommend a specific allocation that's ideal for every U/HNWI – every situation is unique. What I can do, however, is to provide you with a basic starting point. Chart 8.2 details some very basic allocations constructed for a variety of purposes.

Understand that these represent allocations for "ideal" investors – in the real world, they'd be much more complex, and much more specific. I've also included a graph that charts the best, the worst, and the average returns for each of those portfolios over any one year from 1950 through to 2000 (see graph 8.3). It should give you a better understanding of the benefits of asset allocation.

chart 8.2: **Basic asset allocations**

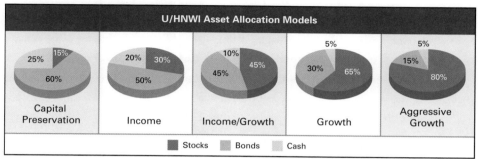

Source: Merrill Lynch

graph 8.3: **Annual returns of ML allocation portfolios**

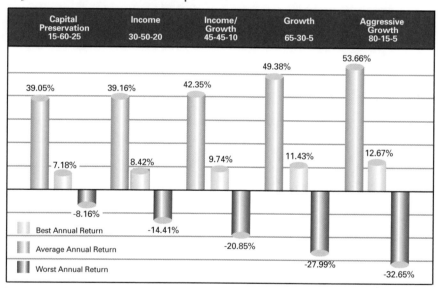

Source: Merrill Lynch Investment Strategy and Product Group/Strategic Planning

Note: Results shown, which are based on indexes, are illustrative and assume reinvestment of income, no transaction costs or taxes, and that the allocation for each model remained consistent. Index sources: Stocks- Standard and Poor's 500; Bonds – 20-Year U.S. Government Bond; Cash – 30-Day U.S. Treasury Bill.

## Asset allocation: rebalancing

Asset allocation isn't a static system. Rather, it requires ongoing management and fairly regular rebalancing. There are two basic systems for doing this: fixed and flexible. A fixed allocation system is exactly what the name suggests: the proportion of assets is pre-established and stays relatively the same no matter what markets may do. Usually such models are established with pre-set purchase and sale criteria which automatically kick in whenever certain portfolio values are met. The main advantage of such a system is the "automatic pilot" type of management it offers. The individual doesn't have to think about, second-guess, or micro-manage the portfolio once the basic allocation decisions have been finalized. A flexible allocation system (sometimes called a "strategic" allocation system), on the other hand, offers target allocation *ranges* rather than set-in-stone percentages for each asset category. It also permits a little more flexibility in allowing the investor to respond to market events or changing life circumstances. In my practice, I've found U/HNWIs are generally evenly divided as to what system they prefer.

Now that you understand some of the general principles behind diversification, we can take a closer look at diversification in action. Here are some of the many methods of diversifying the U/HNWI portfolio.

## Diversification in action: exchange funds

Exchange funds are large, private investment funds that offer U/HNWIs a place to pool their holdings with other U/HNWIs. In exchange for your contribution to the fund (that is, your concentrated holding), you receive a portion of a diversified portfolio. The portfolio is managed by a professional portfolio manager, but is typically constructed as a passive investment, tracking a given benchmark rather than trying to beat it. After a given period of time, or when the fund is terminated, you receive a pro-rated portion of the diversified portfolio.

The diversification advantage offered by exchange funds should be fairly easy to understand: instead of a single concentrated position, each investor receives a slice of a well-diversified pie. But there are a couple of other features that make exchange funds particularly attractive. One of those is the tax advantage of exchange funds. In most jurisdictions, when stock is contributed to an exchange fund, there is no immediate tax liability. That can be a big relief to those who would normally face a huge tax bill if they were to sell a concentrated position. In addition, exchange funds allow for confidentiality. Depending upon the fund in question, filings with regulatory officials may not be required – something executives and owners may find beneficial if selling their concentrated positions would result in a "hubbub" among shareholders. Another advantage of exchange funds is their ability to accept restricted stock – stock that's still in post IPO "lock up" or stock that can't be sold on the open market.

That said, exchange funds are by no means a foolproof diversification option. Many of them demand substantial patience from investors: a minimum investment period of seven years seems to be the industry average. They can also carry sales charges and management fees. Perhaps most importantly, exchange funds can suffer from poor performance. Depending on the breadth of the given fund, an exchange fund may not fairly reflect the index it is supposed to track. And of course, the regulatory rules that allow for the tax-free transfer of stock into an exchange fund are subject to change, potentially taking away one of the advantages of this type of structure.

Despite these drawbacks, exchange funds are often one of the only options available to U/HNWIs with significant holdings in restricted or illiquid stock. Bottom line: exchange funds are a useful way to achieve portfolio diversification for certain U/HNWIs. But they should only be considered after a discussion with a skilled professional well-versed in other diversification options.

### Diversification in action: the stepping out strategy

Asset allocation is easy when you're constructing a portfolio from the ground up. While some U/HNWIs may face such an opportunity (the newly wealthy, for instance), it's not always possible to start a portfolio from scratch. When a portfolio is bogged down in highly concentrated positions – positions in which the low cost base would result in a big tax hit if liquidated – a different strategy is needed.

One method to deal with such situations is a "stepping out" strategy. In a nutshell, the technique involves exchanging or transferring a concentrated position into a customized exchange-traded fund (ETF), a personalized basket of stocks, or a separately managed account, with an eye to adding diversification and deferring taxes. It's a complicated technique, and as of right now, only the largest firms have the expertise to organize such a program. But I expect as more U/HNWIs begin to realize the benefits of diversification, more firms will start to offer such programs.

A very simple stepping out strategy might work something like this. Assume you've worked as an executive at XYZ Corp. (a publicly traded company) for a number of years, and have an investment portfolio of about $15-million. As nice as that sounds, you realize your $10-million holding in XYZ stock constitutes the bulk of your portfolio. So, on the advice of your wealth advisor, you decide to hand over portfolio management to a professional, one who can build a more diversified portfolio for you. Obviously, your manager will want to divest some of your XYZ stock. But instead of selling it all (and incurring a major tax hit), your wealth advisor arranges a stepping out strategy. Initially, your diversified portfolio will be built *around* XYZ – specific investments will be built into your portfolio to complement the qualities of XYZ stock (its position in a given industry, its susceptibility to shifts in interest rates, etc.). At the end of the day, you're left with a diversified portfolio, without having to pay as much tax.

Keep in mind stepping out isn't an exact science. Depending upon the nature of the concentrated position in question, stepping out can be highly complicated, involving alternative investments, segregated accounts, and specialized divestiture strategies. And with some positions, the strategy may not even be possible. Which is why anyone considering it should be prepared to do their homework and find a qualified expert before making any decisions. Stepping out requires a highly skilled specialist, and a firm willing and able to construct such portfolios. Not everyone fits the bill.

## A pound of cure: **hedging strategies**

As I've said before, the best way to minimize concentration risk is to diversify the portfolio. If that's not possible, or if the U/HNWI absolutely wishes to hold a concentrated position, then hedging is the next best thing. Keep in mind, however, these strategies aren't suitable for everyone, and may not even be available depending upon the securities involved. By its very nature, hedging is a more complicated (and sometimes more expensive) strategy than diversification. It's also a more temporary solution: while diversification solves the problem of concentration risk once and for all, the hedging strategies I've listed here are only stop-gap measures, meant to protect a portfolio for a given time. If the ultimate goal is truly to minimize concentration risk, eventually it will be necessary to move on from hedging and start diversifying.

## Puts and calls

Probably the most popular method of hedging a concentrated equity position is to use options. Options are available in two basic forms. A *call* is the right to buy a particular security at a given price on or before a given date. A *put* is the exact opposite – the right to sell a security at a given price on or before a given date. With both calls and puts, what's important is the "strike price" – the stock price at which the purchaser of the option stands to make a profit by exercising the option (an option that would offer its holder a profit if exercised is said to be "in the money"). Both calls and puts may be purchased on the open market, at a percentage of the current price of the underlying stock. As the price of the underlying stock moves either up or down, so too do options on that stock. If the price for the option has gone up since the original purchaser bought it, it may be re-sold to another investor for a higher price.

There are two types of people who use options. On one hand you have the aggressive market traders and speculators – these are the people you see glamorized by Hollywood. On the other hand, you have the conservative, risk-averse investors who use options to protect (or *hedge*) the portfolio against loss. By purchasing a put, a U/HNWI can secure a minimum selling price for a stock, while keeping the opportunity for further gains open. Such a strategy is called a *protective put strategy*: the put functions as a kind of insurance policy, guaranteeing a minimum value for the investor's concentrated holding. Alternatively, an investor may sell calls, selling the right for third parties to purchase some or all of the concentrated position at a certain price. Income provided by the calls can be used to diversify the portfolio, or offset losses in a market downturn. Such a strategy is typically called *covered call writing* ("covered" because the investor has the stock in hand to transfer to another investor should the option be exercised). In either instance, the purpose of using options isn't to make a fortune, but to protect an existing stock position.

## Option collars

One popular hedging strategy that makes use of both calls and puts is the *option collar*. In such a scenario, the investor purchases a put option on a concentrated position. This guarantees a minimum price for the stock for a given period of time – anywhere from a month to a number of years. The investor then sells a call option on the same position. The strike price for the call is usually set much higher than the current trading price, and the expiry date for the options is far in the future. The result is a range of value for the given stock – the "collar."

Should the stock fall below the strike price of the put, the U/HNWI can sell at a guaranteed minimum price. At the same time, the U/HNWI can still participate in any gains – up to the strike price of the call. Ideally, the cost of the put equals the proceeds from the sale of the call, meaning the strategy doesn't have any out of pocket cost. And the strategy can be easily customized through the use of debit or credit collars. Little wonder then this strategy has become immensely popular with options holders or executives looking to hedge large, locked-in stock positions.

graph 8.4: **Option collar at work**

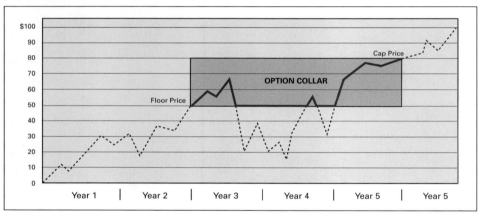

## Case study: a billionaire puts a collar on his portfolio

A recent example of such a strategy can be seen by Microsoft executive and co-founder Paul Allen. Between November 3rd and November 8th of 2000, Allen entered into a number of collared arrangements with one or more financial institutions to secure guaranteed prices for approximately 66.8 million of his Microsoft shares, valued at about $3.5-billion at the time.

Allen's contract provides a classic example of an options collar. Under terms of the contract, Allen secured a "floor value" for his stock, guaranteeing he could sell his shares at a range of prices between U.S. $55.08 to U.S. $63.24 as the various contracts expire between November of 2003 and November of 2005. In exchange for this protection, Allen established a ceiling price for his shares: the contracts give the various institutions the right to buy Allen's stock at prices ranging from U.S. $108.93 to U.S. $167.37 a share. Note that these values are far above Microsoft's trading price at the time of the contract. If Microsoft stock soars over the next few years, Allen can still participate in some of the gains, but only to a certain point.

So far, the move has proven to be a well-timed one. About five weeks after Allen arranged these contracts, Microsoft stock was hit hard – partially because of lowered earnings expectations in the midst of a tech market meltdown, partially because of continued uncertainty about the antitrust suit currently facing the company. In fact, Microsoft shares lost about 40% of their value between November 8th and the end of the year.

This example not only demonstrates the wisdom of an option collar strategy, it underlines the importance Allen places in diversification. As the holder of one of the most concentrated stock portfolios on the planet (he holds almost 150 million shares of Microsoft), the vast bulk of his wealth is at considerable risk. While Mr. Allen may well believe in Microsoft's ability to grow over the next few years, the uncertainty surrounding the technology industry and the company's court case (both of which are largely outside his ability to control) may undermine the value of his holdings. In other words, the time was right for an options collar. The move helps to secure Mr. Allen's wealth, and most certainly allows him to sleep better, knowing he's protected against a sudden drop.

### Hedging with unlisted transactions

With liquid securities (like Microsoft), it's usually possible to hedge a concentrated position through the use of options listed on an exchange. There are times, however, when such a solution may not be possible. There may be no listed options on the stock in question, for example, or the expiration dates or strike prices may not be in line with the U/HNWI's goals. In other situations, the transaction is simply too large for the listed market. Or perhaps the U/HNWI would like to avoid the publicity a large transaction might generate. In such situations, investors must seek an unlisted transaction (sometimes called a "private placement") – an exclusive contract between the investor and a major financial institution. Such a transaction offers many of the same benefits of a listed transaction, but with considerably more confidentiality. Again, only the largest firms can handle such transactions, however.

## Equity monetization

Another hedging strategy that offers executives and other corporate insiders considerable flexibility is *equity monetization*. Such a strategy typically involves a financial structure called a *variable forward contract*. In lay terms, this is a payment made between a financial institution and an individual investor as an advance on the eventual sale of securities. In such a scenario, the U/HNWI receives a loan payment equal to up to 100% of the position's value. The U/HNWI agrees to sell the position at a certain date in the future, and interest charged on the loan is paid back when the position is ultimately sold. Alternately, in lieu of interest, the U/HNWI can accept less cash up front.

For the U/HNWI, variable forward contracts have a number of important benefits. First is the ability to immediately diversify from a concentrated position: proceeds from the loan can be used to construct a more diversified portfolio relatively quickly, without having to wait for lock-ups or other restrictions to expire. Tax deferral is another advantage. Even though you've received a large pool of cash, the fact that you technically still own the stock (remember, the money you receive is a *loan*, not the proceeds from a sale) means you have deferred paying any capital gains tax in most jurisdictions until the contract matures. Such benefits make equity monetization a very attractive strategy for U/HNWIs sitting on large, low cost basis stock positions.

Until very recently, equity monetization had another benefit: confidentiality. It was theoretically possible for executives and other insiders to enter into a variable forward contract and avoid having to report the transaction (because the executive is still the legal owner of the shares, there is no need to report a sale until the windup date). Such practices have come under increasing scrutiny as regulatory bodies and investor rights groups push for more trading transparency. While there are certainly legitimate reasons for U/HNWIs to engage in such a strategy (to minimize concentration risk, to better organize one's estate, etc.), some of these groups consider such a strategy deceptive, as it masks an insider's true trading position. As of right now, it's unclear whether such transactions will continue to be accepted by regulatory authorities (in Canada, such transactions are technically legal, but firms are forced to disclose them). Personally, I don't think that should prevent a U/HNWI from at least *exploring* such a strategy. Yes, you might take some "heat" for diversifying, but you have a right to secure your wealth. The protection a diversified portfolio offers is almost always worth the public scrutiny.

## Case study: diversification for a growing business

If a business invests in another business, the risks of a concentrated position are just the same as they would be with an individual. When that investment is in a small start-up company whose shares are illiquid and volatile, that risk can be extreme.

That was the situation facing a client in one of my firm's Ontario branches a few years back. His business (in which he is a senior executive and part owner) made an investment some time ago in a promising privately-held electronics firm. The investment was a large one for this client's company, totalling about $5-million at the time. Despite the apparent risk, the investment turned out to be a smart one: the electronics company prospered and expanded its business at a rapid pace. Soon it was time for an Initial Public Offering. The IPO sold well, and the company's share price soared, doubling in value within the space of a few months. The client's investment for his company seemed to have paid off, more than tripling its investment of $5-million into an $18-million stake in one of the country's most promising start-ups.

So what was the problem? Well, with such a substantial increase, the client began to worry about hanging on to the investment. Just as importantly, his own company was starting to need cash in order to fuel further growth. Clearly it was time to sell. There was just one catch: the shares were tied up in a post-IPO lock up for a full year. It didn't seem like diversification was really an option for several months at least.

As the client's advisor explained, it is possible to construct a private placement transaction for shares in a post-IPO lock-up. The advisor immediately put the client in contact with divestiture specialists within the firm; they met with the client later that week. Together, they worked on a private contract that would allow the client's company to receive cash for the shares. The client decided to sell the bulk of the stock (about $15-million worth) to our firm at a 7% discount to the current share price. For the client, it was a good move. He was able to ensure the company's initial investment wasn't put at risk by a market downturn.

## A final word on concentration risk

Concentration risk can be a complicated subject. Don't let that discourage or intimidate you. There are highly skilled professionals available to help you navigate through these sophisticated strategies.

# Key concepts: Chapter eight

- While it is possible to minimize risk, it is impossible to eliminate it altogether.

- U/HNWIs face four different kinds of risk: systemic, common, security-specific, and investor. It is the last of these that is the most dangerous.

- There are two general methods for dealing with concentration risk: diversification and hedging.

- In a very general sense, diversification seeks to avoid the problem of concentration, while hedging seeks to remedy its consequences.

- The exact form of diversification is highly individual. It is usually better for U/HNWIs to base allocation decisions on risk tolerance rather than investment goals or age.

- If the portfolio is excessively concentrated in a low-cost-basis position, U/HNWIs may be able to use a stepping out strategy. Such a strategy will help them ease into a diversified portfolio and reduce or defer taxes at the same time.

- Put and call options can be effective tools for hedging concentrated stock positions.

- An option collar may be an effective tool for those U/HNWIs who want to limit downside risk without selling off their positions. Understand, however, that the price of this protection is giving up some upside potential.

- For those unable to use listed options, it is possible to enter into private transactions with brokerages or securities firms to hedge a large position.

- For those executives or insiders who are "locked in" to a concentrated position, an equity monetization strategy may provide an appropriate solution.

# **So** many options . . .

- *The psychology of options*
- *General rules for exercise*
- *Tax treatment of options*
- *Options and your life*

*"Making money is easy — knowing what to do with it becomes a problem."*

**Ring Lardner**

Options, options. So many options . . . and so many people receiving them. A survey by Oppenheimer Funds conducted in 2000 found that a little more than one-tenth of all private sector employees in America (that's about 12 million people) own employee stock options. As for how much wealth we're really talking about, The National Center for Employee Ownership figures that U.S. employees own, or have the option to own, over $800-billion in stock. Not only that, but the entry point for receiving stock options is falling too. In a study of 1,300 companies conducted in January of 2000, global consulting firm Watson Wyatt noted the average lowest salary at which employees receive options was pegged at $58,100. All in all, that's quite a trend.

There are a lot of reasons why more and more executives and employees are receiving options as part of their compensation package. The desire to align the interests of employees with the interests of shareholders is probably the most important of these. By giving management and key personnel a significant stake in the business, shareholders provide incentive for creating shareholder value. Another reason is the spectacular growth of high-tech companies. In order to motivate highly educated, highly driven people to work in an uncertain start-up situation, many high-tech firms have found it necessary to offer enormous options packages. While these companies demand long hours and sometimes offer an uncertain future, they are able to give their executives and employees the chance to one day become U/HNWIs.

# The **controversy** of options

Like it or not, this basic rationale has come under a lot of fire in the financial press – particularly over the past year or so. As compensation for CEOs and other high-level executives goes up and up, some people are wondering whether investors are paying too much for employee stock options. It doesn't help to have highly-publicized options packages being granted immediately prior to a market downturn.

graph 9.1: **Highest-paid CEOs**

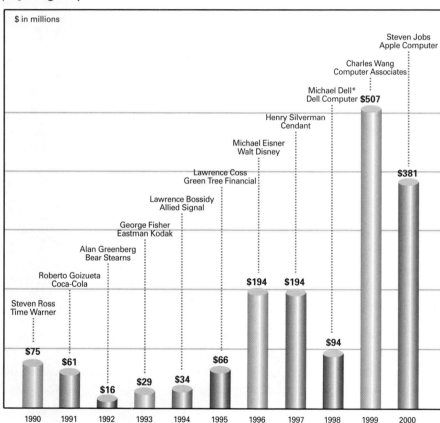

*Though reported in fiscal year 1999, Dell's options were granted in March and July 1998.

Even though most of these executives are cashing out options packages granted a long time ago, it's uncommon these days for a large stock sale to go unnoticed – or uncriticized. In fact, over the past few years, the size of options packages has been the subject of considerable debate. Proponents of such payments say that big options packages are the only way to attract top talent to the corporate boardroom. Opponents, on the other hand, call such compensation outrageous – even immoral. Perhaps more importantly, the opponents of such huge payouts claim they cost shareholders millions.

graph 9.2: **Largest options grants**

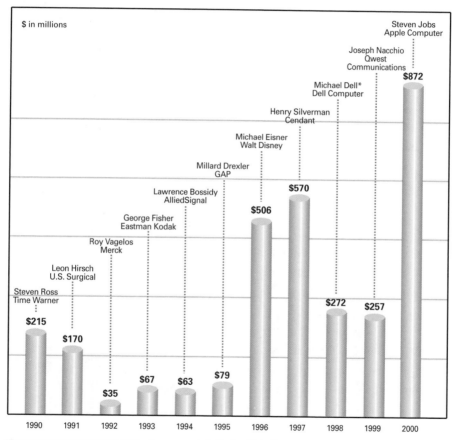

*Though reported in fiscal year 1999, Dell's options were granted in March and July 1998.

The debate over options has been going on for a long time, and it's unlikely it will end anytime soon. There are strong points to be made on both sides, but personally, I find it hard to see how options-based compensation will diminish in the years to come. I don't know if that's a bad thing – those who create wealth are surely entitled to a piece of it, and those who create big wealth are entitled to a big piece. But at the very least, such criticism is an indication of how complicated the issue of options can be.

## Options: the knowledge gap

Unfortunately, it seems many options holders don't fully understand this. A survey conducted by U.S.-based Oppenheimer Funds in 2000 found 37% of options holders claimed they knew more about Einstein's theory of relativity than they did about the tax consequences of their own options packages. Fully 34% didn't know what kind of options they held (there are two distinct varieties in the U.S.), while 29% told pollsters they didn't know how many of their options had vested.

These results indicate a fundamental lack of knowledge about options and their implications on one's net worth. And that has to change. Far from being some kind of financial potion that can make anyone instantly rich, options are a highly sophisticated investment vehicle, often involving extreme financial as well as mental challenges. Clearly, their use demands the utmost attention and care. U/HNWIs with options packages must do everything they can to learn more about their options, and how they can use these specialized financial vehicles to their advantage.

Which is why this chapter is a critical one in *True Wealth*. By the end of this chapter, options holders will have a basic understanding of the rules and regulations regarding options. We'll discuss the psychology of options, and review some of the mental pitfalls options holders can fall into. I'll also describe my basic approach when it comes to handling an options package. Understand, though, that options are a complicated subject – far more complicated than a brief chapter can do justice to. For a full understanding of those challenges, it's absolutely critical for U/HNWIs to to seek personalized investment and tax advice.

## The psychology of options

Wealth management is about managing the mind as much as it is about managing the portfolio. This is especially true when dealing with options. Those who hold significant options positions need to make themselves aware of some of the subtle (and the not-so subtle) psychological pitfalls options can present, and how these pitfalls can potentially leave you in a worse position than before you were granted those options.

### Mental pitfall #1: Not knowing what you own

In order to make clear, rational decisions about your options, you need to learn all you can. First, you should be aware of your intentions regarding your options – what your wealth and lifestyle goals are, and how your options fit into them. You need to know what kind of options you hold, and when those options vest. You should also be aware of some of the exercise alternatives available to you, and have at least a rough idea of how much your options are worth under various valuation methods. Finally, you'll need to understand the tax implications of an options exercise. Knowing these things will ensure your options actually build wealth, instead of working to destroy it.

### Mental pitfall #2: "get-rich-quick" thinking

Back in the days of the Internet millionaire, options were seen as the ultimate in "get rich quick" schemes. Options were often exercised as soon as they were granted. That's not always the best strategy. Options shouldn't be considered the fast track to wealth. Most options have a considerable shelf life – five to ten years is common – and statistically speaking, the longer you hold them, the more your potential for gain. If you're an options holder, teach yourself to avoid "ticker watching" – constantly watching the ebb and flow of the company stock on the Internet while at work – and instead, take a long-term view of your options. Be patient with your options, and give them time to grow.

### Mental pitfall #3: Getting greedy

In other cases, option holders face the exact opposite problem. When company stock is soaring, options holders can get greedy, hanging on to large options packages far longer than is advisable. Once they've exercised, this greed can continue, as former options holders sit on large blocks of stock. It's only when company stock dips do these people realize how dangerous an overconcentrated position can really be. If you hold a significant options position, make sure to investigate your diversification strategies *before* you exercise, and *before* a downturn hits.

### Mental pitfall #4: Letting anxiety get in the way

Fluctuations are par for the course when investing in the stock market. I admit, with many of the highly-volatile companies in which options-based compensation is the norm, those fluctuations can be difficult to tune out. Nevertheless, those with options need to develop a thick skin, become accustomed to seeing their option value – and by extension, their net worth – drop during the course of the day. Tuning out the market's short-term movements is the first step in making sure your options package does you the greatest good.

### Mental pitfall #5: Pre-spending; spending on small stuff

*Options are not cash.* They should not be used as a cash substitute. You should not borrow against them to fund big purchases. Until they are exercised, they are only the *potential* for wealth, and must be treated as such. Probably the best thing for options holders to do is to forget about options when it comes to budgeting and day-to-day expenses. I know that can be tough, particularly when you're looking at that luxury yacht you've fallen in love with. But the less you consider options a part of your present wealth, the less trouble you'll run into.

### Mental pitfall #6: Not keeping yourself grounded

It's easy to get caught up in the excitement of options, and become blind to more important elements of your job or indeed, your life. Understand that your first options package probably won't be your last, and that options typically have a long while before they vest. Understand also that until you actually exercise them, options mean relatively little to your bottom line. And if you remember nothing else, remember this: options should be a reward for a job you love to do. If that job becomes a tedious chore – something you can't stand – then I'm of the opinion that your options are worth very little. These little grounding exercises will help you keep your options package (and your future wealth) in the proper perspective.

## The financial challenge of options

To make sure you get the most from your options, you'll need to carefully consider the financial consequences of the various strategies available to you – preferably well before you exercise. These general guidelines will get you started.

## Exercising your options: **theory vs. reality**

The first thing options holders must learn is how to value their options fairly. Many studies and pricing models have been proposed that look at the valuation of options from a mathematical point of view. In fact, in 1997, the Nobel Prize in economics was given to Myron Scholes of Stanford and Robert Merton of Harvard for their pioneering work on options pricing models. This knowledge has developed to the point where it's possible for options holders to plug their options into a complex computer model and arrive at a fairly accurate valuation of their holding – even if those options are currently "out of the money." It's a little beyond the scope of this book to detail all the math involved in these studies, but the general point goes something like this: *from a mathematical point of view, the longer you hold your options, the more profit you're likely to make.*

That's all well and good, but in the real world, portfolio security, personal emotions, and employment mobility are all issues that get in the way of making a purely mathematical decision. Which is why I've developed some simple rules when it comes to exercising options:

- **Rule #1: take a systematic approach.** I generally recommend a systematic approach when it comes to exercising options. By establishing pre-determined dates for the exercise of your vested options, you can ensure emotions don't factor into the decision to exercise, and gradually whittle down a concentrated position. The exact schedule for such an exercise program could depend on any number of factors – exercise could begin immediately after a chunk of your options vest, or it could happen at a set date, or after a significant life event. The point is to make the schedule regular, and stick to it. I understand such a strategy may leave some money on the table. But remember, the ultimate goal of wealth management for U/HNWIs is *security*.

- **Rule #2: stock first, options second.** If you have both stock and options, sell the stock before the options. It's almost always a better strategy. Why? In most cases, the gain on the options will almost always be much greater.

- **Rule #3: exercise the oldest, cheapest options first.** This one should be common sense. If the oldest options *aren't* the cheapest, things get a little more complicated. In such a situation, I recommend running an options calculator to find out which ones you should sell first. You can find one easily on the Internet, but it's almost always better to run through such scenarios with a financial professional, who will likely be able to outline a number of different exercise strategies with you.

- **Rule #4: think about taxes before you exercise.** With some large options positions, the tax liability can be huge. And if the stock heads downhill after you exercise, it's theoretically possible for the tax bill to exceed the value of your holdings – or even your entire net worth. Obviously, it makes sense to plan as far ahead for this liability as possible.

## Options **and taxes**

Dealing with taxes can be a real challenge for options holders. In many cases, the consequences of an options exercise can force you to sell a good chunk of your position just to cover the taxes. For that reason, I think it's necessary to cover a few of the general rules regarding the way options are taxed in North America. Before we do, however, let me reiterate the importance of finding a qualified accountant or other tax advisor that can discuss the details of your individual tax situation more fully. Professional advice has a funny way of paying for itself.

### Taxation of options: U.S.

In America, the taxation of options depends largely on whether the options are non-qualified options or incentive stock options. With non-qualified options, the rules are relatively simple: appreciation over the strike price is taxed as ordinary income when the options are exercised. After that, any further appreciation will usually be taxed as capital gains. Usually, an employer will withhold tax when options are exercised, making non-qualifieds relatively easy to deal with from a tax planning perspective. That said, options holders could be in for a nasty surprise come reporting season. If the exercise of options bumps the employee into a higher tax bracket, but the employer assumed taxes payable at a lower bracket, the employee will have to make up the difference. Given the large size of options packages, that could make for a hefty bill.

The taxation of Incentive Stock Options (ISOs) is a little more complicated. With ISOs, all gains over the strike price are taxable as a capital gain. What's more, tax is only payable when you sell – as long as you hold the shares for at least two years after your options are issued, or one year after exercise, whichever is longer. That makes ISOs potentially more valuable than non-qualified options. Unfortunately, it also can make them a bigger headache. I know of ISO holders who ran into trouble by holding on to their stock after exercise, ostensibly for tax reasons. Only when the value of their holdings plummeted did they understand how risky such a strategy can be.

Further complicating the matter of options taxation is the Alternative Minimum Tax – a flat 28% tax rate for high-income earners whose deductions bring their income tax below a prescribed minimum level. The rules as to when and where the AMT applies are extremely complicated, and by and large, most options holders don't understand them (75% of options holders said as much in the Oppenheimer Funds survey mentioned above). Detailing appropriate strategies for dealing with the AMT would require much more space than I have here, but suffice it to say, if you find yourself facing such a scenario, go see a tax professional *now*. You could very well be saving yourself a bundle in tax.

### Taxation of options: Canada

Taxation of options in Canada tends to be a little less complicated. When options are exercised in Canada, the option holder is deemed to have received a taxable employment benefit, and must report a portion of this benefit as income. The calculation of the benefit is somewhat complicated, but in general, your tax return will include the fair market value of the shares at the time of exercise, less the cost of the shares, less the cost of the options. Tax may be deferred until the actual sale of the shares – up to an annual limit of $100,000 – as long as certain conditions are met. The employee may also be able to claim a deduction of 50% of the taxable benefit. Again, certain conditions must be met, which makes professional tax advice an absolute must.

## Case study: Taxes? What taxes?

A colleague of mine who's a financial professional in California recently relayed a story involving an options holder (I'll call her Helen here) who came to see him some time ago about establishing a retirement plan. My friend tells me the case is a fairly typical one for many U.S. options holders. I present it here as a study in how the taxation of options can affect exercise strategy. Helen's case revolves around the American tax regulations, but the general principles apply no matter where you live.

Helen was an executive at a large pharmaceutical firm. She had been with the company for a good while, and was starting to think about her retirement. During her employment, she'd taken advantage of a number of employee benefits, including the employee stock ownership plan. She'd also been granted a number of incentive stock options. Those options were granted when the stock was trading near $20, and had another nine months to go before they would have been eligible for preferential tax treatment. Helen's net worth consisted of three major items: her home, her stock portfolio (the bulk of which was invested in company stock), and her unexercised stock options.

As often happens with pharmaceutical companies, one day the company received news of excellent clinical responses for one of its new drugs. Company shares soared on the news, and before long they were trading near $50. Helen was obviously pleased at this turn of events, and being close to retirement, she started to shop for a small vacation property along the Oregon coast. Unfortunately, before she could find the ideal location (but well after she had made up her mind to buy), the market suffered a major drop, and Helen's portfolio was hit hard. Her company's stock traded down to $25 a share – still a significant appreciation over what Helen had bought it for, and Helen's options were still "in the money." But Helen began to worry, and started to see that vacation home slip between her fingers. She decided to do what she considered was the "safe" thing to do: exercise her options and sell before the stock dropped any further.

Under normal circumstances, I might be an advocate of such a move. By taking money off the table, Helen would be ensuring herself a certain quality of life for her retirement. But as my friend explained to me, Helen had forgotten to consider taxes before she made her decision. Because Helen exercised her options early, she was forced to pay ordinary income tax on the proceeds, rather than the much lower capital gains rate. The resulting bill was a hefty one, and as my friend related to me, seemed to make the entire transaction more trouble than it was really worth. On top of it all, my friend tells me the stress this situation created for Helen was considerable.

Helen's story highlights how critical it is for options holders to be aware of the taxation issues surrounding the exercise of their options. Of course, it's not like all is lost for Helen – she still made money from her options, and she still has an enviable net worth, one that is growing steadily. But by not familiarizing herself with the tax laws, Helen cost herself hundreds of thousands of dollars.

But there's another problem here. Helen exercised out of panic – when she started to see the impact of a market drop on her overconcentrated portfolio. While there may or may not have been anything she could have done to diversify out of her *options* position, she could have diversified her *portfolio* (remember, the majority of it was invested in company stock). Perhaps then a market drop wouldn't have caused her to sell her options in the first place. I'm pleased to say that this problem is something my friend is working on with Helen right now. The two are coming up with an exercise strategy that will help Helen avoid future tax problems before they begin.

# Exercising your options: thinking about risk

Helen's story is a good lesson in how risky an options package can be. The technology meltdown of early 2000 through 2001 provides additional evidence of the need for options holders to protect themselves against risks. Need proof? Just take a look at some of the dramatic losses experienced by options holders at some of the biggest technology companies in the world. At its peak on December 29, 1999, Microsoft traded as high as $119.30 a share. Almost a year later (December 21 of 2000), it had dropped to $40.25 a share. Microsoft was not alone. Amazon.com sunk from a high of $106.69 on December 10 of 1999 to $8.10 as recently as April 4 2001. America Online/Time Warner traded at $93.94 on December 13 of 1999, only to fall to $31.75 on January 2 of 2001. But this pales in comparison to the riches–to–rags story experienced by employees and executives at Canada's Nortel Networks. Their stock reached a peak of $124.50. A year later, the stock was trading around $13. In response, Nortel management decided to re-price some 111 million worthless options, giving many of these employees (but not their management executives) another chance to profit. It doesn't seem to have worked. At the time I write this, Nortel stock is trading around $9 a share.

I know, I know – I'm picking on the technology industry. But no matter what industry you work in, if you hold options, you need to be aware of these kinds of risks. Like any equity holder, options holders need to think seriously about minimizing the concentration risk inherent in large options positions.

## Options **and concentration risk**

The most serious risk presented by large options positions is that of concentration risk. With options holders, the problem is compounded by the potential delay between the exercise date and the date the underlying stock is eventually sold.

Although many options holders cash out immediately after exercise, the potential for further gains (and tax deferral) presents a powerful temptation to hang on to super-concentrated positions. This temptation has been the ruin of many an option holder.

I firmly believe every options holder needs to develop an exit strategy — that is, a strategy for easing out of the stock position resulting from an options exercise — before they even consider exercising. This should involve setting an upper and a lower limit for the sale, and clear, measurable criteria that define the circumstances in which a sale will be made. In most cases, it's also a good idea to establish a set selling schedule — this will minimize the role of emotions in any sale decision. Those who already have a significant net worth can afford to be a little more flexible on this point, but in general, I recommend options holders take money off the table sooner rather than later. Beyond these common-sense guidelines, options holders need to take a close look at diversification and hedging strategies, with the intention of minimizing concentration risk. Again, it's about securing wealth, rather than looking for the "big score."

## Case study: A good thing goes bad

The performance of some technology stocks mimics that of an ill-tempered rodeo horse — up and down, up and down. Sure, many technology workers have become used to the rocky ride, but for options holders, this kind of volatility can be a recipe for disaster. A case I recently came across in the paper is a perfect example.

In its heyday, Microsoft was one of the most stable, most reliable growth companies around — that's a considerable accomplishment for a company that had its roots in a small office in Albuquerque, New Mexico. Years of compound growth had transformed many rank-and-file employees into U/HNWIs — and a number of long-serving executives into billionaires. Little wonder why just working for the software giant would lead an otherwise sensible person to take great financial risks.

As the article reported, just prior to the peak of the high-tech boom, many Microsoft employees were adopting extremely aggressive strategies with their options packages. Specifically, some employees were exercising options early to build a sizable chunk of Microsoft stock, then borrowing against that stock for large consumer purchases. This is a risky strategy at the best of times, and downright calamitous on the eve of a market meltdown. When the value of Microsoft stock began to slide, many of the brokerages and financial institutions administering these loans began selling portions of the underlying stock positions to cover the loans. Adding insult to injury was the fact many of these same employees were completely unaware of the tax liability of their exercise. So in addition to having sizeable stock positions liquidated to cover a margin call, these people were left with huge tax bills – and little ability to pay them. Predictably, this strategy ended in disaster for many of these employees: one Seattle-based bankruptcy trustee estimated fully 25 cases came across his desk as a result of Microsoft options gone bad.

The story of these unfortunate employees demonstrates what happens when options holders fail to understand (or rather, fail to acknowledge) the inherent risk of any options package. These Microsoft employees did not diversify their portfolios, and they continued to hang on to excessively concentrated positions even when markets seemed to be taking a turn for the worse. They then compounded their risk by setting up speculative margin loans at a time when the market was ready to take a tumble. To top it all off, they then used the proceeds of those loans not for investment, but as ready cash for luxury purchases. In other words, these employees did everything they could possibly do wrong.

No matter what company they work for, options holders need to be aware of the basic rules that dictate how their options will be taxed, and should ideally make provisions for those taxes long before the decision to exercise. And again, they should seek out professional tax advice as soon as possible, to make sure they don't get caught off guard come reporting season.

## Options and your life

Beyond their financial implications, options can have a significant impact on your life. Of course, these implications can be very personal, but there are two general lifestyle points every options holder needs to be aware of.

### Golden handcuffs

It's easy to get caught up in the excitement of options, and forget what they were originally intended to be: incentive for an employee to stay with a particular company. However altruistic a company may be, most companies don't set up their options plans to make their employees rich. Rather, the primary purpose of every options program is to make it as difficult as possible for employees to leave.

While "golden handcuffs" may make sense for the employer, for the employee, they can be a mixed blessing. I still read stories of Silicon Valley workers slaving away for low base salaries, waiting for their options to vest. No doubt a good many of these people will find the trade-off well worth it. But I wonder whether some of them are sacrificing valuable quality of life in an effort to become rich quick. It's not up to me to tell you what decisions you should make regarding your employment, but to my mind, options should never prevent you from accomplishing what you want to in life. Take it from me – I've seen some bright, intelligent people burn out quickly as they waited for their options to vest. Don't let this happen to you. Ultimately, a healthy, balanced life and a positive mental attitude are worth more than any unvested options position.

### The notoriety of options

Another lifestyle issue with options is their notoriety. Under securities regulations, most North American companies are required to publish a list of the options to which executives and employees are entitled. Recently, shareholders' meetings for many high-profile companies have turned raucous and contentious, as more and more shareholders voice their displeasure with executives taking home generous options packages without earning their keep. At a recent Vodafone annual general meeting, fully a third of shareholders voted against a scheme that would grant its then CEO Sir Christopher Gent eight million options. Such dissent is normally unheard of – but as the market continues to slide, it's becoming increasingly normal. Companies that haven't put the subject of executive compensation up for a vote in the past are coming under increasing pressure to do so, from both individual activists and institutional investors looking for more transparency.

This trend isn't going to go away. As executive compensation soars into the stratosphere, U/HNWIs should expect their compensation to be the subject of public debate. My advice to U/HNWIs in such situations is simple: brace yourself for some static – resistance in the boardroom, catcalls in the AGMs, and criticisms in the press.

## Case study: the notoriety of options

When company stock heads south, options holders often find themselves the target of intense criticism. The case of Vancouver-based 360networks is a classic example.

The general details of the story should be familiar to anyone living through the tech market boom: a promising technology company issues millions of options (31.9 million of them, to be exact) to executives and other company founders at low strike prices (an average of 62.5 cents). After an IPO at $14 CDN, shares start to climb to $35, making many executives fabulously wealthy. Between April 19th, 2000 (the day the company went public) and April 25th, 2001, insiders cashed in almost $1-billion worth of company stock, the bulk of which had been granted by way of options.

As it turned out, this decision was extremely timely – a little too timely for some. Soon after the sales, the stock began a long, drawn-out slide that took it from around $24 to 10 cents. Through it all, insiders and executives continued their selling spree. Over a two-day span in November of 2000, several of the company's vice-presidents decided to cash out *en masse*, collectively selling over 1 million shares. All along the way, these people have had the details of their sales profiled in Canada's national newspapers – often accompanied by blistering criticism of their decision. For many investors, it seemed unethical to sell as the company started to slide. Now that 360networks has filed for protection from creditors, I'm sure those attacks are only going to increase.

I present this case not as a condemnation of what 360networks employees did (given the nature of the company's business, exercising was probably the smart thing to do,). Rather, I present it as an example of the kind of criticism executives should expect. If company prospects turn sour after you exercise a large options position, expect to take some heat. But don't let that deter you from doing what's right. By taking money off the table, you're securing quality of life for yourself and your family, and diversifying your portfolio in an important way. Ultimately, that's more important than any bad press you may receive.

## A last word on options

Make no mistake: however large your options package is, it has the potential to change your life. Treat it with respect. If you have one or more packages of options vesting for you, make sure you take responsibility for your new-found wealth, and spend some time investigating the opportunities available to you *before* you need to exercise.

# Key concepts: Chapter nine

- More and more companies are issuing options as part of their compensation packages. As a result, more employees and executives are becoming U/HNWIs.

- Options have the power not only to change your financial situation, but also the way you think about yourself and your wealth.

- There are several psychological pitfalls options holders find themselves in:

  **pitfall #1:** not understanding the tax and investment implications of options.

  **pitfall #2:** considering options as a get-rich-quick scheme

  **pitfall #3:** getting greedy and not diversifying from concentrated stock positions

  **pitfall #4:** allowing market volatility to affect your decision to exercise

  **pitfall #5:** pre-spending the proceeds from options, or spending proceeds on basic living expenses or luxury goods.

  **pitfall #6:** letting options wealth go to your head

- There are many theories on when to exercise options; from a mathematical point of view, the longer the options are held, the more potential profit.

- In the real world, a regimented options exercise schedule is probably the best strategy for most options holders.

- Options exercise brings a number of tax implications; options holders need to be well aware of these implications before they exercise.

- The large, concentrated positions generated by options demand serious attention. Options holders should limit such risk in their portfolio.

- Options have the power to change your life dramatically. Options holders need to be well grounded, and have a solid understanding of what they want to accomplish with the proceeds of their options.

- Understand the attention the exercise of large options positions can bring upon their owner.

## Resources

Options seem to be a popular topic these days – U/HNWIs looking for more information on them won't have to look too far. Just be careful about what you're reading: rapidly-changing regulations can make the advice in many books and websites out of date.

*Stock Options: An Authoritative Guide to Incentive and Non-qualified Stock Options (2nd Edition*) by Robert R. Pastore

*The Stock Options Book* by David R. Johanson

## Websites

*www.mystockoptions.com* – the premiere online resource for options holders

The National Center for Employee Ownership *www.nceo.org* – excellent information for U.S. residents

ESOP Association Canada *www.esopcanada.org* for Canadian investors

# **Selling** your business

chapter

# 10

*"That men who are industrious and sober and honest in the pursuit of their own interests should after a while accumulate capital, and after that should be allowed to enjoy it in peace, and also if they should choose, when they have accumulated it, to use it to save themselves from actual labor, and hire other people to labor for them, is right."*

**Abraham Lincoln**

**M**any business owners treat their business like a child – caring for it, nurturing it, and giving it the best years of their life. There comes a time, however, when every child must leave the nest.

For many people, selling a long-held business is the most significant financial event of their lives. It's a path to wealth that many people are following, or will be following soon. According to the Canadian Association of Family Enterprise, fully 27% of family business leaders in Canada are planning to retire in the next five years, and another 29% are planning to do so in the next six to ten years. In the U.S., the picture looks much the same. A large survey completed in 1997 by Arthur Anderson and Mass Mutual concluded that nearly 43% of family businesses would change hands over the next five years. By the looks of things, this trend has already started to take place. The value of merger and acquisition activity in the U.S., for example, has grown steadily since 1994. And, while the number of deals has fallen slightly in response to continuing troubles in the technology industry, it is still some 50% higher than it was in 1994.

graph 10.1: **Volume and value of U.S. M&A activity – public and private**

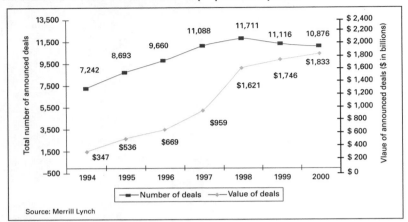

Source: Merrill Lynch

There are four main drivers behind this trend. First and foremost, North America has seen a long period of economic expansion, in which the value of many closely-held businesses has expanded dramatically. Low interest rates have been another factor – cheap money makes it a lot easier for companies and investors to finance acquisitions of high-quality businesses. High stock values are a third factor – these can inflate the value of many of the mergers and acquisitions. The fourth factor has been the rise of private equity funds. As we'll be discussing a little later, many U/HNWIs and other investors are seeking private equity opportunities as a way to diversify and complement existing portfolios with high-performing assets.

Even for those who don't own a business, the financial consequences of this wave of sell-offs will be tremendous. A survey conducted in 1999 by Deloitte & Touche estimates that in Canada alone, some 4.7 million full-time and 1.3 million part time workers owe their employment to a family business. The total revenues from these businesses? Somewhere in the neighborhood of $1.3-trillion. Around the globe, conservative estimates suggest family-controlled businesses account for somewhere between 65% to 85% of all the world's businesses. These statistics illustrate that what happens to the family business is of immense importance to not only the U/HNWIs who own them, but to the entire world.

Despite their apparent frequency, the sale of a closely-held business is anything but an easy task. If the sale of a family business is not planned well in advance, an otherwise stable business can easily go under, wreaking havoc on both family relationships and family accounts. All of which means U/HNWIs who have a business must take special care with their businesses, and become keenly aware of the options available to them for planning their eventual exit from the business.

That, in a nutshell, is what this chapter will tell you to do. It will provide you with a general overview of some of the personal and financial challenges you'll face when you initiate a sale of your business, and will illustrate particular strategies that will help you cope with these challenges. You'll read about how you can prepare for the sale of your business, and some of the financing options available to you when it comes time to sell. Perhaps most importantly, this chapter will also present some valuable case studies about how other U/HNWIs have approached the sale of their businesses. By learning about the decisions these other U/HNWI business owners made – both right and wrong – it should be easier for you to determine how you should sell your business.

## My approach to business divestiture

The first challenge any U/HNWI business owner faces is apathy. The 1999 survey by Deloitte Touche mentioned above discovered nearly 66% of Canadian-based family businesses do not have a written contingency plan in place to provide guidance in the event of an unforeseen death. An equal amount reported they also lacked a plan to deal with an unforeseen disability or incapacity of the owner.

The way I see it, this lack of preparation is probably the most significant financial challenge we will face in years – and I'm speaking not only for the families of the business owners, but for all of North America. With so much money involved in family businesses, this apathy threatens the economics of the entire continent. Which is why I believe it critical for U/HNWI business owners to tackle the issue of business divestiture head-on, and resolve these issues as a central element of their overall wealth management plan.

The subject of business divestiture is a large one. That's why I like to break the subject up into two distinct elements: (a) personal issues, and (b) financial issues. The former deals with issues that affect your life, the lives of your family, or your state of mind. The latter section deals with the financial perspective, and outlines some of the financial options facing business owners when it comes time to sell.

## Personal issues: what makes sense for you?

There are three critical errors business owners can make when considering selling their business: (a) selling too soon, (b) selling too late, and (c) waffling on the sale. To make sure you don't fall into any one of these traps, you'll need to develop some self-awareness. The first step: knowing what you want from your business on an ongoing basis. Are you looking for complete retirement? Or do you envision something else – perhaps a gradual easing out of the business? If you decide to hang on, will you be passing up a favorable market opportunity? Or are you simply going through the motions when it comes to selling, not committing solidly to one decision or the other? Whatever your goals you'll need to be completely comfortable with your decision, so make sure you take the time to consider your options.

Ideally, you'll want to discuss your intentions with your successor (or successors) before making your decision, and finalize arrangements well in advance of the actual sale. You'll want to do the same with your business partners, your family, your employees, and the various stakeholders in the business (creditors, suppliers, clients, etc.). Whatever decision you make, make sure to clearly define your intentions, set a date for your eventual departure, and stick to your plan. Trying to return to a business after you have made the decision to leave can make life extremely difficult for your successor, and can undermine efforts to establish authority or difference between current management and old management. It can also be confusing and unsettling for employees, leaving them unclear as to who is actually in charge. Open, honest communication about your ongoing plans not only ensures a smooth transition from your management to the next, it gives you an opportunity to extract maximum value from the business.

### The emotions of selling a business

For many business owners, the decision to sell is an intensely emotional one. If it is forced upon the owner – as a result of ongoing losses, ill health, or even a divorce – a business sale can initiate an entire range of emotions that non-business owners may find difficult to understand.

Of course, any emotional experience will be highly personal. But speaking from my own experience with business owners over the years, I can say there are a few common emotions associated with the sale of a long-standing business that most former owners share. The most common of these is a sense of *loss*. Depending on the personality, the sale of a business may mean the loss of routine, the loss of control, or even the loss of one's life purpose. In other cases, the business owner can experience extreme *grief* for their business. To some extent, such grief is natural. As any business owner will tell you, a business is more than simply a financial entity, and its exchange for money may leave its former owner feeling empty and alone.

When these emotions spoil the experience of freedom and well-being that is the ultimate goal of any business sale, or cause the owner to second-guess the decision to sell, it can mean big problems. For this reason, it's important for owners to prepare for their emotions as best they can. If you're considering selling your business soon, do yourself (and your wealth advisor!) a favor: give some thought as to how the sale will make you *feel*. Let others know what the sale will mean to you, and keep them informed of your feelings throughout the process. Ideally, you should have a plan of action to deal with such emotions – perhaps taking a long holiday after the sale, or diving into a new business venture. Whatever you come up with, the goal should be to prevent short-term emotions from interfering with what's best for you in the long run.

## Family **matters**

Involving family members in the decision to sell a closely-held business is usually a good idea. *Usually*. If the business is managed as a family concern (or if the family thinks it is), a sale can bring up a number of complicated issues, and a fair bit of conflict too.

In my experience, this is often the most complicated area of business divestiture. Business owners need to tread lightly when involving the family in the decision to sell, and be prepared for conflict. This is particularly the case when owners plan to appoint a family member as their successor. Clarifying your decision with other family members can be a big help in making sure your family isn't torn apart by the jealousies and infighting that can erupt when one family member is handed the business.

In many cases, a family "council" or advisory board can help mitigate these conflicts. In such a scenario, the family organizes a kind of governing body in which family members can voice concerns about the business and formulate solutions that fit everybody. Such a body can be as formal or as informal as is necessary, but keep in mind that it works best in families that sincerely wish to have clear avenues of communication – families that truly want to establish a tradition of consensus when it comes to dealing with their business. Even in a family that does share that tradition, it's a good idea to include some outsiders on the board. Such people can often provide a more objective, more balanced point of view about what the business should do than family members can provide. That perspective can be particularly valuable if the business runs into trouble, and tough decisions have to be made about layoffs, closures, or selling the business to a competitor.

Above all else, it's important for the business owner to understand that *ownership* of a family business and *management* of a family business are two very different things. It can be tough to stay objective about the leadership qualities of your sons and daughters, but this kind of objectivity is absolutely essential if you're looking to build a strong business that will last through several generations. Many well-established firms founder in the second generation under the helm of children whose business skills aren't as well-developed as those of their parents. The advancement of less-than-suitable family managers can quickly turn a progressive, forward-thinking firm into a stale, conservative company that resists change. The moral of the story: while the ownership of the family business might not be in doubt, the management of that business should be approached with the utmost caution, and considered carefully by any owner prior to the sale.

## Case study: A family business gone bad

The pages of business history are full of family feuds; many of these feuds are nasty, hard-fought battles that have little to do with the business, and everything to do with settling scores. A number of particularly poignant examples from Canada have been documented in Gordon Pitts' excellent book *In the Blood: Battles to Succeed in Canada's Family Businesses*. In my mind, this book should be required reading for all business owners – if only to show them what can happen when family pride takes precedence over sound business sense.

To me, the one story in this book that truly leaps off the page is the story of Intercontinental Packers, a large meat packaging and processing company based in the heart of Canada's prairie. Intercontinental was built from the ground up by a hard-working German immigrant by the name of Fred Mendel in the 1940s. Fred's first-born grandson Robert Mitchell had been expected to carry on the family business, but the pressure of being the designated heir took its toll, and Robert committed suicide as a young man. The role of heir then fell to the second-oldest grandson, Fred, who had been working in the business as a management trainee. When the elder Fred died in 1976 at the age of 87, Fred Mitchell took over the family business. He was 29 at the time.

Things at Intercontinental were moving along nicely until family conflict got in the way of the family business. In the early 1980s, Fred met LuAn Gingara. The relationship enjoyed a frosty reception from Fred's immediate family, particularly from Fred's mother, Johanna. When Fred and LuAn decided to marry in 1986, Fred's sister Camille didn't attend. The family's personal relationships – as well as their ability to conduct business together – went downhill from there. In the late 80s, Johanna moved majority ownership of Intercontinental to a family trust, and continued to exert pressure on Fred, who had recently been diagnosed with cystic fibrosis. While a heart-lung transplant in 1990 cured Fred of his ailment, the disease within the family began to grow.

When Fred proposed a consolidation and divestiture of certain business assets in 1994, the simmering feud turned into all-out war, and family relationships began to take on the look of a badly-produced soap opera. Fred resigned his position in 1995 over the growing rancor between himself and other family members. Fred's brother Chip took over, but was quite clearly out of his league – Intercontinental began to bleed red ink at a rapid pace. In 1996, Fred brought a lawsuit against the company. Chip and the rest of the family countersued. In 1996, Fred's sister Camille was charged with uttering death threats. Intercontinental's suppliers, customers, employees, and lenders were all growing increasingly tired of the dog-and-pony show. Under the threat of a complete collapse in the business, the family put their differences aside and allowed Fred back in. In 1997, the business was split into two parts. Fred received the company's pork-processing business, while Johanna, Chip, and Camille received the beef. Fred's portion thrived, and was soon making a profit again. The company was renamed Mitchell's Gourmet Foods, to better reflect the upscale market the company's products were now targeting. The reversal of economic fortunes did little to revive family relationships, however. When Fred died of complications following minor surgery in 1998, he hadn't spoken to his mother in over two years. After Fred's death, LuAn assumed presidency over Mitchell's, and ended up selling a portion of the company to Kitchener-based Schneider Corp. in early 1999.

Seven months later, Johanna died. The acrimony lasted right until the end: two weeks before her death, Johanna had filed suit for a cut of the proceeds from the Schneider sale.

The tragic story of the Mitchells serves as a classic example of how *not* to run a family business. As demonstrated by their sad saga, when a family can't separate their personal issues from what's good for the business, both family and business inevitably suffer. *Don't let that happen to your business*. Clear the air with family members and keep them informed of your intentions. If you've allowed family members to become managers, don't use your personal influence to dictate business decisions. You might end up destroying the business – and the family – you worked so hard to build.

## Financial issues: what makes sense for your wealth?

From a financial perspective, the sale of a business is one of the most complicated financial transactions there is, requiring much organization and planning, and a good deal of professional advice. Here is a brief review of some of the critical issues.

### Financial issues: **preparing the business for sale**

The first part of the divestiture process is to prepare the business for sale. In practical terms, that means maximizing its value. While lengthy preparation is not always possible, ideally, the seller should prepare for the sale of their business well in advance – anywhere between three to five years should allow you to prepare statements, organize the business' finances, and put structures in place that will ensure the transaction will be as smooth and as profitable as possible.

Case in point: the operating practices of your business. Most businesses are managed to minimize the ongoing tax liability of the owner. While this makes sense under normal operating conditions, such a strategy can create problems when the time comes to sell. Simply put, those same strategies that minimize tax liability when you own the business can minimize its book value. Shifting accounting and operating strategies to maximize value may make sense some time before the sale is made.

Valuation of a business is another crucial element of every business sale, and one that often requires extensive preparation. There are many different methods available to evaluate a business. Depending on where you live, some of these might be more acceptable to potential buyers than others. Whatever valuation method you choose, just remember the general principle behind all business valuation is this: the more detailed, the better. In practical terms, that usually means taking the time to have revenue and income statements audited by a professional accountant: audited financial statements make the job easier for the buyer, and are generally well worth the investment.

You'll also want time to write up a valuation report – a detailed overview of business operations and prospects. This is much like a business plan, and should be as detailed and as extensive as possible. The exact contents will vary from business to business and from industry to industry, but some of the more typical areas to cover include:

**business history:** who started it, how it was started, and how it has developed

**analysis of business operations:** how the business makes money

**list of assets and facilities:** including lease arrangements

**description of suppliers:** including credit terms and the history of supplier relationships

**marketing discussion:** describing how the business positions and markets itself

**analysis of competition:** who the competitors are, and their market share

**organization chart:** a list of key personnel, their responsibilities, remuneration, and a discussion of their value to the business

**liabilities:** including legal matters or contingencies

**financial statements:** three to five years of documented financial history

Don't think that just because you know the likely buyer of your business – perhaps a member of your family, or a close business associate – that you should skip the above valuation process. Even if your goal isn't to extract *maximum* value for your business, a sound valuation report will help parties determine a *fair* value. Not only can that help when it comes to keeping your relationship with your buyer on friendly terms, it can make a big difference to your financial future.

## Finding a buyer

With valuation report in hand, you can now take the next step in selling your business: finding a qualified buyer. For some business owners, this will be an easy process. You may well have a buyer in mind when a decision is made to sell – a member (or members) of the family, an existing business partner, or perhaps a trusted employee. If not, you may be able to use advertising or trade sources to find a buyer.

In most other cases, however, it's necessary to employ an intermediary – a broker or other specialist skilled in finding qualified buyers. In the not-too-recent past, intermediaries were only used with larger business sales. Not so anymore. These days, most firms dealing with U/HNWI clients will have a department or division that specializes in finding buyers for small to mid-sized companies. Typically, these experts enter into an exclusive contract to market and sell the business for a given period (usually four to six months). In return for a percentage of the selling price (often called a "success fee" – the fee is usually not charged if the business doesn't sell), your intermediary will assist you in evaluating the business, contacting and screening potential buyers, negotiating terms, and arranging for legal organization and documentation.

Sure, finding an intermediary will probably be more expensive than selling a business on your own. But as I've said before, professional help has a funny way of paying for itself. Particularly with middle-market companies, a skilled intermediary can "level the playing field" between a private seller and a large, well-funded buyer. By providing expertise in business valuation, settlement terms, and financing options, intermediaries can ensure terms of the sale are fair. Perhaps more importantly, the extensive network of business contacts most intermediaries maintain helps ensure sellers receive maximum value for their business. I know in my own firm, for example, it's not uncommon for the business divestiture team to market a business on a global level – canvassing 200 or more potential buyers is par for the course. After that, the team compiles a short list based on price, financing conditions, and other factors. The net result: sellers can be sure they're getting top dollar for their life's work.

## Financing **the purchase**

The structure of the purchase is a primary concern of every business sale. These days, it's rare for a business to be purchased entirely with cash. What follows is a brief list of some of the more common methods for purchasing a business, along with some of the advantages and disadvantages of each.

### Installment purchase

With an installment payment, the buyer and seller agree to an initial lump-sum payment followed by a series of ongoing payments. Installments can be structured over a number of years (anywhere from three to fifteen years is normal), and are usually guaranteed with a promissory note secured by the assets of the business. While such financing can make purchases more affordable for the buyer, it can also be very risky for the seller. If the business isn't run as capably as it was under the previous owner, payments may be delayed or stopped entirely.

### Leveraged buyout

In such a scenario, business assets are used to secure a loan to purchase the business. The buyer typically invests little or no money up front. While the leveraged buyout often presents the seller with the opportunity to realize an immediate gain from the business, it often places a significant burden of debt on the company. If you're planning to sell your business with this method, make sure you can guarantee your business can survive such a burden before entering into such an agreement. Otherwise, you could be putting your wealth in serious jeopardy.

### Earn-out

Earn-outs are usually structured as a bridge between an initial lump-sum payment and the eventual purchase price. Such payments are usually based on the performance of the business, as measured by sales, profit, or some other performance yardstick. Because the earn-out is based on this performance, the seller is typically permitted to continue to operate the business through the earn-out phase. Obviously, that may not suit the needs of the seller or the buyer in all cases.

### Private annuity

If the sale of a business is made to another member of the family, a private annuity may be a viable option. In such a scenario, the seller transfers business ownership to family members in exchange for a series of payments (which are usually made for life). This can be an extremely efficient method of structuring an inter-family business purchase: in most jurisdictions, a carefully-constructed private annuity will not trigger gift or transfer tax, and will result in a minimum of capital gains. And as long as annual payments aren't funded directly from the transferred business, the value of the annuity will be excluded from the seller's estate. But I emphasize the words "carefully-constructed" here. This kind of annuity structure can be highly complicated, and often relies on a tightly-controlled, carefully defined payment schedule. Bottom line: if it's a strategy you and your family are interested in, consult a financial professional and get the job done right.

### Stock purchase

When the buyer is a large, publicly listed company, the most common form of financing is a stock purchase. Such financing has become even more common in the era of inflated stock prices. Although the exact details of such financing can vary widely, a typical stock purchase goes something like this: instead of receiving payment for the business in cash, the business owner accepts the stock of the purchasing corporation. Such financing can be for the entire purchase price, or for a portion, and usually comes with a restriction on the resale of the stock – a two-year ban on resale is standard. With such financing, tax on the sale of the business can usually be deferred in whole or in part until stock is eventually sold (there may be certain "tests" to qualify for such treatment).

From the perspective of wealth management, stock-financed purchases are probably the most challenging type of business sale. First there is the issue of the volatility of the buyer's stock. If it is in a particularly volatile industry, or if the market goes into a tailspin, the seller can see the bulk of the sale proceeds evaporate quickly. If the purchaser's stock is thinly traded, it can be difficult for the seller to eventually unload it. Considering such stock at a discount to its trading price is a reasonable solution to the problem. And of course, upon receipt of the stock, sellers will have to confront the issue of concentration risk. All these issues should be considered before entering into such an agreement.

### Forward agreements and prepaid forward transactions

A common method for handling some of these challenges is through a forward agreement. In such a scenario, the investor enters into an arrangement with a financial institution that guarantees a minimum price when it comes time to sell the position. In return for downside protection, the institution "caps" upside potential: any gain over a certain level goes to the institution, not the investor. Such a structure offers investors the best of all possible worlds, providing both security and opportunity at little or no out-of-pocket cost. In addition, the flexible nature of such agreements mean floor prices, cap prices, and maturity dates can be customized to meet a U/HNWI's personal needs. If the forward agreement is structured as a *prepaid* transaction – that is, the institution writing the contract advances a portion of the current stock price to the investor – the U/HNWI can receive immediate liquidity for an otherwise illiquid, concentrated position. With such advantages, it's easy to see why such agreements are becoming more and more popular among business owners.

## Case study: sale to a publicly traded corporation

When the sale of the business is to a publicly-traded entity, things can become complex fairly quickly. A sale my firm was involved in a couple of years ago is a case in point.

Paul, the client, and his two minority partners were fortunate enough to sell their well-established manufacturing business to a publicly traded U.S. company for about $20-million. The only catch: compensation was largely in the form of shares of the purchasing company. While the purchase certainly left Paul and his partners wealthy on paper, it also presented a real financial challenge. For Paul, his stake in the business represented about 95% of his net worth. Complicating matters was the restriction on the shares: the partners were restricted from selling their shares for six months.

I heard from the advisor involved in the case that Paul was always known for being a pretty level-headed guy – this was certainly no exception. As the sale was being finalized he gave his advisor a call, and they discussed Paul's options. The solution they eventually settled on was a *prepaid forward transaction* – a fairly common strategy for those in Paul's situation. The advisor worked out a scenario where Paul would receive an up-front payment from my firm for about 90% of the current value of his shares (about $13.5-million in this case), while putting a floor price on any downward movement of the shares and a cap price on any upside growth. The payment gave Paul immediate liquidity – he used the proceeds to construct a much more diversified portfolio. Upon maturity of the agreement (in two years), any difference between the stock price and the forward payment will be calculated by the two parties, and appropriate payment made. In the meantime, the restricted shares will be held as collateral, while Paul maintains dividend and voting rights.

At the time I write this, the market has been in a bear phase for the past twelve months. The agreement matures in the Fall of 2002, and while nobody knows for sure what will happen to the markets between now and then, as of right now, it looks like Paul made the right decision. Currently, his shares are trading under the floor price set in the agreement. By utilizing this sophisticated strategy, Paul was able to achieve some immediate diversification, and protect himself from market volatility. And, even though I understand he's a level-headed guy, it's my belief he also managed to find a way to retain his sanity in the middle of a bear market. It's hard to put a price on that.

Paul's case is just one example of the wide variety of financing and investment options available to business owners. If your business is in the process of being bought out by another business, don't become complacent and accept payment in shares without thoroughly investigating your options with a skilled financial professional first – one who works closely with legal and accounting professionals experienced in the area. As Paul's case demonstrates, the time and energy you spend now will be well worth it.

## A final word on selling your business

It's easy to let your emotions prevent you from making a sound business decision regarding your business. It's also easy to let financial considerations prevent you from doing what you truly want to do with your business. Make a promise to yourself not to compromise either, and you'll be well on your way to securing *true wealth*.

## Key concepts: Chapter ten

- There are many good reasons to sell a business. The primary reason is to diversify your wealth.

- Those who become wealthy suddenly face significant challenges when it comes to managing that wealth on an ongoing basis. Some of those challenges are personal in nature, some of them are financial.

- The first (and ultimately the most important) decision for business owners is deciding what they want from the business.

- Selling a business is an emotional experience; business owners should prepare themselves for those emotions and be on guard against their emotions interfering with sound business judgement.

- If there are family members involved with the business, business owners should be extra cautious, and clearly communicate their intentions well before the eventual sale.

- Before the business is ready to be sold, the business owner must prepare operating statements and a valuation report.

- Finding the right buyer is an important part of the selling process. There are many avenues for finding a buyer, but probably the most effective (particularly for medium-to-large businesses) is utilizing the services of a qualified business broker.

- When it comes to financing, there are many options, some of which are more advantageous to the buyer than the seller.

- Because of their complexity and the number of financial planning issues that are raised by them, stock-based purchases demand special attention from the seller.

## Resources

Books on how to sell your business can be found in most bookstores, but it's best to approach them with a degree of caution. In my experience, U/HNWIs usually need more sophisticated advice than many of these books provide. Here are some suggestions that should actually be of value.

*Unlocking the Value of Your Business* by Thomas W. Horn

*In the Blood* by Author Gordon Pitts

*How To Sell Your Business – And Get What You Want* by Colin Gabriel

## Websites

Ambrecht & Associates Resources Pertaining to Family Business Succession Planning *www.taxlawsb.com/resources/FamBus.htm* – articles and resources on selling a family business

The Family Firm Institute *www.ffi.org* – articles, information, and contacts for family businesses

National Network of Estate Planning Attorneys *www.netplanning.com* – loads of information from estate planning specialists

*www.buysellbiz.com* – information on buying, selling, and financing

# The case for and against mutual funds

- Asset "evolution"
- The case against mutual funds revisited
- The case for mutual funds

*"Surely there comes a time when counting the cost and paying the price aren't things to think about any more. All that matters is value – the ultimate value of what one does."*

**James Hilton**

There has been a lot of talk in financial circles over the past few years about the pros and cons of mutual funds. Usually, the talk goes something like this: for *novice* investors, mutual funds are a great benefit, offering diversification, active management, and reasonably low cost all in a single investment. By the time you become a U/HNWI, however, you shouldn't waste your time looking at funds at all.

Personally, I believe such arguments are oversimplified, and perform a grave disservice to U/HNWIs. It's true, mutual funds are far from the financial cure-all that some people have claimed them to be. But then again, no investment is. There is nothing inherently *right* or *wrong* about any investment – they all have their place in certain portfolios under certain circumstances. So rather than whitewash mutual funds as an investment vehicle, I believe it's time U/HNWIs took a closer look at of some of the benefits – and some of the drawbacks – of funds, in order to formulate a more objective opinion.

## The myth of asset "evolution"

Most financial types frame the development of wealth in terms of an "evolution": a natural process in which the portfolio develops from simple, easy to understand investments to more complex products and strategies.

In such a system, those just starting their portfolios are at the bottom of the evolutionary ladder. For these investors, mutual funds are the logical choice – they have low investment minimums, they don't require a lot of ongoing supervision, and they offer diversification at a relatively low cost. As the portfolio grows, investors "evolve": direct investing in stocks, bonds, and other vehicles becomes the norm. Eventually, these investors may look to some kind of hybrid fund product that provides limited professional management but whose high minimums offer a degree of exclusivity. After that, investors progress to sophisticated, complex investments – hedge funds, segregated management, options and futures. Again, the central idea behind the system is *evolution*: at each stage, the investor moves into more sophisticated, supposedly "better" investment products. Once an investor reaches a certain level, there is no need for the investor to revisit the products and strategies meant to service the less "developed" among the investment population.

chart 11.1: **Evolutionary pyramid**

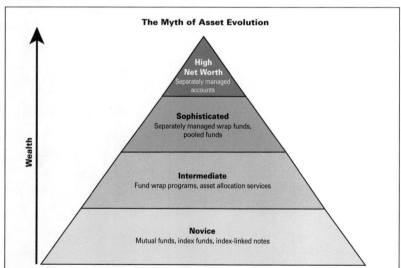

You should be able to tell by my tongue-in-cheek tone that I don't necessarily prescribe to this view. Let me be blunt: I don't believe any investment should be *excluded* from the financial planning process simply because the portfolio has "evolved" to a certain level. It's true, once your portfolio surpasses the $1-million mark, certain financial options are available to you that may not have been available before. And these options may make more sense than traditional financial products in many circumstances. But that doesn't mean you should ignore anything.

## My approach to mutual funds

U/HNWIs are better served by considering investments *objectively*. What judgements there are should be based on life circumstances (age, risk tolerance, financial goals, etc.) and practical considerations (diversification issues, tax or transaction costs, etc.) rather than snobbery or some pre-determined hierarchy of assets. Simply put, prejudice or bias against an entire investment class shouldn't be part of the equation.

That aside, it is possible to examine some of the benefits and drawbacks of funds, and make some general comments about the specific charges levied against them. And that's the purpose of this chapter. This chapter will take a close look at the three most common arguments made against funds, and couple those arguments with a brief rebuttal. After that, I'll present some recent innovations from the fund industry that should make it clear why U/HNWIs should take a second look at mutual funds when it comes to constructing their portfolios. By the end of this chapter, you should be better able to objectively determine whether funds suit your needs.

## The case against funds revisited: a rebuttal

We'll start our discussion with some of the central arguments behind why some financial professionals are down on funds. After each explanation, you'll find my comments on the specific point in question.

### The case against funds I: **"funds cost too much"**

One of the primary objections levied against mutual funds is their cost. An important issue, to be sure. But before we're ready to talk seriously about the issue, we need to understand how fund companies charge investors for their product.

There are two ways investors are charged for mutual funds. The first of these is the "load" or sales charge billed by the financial professional (and/or their firm) for purchasing the funds. In the early days of mutual funds (that is, prior to 1987), this charge could be hefty – in some cases as much as 9% of the total investment. Over the past several years, however, many professionals have been reducing these fees or waiving them altogether. In addition to these sales charges, all funds charge unitholders ongoing fees for professional management and other expenses such as marketing and administration. This is usually expressed as the Management Expense Ratio, or MER. While this number may seem small, it means big dollars for the fund companies – MERs are charged on assets under management, and taken off the top of any performance the fund may realize.

The argument about funds costing too much usually comes down to whether these fees are "fair." While few investors would question the need for fund companies to charge something for administration and management, many have begun to question the payments they make to the various salespeople who channel investors into their funds. These costs can boost a fund's MER dramatically, accounting for anywhere between 0.25% to 1.0% of a fund's MER.

While the issue of fund fees is more of an issue in some jurisdictions than it is in others (the average MER of a large-cap equity fund in the U.S., for instance, is about 1.5%. In Canada, it's approaching 2.3%), there can be little doubt high MERs are the enemy of U/HNWIs looking to build and maintain their wealth. Over time, a high MER can erode a decent amount of wealth invested in a fund. So much so that over a 30-year time period, an MER of 3.5% can destroy almost 65% of a fund's potential value (that is, there would be a 65% difference between what the fund *might* have been worth and what it actually is worth). Of course, this is an extreme example – few funds have MERs that high – but it does demonstrate the danger of high fees.

The question of cost should be an important consideration for all investors (and all financial professionals). But as with many arguments, the case isn't as clear cut as it first seems. There is *wide* variation in the MERs charged by fund companies (in fact, many fund companies use low fees as a way to gain an advantage over their peers). Ultimately, the solution to the problem of high fees is to vote with your wallet: by steering away from some of the most notable offenders, it is entirely possible for U/HNWIs to reduce costs and still build a high-quality portfolio. With the development of "I" or "F" class funds it's possible to keep fund MERs to a bare-bones minimum. This is just one example of how fund companies are starting to offer products that are more affordable, and more in line with the specific needs of U/HNWI clients.

As an aside, I can't help but wonder whether the real problem some investors have with fund fees is the fact they have to pay anything at all. That's an unfortunate position. When it comes down to it, what fund companies are selling is professional management. Unlike other services or products, such as a car, a television set, or a new pair of shoes, it's difficult to hang a price tag on the value of that management – everyone has a different opinion about how much it's worth. Most of the U/HNWIs I work with place a considerable value on professional management, and are willing to pay for it. As the saying goes, in this life, you usually get what you pay for. That's as true with advice as it is with cars, houses, clothes, or anything else in life.

## The case against funds II: **"the managers can't beat the index"**

Another argument against funds revolves around the question of whether fund managers actually add value to the portfolios they manage. If value means the ability of a given manager to outperform a given investment index, there's been a lot of research that suggests many funds don't make the grade. Given the money an investor pays for the privilege of *not* beating an index, it seems the logical decision would be to forget about funds and instead put your money in an index-type investment.

Let me be up front about this one: I'm usually not a fan of passive investing. Even I have to admit that as far as performance goes, passive investments have sometimes performed remarkably well compared to actively managed investments. But common sense should tell us that's not the way it's always going to be. For proof, I asked a colleague of mine at Morningstar to run through some numbers, and see how many Canadian equity funds have actually beaten the benchmark TSE 300 Index. The results were astonishing. *Over the past year, 91.2% of all funds in the Canadian equity category have beaten the TSE 300.* Longer term numbers are less astonishing, but still fit the general pattern: over a 2–year time frame, 69.2% of funds beat the index; over a 3–year period, 56.1%. The numbers drop off after that, but nevertheless, even over 15 years, a full 40.0% of all funds beat the index. To me, this is sure-fire proof that active management has its benefits.

table 11.2: **Percentage funds beating benchmark index return 15 years to Aug. 31, 2001**

| Period | Canadian Equity | | US Equity | |
|---|---|---|---|---|
| | # Funds in Category | % of Funds Outperforming the TSE 300 | # Funds in Category | % of Funds Outperforming the S&P 500 |
| 1 Year | 307 | 91.2% | 252 | 39.7% |
| 2 Years | 250 | 69.2% | 167 | 36.5% |
| 3 Years | 180 | 56.1% | 120 | 26.7% |
| 4 Years | 139 | 46.8% | 96 | 14.6% |
| 5 Years | 109 | 44.0% | 78 | 15.4% |
| 6 Years | 92 | 45.7% | 66 | 16.7% |
| 7 Years | 89 | 42.7% | 56 | 10.7% |
| 8 Years | 83 | 43.4% | 50 | 10.0% |
| 9 Years | 75 | 40.0% | 36 | 5.6% |
| 10 Years | 70 | 47.1% | 34 | 2.9% |
| 11 Years | 68 | 50.0% | 30 | 6.7% |
| 12 Years | 65 | 56.9% | 28 | 7.1% |
| 13 Years | 54 | 50.0% | 26 | 3.8% |
| 14 Years | 48 | 45.8% | 24 | 4.2% |
| 15 Years | 40 | 40.0% | 22 | 4.5% |

Source: ©2001 Morningstar Research Inc.

Note: IFSC Fund Categories Canadian Diversified Equity and U.S. Equity. Funds with a specific capitalization focus and index funds were excluded.

As could be expected, the numbers show a much different story for those funds investing in the U.S. It seems many actively-managed funds can't keep up to the broadly-based S&P 500. But again, look at the overall pattern: *over the short term, a good many funds do manage to beat the index.* The simple fact of the matter is, if the investor has a relatively short investment horizon (say, anything less than five years) investing in any index can be a risky proposition. There's just too much that can happen, too much to be uncertain about. And even beyond that, the fact that there are indeed managers out there who are beating the index suggests we should go look for them.

In a perfect long-term world – a world where we wouldn't ever need to liquidate our positions to purchase a new house, fund a grandchild's education, or deal with an unforeseen financial emergency – passive investing might make some sense. But let's face it: most of us don't live in that kind of world. For most U/HNWIs, shorter time horizons and big purchases can make demands on the portfolio, demands that require a little more security than index investing can provide.

That brings up my next big point about passive investing. Performance is only one part of the picture when it comes to wealth management. And while there may be debate about whether index funds offer better performance than actively managed funds, there can be little doubt they offer little if anything in the way of risk management. Here in Canada, we are more than aware of the risk involved with tracking an index: after the spectacular rise and fall of fiber-optic giant Nortel Networks (which at its height made up some 35% of the supposedly broadly-based TSE 300 index ) any argument about the security offered by an index will most likely have investors laughing. As it became apparent that Nortel's earnings estimates were way out of line with reality, the stock started to slide, taking down the entire index with it. After all was said and done, the darling of the Canadian stock market had dropped from $124.50 to less than $9.00 a share, while the index shed some 37% of its value. The company is now only about 6% of the TSE 300 Index. So much for the safety of the index. All the while, the large majority of actively managed equity funds have significantly outperformed the index.

I understand such a case may be more unlikely with more diversified indices (the S&P 500 or the Russell 2000, for example). At the same time, any passive investor who put money in the Nasdaq index thinking it would be safer than investing in a diversified portfolio has learned a hard lesson over the past year or so. Make no mistake: index investing can be risky. With an index, you really don't have anyone keeping an eye on your investments. Unless you want to bail out of your investment altogether, you have to take your lumps and accept whatever happens to the market as a whole. By selecting active managers, you're not always guaranteed that you will outperform the index. But who made that the measure of investment success? As I've said throughout this book, *for U/HNWIs, security is ultimately a more pressing concern.* By selecting conservative managers who care about the volatility they subject their clients to, U/HNWIs can better protect themselves against the volatility that's common with an index.

## The case against funds III: **"separate accounts are superior"**

Separate accounts are often presented as an alternative – and a more sophisticated alternative, at that – to mutual funds. I use the term "separate accounts" to describe a wide variety of different investment products – pooled accounts, wrap accounts, discretionary managed accounts, segregated accounts, etc. Such products go under a multitude of names, but they all offer some form of "exclusive" investment management, where the assets of the individual are held separate from the assets of the group. This kind of exclusion can take a variety of different forms, but in the typical scenario, the investor owns the underlying securities held within a portfolio managed by a professional, rather than owning an interest in a collective asset pool.

Separate accounts have been around for almost as long as U/HNWIs have been investing, but in recent years, their popularity has grown dramatically. They now account for some $271-billion worth of assets in America. That's a considerable number, to be sure, but it's still a far cry from the $7-trillion invested in mutual funds. Over the past few years, many mutual fund companies and most brokerage houses and investment firms have been creating their own customized wrap programs, so I'm sure this number will rise.

It's easy to see the appeal of these kinds of products. Because they are separately managed, you can be sure you're getting a customized portfolio based on your exact needs, managed for your benefit, not the benefit of the company selling it. With a separate account, buying into a large, unrealized capital gain is never a real problem, and offsetting gains with losses is at least possible, although this depends largely on the manager you're working with. You have a lot more flexibility with a separate account – some managers may permit existing holdings to be worked into a separate account, or may permit investors to make certain exclusions to account for ethical considerations.

These are all significant benefits, and should be seriously considered by any U/HNWI looking to manage their wealth effectively. But separate accounts also have some drawbacks. Investing in separate accounts often requires a high minimum investment – anywhere between $100,000 and $5-million per manager depending on the exact structure.

That's usually not a problem for U/HNWIs looking to put all their money in a single account, but if diversification among multiple managers with different investment styles is important (which it should be), these minimums can be bothersome. Another potential drawback is the documentation and reporting for separate accounts. While most separate account managers can provide excellent quarterly performance reports, in most cases you won't be able to track your performance in the daily paper.

graph 11.3: **Rise in separate accounts in U.S.**

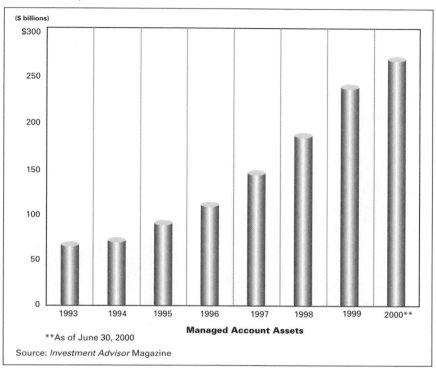

($ billions)

**Managed Account Assets**

**As of June 30, 2000

Source: *Investment Advisor* Magazine

But what about the big issues – performance and fees. Which product is better? Unfortunately I don't have a clear answer for you – and neither does anyone else. Despite what you might read in the marketing material, there is very little evidence of the inherent superiority in the performance of separate accounts over mutual funds. Simply put, there are excellent managers in *both* camps. As for cost, there are simply too many variables involved to make a clear comparison. Generally, separate accounts offer lower fees than many mutual funds, although many mid-tier wrap programs charge fees that are higher. Select a good-quality, low-fee fund – a fund which allows discounted MERs for larger investments – and you'll probably be close to the fees of a separately managed account.

# The case for funds revisited: industry innovations

I admit, these are fair criticisms of mutual funds. But as the saying goes, there are two sides to every story. Instead of simply listing the same old benefits that have been discussed before (diversification, professional management, simplicity, etc.), I'd like to approach the case for funds in a different way. Here are some recent fund innovations that have made mutual funds a lot more attractive to U/HNWIs. Taken together, I think these developments are a strong case in defense of mutual funds.

## The case for funds I: "I" and "F" class-structured funds

A new class of funds looks to make one of the central arguments against mutual funds moot. Traditionally, fund MERs have paid for three things: management fees, operating expenses, and the ongoing advice of the broker/dealer. I-class and F-class funds essentially unravel the MER of a given fund into these distinct components, with the intention of rebating the portion that pays the trailer fee to the broker/dealer. The rationale is twofold. Many mutual fund clients are already paying for advice as part of a fee-based portfolio program. Charging a trailer fee would be doublecharging these people for the same advice. In addition, the actual advice given on a large purchase may well be out of whack with the total fees charged for that advice. In this way, an I- or F-class fund is like a "bulk rate" on the MER in consideration for the size of the investment.

Each fund company treats its I- and F-class funds slightly differently. The exact amount of the savings will of course differ from fund to fund, but anything from a 0.75% to a 1.0% reduction in fees is typical. This would bring the total MER down to the 0.75% to 1.5% range for most funds. Generally, the most significant discounts will be with the I-Class Funds, but they require a significant commitment – $1-million or more is not uncommon. F-class funds aren't quite as cheap, but have lower minimums and still offer significant savings over standard mutual funds. More and more wealth advisors are using them in fee-based accounts.

I've had several conversations with various fund industry insiders on the topic, and they confirm that fund companies have introduced these I- and F-class funds in large part to make their products much more attractive to U/HNWIs. The discounted rate brings fund fees on par with other alternatives such as separate accounts and other forms of discretionary management. In other words, it makes funds a reasonably-priced alternative to more exclusive forms of managed money, and gives U/HNWIs an excellent opportunity to access some of the best managers in the business.

If you haven't yet heard of class-structured funds, you're not alone. Delays with back-end administration and the signed agreements between fund companies and dealers (who must agree to give up their portion of the MER) have prevented these funds from taking off in a big way. In fact, the Canadian publication *Investment Executive* estimated that as of December 31, 2000, a mere $9-billion was allocated to F-class shares in Canada, out of an estimated $350-billion allocated to long-term assets. But as more and more financial professionals switch to fee-based asset management (an inevitability, in my opinion), it's clear that class-structured funds are an idea whose time has come. By eliminating an embedded fee for something these investors are already paying for, class-structured funds make it easier for U/HNWIs to invest in mutual funds with a clear conscience.

## The case for funds II: **Corporate-class ("umbrella") funds**

Corporate class funds are another industry innovation that have made mutual funds significantly more attractive to U/HNWIs. The structure of the typical corporate class fund is fairly simple to understand. A fund company issues a single fund with a variety of different share classes. Each class represents a different portfolio – class 1 might represent a diversified global equity portfolio, class 2 might represent an international bond portfolio, and so on. Under the tax laws of most jurisdictions, investors have the ability to switch from class to class – essentially from portfolio to portfolio – without triggering a taxable event, deferring tax until the investor sells out of the fund family. I know most of the major mutual fund companies in Canada have developed such structures (AGF, AIC, AIM/Trimark, C.I. Group (the pioneer in Canada), Dynamic, Fidelity, Franklin/Templeton, Mackenzie, just to name some of the major ones). I also know that the reason behind the development was largely the projected demand of U/HNWIs. If you live in the U.S., you'll need to work closely with a qualified wealth advisor to be able to access such funds. Your advisor will then work with an appropriate fund wholesaler to see if there's a corporate-class fund that's suitable for your situation.

For disciplined, patient investors, corporate class funds are a major financial development in the effort to secure wealth. Corporate class funds present U/HNWIs with a dramatic opportunity to formulate an effective asset allocation strategy without incurring a tax hit every time rebalancing is necessary. With a corporate class fund, there are only two times at which an investor could face the taxman: at the fund's yearly distribution to investors (typically a rare event), or when the investor actually sells out of the corporate family. The long-term compounding of that extra money that would have normally been carried away by the taxman can make a big impact on your bottom line.

graph 11.4: **The power of tax deferral**

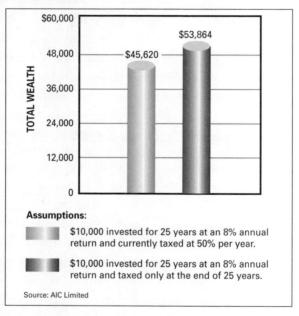

Assumptions:

$10,000 invested for 25 years at an 8% annual return and currently taxed at 50% per year.

$10,000 invested for 25 years at an 8% annual return and taxed only at the end of 25 years.

Source: AIC Limited

Understand that corporate class funds do have some drawbacks. First and foremost, they make it a lot more tempting to time the market, and that's rarely a good idea. Eventually, that will weigh on returns. In extreme cases, when one class of a corporate class fund experiences a large number of redemptions, it can force managers to sell positions to cover the redemptions. True, that's an extremely unlikely scenario, but if it happens, it could restrict performance. Because some of these funds are relatively new, it's unclear whether these will be major drawbacks. I suspect not, but until there's conclusive evidence either way, it's probably a good idea to get the full story from a qualified professional before investing in a corporate class fund.

## The case for funds IV: **Managed yield funds**

Managed yield funds are another innovation that's causing U/HNWIs to re-think their approach to mutual funds. In Canada, they've largely been pioneered by Mackenzie Financial and Franklin/Templeton, and are specifically targeted to conservative investors looking for tax relief. The central benefit of these funds is their tax treatment: distributions from a managed yield fund are taxed as capital gains rather than interest. That can be a great benefit for investors looking for an ultra-secure income stream or a short-term parking place for capital without paying a lot of tax.

The exact structure of these funds is a little complicated, and differs slightly depending on the company involved. Typically, a managed yield fund invests in a diversified portfolio of equities, then uses short-term options to hedge against most of the risk associated with those equities. The net result is a portfolio that approximates the risk-return profile of higher-yield short-term investments (such as banker's acceptances), yet distributes income that is technically classified as a capital gain. At the time I write this, the category is brand new, so it's tough to predict what kind of income they'll provide for their investors. But for what it's worth, industry insiders say the average yield should be somewhere in the neighborhood of 4.0% to 4.5%. And because that's in the form of capital gains or dividends, the taxman takes a lot less. Investors would have to look for a decidedly higher yield in a comparable fixed-income investment to come close to that.

A comparison of the performance offered by a managed yield fund and a comparable fixed-income investment will illustrate the benefit of these new funds. Let's assume a managed yield fund comes in at the low end of its expected returns, offering investors 4.0% over the year. At the time I write this, a three-year bond returns about 4.5%. At first glance, the bond seems the better investment. But what about taxes and inflation? Assuming a tax rate of 45% (a typical high-end tax bracket in Canada), the bond would leave you with an after-tax return of 2.48%. Add in an inflation rate of 2.7% (about where inflation is right now), and you're actually *losing* money. The managed yield fund, on the other hand, would leave you with three times as much: because the fund's return has only a 50% inclusion rate (being capital gains), the after-tax return would be 3.1%. After inflation, you're looking at a return of 0.4%. I admit, this isn't going to do much to build long-term wealth, but if you're looking for a secure place to put your money – a temporary parking place for the proceeds of a business sale or the exercise of a large options position – the managed yield fund is clearly the better choice.

For U/HNWIs, managed yield funds offer an excellent way to keep on top of one's tax bill without sacrificing much in the way of security. But because most managed yield funds do invest in equities (albeit in a round about way), the risk–return profile of a managed yield fund isn't quite the same as an ultra–conservative Treasury Bill. But it's very close. Bottom line: for U/HNWIs looking for a secure, short–term source of income, these funds deserve a close look.

## The case for funds III: **Exchange-traded funds**

Another industry innovation U/HNWIs have found valuable is the exchange-traded fund, or ETF. ETFs have been around in one form or another for some time in the U.S.: Barclay's, State Street, and Dow Jones offer many different types, and at last count there is over $57-billion invested in them. But they are only now beginning to make a big splash in other markets – in Canada, for example, they account for only about $6-billion of all invested assets. But that number is expected to climb – and climb rapidly. The total assets in ETFs in America is expected to hit $400-billion within five years.

So what are they? ETFs are "baskets" of stocks that track a well–established index (or portion of an index). Because they trade on an exchange (just like a stock), ETFs will fluctuate in price according to the day's demand. In theory, that demand will rise and fall in conjunction with the price of the underlying securities which the ETF represents, but there can be instances when an ETF trades at a slight premium or discount to the price of its underlying securities. This is a little different from the average mutual fund, which is priced only at the end of the day, and follows the price of its holdings to the letter.

There are a number of benefits to ETFs. Cost is one. Because they utilize a stock exchange to facilitate sales, ETFs come with rock-bottom management fees. Fees for broad-market ETFs in North America are in the neighborhood of 0.08% to 0.60%. That's far below the fees charged for actively managed products. That can make ETFs extremely attractive to price-conscious investors. Another benefit is the fact they trade on an exchange. This feature allows ETF investors to employ a variety of strategies that simply aren't possible with mutual funds (selling short, placing limit or stop loss orders, or purchasing options contracts to name just a few examples). In addition, investors don't have to pay bulky redemption or load charges with ETFs – a simple commission is all that's required (or they can be purchased within a fee-based account). The tax efficiency of ETFs is another benefit. Because ETFs typically track an index (or a sub-index, as the case may be), the only selling going on is when a given stock is removed from an index. That helps reduce distributions to investors, which in turn helps to limit the investor's exposure to taxes. Finally, the structure of an ETF promotes maximum use of investor dollars. Most ETFs have a mandate to be fully invested in the underlying index, meaning performance won't be dragged down by excess cash. And because ETFs trade on an exchange, unit redemptions don't have to be financed by the fund itself – meaning fund managers won't have to liquidate positions just to cover redemptions.

Yes, these are all benefits. But as they exist right now, ETFs are still passive investments. (There is talk of the SEC in the U.S. investigating the possibility of actively-managed ETFs, but such discussion is still at a preliminary stage.) As passive investments, ETFs are susceptible to the same drawbacks I outlined in the argument against index investments above. So why am I now taking the exact opposite position? Because of the flexibility of ETFs. Unlike index units, ETFs offer investors the ability to invest in micro-portions of the market – a specific market sector, for instance, or a geographic area that would be hard to invest in otherwise. While most U/HNWIs probably don't need this level of diversification, it's nice to know the flexibility is there should you need to protect yourself against other, more concentrated positions elsewhere in the portfolio. On top of that, the fact that ETFs are traded on an exchange allows investors to get into and out of those micro-portions of the market extremely quickly – much more quickly than would otherwise be possible. Again, that kind of flexibility isn't something every U/HNWI needs, but it's nice to know that it's there.

## A **final word** on mutual funds

There is nothing inherently "good" or "bad" about mutual funds or any other investment. Investors must judge the benefits and drawbacks of each asset class against their personal goals in order to determine the best fit possible.

## Key concepts: Chapter eleven

- There is nothing inherently good or bad about any investment. Each has distinct benefits and drawbacks that must be carefully considered.

- The case against mutual funds is usually expressed as an "evolution": This is a simplistic way of looking at the issue of whether funds belong in your portfolio.

The case against funds I: cost

> **Myth:** the loads and other fees associated with funds make them more expensive than other investment alternatives.

> **Fact:** there is a wide variation in the costs of various mutual funds. Investors can select funds that offer reduced fees.

The case against funds II: active/passive investing

> **Myth:** active fund managers rarely outperform the index.

> **Fact:** Passive investments offer little opportunity to minimize risk. This is ultimately a more important issue than the issue of performance.

The case against funds III: separate accounts

> **Myth:** U/HNWIs are better served by separate accounts.

> **Fact:** Separate accounts have their benefits, but when it comes to performance and cost, there is little difference between funds and separate accounts.

- There are a number of recent developments in the mutual fund industry that should cause U/HNWIs to reconsider the benefits of funds.

- Class-structured funds: I- and F-class funds offer U/HNWIs the opportunity to secure significantly lower fees for many popular mutual funds.

- Corporate class ("umbrella") funds: these funds offer the ability to move in and out of tax-deferred portfolios without triggering a taxable event. This makes them an excellent tool for asset allocation and tax-deferral strategies.

- Managed-yield funds: for U/HNWIs looking for a secure income source, managed yield funds offer a tax-efficient place to park short-term assets.

- Exchange traded funds: ETFs offer an extremely liquid, extremely flexible method for securing exposure to select markets.

## Resources

The problem for U/HNWIs looking for information on mutual funds isn't the lack of information – it's the lack of good information. Here are some resources that buck the general trend.

Nick Murray's **Simple Wealth, Inevitable Wealth**

Gordon Pape's **Investing Strategies 2000: Mutual Funds and Beyond**

**The Wealthy Boomer: Life After Mutual Funds** by Jonathan Chevreau

## Websites

The New York Times on the Web **www.newyorktimes.com** – an excellent mutual fund section

The Washington Post **www.washingtonpost.com** – another good fund site

The Globe and Mail mutual fund site **www.globefund.com** – top-quality information for Canadian investors

The National Post **www.nationalpost.com** – look under "Financial Post"

USA Today newspaper **www.usatoday.com**

Fidelity Investments **www.fidelity.com** – a good general fund resource

Fidelity Investments Canada **www.fidelity.ca** – for Canadian investors

The Fund Library **www.fundlibrary.com** – loads of info on funds for Canadian investors

**www.smartmoney.com** – informative articles and other resources

**www.bloomberg.com** – statistics and up-to-date market information

# **Alternative** investments

- *Trends in alternative investments*
- *Rationale for alternative investments*
- *Portfolio enhancers*
- *Portfolio diversifiers*

*"If you must play, decide upon three things at the start: the rules of the game, the stakes, and the quitting time."*

**Chinese proverb**

N ow that you understand some of the ins and outs of the more traditional asset classes, it's time to turn our heads to more sophisticated investments. Investments that were tailor-made for U/HNWIs.

Far from being a mere substitute for more traditional investment vehicles (stocks, bonds, funds, etc.), I see alternative investments as a complement to an already well-diversified core portfolio. Because of their complexity, they must be considered carefully, and structured in co-ordination with the performance of other investments in the portfolio. Such an approach fits well with one of my core investment principles for U/HNWIs: to ensure security through a carefully managed diversification strategy.

This chapter will provide a basic overview of alternative investments. We'll discuss the two basic categories of alternative investments – portfolio enhancers and portfolio diversifiers – and show how each of these can be of use to you. By the end of this chapter, you should have a general understanding of the reasons why U/HNWIs should invest in alternative investments, and be able to determine whether they're suitable for you. But as with many other topics in *True Wealth*, keep in mind that I have space for only a very basic overview. Before you're ready to put your money into alternative investments, you'll need to consult a qualified professional, one who's familiar with these products and has helped U/HNWI make alternative investment placements before.

# Trends in alternative investments

By all accounts, more and more U/HNWIs are becoming interested in alternative investments. The 2001 edition of the annual Merrill Lynch/Cap Gemini *World Wealth Report* estimates that there is over $1-trillion invested in alternative investments around the world. The growth of these assets has exploded over the past five years: hedge fund assets have grown at an average rate of 13% a year during the last five years, while commitments to private equity funds have grown by over 35% over the same period. North American investors are by far the most hungry for alternative investments, accounting for almost 87% of the world's investment in these products. Most of this money (about 62% of it, for a total of $720-billion) is invested in private equity and venture capital opportunities, with hedge funds second (accounting for about $400-billion) and managed futures a distant third ($40-billion).

chart 12.1: **Alternative investment funds assets**

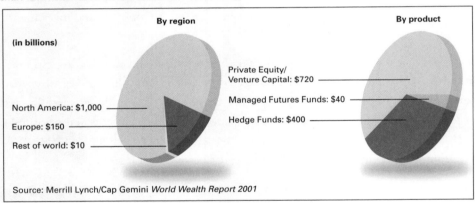

**By region**

(in billions)

North America: $1,000
Europe: $150
Rest of world: $10

**By product**

Private Equity/Venture Capital: $720
Managed Futures Funds: $40
Hedge Funds: $400

Source: Merrill Lynch/Cap Gemini *World Wealth Report 2001*

This growing demand is being driven by a relatively small number of U/HNWIs. Cap Gemini estimates less than 20% of U/HNWIs hold alternative investments, and of those who do, alternative investments comprise a relatively small percentage of the total portfolio. But as the report authors suggest, these numbers are sure to grow over the next several years. As U/HNWIs pass on the word about the benefits of alternative investments, there is sure to be more interest.

And as traditional mutual fund companies launch their own alternative asset products or buy out well-established firms in the industry (industry leader Tremont Investment Management was recently purchased by mutual fund giant Oppenheimer Funds), things are going to get more competitive. That likely means lower minimum investment requirements and looser liquidity restrictions, which should mean even more growth in the years to come.

graph 12.2: **Average portfolio allocation to alternative investments**

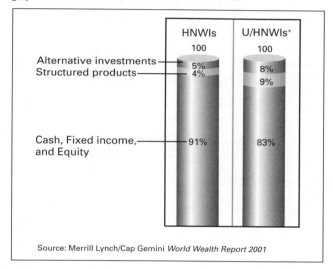

Source: Merrill Lynch/Cap Gemini *World Wealth Report 2001*

*Note: Cap Gemini defines an ultra-high-net-worth individual as having $30-million of investable assets

As for performance, this is the area in which alternative investments have truly excelled. Over the past five years, hedge funds and private equity opportunities have offered performance far superior to that of most major market indices.

Alternative investments have also demonstrated their ability to offer performance that moves independently of the performance experienced by standard equity markets. In 2000, for instance, while the S&P 500 was busy posting an 8.1% loss and the tech-heavy Nasdaq was off by some 39%, the average hedge fund posted an 11.3% gain. The returns for venture capital funds were even higher, at 41.0%.

graph: 12.3: **Average returns of hedge funds 1996-2000**

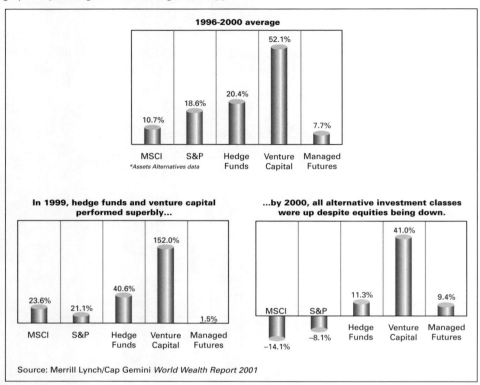

Source: Merrill Lynch/Cap Gemini *World Wealth Report 2001*

Note: Taxes and sales charges are not taken into account, therefore the figures do not give a measure of return to the investor, only a measure of relative performance.

Perhaps more important than performance is the relative volatility of alternative investments. Here again, many classes of alternative assets compare favorably to more traditional asset categories. In fact, from 1990–2000, "fund-of-fund" type hedge funds averaged an annual standard deviation of 13.1, compared to 13.9 for the S&P 500. That might seem like a nominal difference, but in practical terms, that means hedge funds as an asset class offer lower volatility (that is, *less risk*) than the overall stock market.

graph 12.4: **Volatility: annual standard deviation of various indices 1990-2000**

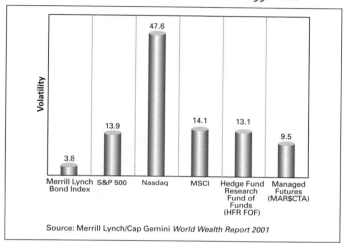

Source: Merrill Lynch/Cap Gemini *World Wealth Report 2001*

What's more, hedge funds have a proven track record of offering "safe haven" in times of market turmoil. I asked a close colleague of mine at Tremont Investment Management for a comparison of hedge fund performance to the performance of the overall market during select market downturns over the past seven years or so. The results were surprising. As chart 12.5 shows, if you're looking for protection, you can find it in hedge funds.

table 12.5: **Performing under pressure**

|  | Feb./Mar.'94 | Nov. '94 | Jul. '96 | Mar. '97 | Aug. '97 | Oct. '97 | Aug. '98 |
|---|---|---|---|---|---|---|---|
| **S&P 500 Index** | **-7.04%** | **-3.40%** | **-4.42%** | **-4.11%** | **-5.60%** | **-3.34%** | **-14.64%** |
| *Strategy* | | | | | | | |
| Market Neutral | 1.12% | 0.07% | 2.50% | 1.54% | 1.20% | 1.72% | -0.90% |
| Arbitrage | 1.16% | -1.12% | 0.36% | 1.29% | 1.56% | 1.37% | -2.79% |
| Special Situations | 2.50% | -1.38% | -0.43% | -0.08% | 2.39% | -1.27% | -4.16% |
| Equity Trading | 0.38% | -0.76% | -0.07% | 0.41% | 3.34% | -0.11% | -1.24% |
| Fixed Income | 0.77% | -0.02% | 1.31% | 0.27% | 0.61% | 0.23% | -4.94% |
| Short Seller | 16.83% | 3.67% | 9.52% | 10.32% | 1.17% | 4.33% | 15.14% |
| Commodity Trading Advisor | 3.96% | 2.53% | -1.93% | 0.49% | -2.85% | -0.81% | 8.41% |
| Value | 2.50% | -1.38% | -0.43% | -0.08% | 2.39% | -1.27% | -4.16% |
| Other | -4.98% | -1.48% | -2.23% | -1.58% | 0.82% | -1.31% | -8.69% |
| **All Hedge Funds (average)** | **-1.23%** | **-0.48%** | **-0.79%** | **-0.27%** | **0.61%** | **-0.30%** | **-4.75%** |

Source: *Taming Hedge Fund Hysteria* by Robert Parnell, Tremont Investment Management Inc.

With all these benefits, it's little wonder why many U/HNWIs have such a healthy appetite for alternative investments. But for my own part, I like to recommend alternative investments for reasons other than just performance. While it's hard to argue with the returns these investments have offered recently, I believe the reason alternative investments should be in a U/HNWI portfolio isn't necessarily for their performance, but for their ability to provide an additional layer of diversification to a traditional portfolio. That makes a portfolio more secure – something all U/HNWIs should strive for.

## My approach to alternative investments

I take a different approach to alternative investments than many financial professionals. Instead of focusing on a small group of exclusive investments that U/HNWIs should invest in simply because they are able to, I prefer to focus on the *end purpose* of these assets in the U/HNWI portfolio. This ensures factors like status, performance, or novelty – factors which can all affect a U/HNWI's decision to place a portion of their wealth in alternative investments – play no role in the investment decision.

Such an approach suggests two distinct categories of investment that every U/HNWI needs to investigate. The first, portfolio enhancers, offers specialized equity opportunities in existing concerns with the potential for dramatic performance. The second, portfolio diversifiers, are investments primarily intended to add additional diversification to the U/HNWI portfolio – although they too can offer performance that is far superior to that of traditional asset classes.

As for the exact percentage of the U/HNWI portfolio that belongs in alternative investments, well, that's difficult to say. Perhaps more than with other asset classes, the question ultimately comes down to an individual's risk tolerance. If hard pressed, I would say that as a general rule, no more than 10-15% of the total portfolio should be placed in alternative investments. For those with substantial wealth, these numbers can be a little more flexible, but in no case do I believe more than 25% of the portfolio should be allocated to these kinds of investments.

I have some other principles when it comes to alternative investments. Generally, I believe most U/HNWIs would be better served by investing in a well-diversified "fund-of-funds" type of hedge fund. For wealthier, more aggressive U/HNWIs, private equity is certainly an option, but it should be approached with caution: I've seen more than one private equity deal that has offered a lot more risk than was really wise for the U/HNWI to accept. This cautious approach may not be what some U/HNWIs are looking for with alternative investments, and that suits me fine. As I've said throughout *True Wealth*, the end goal of wealth management for U/HNWIs isn't all-out performance, but rather ongoing security of their wealth and their quality of life – the kind of security that comes with consistent returns. This mindset necessitates a conservative approach to investing – particularly when it comes to alternative investments.

Let's take a look at the two broad categories of alternative investments, and review some of the basic benefits they offer to U/HNWIs.

## **Portfolio** enhancers: private equity

There is a wide range of private equity investments, and a wide variety of structures through which to make them. At their most basic level, however, most private equity investments entail some form of ownership in a commercial enterprise not registered for public sale. Most U/HNWIs will invest in private equity through a private limited partnership. In such an arrangement, a pool of capital is overseen by a general partner – most often a firm of professional managers, hopefully with a proven track record in identifying and managing such opportunities. These partnerships require significant commitments from their investors ($1-million is a common figure, although I've seen specialized structures that allow for investments of as little as $250,000). Often there is low liquidity with such investments – a two or three-year commitment is normal.

In theory, private equity partnerships can invest in almost any enterprise. In practice, most private equity deals fall into one of two general categories. The first is the venture capital fund, which specializes in providing operating capital for start-up companies (over the past few years, a lot of these have focused on the technology industry – although this has changed dramatically with the tech stock meltdown of 2000-2001). Buyout funds are the second category. These specialize in the purchase of larger businesses, usually within mature industries, with the hopes of reselling those businesses to another buyer. There are many subdivisions within the overall buyout category – funds that specialize in mezzanine financing, for example, or distressed equity funds which invest in companies undergoing bankruptcy or other restructuring.

There has been an explosion in the demand for private equity over the past several years. In 1996, fundraising commitments in the U.S. were about $45-billion. By the year 2000, they had topped $163-billion. In the early nineties, this growth was fueled by investors looking to find a way into the top buyout firms of the late 80s. Up until recently, it has been driven by the demand for exposure to promising technology companies.

The main benefit of private equity is its potential to enhance portfolio performance. Most private equity partnerships have the potential to earn returns far in excess of traditional equity investments. As mentioned above, while the five-year returns for the S&P 500 averaged 18.6%, five-year returns for venture capital funds were somewhere in the neighborhood of 52.1%. In 1999, while the S&P 500 was busy posting a 21.1% return, venture capital offered its investors a whopping 152.0% return. These numbers make it easy to understand why so many U/HNWIs are interested in private equity.

graph 12.6: **Commitments to private equity funds in the U.S.**

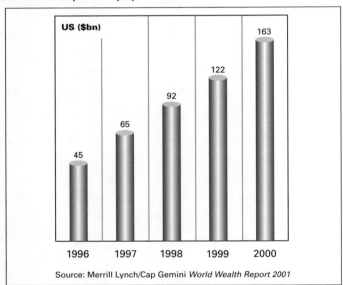

**US ($bn)**

| | | | | 163 |
| 45 | 65 | 92 | 122 | |
| 1996 | 1997 | 1998 | 1999 | 2000 |

Source: Merrill Lynch/Cap Gemini *World Wealth Report 2001*

Despite these stunning returns, private equity is not without its drawbacks. First and foremost are the high investment minimums – anything between $10-million and

$20-million is a common entry level with buyout funds. While many U/HNWIs can certainly afford such investments, for all but a few it would leave little else in the portfolio. As I've said before, that kind of concentration is rarely a good idea. The second problem is the demand for private equity. There has been a big surge in the number of U/HNWIs looking to invest in this asset class – meaning venture capital firms have been drowning in cash, forcing some to close their doors to new investors. Another problem with private equity is the relative lack of transparency. While there are regulations that require mutual fund managers to make timely disclosures of what they're actually doing, there are no rules that say hedge fund managers have to do the same. And of course, the illiquidity of private equity makes it unsuitable for those who might need access to funds quickly.

But to my mind, the most significant consideration with private equity is the quality of the managers. There can be a dramatic variation between the quality of management in the private equity business – and the lack of regular reporting can make it difficult to assess that quality. One answer to this problem is a private equity "funds of funds" – a fund that offers investors a broad sample of private equity and buyout funds operating within specific niche segments. The advantage of such a structure should be obvious: diversification. Another is the ability to get around high minimum investment requirements. Particularly with buyout funds, the ability for funds-of-funds to pool contributions from a number of different limited partners provides the U/HNWI of more modest means with greater access to this asset class. That said, the costs associated with funds-of-funds can be a bit of a drawback. Depending on the structure of the fund in question, investors in private equity funds-of-funds end up paying fees twice – once to the fund-of-funds manager, and again to the managers of the funds held within the fund of funds. Despite this drawback, it seems many U/HNWIs like the idea of a private equity fund-of-funds. Like the alternative investment market in general, their growth seems to be explosive.

## Private equity plus: **direct investment or "angel" investing**

For UHNWIs and the Superwealthy, private equity can take the form of a direct investment. Such investments typically go by the name of "angel" investments – the investor taking on the role of an "angel" who graces the business with a blessing of capital.

There's no doubt about it – direct investment is more risky than other forms of private equity. That said, there is a potential for even greater returns. Performance data on these opportunities is sketchy (part of the reason why it's called *private* equity) but if the anecdotal evidence I've heard is any indication, the potential returns can be enormous. By making large amounts of capital available to companies that would have a difficult time securing it elsewhere, angels are in a unique position to secure large amounts of equity from their investments. If that company hits the big time and eventually goes public, angels can make a significant fortune in a relatively short time. I remember meeting one U/HNWI who had borrowed against a number of commercial properties he owned to make an investment in a small software development company. Five years later, the firm was bought out by one of the big players in the industry, to the tune of $600-million.

Not everyone is cut out to be an angel investor, however. First and foremost, angel investing requires massive amounts of capital – the kind of capital that raises the eyebrows of even the wealthiest U/HNWI. Even if money isn't really an object, angel investing requires a certain mindset that not everyone shares. The angel investors I've met have all had extensive contacts in the business community, and the majority of them have been successful owners and operators of large, growing businesses. They have all been extremely adept at identifying and assessing unique business opportunities, not only from the perspective of the balance sheet (which is the easy part), but from the perspective of business "intangibles" – the quality and drive of the management, the value of the business idea, etc. Every single one of them has an uncommon tolerance for risk, a tolerance that is far, far beyond the tolerance of the average U/HNWI. Most important of all, the angels that I've met have a unique visionary quality. They have a knack for seeing the opportunity that lies just beyond the challenges a young business must face. And they believe wholeheartedly in what they are doing. That's not to say they are motivated purely by altruism, or by the idea of doing "good" for a given company. But by and large, they believe in their investments in a way that goes far beyond the average U/HNWI. Angels are almost always passionate, driven people, people who take a certain joy in being part of a burgeoning enterprise, and are willing to back up their beliefs with dollars. These qualities make angel investing an unrealistic option for all but a few U/HNWIs.

Personally, I think that's for the best. Simply put, the vast majority of U/HNWIs are much better served with opportunities that require a little less capital, a little less involvement, and a lot less risk. With private equity partnerships and funds-of-funds, investors have the protection of a layer of professional management between them and their investment, and in some cases, the advantages of diversifying across a wide variety of opportunities. That's most likely not the case with angel investing. And of course, angel investing usually results in concentrated positions – something I'm opposed to. But most importantly, angel investing is a kind of investment that dramatically shifts the goal of wealth management from *security* to *performance*. Again, that's the opposite of the philosophy I believe U/HNWIs need to take with their wealth.

# **Portfolio** diversifiers: hedge funds and managed futures

The second category of alternative investments is portfolio diversifiers, and they are meant to add another level of diversification to an already well-diversified portfolio. There are two products of particular interest to U/HNWIs within this general category: hedge funds and managed futures. Let's take a look at each.

## Hedge **funds**

The genesis of the hedge fund dates back to 1949, when *Fortune* magazine editor and Wall Street guru Alfred Jones conceived of a fund that used both long and short positions in equities in a single investment. Since then, hedge funds have developed into a diverse investment category that offer investors both conservative and aggressive choices. That said, the end goal of most hedge funds is the same: to deliver solid performance in nearly any market condition.

Most hedge funds operate as limited partnerships (typical in the U.S.), or offshore investment corporations (the typical structure elsewhere), and usually require large minimum investments (sometimes as high as several million dollars). The general partners in these limited partnerships are roughly equivalent to the fund manager in a common mutual fund, handling all day-to-day trading activity. Because they are largely unregulated (part of the reason why they operate as limited partnerships), hedge fund managers usually have a broad license to conduct their business in any way they see fit.

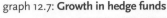

graph 12.7: **Growth in hedge funds**

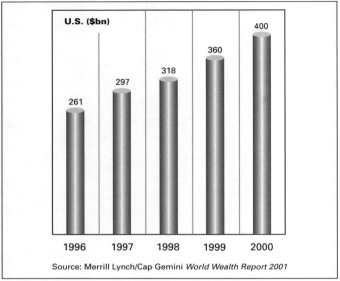

In practical terms, this means a hedge fund can invest in just about anything, from equities to futures to international currencies to distressed assets or debt. Hedge funds can also utilize sophisticated investment strategies such as leverage or derivative investing. In addition, while securities regulation often limits the size of a given investment for mutual funds, hedge funds face no such restriction, meaning they can load up on a given investment if management thinks such a move is a good idea. The freedom hedge funds enjoy has led to the development of a wide variety of hedge fund styles, each with their own benefits and drawbacks. Chart 12.8 lists a few of the most common.

Hedge fund managers are a very distinct breed. To be blunt, they are typically the *crème de la crème* of the investment world, often having left traditional mutual funds to manage hedge funds instead. Because of the incentive-based compensation that's standard in the hedge fund business, these people can make a substantial fortune if they deliver top performance. But that's not to say that all of them do. Perhaps more with hedge funds than with other managed investments, the quality of this management is a key component to the ultimate success of the investment, making an assessment of the fund manager a key component of the investment process.

table 12.8: **Hedge fund styles**

**Hedge fund investment styles**

Since the first hedge fund was introduced, many different investment strategies and styles have been used. Here are some of the most common types:

**MARKET NEUTRAL** 50% short/50% long in equities

**CONVERTIBLE ARBITRAGE** long on a convertible security, short on the underlying security

**GLOBAL MACRO** focus on global macroeconomic changes

**GROWTH** looks for growth potential in earnings and revenues

**VALUE** investments based on assets, cash flow and book value

**SECTOR** focus on particular economic or industry sectors

**DISTRESSED SECURITIES** invests in companies undergoing reorganization or in bankruptcy

**EMERGING MARKETS** invests in emerging foreign market equity or debt

**OPPORTUNISTIC** trading oriented, takes advantage of market trends and events

**LEVERAGE** employs leverage to invest in fixed-income instruments

**SHORT** only takes short positions

Source: *Investment Executive*

A recent comparison between mutual fund and hedge fund performance in *Investment Advisor* magazine highlighted the difference a quality hedge fund manager can make. Between 1988 and 1998, mutual funds showed a 12% performance gap between funds in the top quartile and funds in the bottom quartile. For buyout-type hedge funds, the difference between top and bottom was 20%. For venture capital funds, the gap was a whopping 30%. Proof positive of the importance of a thorough manager review before signing on to any hedge fund.

It's easy to be intoxicated by hedge fund performance. But to me, the main benefit of hedge funds (and the real reason why they deserve serious attention from U/HNWIs) is their potential to provide strong performance when the market is in a tailspin. Unlike mutual funds and other traditional investments, where the goal is *relative* performance, hedge funds try to achieve *absolute* performance – solid returns no matter what the market may be doing. Let me give you an example. As most investors are well aware, the year 2000 was a challenging one. The broadly-based

S&P 500 index dropped 8.1%, while the technology-heavy Nasdaq shed some 39% of its value. But by all accounts, hedge fund investors were doing just fine, enjoying an 11.3% gain (that's on top of a 40.6% advance the year before that). This kind of non-correlated performance can be a real lifesaver when positions in traditional asset classes are dragging the portfolio down. This potential for solid performance in all parts of the market cycle is also something that makes hedge funds a little different than private equity, and in my mind, makes hedge funds of inherently more value to the U/HNWI.

A lot of financial professionals take an "evolutionary" approach to hedge funds: as the U/HNWI portfolio grows, hedge funds are a natural next step. I'm not so sure I agree with this idea. It's true, the benefits of a hedge fund can be very appealing, but their inherent risk, low liquidity, and high minimums can make them unsuitable for some individuals no matter how large the portfolio may be. Personally, I'd be hesitant to place a large investment in a single hedge fund – even if that investment is meant for the aggressive, "high-risk" portion of an otherwise well-diversified portfolio. Instead, I like to invest in two or more, preferably of complementary styles and investment mandates. A relatively recent innovation I find particularly appealing is the hedge fund "fund-of-funds" – a hedge fund whose holdings consist of other hedge funds. These funds give investors access to the same high-powered investment strategies as other hedge funds, yet reduces some of the risk inherent in hedge funds that are heavily weighted to a particular investment style. Like private equity funds-of-funds, the fees for such funds are typically higher than the average hedge fund (which can be high enough by themselves). But in my mind, the ability to diversify is something that's well worth paying for.

Make no mistake: despite what their recent performance might suggest, hedge funds can be risky investments. By taking up futures and options positions, engaging in leverage, trading currencies, and shorting equities, the average risk profile of a hedge fund far outweighs that of an average mutual fund. The high-profile floundering of Long Term Capital in 1998 is a prime example of how such strategies can run into trouble, and by no means is it the only example. And as I mentioned above, they are largely unregulated, which means receiving timely and accurate information about them can be something of a challenge. Both these factors make hedge funds less than ideal for those U/HNWIs with a low risk tolerance. And downright dangerous for those U/HNWIs who don't want to consult a professional first before investing in one.

## Managed **futures**

A further class of portfolio diversifier is the managed futures fund. In the past, these specialized funds invested in highly volatile commodities such as resources (oil, base metals, lumber etc.) and agricultural products (wheat, soybeans, pork bellies, etc.). In recent years, they have also included financial products such as options, equity futures, and foreign currencies in their portfolios. They are a relatively small part of the alternative investment universe, accounting for only $44-billion of the $1.1-trillion invested in alternative investments.

For U/HNWIs, managed futures offer a very significant benefit, and that is *negatively-correlated* performance. The performance of commodities and currency futures often runs counter to the market cycle of traditional investments; as such, the performance of managed future funds is often the opposite of other investments in the U/HNWI portfolio. As I showed you above, in the year 2000, managed futures funds offered investors some degree of protection against market volatility. While the MSCI world equity index (an appropriate benchmark for funds that invest all over the world) dropped 14.1%, for instance, managed futures funds performed well, posting a 9.4% gain. That sounds good, but with managed futures, performance can just as easily go the other way. Performance from 1999 provides another example: the MSCI posted a 23.6% return, while managed futures eked out a meagre 1.5%. This kind of *negative* correlation is different from the non-correlated performance offered by hedge funds. As mentioned, negative correlation means that statistically, two assets offer opposite performance. With *non*-correlated assets, there is no statistical link between the performances whatsoever. Depending on what the overall portfolio needs, one may be more suitable than the other.

In practice, managed futures funds have an important role to play for some U/HNWIs. Their negative correlation to traditional asset classes offers an opportunity to create a portfolio that is more protected against significant shifts in the broader market. That makes them a good choice for those U/HNWIs seeking absolute, 100% diversification, or those who are looking for a way to diversify a portfolio that is highly concentrated in a single stock that tends to move closely with the market itself. That said, the negative correlation can often create a drag on portfolio performance when times are good – and that can be a hard pill for many U/HNWIs to swallow. For this reason, I consider managed futures to be a secondary option. They certainly have their place in some special situations, but for most U/HNWIs, there are better diversification opportunities out there.

## A final word on alternative investments

There is nothing inherently "good" or "bad" about alternative investments. And there is no rule that says they *must* be in your portfolio. But if you do invest in alternative investments, professional advice is a must. Unlike traditional investments, the dollars involved in alternative investments are often large, the risks are often acute, and the transparency is often lacking. Before signing any offering memorandum or prospectus, make sure you get a professional opinion.

# Key concepts: Chapter twelve

- The assets invested in alternative investments are growing, and growing quickly.

- Alternative assets offer the potential for solid growth; the primary purpose of alternative investments, however, is to provide added diversification.

- There are two types of alternative investments: portfolio enhancers and portfolio diversifiers.

- While the exact portion of the U/HNWI portfolio allocated to alternative investments should vary with the individual's risk tolerance, no more than 10-15% of the total portfolio should be allocated to alternative investments. For wealthier, more aggressive U/HNWIs, that total should not exceed 25%.

- Private equity is the primary portfolio enhancing asset.

- There are two basic types of private equity investment: venture capital funds and buyout funds. Each has benefits and drawbacks.

  - The main benefit of private equity is the ability to enhance performance. This enhanced performance comes at the cost of added concentration, lower liquidity, and the difficulty in selecting top-performing managers.

  - Direct private equity investing is commonly called "angel" investing. It should be left for only the most wealthy, most aggressive U/HNWIs.

  - There are two primary assets within the portfolio diversifier category: hedge funds and managed futures funds.

- There are many different types of hedge funds; each with benefits and drawbacks.

  - The primary benefit of all hedge funds is to provide strong performance when traditional markets are down. This benefit comes at the cost of low liquidity, high minimum investments, and higher risk.

- Managed futures represent a small portion of all alternative investments. Their main benefit is to offer negatively-correlated performance relative to traditional markets. This feature makes them a good choice for those looking to diversify against a large stock position that moves in lock-step with the broader market.

## Resources

Looking for more information on alternative investments? The best thing to do is to search for something on the specific investment you have in mind. Here are some good places to look for more information on the two main types of alternative investments, hedge funds and private equity.

*Getting Started in Hedge Funds* by Daniel A. Strachman

*Investing in Hedge Funds* by Joseph G. Nichols

*Venture Capital and Private Equity: A Casebook* by Joshua Lerner and John Lerner

*Angel Financing: How to Find and Invest in Private Equity* by Gerald A. Benjamin and Joel Margulis

## Websites

Planet Hedge Fund *www.planethedgefund.com* – an online community for anyone interested in investing in hedge funds or alternative investments

Alternative Investment News *www.iialternatives.com* – search here for articles on alternative investments

*www.privateequity.com* – information on private equity firms in the U.S.

# **Being a** tax-wise investor

- *Levels of tax responsibility*
- *Taxes and the individual*
- *Taxes and the portfolio*
- *Taxes and the professional*

*"Next to being shot at and missed, nothing is quite as satisfying as an income tax refund."*
**F. J. Raymond**

L et me ask you a question. Do you know of anyone who is looking to pay *more* tax? I don't. I have, however, met several who fail to incorporate even the most basic tax planning strategies in their overall financial plan. Which leads me to wonder: do these people in fact feel they should be paying more?

Tax planning can be one of the most effective, most cost-efficient ways of both securing your wealth and building upon it. It's true, as governments close tax loopholes, end tax-advantaged investment programs, and generally clamp down on the use of domestic and offshore tax-reduction structures, there are less opportunities for U/HNWIs to develop tax planning strategies. But to me, this is a poor excuse for ignoring the subject of tax planning altogether.

I think it's high time for U/HNWIs to learn more about tax planning, and about taxes in general. This chapter will provide a brief overview of some of the important concepts surrounding taxation, and will outline my three-tiered approach to the subject of tax planning. It will review some of the basic tax rules in both the United States and Canada, and discuss some of the things U/HNWIs need to keep in mind when thinking about tax planning. After that, it will explain some of the practical decisions and strategies U/HNWIs can enact to reduce the amount of tax they pay. Finally – and perhaps most importantly – this chapter will provide guidance on how you can ensure the financial professionals you work with are sensitive to taxation issues.

Before we get into all that, however, you should understand that tax planning strategies tend to be highly personal. Most of them – the good ones, anyway – focus on the unique opportunities and challenges facing the individual. By their very nature, they are not the kind of strategies that can be applied to every situation without significant modification. So instead of discussing detailed descriptions of complicated strategies that may or may not be relevant to you, I'll concentrate more on tax planning *concepts*. These should help you secure a mindset that's conducive to saving tax – and saving wealth.

## My approach to tax-wise investing

Tax planning has the reputation for being highly complicated, highly confusing, and, when push comes to shove, highly *boring*. Maybe that's true, but the way I see it, tax planning starts with a rather simple idea. At the root of all tax planning is the understanding that *it's not just the money on the account statement that matters, but rather the money that makes it into your wallet*. Before they implement any tax planning strategy, U/HNWIs need to think about income in the right way – that is, in terms of after-tax dollars. This simple philosophy is the foundation for all tax planning strategies, and it's something I try to impress upon every U/HNWI client I work with.

The way I see it, tax planning is ultimately about *responsibility*. Even though they should always seek professional advice when it comes to tax matters, U/HNWIs need to take responsibility for the financial decisions and behaviors that affect their tax situation. This responsibility exists on three distinct levels. The first of these is the individual level: U/HNWIs must take responsibility for their own tax knowledge, and do what they can to learn more about the tax laws in their jurisdiction. They should also make themselves aware of some of the specific tax challenges facing them. The second is the portfolio level: U/HNWIs must take responsibility for their own financial behavior, and learn how the decisions they make about their investments will affect the taxation of their wealth. The third is the professional level: U/HNWIs must take the responsibility to find and work with professionals who are committed to minimizing tax. Taken collectively, this co-ordinated approach can help ensure U/HNWIs keep more of what they earn.

Understand, however, that taxes shouldn't always be at the top of any U/HNWI's mind. While the tax implications of a given investment are an important part of the investment evaluation, they are not the only consideration. This leads to one of my fundamental principles regarding tax planning: *just because a given investment offers tax advantages, that's not a good enough reason to invest.* This is part of what I mean when I talk about "tax-wise" investing. U/HNWIs need to develop a certain degree of *wisdom* when it comes to taxes – the wisdom to determine which tax planning strategies make sense, and which strategies are more trouble than they're worth.

## Tax planning level 1: the individual

Because most taxes are ultimately based on the individual's unique financial circumstances, tax-wise investing starts with a thorough knowledge of your personal tax situation. By becoming familiar with only a few key elements of your overall financial picture, you'll be able to make better-informed financial and lifestyle decisions – decisions that could make a big difference to your bottom line.

### Basic **information**

For starters, you need to be aware of the specific features of your individual tax situation that apply to you and you alone – the number of dependents you have, the contributions you make to tax-deferred retirement plans, your charitable bequests in a given year, etc. You'll also want to examine some of the specific strategies available for reducing your income – through the use of tax deferred retirement savings plans, for instance. It's beyond the scope of this book to provide you with a complete summary of all the deductions and credits you can claim on your tax return. There are, however, a number of comprehensive (yet quite readable) publications that focus on this subject. Quite frankly, one or more of them deserves to be on the shelf of every U/HNWI.

### Tax **brackets**

In order to fully understand their individual tax situation, it's essential for U/HNWIs to understand how income is taxed in their jurisdiction. A good place to start is by familiarizing themselves with the way tax brackets work. I haven't the room to list all the tax brackets for all areas of the world; what follows are the tax brackets for individuals in select jurisdictions in North America. The exact brackets may be slightly different where you live, but they should give you a general understanding of how the system works.

table 13.1: **Individual marginal tax rates U.S./Canada for Salary or Interest Income**

| 2002 Projected Personal Income Tax Rates | | | | | | | |
|---|---|---|---|---|---|---|---|
| Salary/Interest (see notes) | California (1,2,6) | Florida (1,6,8) | New York (1,6) | Washington (1,6,9) | British Columbia (5,7) | Alberta (5,7) | Ontario (5,7) |
| $0 to $7,400 | 11.00% | 10.00% | 14.00% | 10.00% | 0.00% | 0.00% | 0.00% |
| $7,401 to $12,000 | 11.00% | 10.00% | 14.00% | 10.00% | 22.10% | 26.00% | 22.05% |
| $12,001 to $12,014 | 16.00% | 15.00% | 19.00% | 15.00% | 22.10% | 26.00% | 22.05% |
| $12,015 to $16,000 | 17.00% | 15.00% | 19.00% | 15.00% | 22.10% | 26.00% | 22.05% |
| $16,001 to $21,600 | 17.00% | 15.00% | 19.50% | 15.00% | 22.10% | 26.00% | 22.05% |
| $21,601 to $22,000 | 17.00% | 15.00% | 19.50% | 15.00% | 22.10% | 26.00% | 22.05% |
| $22,001 to $26,000 | 17.00% | 15.00% | 20.25% | 15.00% | 22.10% | 26.00% | 22.05% |
| $26,001 to $28,476 | 17.00% | 15.00% | 20.90% | 15.00% | 22.10% | 26.00% | 22.05% |
| $28,477 to $30,754 | 19.00% | 15.00% | 20.90% | 15.00% | 22.10% | 26.00% | 22.05% |
| $30,755 to $40,000 | 19.00% | 15.00% | 20.90% | 15.00% | 31.20% | 32.00% | 31.10% |
| $40,001 to $44,942 | 19.00% | 15.00% | 21.85% | 15.00% | 31.20% | 32.00% | 31.10% |
| $44,943 to $45,000 | 21.00% | 15.00% | 21.85% | 15.00% | 31.20% | 32.00% | 31.10% |
| $45,001 to $46,400 | 21.00% | 15.00% | 21.85% | 15.00% | 31.20% | 32.00% | 31.10% |
| $46,401 to $53,650 | 33.00% | 27.00% | 33.85% | 27.00% | 31.20% | 32.00% | 31.10% |
| $53,651 to $61,510 | 33.00% | 27.00% | 33.85% | 27.00% | 31.20% | 32.00% | 33.00% |
| $61,511 to $62,387 | 33.00% | 27.00% | 33.85% | 27.00% | 37.70% | 36.00% | 39.40% |
| $62,388 to $63,370 | 35.00% | 27.00% | 33.85% | 27.00% | 37.70% | 36.00% | 39.40% |
| $63,371 to $70,000 | 35.00% | 27.00% | 33.85% | 27.00% | 37.70% | 36.00% | 43.40% |
| $70,001 to $78,845 | 35.00% | 27.00% | 33.85% | 27.00% | 39.70% | 36.00% | 43.40% |
| $78,846 to $85,000 | 36.30% | 27.00% | 33.85% | 27.00% | 39.70% | 36.00% | 43.40% |
| $85,001 to $90,000 | 36.30% | 27.00% | 33.85% | 27.00% | 40.70% | 36.00% | 43.40% |
| $90,001 to $100,000 | 36.30% | 27.00% | 33.85% | 27.00% | 40.70% | 36.00% | 43.40% |
| $100,001 to $112,150 | 36.30% | 27.00% | 33.85% | 27.00% | 43.70% | 39.00% | 46.40% |
| $112,151 to $170,950 | 39.30% | 30.00% | 36.85% | 30.00% | 43.70% | 39.00% | 46.40% |
| $170,951 to $305,350 | 44.30% | 35.00% | 41.85% | 35.00% | 43.70% | 39.00% | 46.40% |
| $305,350+ | 47.90% | 38.60% | 45.45% | 38.60% | 43.70% | 39.00% | 46.40% |

Source: KNV Chartered Accountants

1) Married filing joint. The tax rates only include Federal and State taxes, other city taxes may apply. The Federal portion of the tax rate has been adjusted for estimated inflation of 2.7%.
2) The State of California tax rate has been adjusted for an estimated inflation rate of 4.5%.
3) The rates are for property that has been held for greater than one year.
   If the property has been held for less than one year, see the salary and interest rates.
4) The rate will be reduced by a further 2% when the property sold has been held for more than 5 years.
5) The tax rates are based on the tax legislation proposed up to July 31, 2001 and will be subject to inflation.
6) The rates shown are applicable to taxable income stated in U.S. dollars.
7) The rates shown are applicable to taxable income stated in Canadian dollars.
8) Florida does not charge state personal income tax. Florida assesses an intangible tax based on the gross value of intangible assets owned by residents of the state.
9) Washington does not charge state personal income tax.

Even the most basic knowledge of these tax brackets could help reduce the tax you pay. With this knowledge, you can project tax liability for a given year, and potentially plan some of the larger events and specific investment decisions around that projected liability. If you know you're at or near the top tax bracket in your jurisdiction, for instance, you could be able to delay a taxable event (the exercise of an options package, for instance, or withdrawing a large lump sum from your investment portfolio) until such time as your income is a little lower. Working with an accounting and/or tax specialist will help you take advantage of such situations, but taking responsibility for knowing about them yourself will help ensure you get the advice you need when you need it.

## Alternative minimum tax: **the danger of being a U/HNWI**

Another important tax topic every U/HNWI needs to become familiar with is the Alternative Minimum Tax, or AMT. The exact name of this tax may be different from jurisdiction to jurisdiction, but the general concept is the same most everywhere. The AMT is a flat tax levied against those taxpayers who have reduced their taxable income below a specified point through the use of complicated deductions and sophisticated tax-reduction strategies. While such laws theoretically apply to any taxpayer, in practice, it's obvious that they are clearly targeted against U/HNWIs.

The first step is to familiarize yourself with the specific tax regulations that relate to the AMT in your jurisdiction. Pay particular attention to the criteria which will be used by tax authorities to determine whether the AMT should be levied against you, as well as to the specific level of tax at which the AMT will kick in. If you're considering investing in complicated tax shelters – or if you've invested in one already – you'll want to double-check the specific regulations that apply to your deduction of those investments. It's a good idea to treat the prospectus or offering memorandum with a healthy dose of skepticism here, and seek a professional opinion. There have been a number of notable cases where promises made in a prospectus of attractive tax deductions have been revealed to be nothing more than hot air.

It should go without saying that if you have even the slightest inkling that you may be hit with the AMT, you need to seek professional tax help *now*. Contrary to what you might assume, there are strategies that can help you avoid the AMT (you may be able to boost income to eliminate the threat of the AMT, for example). But the more time you waste, the fewer opportunities will be available to you. What's more, in most jurisdictions, the specific rules governing the AMT are extremely complicated, and getting them wrong could cost you a bundle. Professional advice is the only way to ensure the AMT doesn't impact your net worth.

## Tax planning level 2: the portfolio

The second level of tax planning responsibility takes place on the level of the portfolio. By learning how to make tax-wise investment decisions, U/HNWIs can limit tax and keep more of what they earn. Again, the amount of information on this topic would easily fill a library, so instead of listing all the possible options available to U/HNWIs, I've kept to some of the central concepts that promote tax-wise investing. For more detailed information, you'll want to consult with a qualified professional.

### Not all income **is created equal!**

At some time or another, most U/HNWIs will be living off the income of their investment portfolios. For that reason, it's essential that U/HNWIs understand the difference in the way various forms of investment income are taxed in their jurisdiction. This knowledge will make it easier to make appropriate decisions regarding the structure of ongoing income payments from an investment portfolio. It should also make it easier to keep more of your money.

Most jurisdictions give certain forms of income preferential tax treatment. Usually, capital gains receive the biggest tax break, ostensibly to encourage investment in businesses and keep people employed. Dividends usually receive a smaller tax break, ostensibly because dividend income comes from corporate profits, and is assumed to have been subject to tax at the corporate level.

Interest income is usually taxed at a relatively high rate, usually as high as everyday income from salaries, rent, etc (see chart 13.1). I don't have the room to list all the rates for all the different jurisdictions of the world, but charts 13.2a and 13.2b list the rates for some of the major jurisdictions in North America. It should provide you with a general understanding of the way most jurisdictions work.

table 13.2a: **Income tax rates: dividends**

| 2002 Projected Personal Income Tax Rates | | | | | | | | |
|---|---|---|---|---|---|---|---|---|
| **Dividends**<br>**(see notes)** | | **California**<br>(1,2,6) | **Florida**<br>(1,6,8) | **New York**<br>(1,6) | **Washington**<br>(1,6,9) | **British Columbia**<br>(5,7) | **Alberta**<br>(5,7) | **Ontario**<br>(5,7) |
| $0 to | $7,400 | 11.00% | 10.00% | 14.00% | 10.00% | 0.00% | 0.00% | 0.00% |
| $7,401 to | $12,000 | 11.00% | 10.00% | 14.00% | 10.00% | 4.50% | 7.80% | 4.70% |
| $12,001 to | $12,014 | 16.00% | 15.00% | 19.00% | 15.00% | 4.50% | 7.80% | 4.70% |
| $12,015 to | $16,000 | 17.00% | 15.00% | 19.00% | 15.00% | 4.50% | 7.80% | 4.70% |
| $16,001 to | $21,600 | 17.00% | 15.00% | 19.50% | 15.00% | 4.50% | 7.80% | 4.70% |
| $21,601 to | $22,000 | 17.00% | 15.00% | 19.50% | 15.00% | 4.50% | 7.80% | 4.70% |
| $22,001 to | $26,000 | 17.00% | 15.00% | 20.25% | 15.00% | 4.50% | 7.80% | 4.70% |
| $26,001 to | $28,476 | 17.00% | 15.00% | 20.90% | 15.00% | 4.50% | 7.80% | 4.70% |
| $28,477 to | $30,754 | 19.00% | 15.00% | 20.90% | 15.00% | 4.50% | 7.80% | 4.70% |
| $30,755 to | $40,000 | 19.00% | 15.00% | 20.90% | 15.00% | 15.90% | 15.30% | 16.00% |
| $40,001 to | $44,942 | 19.00% | 15.00% | 21.85% | 15.00% | 15.90% | 15.30% | 16.00% |
| $44,943 to | $45,000 | 21.00% | 15.00% | 21.85% | 15.00% | 15.90% | 15.30% | 16.00% |
| $45,001 to | $46,400 | 21.00% | 15.00% | 21.85% | 15.00% | 15.90% | 15.30% | 16.00% |
| $46,401 to | $53,650 | 33.00% | 27.00% | 33.85% | 27.00% | 15.90% | 15.30% | 16.00% |
| $53,651 to | $61,509 | 33.00% | 27.00% | 33.85% | 27.00% | 15.90% | 15.30% | 16.00% |
| $61,510 to | $62,387 | 33.00% | 27.00% | 33.85% | 27.00% | 24.10% | 20.30% | 23.40% |
| $62,388 to | $63,370 | 35.00% | 27.00% | 33.85% | 27.00% | 24.10% | 20.30% | 23.40% |
| $63,371 to | $70,000 | 35.00% | 27.00% | 33.85% | 27.00% | 24.10% | 20.30% | 23.40% |
| $70,001 to | $78,845 | 35.00% | 27.00% | 33.85% | 27.00% | 26.60% | 20.30% | 23.40% |
| $78,846 to | $85,000 | 36.30% | 27.00% | 33.85% | 27.00% | 26.60% | 20.30% | 23.40% |
| $85,001 to | $90,000 | 36.30% | 27.00% | 33.85% | 27.00% | 27.80% | 20.30% | 23.40% |
| $90,001 to | $100,000 | 36.30% | 27.00% | 33.85% | 27.00% | 27.80% | 20.30% | 23.40% |
| $100,001 to | $112,150 | 36.30% | 27.00% | 33.85% | 27.00% | 31.60% | 24.10% | 28.60% |
| $112,151 to | $117,400 | 39.30% | 30.00% | 36.85% | 30.00% | 31.60% | 24.10% | 28.60% |
| $117,401 to | $170,950 | 39.30% | 30.00% | 36.85% | 30.00% | 31.60% | 24.10% | 31.30% |
| $170,951 to | $305,350 | 44.30% | 35.00% | 41.85% | 35.00% | 31.60% | 24.10% | 31.30% |
| $305,350+ | | 47.90% | 38.60% | 45.45% | 38.60% | 31.60% | 24.10% | 31.30% |

Source: KNV Chartered Accountants

1) Married filing joint. The tax rates only include Federal and State taxes, other city taxes may apply. The Federal portion of the tax rate has been adjusted for estimated inflation of 2.7%.
2) The State of California tax rate has been adjusted for an estimated inflation rate of 4.5%.
3) The rates are for property that has been held for greater than one year.
   If the property has been held for less than one year, see the salary and interest rates.
4) The rate will be reduced by a further 2% when the property sold has been held for more than 5 years.
5) The tax rates are based on the tax legislation proposed up to July 31, 2001 and will be subject to inflation.
6) The rates shown are applicable to taxable income stated in U.S. dollars.
7) The rates shown are applicable to taxable income stated in Canadian dollars.
8) Florida does not charge state personal income tax. Florida assesses an intangible tax based on the gross value of intangible assets owned by residents of the state.
9) Washington does not charge state personal income tax.

table 13.2b: **Income tax rates: capital gains**

| 2002 Projected Personal Income Tax Rates | | | | | | | |
|---|---|---|---|---|---|---|---|
| Capital Gains (see notes) | California (1,2,3,6) | Florida (1,3,6,8) | New York (1,3,6) | Washington (1,3,6,9) | British Columbia (5,7) | Alberta (5,7) | Ontario (5,7) |
| $0 to $7,400 | 11.00% (4) | 10.00% (4) | 14.00% (4) | 10.00% (4) | 0.00% | 0.00% | 0.00% |
| $7,401 to $12,000 | 11.00% (4) | 10.00% (4) | 14.00% (4) | 10.00% (4) | 11.05% | 13.00% | 11.03% |
| $12,001 to $12,014 | 11.00% (4) | 10.00% (4) | 14.00% (4) | 10.00% (4) | 11.05% | 13.00% | 11.03% |
| $12,015 to $16,000 | 12.00% (4) | 10.00% (4) | 14.00% (4) | 10.00% (4) | 11.05% | 13.00% | 11.03% |
| $16,001 to $21,600 | 12.00% (4) | 10.00% (4) | 14.50% (4) | 10.00% (4) | 11.05% | 13.00% | 11.03% |
| $21,601 to $22,000 | 12.00% (4) | 10.00% (4) | 14.50% (4) | 10.00% (4) | 11.05% | 13.00% | 11.03% |
| $22,001 to $26,000 | 12.00% (4) | 10.00% (4) | 15.25% (4) | 10.00% (4) | 11.05% | 13.00% | 11.03% |
| $26,001 to $28,476 | 12.00% (4) | 10.00% (4) | 15.90% (4) | 10.00% (4) | 11.05% | 13.00% | 11.03% |
| $28,477 to $30,754 | 14.00% (4) | 10.00% (4) | 15.90% (4) | 10.00% (4) | 11.05% | 13.00% | 11.03% |
| $30,755 to $40,000 | 14.00% (4) | 10.00% (4) | 15.90% (4) | 10.00% (4) | 15.60% | 18.00% | 15.55% |
| $40,001 to $44,942 | 14.00% (4) | 10.00% (4) | 16.85% (4) | 10.00% (4) | 15.60% | 18.00% | 15.55% |
| $44,943 to $45,000 | 16.00% (4) | 10.00% (4) | 16.85% (4) | 10.00% (4) | 15.60% | 18.00% | 15.55% |
| $45,001 to $46,400 | 16.00% (4) | 10.00% (4) | 16.85% (4) | 10.00% (4) | 15.60% | 18.00% | 15.55% |
| $46,401 to $53,650 | 26.00% | 20.00% | 26.85% | 20.00% | 15.60% | 18.00% | 15.55% |
| $53,651 to $61,510 | 26.00% | 20.00% | 26.85% | 20.00% | 15.60% | 18.00% | 15.55% |
| $61,511 to $62,387 | 26.00% | 20.00% | 26.85% | 20.00% | 19.85% | 18.00% | 19.70% |
| $62,388 to $63,370 | 28.00% | 20.00% | 26.85% | 20.00% | 19.85% | 18.00% | 19.70% |
| $63,371 to $70,000 | 28.00% | 20.00% | 26.85% | 20.00% | 19.85% | 18.00% | 21.70% |
| $70,001 to $78,845 | 28.00% | 20.00% | 26.85% | 20.00% | 19.85% | 18.00% | 21.70% |
| $78,846 to $85,000 | 29.30% | 20.00% | 26.85% | 20.00% | 19.85% | 18.00% | 21.70% |
| $85,001 to $90,000 | 29.30% | 20.00% | 26.85% | 20.00% | 20.35% | 18.00% | 21.70% |
| $90,001 to $100,000 | 29.30% | 20.00% | 26.85% | 20.00% | 20.35% | 18.00% | 21.70% |
| $100,001 to $112,150 | 29.30% | 20.00% | 26.85% | 20.00% | 21.85% | 19.50% | 23.20% |
| $112,151 to $170,950 | 29.30% | 20.00% | 26.85% | 20.00% | 21.85% | 19.50% | 23.20% |
| $170,951 to $305,350 | 29.30% | 20.00% | 26.85% | 20.00% | 21.85% | 19.50% | 23.20% |
| $305,350+ | 29.30% | 20.00% | 26.85% | 20.00% | 21.85% | 19.50% | 23.20% |

Source: KNV Chartered Accountants

1) Married filing joint. The tax rates only include Federal and State taxes, other city taxes may apply. The Federal portion of the tax rate has been adjusted for estimated inflation of 2.7%.
2) The State of California tax rate has been adjusted for an estimated inflation rate of 4.5%.
3) The rates are for property that has been held for greater than one year. If the property has been held for less than one year, see the salary and interest rates.
4) The rate will be reduced by a further 2% when the property sold has been held for more than 5 years.
5) The tax rates are based on the tax legislation proposed up to July 31, 2001 and will be subject to inflation.
6) The rates shown are applicable to taxable income stated in U.S. dollars.
7) The rates shown are applicable to taxable income stated in Canadian dollars.
8) Florida does not charge state personal income tax. Florida assesses an intangible tax based on the gross value of intangible assets owned by residents of the state.
9) Washington does not charge state personal income tax.

With the knowledge that certain forms of income receive privileged tax treatment, you're able to make better-informed decisions about what investments you need to accomplish your specific goals. In most cases, you'll be able to adjust your portfolio to select investments that take maximum advantage of these different rates of taxation: if you're looking for income, for example, it may make a lot of sense to steer the portfolio towards dividend-yielding common and preferred shares rather than piling up CDs, GICs or bonds. Of course, there are factors to consider other than simply taxation, but by knowing how the income you receive will be taxed, you'll be better able to fine-tune your portfolio to your exact needs.

## Understanding **tax efficiency**

If you're a U/HNWI who invests in mutual funds or other pooled products, you'll want to know a little more about *tax efficiency*. That's the general name for the measurement of how good a mutual fund or other pooled product is at keeping investment capital away from the taxman. A fund is said to be 50% efficient if the investor gets to keep 50% of the income it generates. A fund is 100% efficient if investors keep 100%. You get the idea.

What makes tax efficiency so important? Well, over the course of time, taxes can steadily drain away your capital, diminishing the compounding power of your wealth. Obviously, it makes sense to keep as much of that capital working for you as possible. Graph 13.3 on the following page provides a simplified example to make the point clear. You'll notice it compares three investments: (1) a standard interest-bearing CD or term deposit, (2) a mutual fund with an aggressive trading strategy (resulting in annual distributions of 10% a year), and (3) a mutual fund following a buy-and-hold strategy with no annual distributions. Just so we can compare apples to apples, I've assumed the average annual return for each of these investments to be 12% – that's unrealistic for fixed-income investments like term deposits or certificates of deposit, but my goal is to keep the math simple so you can see exactly what I'm talking about. The basic message should be clear: the more efficient a fund is at deferring taxes, the more your wealth is allowed to compound. The more your wealth is allowed to compound, the more money you'll eventually have in your pocket.

Given this information, it's sensible to lean toward those funds and other pooled products that have a track record of tax efficiency. In practical terms, that often means selecting funds with a mandate that allows for at least some investment in tax-advantaged vehicles. But remember, tax efficiency is only one measure of an investment's suitability – there are many other factors to keep in mind before deciding on a particular investment.

graph 13.3: **The power of tax deferred compounding**

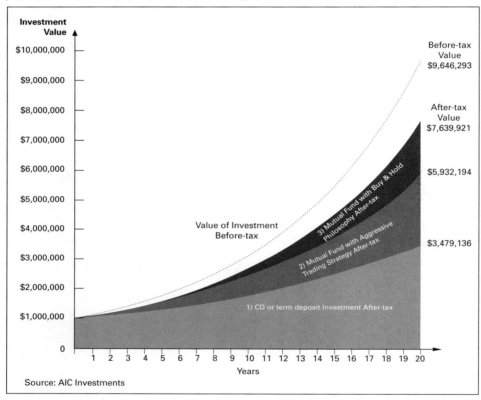

Understand too that tax efficiency can sometimes be a bad thing. Because most funds with high tax efficiency go several years without distributing income to investors, they may be hiding large deferred capital gains. These gains may result in sizable distributions when these positions are eventually liquidated. Most top-quality fund managers are well aware of specific strategies to limit such unrealized gains and prevent them from ever being a problem; nevertheless, it's something to investigate when looking at a fund with a long record of minimal distributions.

**Tax efficiency and your managers**

In the war against taxes, your managers are your first line of defense. Many times, their decisions are the ones that will ultimately determine how much of your wealth you will keep, and how much will go to the taxman. For this reason, U/HNWIs need to learn how to assess the tax sensitivity of various managers, and determine what kind of effect the investment style of various managers will have on their portfolio.

It's sad, but true: many professional money managers take a "not my problem" approach to taxes. Fortunately, these people are usually easy to identify. All you have to do is look at your manager's trading record, and determine if the manager in question likes to "turn over" his or her portfolio (that is, sell off various positions) on a regular basis. Most of the time, the rate of change in the portfolio will be the single most important factor in determining tax efficiency, so it's usually a wise idea to treat those managers who like to turn over the portfolio with a higher degree of caution.

As I mentioned above, I tend to lean toward those managers who limit portfolio turnover when I construct U/HNWI portfolios. That said, outstanding performance can sometimes be worth the extra tax hit. Some aggressive managers are so good at what they do that the distributions they generate are worth forgiving. But at the very least, you'll want to know what you're getting into before you invest in such a fund. That way, you can prepare for the added tax liability in other parts of your portfolio – like selecting tax-advantaged investments for your income-generating assets (municipal bonds would be a good example for U.S. investors), or offsetting gains with losses (sometimes called "tax-harvesting").

Of course, the best managers understand that it's their job to do this for you – at least to the extent that they *can* do it for you. Tax harvesting, crystallization of gains, and other sophisticated tax-minimization techniques should be the hallmarks of every money manager. To my mind, these activities speak as much about the individual as they do about their money management skills: an awareness of tax issues suggests the manager understands that he or she is the *steward* of your wealth, and must do everything possible to protect that wealth from forces that might take it away. Ideally, that's the kind of person you want managing your wealth – someone who truly cares.

### Apples to apples: Looking twice at performance figures

Most U/HNWIs don't need any motivation to monitor the performance of their investments. But in my experience, a good many U/HNWIs don't fully understand what they're looking at when they look at performance figures. Specifically, there seems to be considerable confusion regarding *after*-tax and *before*-tax performance figures. Such confusion makes it difficult to evaluate performance properly, making timely and proper investment decisions more difficult.

In many jurisdictions, the performance figures that make it into investment publications and advertisements are *before*-tax returns, making it difficult for investors to come to a fair evaluation of the value of the given investment. In recent years, there has been improvement on this issue. In the U.S., for instance, the Securities and Exchange Commission has required mutual fund and other investment managers to report *after*-tax returns as of January of 2001. So far, that's a move that hasn't been followed in other jurisdictions. But there's little doubt that the writing is on the wall.

What does it matter whether a fund reports after-tax or before-tax income? Some statistics will provide an answer. As we've discussed throughout this chapter, many mutual funds and other pooled products are in the habit of issuing annual distributions to investors. In 1999, the SEC estimated U.S. mutual funds distributed about $238-billion in capital gains, and $159-billion in taxable dividends. What does that really mean? While the exact amount of tax payable varies from fund to fund, estimates are that as much as 2.5% of the average U.S. equity fund's return is lost to taxes each year (that's more than most funds in the U.S. charge in fees!).

This is essential information to have in hand when trying to evaluate a given fund, a discretionary manager, or other investments. If you're looking at fund performance, and you see Fund A offers returns 2.5% higher than Fund B, you're likely to select Fund A for your portfolio. If so, you'd be duped. So make sure you're aware of what kind of performance figures you're looking at when it comes time to evaluate your funds.

### The offshore tax haven: the end of the "quick fix" tax solution

In the past, one strategy available to U/HNWIs looking to reduce their tax exposure was to establish an offshore account. Several jurisdictions around the world – Switzerland, the Channel Islands, and various nations in the Caribbean – have enjoyed long-standing reputations as jurisdictions where tax and tax reporting laws are either lax or non-existent. These features have traditionally made them ideal places to hold assets that would normally be subject to a high rate of tax in a U/HNWI's home jurisdiction.

There are many ways in which an offshore account might be used to reduce tax. In the most basic scenario, the U/HNWI would establish an account registered in one of the known tax havens, then transfer the proceeds of unreported or under-the-table transactions to that account. A credit card or debit card linked to that account would then be issued, giving the U/HNWI ready access to a large pool of untaxed cash. The jurisdiction in which the account was domiciled was under no obligation to report purchases made to the card, so there was little way the home jurisdiction could know exactly what was going on.

Today, setting up an offshore account to avoid tax at home is more likely to result in a conviction for tax evasion than it will in tax savings. Over the past several years, two simultaneous developments have worked to close off these opportunities for tax savings. First and foremost is the trend among Western nations to insist on rigorous reporting of foreign income from their citizens. To be honest, this was always the rule, but in the age of debit cards, instantaneous funds transfer, and electronic tracking, it's become much easier (and much more affordable) to track down offenders than it was in the past. Secondly, some high-profile international agencies have put increasing pressure on tax havens to rescind the kinds of policies formally used by U/HNWIs to avoid tax. Admittedly, the primary reason for this was to make it difficult for criminals to stash their cash. But make no mistake, a secondary (if unstated) goal was to make it harder for U/HNWIs to hide assets from the long arm of the taxman. As a result of these developments, the governments of these jurisdictions have begun to change their tax laws. Most of the well-established financial institutions in these jurisdictions are now beginning to comply with disclosure requests from the tax departments of the Western nations. Which will make it increasingly difficult, if not impossible, for a U/HNWI to use an offshore account to avoid tax back at home.

Let me be blunt: setting up such an offshore account for the express purposes of tax avoidance is a *very* bad idea. Most banks and other financial institutions in these jurisdictions won't even consider engaging in such tax avoidance schemes any more. And even if you were to find one that did, it's become easy for auditors back home to trace your electronic footprints. What's more, foreign jurisdictions are starting to co-operate with each other on a level they never did before. Couple that with the usually hefty fines for non-disclosure most well-developed nations apply to tax evaders, and you have a pretty strong argument against the idea of offshore tax havens.

Don't get me wrong: there are still some legitimate uses for these jurisdictions. If you have a business that generates significant offshore revenue (an e-commerce company would be a good example), an offshore trust might reduce the taxes you pay. An offshore account can in some cases offer a way to protect assets from potential creditors – protection that wouldn't be possible with a domestic structure. This isn't a concern for all U/HNWIs, but for those who own a business, it can be a useful strategy. And of course, for those serious about reducing their taxes, these jurisdictions still exist as possible places to take up permanent residence. Such a decision shouldn't be taken lightly, however. In Canada, for instance, the decision to leave would necessitate severing a number of personal and financial ties at home, and incurring a withholding tax of between 15%-20% on almost everything you own. For this reason, you'll want to consult closely with a legal and an accounting experts who have had considerable experience in the intricacies of such a move well before you make a final decision.

The main reason I bring up the subject of offshore accounts isn't to present a viable tax-reduction strategy, but rather to discuss the *concept* of tax shelters in general. Personally, I see the demise of the offshore tax haven constituting the demise of an entire way of thinking about tax planning. Offshore accounts and other tax shelters tempted U/HNWIs to take a "quick fix" approach to a very complicated problem. That's not what tax planning is really about. Rather, all U/HNWIs should be committed to modifying their investment behavior to prevent taxation from becoming a problem in the first place.

## Tax planning level 3: the professional

The final level of tax planning responsibility has to do with the people with whom you entrust your wealth. U/HNWIs need to accept responsibility for finding skilled professionals who know about the tax challenges of wealth, and who are willing to co-ordinate sophisticated tax and investment strategies with a team of tax specialists. Working with a professional who has a strong and thorough grasp of relevant tax regulations will allow U/HNWIs to overcome many tax challenges before they even become an issue.

## Taxes and your wealth advisor

I've spoken about some of the qualities U/HNWIs need to look for in a wealth advisor throughout this book. Tax awareness is one of the most critical. Here's a basic list of some of the tax-related qualities every wealth advisor dealing with U/HNWIs should exhibit.

- **Tax knowledge.** Your wealth advisor should show a keen awareness of tax laws, and should be interested in talking about them with you. To me, this is an absolutely fundamental requirement of all professionals working with U/HNWIs.

- **Tax foresight.** Your wealth advisor should demonstrate a considerable degree of foresight in preparing you for the tax challenges that may one day affect your individual situation.

- **Tax and your portfolio.** Your wealth advisor should be able to discuss the tax implications of investments you hold, and be able to suggest suitable alternatives that maximize after-tax dollars.

- **Tax strategies.** Your wealth advisor should be knowledgeable about specific tax-reduction strategies that might be available to you, and should show an active interest in promoting them.

- **Tax and your estate plan.** When discussing estate planning, your wealth advisor should demonstrate a keen awareness of the complex tax challenges involved in organizing a U/HNWI estate, and should be able to offer a variety of solutions for overcoming these challenges.

- **Tax and your business.** If you're a business owner, you'll want to work with a wealth advisor who is well versed in the unique taxation challenges of business divestiture, and has access to tax specialists who can co-ordinate a tax efficient exit strategy for you.

- **Tax specialists.** Your wealth advisor should know where to obtain more specialized advice when necessary. The more complex your financial situation, the more critical this network of specialists will be, so make sure to ask about it.

- **Tax meetings and reviews.** Your wealth advisor should demonstrate a willingness to meet with you on a semi-regular basis to discuss your ongoing tax situation.

Probably the only way to evaluate whether the professional you're working with has these qualities is through a one-on-one interview. You'll find more information about that in the appendix at the back of this book.

### Taxes and your financial services firm

Another important element of this evaluation should be a close look at the firm with which your financial professional is affiliated. Again, the best way to approach the topic is through the use of a brief checklist.

- **Tax sensitivity.** The firm should demonstrate a thorough understanding of tax-related issues in a variety of contexts (investment, estate planning, business succession, etc.). You'll be able to tell if it does by taking a close look at some of its marketing materials, and looking for any mention of tax strategies.

- **Tax attitude.** The firm should foster an attitude that is attentive to the after-tax needs of its clients, and encourages its employees to do the same. Having tax specialists on staff is a good indication that the company is serious about minimizing taxes for its clients.

- **Tax education.** Ideally, you'll want to work with a firm that's committed to educating clients about tax-planning opportunities, and follows up that commitment with tax-specific publications, seminars, and training sessions.

- **Tax services.** More and more firms that work with U/HNWIs are taking their commitment to tax planning a step further, offering U/HNWIs low-cost, in-house tax planning services and access to specialized tax-advantaged investments. Such resources will make it easier for U/HNWIs to keep on top of their tax matters.

Again, it's a good idea to ask about these issues during the initial meeting with your prospective wealth advisor. By sorting these issues out well before any tax-related planning, you'll know whether you'll have to look for outside tax help.

## A final word on tax-wise investing

If I could give one piece of advice to U/HNWIs about tax-planning, it would be this: *buy the best professional help you can afford.* As I've said throughout *True Wealth*, professional advice has a way of paying for itself. This is especially the case when it comes to taxes.

# Key concepts: Chapter thirteen

- Tax planning is one of the most effective, most cost-efficient ways of securing and building upon your wealth.

- Even though many tax loopholes and other tax-advantaged strategies have been eliminated, there is no excuse for ignoring the subject of taxes.

- It's not the money that's on the account statement that matters. Rather, it's the money that makes it into your wallet.

- Tax planning is ultimately about responsibility. That responsibility has three levels:

  (a) the individual. U/HNWIs need to learn about tax regulations and tax planning strategies.

  - U/HNWIs need to develop a general knowledge of their individual tax situation.

  - U/HNWIs also need to understand the tax bracketing system in their jurisdiction

  - Alternative Minimum Tax is a significant threat to many U/HNWIs. For this reason, U/HNWIs need to familiarize themselves with it, and work with skilled professionals to formulate effective strategies to avoid it.

  (b) the portfolio. U/HNWIs need to understand how investment practices will affect the taxation of their wealth.

  - Not all income is taxed in the same way. U/HNWIs need to have a general understanding of the ways capital gains, dividends, and income is taxed in their jurisdiction.

  - Tax efficiency is the measure of how much income from a mutual fund or other pooled products the U/HNWI gets to keep. It is an important issue to keep in mind when selecting these investments.

  - The individual style of the fund manager can have a big impact on tax efficiency. In most cases, it makes sense to select those managers who limit portfolio turnover.

  - Performance figures can be deceiving. When evaluating a given investment, it's important to compare after-tax performance figures. This will help formulate a true understanding of an investment's worth.

  - Offshore tax havens are largely a thing of the past. U/HNWIs would be wise to look elsewhere for strategies that will reduce taxes.

  c) the professional. U/HNWIs need to work with qualified professionals who are aware of tax planning issues. These professionals should work for firms who are committed to helping clients overcome the tax challenges of wealth.

## Resources

Taxes can vary dramatically from jurisdiction to jurisdiction. This makes recommending a single, comprehensive tax planning guide useful to all U/HNWIs everywhere almost impossible. Included below are some suggestions for U/HNWIs living in North America.

***Ernst & Young Tax Guides for U.S. and Canadian citizens***

## Websites

Canada Customs and Revenue Agency *www.ccra-adrc.gc.ca*

The Digital Daily – published by the IRS *www.irs.ustreas.gov*

# section3

## Passing on wealth

With wealth comes responsibility.
A responsibility to protect your wealth
for the next generation and the
community at large. Welcome to your
wealth stewardship.

# Estate planning for U/HNWIs

- *Trends in estate planning*
- *Essential principles of estate planning*
- *Basic goals of an estate plan*
- *Basic features of an estate plan*

*"If rich men would remember that shrouds have no pockets, they would, while living, share their wealth with their children, and give for the good of others, and so know the highest pleasure wealth can give."*

*Tryon Edwards*

N o, we don't generally want to talk about it. Some of us don't even want to *think* about it. But there's no denying it – it's going to happen. And unless you plan ahead, it's going to be expensive. I'm talking, of course, about our eventual demise.

It's easy to see why estate planning is the one area of personal finance that tends to get short shrift from investors. Not only does it touch upon a subject that's emotionally sensitive, but it is often a complicated process. Generally, estate planning involves subjects that lie beyond the expertise of the average investor, and deals with topics most of us have neither the aptitude nor the inclination to learn about. Worst of all, it inevitably costs money, and results in little or no tangible benefit – to our heirs perhaps, but not to us. All of which makes many U/HNWIs consider estate planning a tedious chore.

Like it or not, our death is likely to be the single most important financial event in our life (ironic, but true). If we fail to plan adequately for the transfer of our wealth, we risk squandering an opportunity to make a real difference to the causes we care about. We also risk leaving the people we care about in a dangerous financial position. I'm sure that's not the kind of inheritance most of us are looking pass on.

On the whole, I've found the U/HNWIs I've worked with to be at least *aware* of these issues. For the most part, U/HNWIs understand how important it is to plan ahead for this transfer of wealth, and have taken some tentative steps to ensure this transfer doesn't result in a crippling tax liability for their heirs. Even so, I've found few U/HNWIs are doing everything they can in this area. This chapter will provide you with an overview of some of the most crucial elements of your estate plan, and explain some of the general ideas that go behind constructing a sound estate plan. The chapters that follow will detail some of the specific estate planning strategies and opportunities available to U/HNWIs. By the end of this section, you should be well aware of what you need to do to ensure your estate plan is the best it can be.

Understand, however, that estate planning for U/HNWIs is an extremely complicated subject. So complicated, in fact, that it's impossible for me to give the topic the attention it truly deserves in these short pages. When it comes time to formulate their estate plans, most U/HNWIs will have to rely on the specialized advice of a number of investment, tax, and legal professionals. Many wealth advisors have put together teams of estate planning experts to help this process. In my practice, I've often consulted closely with David Temple, an estate planning specialist in my firm's Vancouver office. His knowledge of all elements of the estate planning process has proven a great help to many of my U/HNWI clients over the years. I've relied upon David's expertise extensively throughout all the chapters in this section.

## Trends in estate planning

Estate planning is bound to become a very popular financial planning topic over the next several years. In the most recent edition of its annual survey of the wealthy in America, U.S. Trust estimated over $5-trillion will change hands over the next 20 years, with over $1-trillion of that to be transferred by the end of the decade.

Most U/HNWIs seem to have made at least rudimentary preparations for this transfer. Fully 84% of those surveyed in the U.S. Trust study responded they had a will in place, while 70% responded they had an estate plan. The majority have discussed that plan with their spouse (89%), and most have familiarized themselves with both federal (79%) and state-level estate taxes (72%). This is all good news, but there are other results that indicate U/HNWIs may have some work to do when it comes to of estate-planning awareness. Only 55% have run through an estimation of the taxes owing on their estate at death. An identical number have placed property into trusts (a core estate planning strategy for U/HNWIs). Perhaps most important of all, only 34% have discussed the contents of their estate plan with their children.

table 14.1: **Estate planning actions taken by U/HNWIs**

| Estate Planning Action | |
| --- | --- |
| Discussed their estate plan with their spouse | 89% |
| Named an executor of their estate | 86% |
| Consulted an attorney | 83% |
| Familiarized themselves with federal estate tax laws | 79% |
| Consulted an accountant | 73% |
| Familiarized themselves with estate laws in their state | 72% |
| Have an estate plan | 70% |
| Named a guardian for their children | 68% |
| Named a trustee for their estate | 67% |
| Put some property into trusts | 55% |
| Developed an estimate of the amount their taxes are likely to total at their death | 55% |
| Consulted an estate planning professional other than an accountant or an attorney | 43% |
| Discussed their estate plan with their children | 34% |

Source: U.S. Trust *Survey of Affluent Americans*

On the whole, U/HNWIs are planning to leave a fairly varied portfolio to their heirs. The bulk of those inherited assets will be investment-grade securities, comprising 50% of the average U/HNWI estate. Investment real estate will be the next biggest chunk, at 20%. And who will be the primary beneficiaries of these estates? Fully 85% of those U/HNWIs surveyed planned to leave the bulk of their assets to their surviving spouse. If they die after their spouse, the average U/HNWI plans to leave about 64% of their wealth to their children, with the remainder going to a variety of relations and other causes.

These statistics prove that when it comes to estate planning, the problem for many U/HNWIs isn't the *complete lack* of a plan, it's the *lack of a complete* plan. While it seems most U/HNWIs have some of the elements of a good estate plan in place, when it comes to some of the more intricate methods of organizing one's estate, there is a significant gap between what U/HNWIs should be doing and what they actually are doing. For that reason, I think it's a good idea to review some of the basic philosophies that make up a sound estate plan.

chart 14.2: **Estate assets of U/HNWIs**

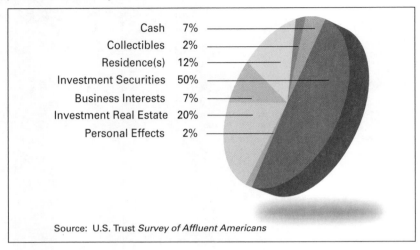

| | |
|---|---|
| Cash | 7% |
| Collectibles | 2% |
| Residence(s) | 12% |
| Investment Securities | 50% |
| Business Interests | 7% |
| Investment Real Estate | 20% |
| Personal Effects | 2% |

Source: U.S. Trust *Survey of Affluent Americans*

chart 14.3: **Disposition of assets U/HNWIs**

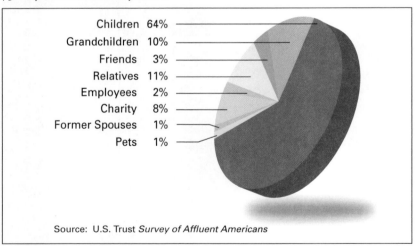

| | |
|---|---|
| Children | 64% |
| Grandchildren | 10% |
| Friends | 3% |
| Relatives | 11% |
| Employees | 2% |
| Charity | 8% |
| Former Spouses | 1% |
| Pets | 1% |

Source: U.S. Trust *Survey of Affluent Americans*

# My approach to estate planning

Estate planning is a highly individual process. But there are some big-picture ideas that go behind every U/HNWI estate plan. I've boiled these down to four essential principles:

### Principle #1: different needs/responsibilities/opportunities

The estates of U/HNWIs are more complicated than those of non-U/HNWIs. And because most U/HNWI estates involve far more money than could ever be reasonably spent in a lifetime, there is more responsibility, too. For this reason, it's essential for U/HNWIs to have a personalized estate plan that specifically addresses these needs and responsibilities, while taking advantage of the opportunities available to U/HNWI estates.

### Principle #2: intentions first

It is my belief that estate planning is not a time for compromise. Your intentions are the single most important factor in determining what estate planning strategies you should use. If you have to sacrifice some taxes or other fees in order to do what you really want to do with your estate plan, then so be it.

In my experience, a lot of U/HNWIs get this one backwards. They spend much time and considerable sums of money organizing their estates in a tax-efficient manner, and for the most part, these people get what they pay for. But when I check their plan against their goals – when I ask them what they're actually looking to accomplish when they pass on their wealth – it's obvious their plan doesn't address their intentions. Make sure you don't fall into the same trap.

### Principle #3: estate planning is an ongoing process

Too many U/HNWIs take a "once and for all" approach to their estate plans. Such an approach is shortsighted and dangerous. Truth be told, an out-of-date estate plan is just as dangerous (and in some cases, even more so) than no estate plan. For this reason, U/HNWIs should establish a schedule for reviewing their wills.

It's tough for me to give U/HNWIs a precise schedule for such revisions. At a bare minimum, your will needs to be reviewed at least every two years, even if there have been no significant changes in your life or your financial circumstances. That doesn't necessarily mean modifications need to be made, but at the very least, you should take the time to sort out your intentions and to review your situation with a skilled professional.

### Principle #4: communication is key

Communication is the key to every successful estate plan. Which is why U/HNWIs should discuss their intentions thoroughly with their immediate family, and with other significant heirs to their estate. There are many ways to do this: either through casual one-on-one conversations or more formal family meetings. Whatever method you choose, such involvement and communication will help avoid the emotional and financial disasters that can erupt over the considerable sums most U/HNWIs leave behind. The alternative to such communication can be ugly – as we'll see in the following case study.

## Case study: Silence breeds legal battles

It should be obvious how dangerous it can be to keep one's family "out of the loop" when it comes to an estate plan. The debacle surrounding Seward Johnson's estate (Seward was the son of the founder of Johnson and Johnson's empire) is a case in point. As a director of J&J from 1921 to 1971, Seward had amassed a large block of Johnson & Johnson stock (around 7 million shares). When he passed away in 1983, he left an immense fortune – somewhere in the neighborhood of $500-million.

Upon Mr. Johnson's death, it was revealed he had written a total of 22 wills in the last 12 years of his life – four of those in the last two months. In the most recent will, Mr. Johnson had overlooked five of the six children from his first marriage, as well as a charitable foundation Mr. Johnson had founded (in his second-to-last will, he had left the foundation $70-million). Instead, he had left the bulk of his assets to his third wife, Basia, whom he had married at the age of 76 (she was 34 at the time). Under terms of the will, Basia was given a life interest in the estate, which would have resulted in a yearly income of about $50-million, as well as the opportunity to borrow unlimited amounts from the estate. Another provision set aside $20-million for the descendants of Basia's father, who were living in Poland.

Needless to say, these provisions came as a complete shock to Seward's children. After finding out they had been disinherited, the children initiated a legal challenge of their father's will, labeling Basia an emotional bully who had coerced her husband into writing a will more favorable to her. Basia fought back by labeling the children greedy golddiggers, presenting the will as evidence of their father's disappointment and embarrassment in them. Shortly after court documents were filed, the case was settled, to the tune of $159-million. Not surprisingly, legal fees for the settlement came in at about $10-million.

It's not my place to say whether the intended distribution of Mr. Johnson's estate was a fair one or not. But what I can say is that the secrecy surrounding those intentions certainly helped to ensure his children wouldn't accept them. While it's not always possible to prevent children from feeling they were mistreated in your will, it is possible to talk to them about it before hand. Sure, this might be uncomfortable, but when it comes right down to it, it's a responsibility U/HNWIs need to accept.

## Case study: good planning; poor communication

Another problem arising from poor communication is leaving heirs unprepared for their wealth. A case I heard about from a colleague of mine in Alberta will illustrate the point.

My colleague had worked with Jim, a successful owner of an oil rig service and repair company in the Edmonton area, for a number of years. Like many business owners in that province's booming oil and gas industry, Jim had built up a substantial net worth. But Jim had lived large through his whole life, and had been in poor health for some time. So while Jim's death at the relatively early age of 58 was a shock to his many friends and family members, it certainly couldn't be called a surprise.

Thankfully, my colleague had drafted an estate plan for Jim some years before, and the two of them had kept it up to date. A well-prepared succession plan ensured the family was able to sell Jim's business at a fair price – more than enough to secure an excellent quality of life for Jim's wife (who received the bulk of the wealth) and to leave a substantial inheritance to each of Jim's three children, Tammy, Dawn, and Jim Jr., (who received about $1-million each). In other words, it seemed like the perfect estate plan.

Perfect in all but communication. My colleague was a little reluctant to go into the exact details, but suffice it to say that over the years, Jim hadn't seen eye-to-eye with his son – particularly when it came to the subject of a suitable career. Three years prior to his father's death, Jim Jr. had left Alberta to study art in Vancouver. The tension resulting from the decision had prevented Jim from telling his son about his estate planning intentions. The result was a son who was completely unprepared for his new fortune.

Almost immediately, this lack of preparation became evident in the kinds of financial decisions Jim Jr. made. Against the advice of his mother, Jim Jr. used a considerable chunk of his inheritance to purchase two rental properties and a loft-style condo in a trendy area of Vancouver. As my colleague explained, Jim Jr. thought he was doing the right thing: a wave of migration from both within Canada and from overseas was making the area an extremely attractive place to live. The idea was to pursue his career in art while he lived off the rental income from his two other properties.

Things didn't quite work out that way. It turned out that Jim Jr. wasn't exactly cut out to be a landlord – finding tenants, making repairs, and the other hassles of real estate didn't leave a lot of time for art. If that weren't enough, property values in Vancouver had begun to decline, and while Jim Jr.'s tenants did provide him with an income, property taxes and repairs burned through most of that fairly quickly. To top it all off, his loft turned out to be one of Vancouver's infamous "leaky condos," requiring several thousand dollars in additional repairs. Faced with the mounting possibility of his own bankruptcy, Jim Jr. decided to sell one of his properties and his condo – both at a considerable loss – and move into one of his own apartments. All told, Jim Jr.'s foray into real estate had cost him well over half his inheritance.

To be fair to the father in this story, it's often difficult to foresee what kinds of decisions your heirs will make with the money you leave them. But at the very least, Jim should have discussed his intentions fully with his son, and helped him prepare for the eventual responsibilities of his wealth. By involving my colleague in such discussions, Jim would have also given his son something much more valuable than money – a source of financial advice. This would have given Jim Jr. someone to consult with before making rash decisions about his wealth.

## The basic goals of an estate plan

Estate planning is a highly personal process, driven more by the specific needs of the individual than by some kind of a cut-and-dried idea of what constitutes a "good" estate plan. But every well-designed estate plan should cover the following basic goals:

### Goal #1: Financial security for heirs

An estate plan is essentially an extended financial plan for your heirs. Ideally, your estate plan should provide your immediate family (your spouse, your children) with the means to secure a high quality of life for a given number of years.

## Goal #2: Retention of control

An estate plan makes it possible for you to do what you want with your money. All else is secondary. Whatever your goals for your money, your estate plan should strive to make them happen in the best possible way. Keep this in mind whenever you feel bogged down by the complicated legal and tax challenges that U/HNWI estate plans often generate.

## Goal #3: Minimization of tax

Another goal of all estate plans is the minimization of tax. The reason is simple: less money for the taxman means more money for heirs. That said, there are many strategies for accomplishing this goal – and not all will be suitable for every individual. Which makes a careful review of tax saving opportunities an important part of every estate plan.

## Goal #4: Estate liquidity

Another important goal of all estate plans is liquidity. I hate to say it, but if you're like most U/HNWIs, your death won't be cheap. Every estate plan should account for the bills, taxes, and fees that accompany every death, and provide executors with with a certain level of immediate liquidity. Otherwise, they may have to sell assets to pay taxes or fees.

## Goal #5: Business succession plan

For U/HNWIs who are business owners, the estate plan should include provisions that clearly dictate plans for the sale or transfer of a closely-held business. Ideally, such provisions should allow the family to obtain maximum value for the business without disrupting the viability of the business itself. Depending on the needs of the individual, this may involve a buy-sell agreement with existing partners, the identification of other potential buyers, or the complete liquidation of the business. Whatever option you choose, this process should be clearly defined and prepared for well in advance.

**Goal #6: "Bulletproofing"**

Finally, every estate plan needs to be "bulletproofed." That is, it needs to be constructed to withstand potential legal challenges from heirs, creditors, or the taxman. The exact form of this preparation will depend on the complexity of the U/HNWI's circumstances. But at the very least, this means every estate plan needs to be thoroughly reviewed by appropriate tax and legal professionals before being considered complete.

# The basic features of an estate plan

We'll discuss many of the practical strategies for achieving the above goals in the following chapters. In the meantime, it's important for U/HNWIs to be aware of some of the basic features of every estate plan.

## Your **will**

I once heard a story that the shortest legal will on record was written in Japan. It consisted of three words: *all to wife*. While the brevity and clarity of such a will is certainly admirable, most U/HNWIs will need something a little more complex. It's a little beyond my scope to provide a run-down of all the legal details that govern wills in your jurisdiction, but what I can do is to review some basic points that U/HNWIs often overlook when writing their wills.

First things first: all U/HNWIs need a will. End of discussion. Most jurisdictions have pre-set rules that prescribe who gets what in cases where the deceased has no will (typically called "dying intestate"). Needless to say, these schedules often don't reflect the complicated family situations of the age, and have little or no regard for tax-efficiency. This means those U/HNWIs who pass away without a will are doing their families and their communities a tremendous disservice, squandering their wealth and potentially condemning their families to a lifetime of financial hardship. Such oversight is absolutely opposed to the philosophy of responsibility that I advocate. This is why I make it my personal duty to ensure that all of my clients have a proper will in place. I shouldn't have to say any more than that.

One of the purposes of your will is to establish how you want your assets distributed to your beneficiaries. These decisions are of course highly personal, but no matter what your wishes, you'll need to pay particular attention to the exact legal wording of your bequests. In certain jurisdictions, legal language may force a particular distribution of a given asset if one of your beneficiaries predeceases you (the most common case is to automatically pass on the asset to the beneficiary's heirs). Such automatic re-distribution may not be what you're looking for. Which brings up a second point about wills. It's important to think of a number of "what if" scenarios before finalizing your bequests. In most jurisdictions, if a provision in the will is no longer applicable (you sold that car you had originally destined for your nephew, or your uncle Harry has predeceased you and can no longer inherit your collection of antique stamps), it will simply be ignored. But that can lead to unnecessary complications and delays. It can be very costly to update a will every time a beneficiary change is necessary, so make sure to name some alternative beneficiaries in your will.

Another important consideration to keep in mind is what you *won't* be able to do in your will. Many jurisdictions establish certain minimums to which spouses and close family members are entitled, and most jurisdictions require your estate to continue providing adequate support for your dependents (note this law applies only to *dependents*). In addition, wills have no jurisdiction over assets that already have other legal means of being distributed: property that is jointly owned, or a business that has a buy-sell agreement, or even RRSPs with a named beneficiary are common examples. Finally, most jurisdictions now have laws that prevent the draconian "power-beyond-the-grave" provisions that were possible in previous generations. If you're looking to have your will establish certain complicated conditions upon which your beneficiaries will or will not inherit, you can forget about it.

A last word on wills: your last will and testament is no place to save a couple of bucks. Sure, a properly legalized will costs more than a $29 software kit or a stack of pre-fab forms. But trust me on this one: the complexity of a U/HNWI estate demands more rigorous attention than the do-it-yourself approach can provide. As I've said throughout *True Wealth*, professional advice has a funny way of paying for itself. This is as true of wills as it is of any element of your wealth management plan.

## Your **executor**

The second purpose of your will is to appoint an executor. Think of your executor as the "manager" of your estate. This person will have four key responsibilities:

- **Arranging your funeral.** Your executor will be responsible for making funeral arrangements. If you've left no instructions or a statement of wishes regarding your funeral, your executor will work closely with your family and make appropriate arrangements. If no family is present, your executor will make those decisions alone.

- **Managing your estate.** Your executor will be responsible for locating estate assets and registering them in the name of the estate, in preparation for their distribution. Depending on the provisions of your will, your executor may also be responsible for overseeing the management of those assets until they are distributed to heirs.

- **Paying bills, fees, taxes, and debts.** Your executor is in charge of paying all bills, fees, and taxes related to your estate, as well as settling any outstanding debts. Depending on your jurisdiction, this may involve filing a terminal tax return.

- **Distributing assets.** Your executor will also be responsible for making timely and appropriate distributions of assets to your heirs. This of course will be done according to the provisions of your will.

In most jurisdictions, executors are entitled to a basic fee for their service. In theory, this entitlement applies to both professional and lay executors, but in reality, executors who are close friends or family members often don't charge for their services. The exact amount depends on the jurisdiction, but in most cases executors can charge anywhere from 3% to 5% of the value of the estate. This is only a very rough guide: most of the time this fee will vary according to the *complexity* of the estate rather than its *value*.

The choice of an executor is largely a personal one, but the decision should not be made casually. Here's a quick review of some important points when deciding on your executor. First and foremost: make sure to discuss the matter closely with your prospective choice well in advance. Many think being appointed an executor is an honor, but in reality, it is more of a job. Perhaps more importantly, accepting the role of executor often means accepting legal responsibility for the ongoing management of estate assets – something not everyone is willing to accept. Number two: make sure to assign a back-up choice. This should be common sense, for the reasons we discussed above in regard to naming alternative beneficiaries. Number three: don't automatically assume a close friend or family member is the best choice. They'll likely be busy grieving, and may not be able to make proper financial decisions while dealing with their emotions. Not only that, they may run into conflicts of interest or family members who question their judgement or actions. If you insist on appointing a family member as your executor, then it probably makes sense to select a co-executor – someone outside the family who has an objective viewpoint and provides balance to the family member's decisions.

These days, the responsibilities of the executor require a fair bit of investment acumen. This is even more the case for executors of a U/HNWI estate. In practical terms, that means you should choose someone with considerable experience in managing money – a trusted business associate, or perhaps a professional the family has known for some time. If your will involves complicated trusts, or might be subject to legal challenge, then a professional executor makes sense. Professional executors are usually accountants, lawyers, or members of a trust company, making them capable administrators of your estate. When the estate involves managing assets for a number of years, or the disbursement of business assets, a professional trustee can be counted on to make decisions that are in *everyone's* best interests. Professional executors typically charge a percentage on estate assets under a certain amount, and a lower percentage on anything above that. That's a little more than what family members typically charge, but as I've said before, professional advice tends to pay for itself.

## Power **of attorney**

No estate plan is complete without a power of attorney. True, your power of attorney is technically a *living* consideration: it deals with events and issues you'll face while still alive. But to my mind, the purpose of such a document is much the same as a will. That is, it documents your wishes, and is to be used at a time when you won't be able to express those wishes yourself. For this reason, I typically recommend my U/HNWI clients organize and assign their power of attorney while considering their estate plans.

Much like your executor, your power of attorney is in an immensely powerful position. In theory, this person has the power to enact any financial decision you would make yourself – including the power to buy or sell investments or real estate, make charitable contributions, loan money, etc. Obviously, this kind of power is easy to abuse. That's why it's often a good idea to write some limitations as to what decisions your power of attorney is entitled to make. Another solution is to appoint joint powers of attorney, or to make the decisions your power of attorney makes subject to review by a third party.

Spurred on by the changing values of their residents, many jurisdictions are now scrapping the old laws that supervise powers of attorney in favor of new laws that allow for broader powers over the individual's health and welfare (British Columbia's Representation Agreement Act is a good example). Make sure to investigate what the standard is in your jurisdiction, and make appropriate arrangements.

## A final word on estate planning

While estate planning can be a complicated subject, it revolves around a very simple idea. As a U/HNWI, you have a responsibility to be a capable *steward* of wealth – that is, to protect wealth for the next generation. In order to ensure that wealth actually passes into their hands, you have an obligation to keep it organized, and take advantage of specific opportunities that will ensure it is in an environment where it can grow.

# Key concepts: Chapter fourteen

- Our death is likely to be the single most important financial event in our life.

- Most U/HNWIs seem to have taken at least basic steps towards organizing their estates, but more can be done.

- Estate planning is guided by four simple principles:

    (a) U/HNWIs have unique financial needs; their estate plans must be equally unique

    (b) the primary goal of any estate plan is to satisfy the intentions of the U/HNWI

    (c) estate planning is an ongoing process requiring monitoring and periodic reviews

    (d) U/HNWIs need to communicate their intentions for their estate plan with family and friends well before that plan is finalized

- There are five basic goals of every estate plan

    (a) retention of control – to make your intentions possible

    (b) minimization of tax – less tax means more money for your heirs

    (c) liquidity – to satisfy the immediate needs of your heirs, and to prevent assets from being sold to pay taxes and fees

    (d) business succession plan – a must for all U/HNWIs with a business

    (e) bulletproofing – to ensure your intentions can survive legal challenge

- No matter how complicated the estate, every estate plan has basic features in common. U/HNWIs need to familiarize themselves with these features.

- The importance of a will suggests it requires qualified legal advice.

- Your executor is the manager of your estate. This person has a number of important duties; as such, U/HNWIs should think carefully about their choice, and have a back-up choice.

- No estate plan is complete without a power of attorney document. Even though power of attorney is a living consideration, its similarity to your will suggests you assign it while constructing your estate plan. Your power of attorney is in an immensely powerful position; it makes sense to be prudent about your selection.

## Resources

Estate planning relies heavily on the estate and tax regulations of the jurisdiction in which you live. Once again, that makes a single comprehensive book or website that all U/HNWIs would find useful impossible. Here are a few selections for North Americans, as well as some general estate planning material that explains some of the central concepts common to all estate plans.

**You Can't Take It With You** by Sandra Foster

***Beyond the Grave: the Right Way and the Wrong Way of Leaving Your Children Money*** by Gerald M. Condon and Jefferey L. Condon

***The Artful Dodger's Guide to Planning Your Estate*** by Thomas Hart Harley

***Funding Your Dreams Generation to Generation*** by Carol Akright

***How to Inherit Money*** by Michael Alexander

## Websites

Nolo ***www.nolo.com*** – law in everyday English

***www.estateplanninglinks.com*** – loads of links on estate planning

Wills on the Web ***www.ca-probate.com/wills.htm*** – real wills of the famous and not-so-famous

# Dealing with estate taxes

- *Tax treatment of your estate*
- *Rules for dual jurisdictions*
- *Probate taxes*
- *Tax minimization strategies*

*"Noah must have taken into the Ark two taxes, one male and one female, and did they multiply beautifully: next to guinea pigs, taxes must have been the most prolific animals."*

**Will Rogers**

Looking to turn a mild-mannered, even-tempered U/HNWI into a raving lunatic? Here's what you do. First, take a complicated, technical subject like estate planning. Then combine it with a topic that's often beyond our power to even control – like taxes. What do you get? A subject that will make even the most gentle U/HNWI furious.

You'll forgive me for trying to take a light approach to a difficult subject. In reality, estate taxes are anything but funny. The high values of many U/HNWI estates often result in excessive tax bills – as much as 55% in some jurisdictions. Without prior planning, there's a good chance a substantial portion of the estate will be lost to these taxes. By not incorporating some basic tax-planning strategies into your estate plan, you risk leaving behind an estate that offers little or nothing to your beneficiaries. Fail to plan for probate, and you could actually leave a financial burden for your heirs.

Like it or not, estate planning means planning for taxes. This chapter will give you a basic grounding in what's likely to happen to your estate from a tax perspective, and will provide a general survey of some common techniques to minimize the tax owing on your estate. Reading through this chapter can serve as a good starting point prior to discussing the matter more fully with your financial professional. It should help you ensure you're doing everything you possibly can to keep taxes from eating away a substantial portion of your estate.

## Taxes and your estate – the basic rules

We'll start with a brief review of some of the important rules that govern the taxation of estates in both the U.S. and Canada. This basic knowledge will let you know what you're up against when it comes time to organize your estate. At the same time, the subject of tax could easily fill an entire volume (in fact, it fills several!), so what you're getting here is only the most basic survey. You'll want to follow up with a tax specialist for the details.

### Estate taxes in the U.S.

In the U.S., estate taxes are calculated as a percentage of the *total value* of the estate. The amount of that taxation is in some cases extreme: estate taxes can top 55% in some states. Combined with the punitive generation-skipping transfer tax (GSTT – imposed on transfers to heirs two or more generations younger at a flat rate of 55%), these taxes can devastate a U/HNWI estate.

Thankfully, there are a number of credits available to offset U.S. estate taxes. When assets are left outright to a spouse who is a U.S. resident, the spouse may claim an unlimited "marital deduction" which offsets tax on all assets transferred. In addition, all U.S. citizens may claim a "Unified Credit" that completely offsets any tax owing on estates of up to $675,000 in value. That doesn't do much to help U/HNWIs, but this credit is expected to rise in stages up to $1,000,000 by 2006. In addition, similar deductions exist when assets are transferred to specialized trusts.

The United States government tinkers with estate law on a fairly regular basis. Over the past several months, that tinkering has become substantial, and has caused no end of grief to U/HNWIs and financial professionals alike. At the time I write this, there is ongoing debate over whether President Bush will eliminate the estate tax altogether – or at least reduce it for highly valued estates. Such a move would certainly be welcome news to some U/HNWIs, but recent reports from Washington suggest there may be a substantial backtracking on some of the administration's previous commitments. It's difficult to say just how all the political wrangling will resolve itself, but until the proposed changes actually become law, it would be wise for U/HNWIs to assume at least a basic estate tax liability in their estate planning calculations.

## Estate taxes **in Canada**

Even though estate taxes in the proper sense were eliminated in Canada back in the early 1970s, don't think the government doesn't want to get its share of your estate. In Canada, taxes on estates are now based on the *undeclared profits* accrued to the assets in the estate, rather than the total estate value. The valuation of assets is based on the increase between the day those assets were acquired and the day of death. For those assets acquired before 1972, valuation will be calculated based on the value of the assets on December 31st, 1971 – the day the capital gains tax came into existence. What's more, your executor must file a "terminal tax return" that declares all income for the year of your death. Any taxes that might be owing on that income will be payable by the estate.

That's not to say there aren't remedies for these taxes. Certain assets may be passed to beneficiaries in Canada without tax, given certain conditions. Your principal residence is an example. Most assets can be left to your spouse at the original cost of the assets, meaning tax will be deferred until the death of the second spouse (this is commonly called a spousal rollover). There are special rules regarding RRSPs and RRIFs, but in most cases, it is at least possible to transfer these plans free of tax when the beneficiary is a spouse, and in some specialized cases, if the beneficiary is a dependent child or dependent grandchild. U/HNWIs who own qualified small businesses or qualified farm properties may be able to utilize a special $500,000 capital gains exemption, though the operative word here is qualified – there are a number of tests the business must pass before the deduction is granted. A qualified farm property can also be transferred to the children of the deceased without triggering any taxable capital gain. Obviously, these rules make the selection of beneficiaries an important part of all estate planning in Canada.

When the beneficiary is not a spouse – as will be the case with all married U/HNWIs when the second of the two partners dies – the rules become more complicated. In the majority of cases, Canada Customs and Revenue will apply deemed disposition rules to most assets. That doesn't mean the government will actually force your heirs to sell anything, but heirs will face a tax bill as if it had. In most cases, it's the estate that's liable for any tax, not the beneficiary. That means if an estate doesn't have the cash to pay its taxes, your executor may have to liquidate some assets to pay the tax bill.

Like its counterparts around the world, the Canadian government is notorious for tinkering with the tax laws. In recent years, there have been rumors of a re-introduction of a tax on the *value* of an estate rather than the current system of tax on the *gains* on assets contained within it. It's tough to say if that will happen, but in my mind, it's never a good idea to base your financial plans on speculation. Better for Canadian U/HNWIs to construct an estate plan that solves today's challenges, rather than one that hopes to solve something that may or may not come to pass.

## Taxation of assets **in dual jurisdictions**

If you're a U/HNWI who spends a significant part of the year away from your country of residence, estate planning can be complex. If you've acquired assets in the second country, you'll need to review the important laws and regulations regarding the taxation of those assets upon your death. Here is a brief overview of some of the important regulations facing Canadian residents who own property in the U.S. – a fairly typical situation for Canadian U/HNWIs. Again, the rules and regulations will differ depending on the two jurisdictions where you own property, but the general principles should give you a basic understanding of what you may be subject to.

Generally, the U.S. government wants its share of money on assets domiciled within its borders. This includes interest, dividends, and capital gains generated by most forms of real estate, U.S. equity securities, and most (but not all) debts of U.S. issuers. This general rule is subject to a variety of tax treaties, and can differ for residents of different countries. Even so, it should be clear that such regulations could expose a non–U.S. resident to "double taxation": once by their home jurisdiction, once by Uncle Sam.

That's not to say foreign taxpayers have no recourse. In general, worldwide estates valued under U.S. $675,000 are exempt from U.S. tax. If the worldwide estate of a Canadian resident is under U.S. $1.2-million, U.S. estate tax is limited to U.S. real property and certain business assets. Under U.S. law, Canadian residents cannot claim the same unified credit or marital credits in the form they are available to U.S. residents. Most Canadians will have access to a portion of the unified credit equal to the greater of U.S. $13,000 or $220,550 multiplied by the value of the U.S. gross estate divided by the value of the worldwide gross estate (see diagram 15.1). In practical terms, this means there is little relief for U/HNWIs with substantial worldwide assets but few U.S. taxable assets.

diagram 15.1: **U.S. unified credit calculation for Canadians**

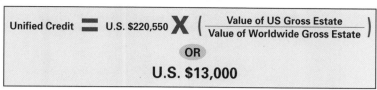

Canadians are also entitled to a marital credit equal to the lesser of (a) U.S. estate tax payable on the property left to the spouse, or (b) an amount equal to the unified credit as calculated above. In addition, Canada Customs and Revenue provides a Canadian tax credit for U.S. estate taxes paid – this helps reduce exposure to double taxation. That looks good on paper, but in practice, this credit often isn't all it's cracked up to be. Because of the different deferral opportunities available in Canada, it's quite possible there will be no Canadian taxes against which the U.S. estate tax credit may be applied.

## Probate: **another form of estate tax**

Probate taxes are another form of estate tax that U/HNWIs need to deal with. Probate is the general name for the legal process undertaken by the court to itemize and approve the transfer of assets upon your death. As such, it is often a legal necessity: many financial institutions will not transfer assets until they receive a copy of the official probate document. Every jurisdiction handles probate a little differently, but at the very least, it seems to me all U/HNWIs need to have at least a general understanding of how the system works.

In some jurisdictions, there may be some question about whether probate is even legal. Such was the case in Canada until very recently. Back in 1998, The Supreme Court of Canada decided that Ontario probate practices were actually an illegal tax on estates. The exact details of the case were fairly technical, but suffice it to say the final decision was something estate planners could understand – and be happy about. Unfortunately, the issue was quickly resolved with the passing of a new probate law (probate is *officially* a tax now). Call it by whatever name you want, probate is a significant threat to all U/HNWIs. While smaller estates are often protected by flat fees and exemptions, the size of most U/HNWI estates almost ensures heirs will pay a hefty probate bill.

table 15.2a: **Probate tax schedule in Canada**

| Province | Value of Estate | Probate Costs |
|----------|-----------------|---------------|
| British Columbia | Under $10,000<br>$10,000 – $25,000<br>$25,001 – $50,000<br><br>Over $50,000 | No fees<br>$208<br>$208 + $6 per $1,000 or fraction thereof<br>$358 + $14 per $1,000 or fraction thereof in excess of $50,000 |
| Alberta | Up to $10,000<br>$10,001 – $25,000<br>$25,001 – $125,000<br>$125,001 – $250,000<br>$250,001+ | $25<br>$100<br>$200<br>$300<br>$400 |
| Saskatchewan | | $7 per $1,000 or fraction thereof (no maximum) |
| Manitoba | Under $10,000<br>Over $10,000 | $50<br>$50 + $6 per $1,000 or fraction thereof in excess of $10,000 |
| Ontario | Under $50,000<br><br>Over $50,000 | $5 per $1,000 or fraction thereof<br>$250 + $15 per $1,000 or fraction thereof in excess of $50,000 |
| Quebec | | Probate not required for notorial Wills; flat fee of $69 for English form Wills |
| New Brunswick | Up to $5,000<br>$5,001 to $10,000<br>$10,001 to $15,000<br>$15,001 to $20,000<br>Over $20,000 | $25<br>$50<br>$75<br>$100<br>$5 per $1,000 or fraction thereof |

Source: Merrill Lynch

Every jurisdiction takes a slightly different approach to the way it charges probate taxes, but in general, they are structured on a sliding scale: the more your estate is worth, the more you pay. The chart here details probate taxes for Canadian provinces. Although the precise categories will change according to where you live, the general structure should serve as a good example of how probate works.

table 15.2b: **Probate tax schedule in Canada**

| Province | Value of Estate | Probate Costs |
|---|---|---|
| Nova Scotia | Up to $10,000<br>$10,001 to $25,000<br>$25,001 to $50,000<br>$50,001 to $100,000<br>$100,001 to $150,000<br><br><br><br>$150,001 to $200,000<br><br><br><br>$200,001 + | $70<br>$150<br>$250<br>$700<br>$700 +$12 per $1,000 or fraction thereof in excess of $100,000<br>$700 + $12 per $1,000 or fraction thereof in excess of $150,000<br>$700 + $12 per $1,000 or fraction thereof in excess of $200,000 |
| Prince Edward Island | Up to $10,000<br>$10,001 to $25,000<br>$25,001 to $50,000<br>$50,001 to $100,000<br>Over $100,000 | $65<br>$115<br>$215<br>$415<br>$415 + $4 per $1,000 or fraction thereof in excess of $100,000 |
| Newfoundland | Under $1,000<br>Over $1,000 | $80<br>Value of estate multiplied by 0.005 + $75 |
| Yukon | | $140 regardless of estate size |
| Northwest Territories/ Nunavut | Up to $500<br>$Up to $1,000<br>Over $1,000 | $8<br>$15<br>$15 + $3 per $1,000 or fraction thereof in excess of $1,000 |

Source: Merrill Lynch

It should be obvious how threatening probate can be to U/HNWI estates. But besides the money, what makes probate threatening is how it can delay the transfer of assets to your heirs. It's not uncommon for probate to take weeks or even months, and until the process is completed, assets usually can't be transferred. In extreme cases, probate can be a "catch 22" for your heirs: heirs may need quick access to cash to pay taxes owing on the estate, but may be unable to do so because the estate is tied up in probate.

So how does a U/HNWI deal with probate? There are a number of different strategies, some of which we'll discuss below. By and large, they all focus on the idea of holding assets *outside* the estate (remember, probate taxes are charged only on those assets in the estate). If your estate is a large one, keep this general principle in mind: transferring assets to various financial structures outside of your estate will save your estate thousands of dollars.

## Tax minimization strategies

Despite what governments would have us believe, estate planning opportunities do exist. Estate taxes and other fees can be minimized by taking advantage of certain financial structures and tax-deferral strategies. We'll deal with two of the most sophisticated strategies – trusts and charitable giving – in following chapters. In the meantime, here are some other steps U/HNWIs can take to reduce the tax payable upon their death.

### Transfers or gifts

Probably the most simple way for U/HNWIs to reduce the size of their estates is to give their money away through "strategic giving." The concept is simple: you have more money than you'll ever need, so instead of forcing heirs to wait for their inheritance, you give some of it to them now. By doing so, you can enjoy seeing the benefit of your inheritance during your lifetime and reduce the tax liability you leave behind.

Notice I said *reduce* – not eliminate. In most jurisdictions, there are limits to what you can give away in any year without incurring some kind of tax or penalty. In the U.S., for instance, taxpayers may gift up to $10,000 to one individual per year. Although that number might be a rather insignificant chunk of a U/HNWI estate, given enough beneficiaries and enough time, it's theoretically possible for U/HNWIs to whittle down the tax liability on their estates through this kind of giving.

Be aware, however, that there are very stringent rules designed to prevent one from using strategic gifting to avoid paying taxes altogether. In most jurisdictions, excessive gifts or transfers will result in a tax liability for the giver: the tax authorities will commonly deem assets disposed at Fair Market Value and give you a tax bill for any capital gain. If the gift is to certain related minors, most jurisdictions will attribute income from the proceeds of the gift back to the giver – this to discourage paper transfers of assets that really don't result in any change of control. These and other types of rules fall under the general name of income attribution rules, and they will differ according to the situation and the jurisdiction. I've included the *income attribution* rules for Canadian immediate family members in chart 15.3. Once again, the rules affecting you might be a little different, but the general structure should give you a good idea as to how a simple gift can trigger a hefty tax liability.

table 15.3: **Income attribution schedule, Canada**

**Transfer of Interest-Earning Types of Assets (e.g. Cash Accounts, GICs, T-bills)**

| Connected person receiving assets | Does deemed disposition trigger immediate capital gain? | Who reports future interest income on their own tax return? |
|---|---|---|
| Spouse | NO | Person who transferred assets |
| Child under 18 | NO | Person who transferred assets |
| Child over 18 | NO | Adult child |

**Transfer of Appreciable Assets (e.g. Stocks, Bonds, Real Estate)**

| Connected person receiving assets | If deemed disposition triggers immediate capital gain, who reports it for tax purposes? | Who reports future interest dividends on their own tax return? | Who reports future capital gains on their own tax return? |
|---|---|---|---|
| Spouse | No deemed dispostion *(unless transfer at FMV)* | Person who transferred assets *(unless transfer at FMV)* | Person who transferred assets *(unless transfer at FMV)* |
| Child under 18 | Person who transferred assets | Person who transferred assets | Minor child |
| Child over 18 | Person who transferred assets | Adult child | Adult child |

*Note that the attribution rules become irrelevant after the death of person who transferred assets.
Source: Merrill Lynch

If you're planning on giving away a significant portion of your estate before you die, make sure to consider the decision carefully. First, you'll need to be completely comfortable with relinquishing control over an asset. While most of us are prepared for that when we give cash or securities, we may not be when we give real estate or business assets. Second, you'll also need to ensure you can afford to part with the assets. That's usually not a problem with more modest gifts, but I have known of a few cases where the gifts were so substantial that it impacted the giver's ability to provide for themselves.

## Life **insurance**

For many people, life insurance is all about financial protection for one's family. That's usually not a pressing issue for most U/HNWIs, but that doesn't mean U/HNWIs should simply ignore the subject altogether. Structured properly, a life insurance policy can offset taxes owing on other portions of the estate, help the U/HNWI avoid probate, and provide tax-deferral opportunities that would be otherwise unavailable. That makes it one of the building blocks of any U/HNWI estate plan.

In the most basic scenario, the proceeds from a life insurance policy can offset taxes owing on other portions of the estate. Because the total value of policy premiums will most likely end up being much lower than the total value of the insurance, you may end up paying for estate taxes using "discounted" dollars – dollars that you were able to buy from the insurance company for less than a dollar. In most jurisdictions, policies can be structured to provide a tax-free benefit, and if a policy is held outside the will, proceeds won't be tied up by probate, meaning your heirs have an immediate source of cash after your death. This could be the perfect solution to a stock portfolio with a low cost basis, for example, or an asset heirs might find difficult to liquidate at fair value (a vacation property, for example).

In recent years, one particular form of insurance – universal life – has seen increasing popularity as an estate planning tool. Essentially, a universal life policy is an insurance policy with a tax-sheltered savings account attached to it. Like a registered tax deferral account (a 401-k in the U.S., or an RRSP in Canada), investment savings compound tax free within a universal policy. That makes universal life particularly attractive to high-income earners who have already "maxed out" other tax-deferral options, and are looking to save more.

Even with all these benefits, life insurance isn't always the best solution for every U/HNWI. In many cases, those in poor health may be rejected as ineligible by an insurance company. In others, ill health may cause the premiums to be so high the policy becomes unaffordable. That's why I suggest U/HNWIs purchase insurance as early as they can – preferably well before the age where medical conditions become a problem.

## Joint **ownership**

Joint ownership can be an effective solution to probate taxes. In such a scenario, the U/HNWI establishes equal ownership of a given asset with another party. Upon the death of the U/HNWI, assets pass to the second owner directly, without having to pass through probate. Not only will this save money, it will speed up the transfer of assets.

Depending on your jurisdiction, there are different types of joint ownership, and different regulations as to what kind of assets can be jointly owned. In Canada, for example, if ownership is registered as "joint ownership with rights of survivorship," the asset will pass automatically to the co-owner without having to go through probate. Ownership registered as "tenancy in common," however, won't – it will be governed by provisions in the will. Certain assets may have different rules when it comes to registering them jointly. In Canada, government savings bonds may only be registered jointly upon maturity, for instance, while RRSPs and RRIFs can't be registered jointly at all.

While joint ownership may help you avoid probate, it probably won't help you with taxes. Most of the time, the original owner will be responsible for income generated from the asset (of course, this will be subject to the income attribution rules of your particular jurisdiction). And if there's a capital gain on the asset at the time it is registered jointly, the original owner will most likely be liable for the bill. In addition, many jurisdictions have taken steps to ensure thinly-disguised joint ownerships are actually classified as gifts or transfers, and subject to appropriate gift taxes.

But to my mind, the main drawback of joint ownership is a practical one. Joint ownership forces a U/HNWI to relinquish control over a given asset – that control is something most U/HNWIs aren't prepared to sacrifice. If you're not in the habit of working with a partner when it comes to making financial decisions (if the asset owned is real estate, for instance, you'll have to obtain consent if you ever want to sell), you're probably better off investigating other probate reduction strategies. And of course, there's the issue of risk. If your second owner becomes embroiled in bankruptcy proceedings or a divorce, for instance, joint assets may be involved in any settlement. The same scenario applies if you and your joint owner have a "falling out." In extreme cases, a second owner may liquidate the asset, or ask the court to force a sale in order to settle differences. All of which means joint ownership is a strategy that should be carefully considered before any decisions are made.

## Estate freeze

One sophisticated tax reduction strategy available to U/HNWIs is an *estate freeze*. For those U/HNWIs who own an operating business or a holding company, such a strategy can be a highly effective method to limit tax owing upon death.

There are many ways to implement an estate freeze. The general idea behind them all goes something like this: an investor locks in ("freezes") the value of an asset at its present value, retaining control over the asset but transferring future growth (and the taxes on that growth) to the next generation. This is commonly done through a reorganization of the shares of an existing operating company. In such a scenario, the U/HNWI exchanges existing common shares for special "freeze-preferred" shares of equal value. All existing value would be captured in the preferred shares (which would retain voting rights), while all future growth would accrue to the new class of common shares. In essence, the tax liability of the estate is frozen at its present value, while the U/HNWI retains control.

In most cases, such a reorganization can be structured without triggering any immediate tax liability. But it's a complicated strategy, meaning professional tax and legal advice will almost always be required. The key is to establish *equal value* between the common shares and the freeze preferred shares. In practical terms, that usually means assigning special characteristics to the freeze preferred shares, such as:

(a) **redemption feature:** the holder is able to redeem the preferred shares at the original value for which they were exchanged.

(b) **dividend entitlement:** the holder of preferred shares is entitled to dividends, payable at the discretion of the company's board of directors.

(c) **preferential consideration:** preferred entitlement upon liquidation of the company.

(d) **price adjustment:** the shares hold a price adjustment clause.

An estate freeze makes sense in a variety of circumstances, but not in every one. If the ability to meet anticipated future needs is even remotely in question, it's best not to initiate an estate freeze. If the U/HNWI is separated or divorced – or if an existing marriage is unstable – a freeze may cause more harm than good (this is particularly true of those U/HNWIs with children from a second marriage).

Another potential problem is the timing of a freeze: on one hand, it makes sense to freeze as *soon* as possible to minimize tax; on the other hand it makes sense to freeze as *late* as possible in order to ensure an appropriate lifestyle for the U/HNWI. Finding an appropriate balance can be extremely difficult, which is why it's important to run through possible scenarios with a qualified professional before making any final decisions.

## Case study: Wasting freeze whittles down liability

When the target of an estate freeze is a business, the freeze can take the form of a "wasting freeze," in which tax liability is not only frozen, but is gradually diminished through the use of tax-advantaged corporate dividends and share redemptions. A client of mine recently incorporated such a strategy. Here's a brief review of what happened.

Gary owns a large agricultural operation (a nursery) on the outskirts of a Vancouver suburb. Like many U/HNWIs, Gary has built up a substantial portfolio in addition to his business assets. Gary has always been a buy-and-hold investor – I suppose that's natural for someone who grows trees for a living. While that's a good strategy for his portfolio, the low cost basis of most of his assets would mean a big tax hit for his heirs. This problem was something that Gary wanted to address in his estate plan.

As I explained to him at the time, one possible solution would be for Gary to transfer a good chunk of his portfolio to his business. At the time, I recommended transferring investments with a fair market value of $1-million and a cost base of $100,000 to the business. The business would then issue a $100,000 note and 900 preferred shares with a redemption value of $1,000 each back to Gary (such a transaction is fully authorized under section 85 of the Federal Income Tax Act).

Such a transaction should save Gary's heirs a lot of tax. If all goes according to plan, the company's investments will generate investment income of about $75,000 a year, and generate an annual tax refund of $20,000. Each year, the company will redeem 60 of Gary's preferred shares, on which Gary will pay a rate of 36% tax. Over the course of time, tax liability will be considerably diminished – in ten years, his heirs will have to deal with an accrued gain of $300,000 instead of $900,000. More importantly, if Gary's company sells the investments for capital gains sometime in the future, Gary's preferred shares can be redeemed out of the company's capital dividend account, and transferred free of tax to Gary, leaving no liability for his heirs. This is a great way to not only freeze taxable gains, but gradually eliminate them over time.

## Holding **companies**

Another strategy for U/HNWIs who own their own businesses is to create a qualified "holding company," and then transfer ownership of an existing company to the holding company. In the past, such a structure allowed for dramatic tax savings for those U/HNWIs who were in the top tax brackets. However, recent calibrations between the tax rates for corporations and individuals in many jurisdictions have eroded such savings – to the point where a U/HNWI might pay *more* tax by transferring assets to a holding company.

Even so, there are still a number of advantages to using a holding company. During the U/HNWI's life, a holding company makes it easier to shuffle cash from an operating division to other businesses in the same corporate group. Such a move goes by the name "recycling" and can often be executed free of tax. A holding company can also make it easier to divert income to members of the family who enjoy lower marginal tax rates – although such a strategy would be subject to stringent attribution rules. For estate planning purposes, a holding company makes it possible to distribute assets without probate, although this would require the drafting of two wills. The exact legal structure of such a strategy is complicated, but in essence, one will would cover assets which require probate, and another will would contain the company shares.

A holding company could also be used by a Canadian U/HNWI to avoid U.S. estate tax. In such a scenario, U.S. assets could be held by a Canadian-based holding company. Because the taxpayer would technically hold only the shares of the holding company, the value of the U.S. assets would not be included in the calculation of the U.S. estate. In theory, the IRS should respect such a structure, but as American U/HNWIs well know, the IRS can be ruthless in its interpretation of the American tax code. There's nothing to say it won't start taking a dim view of such a tax structure – particularly if there are more and more U/HNWIs using it for the purposes of avoiding U.S. estate tax.

As good as all this sounds, setting up a holding company may be more trouble than it's actually worth. Anyone wishing to implement such a strategy needs to be aware of the costs of both establishing and maintaining that corporation. Understand as well that the rules and regulations governing holding companies are strict, so you'll need to take great care to follow them to the letter. Bottom line: make sure to consult closely with your tax and legal advisors to determine whether such a strategy would make sense for you.

### Family limited partnership (FLP)

The basic concept of an FLP is simple enough to understand: a family creates a business organization owned by family members that holds certain family assets. A family business is a prime example, but in theory, an FLP can own almost anything. In the typical case, parents become general partners, retaining full control and much of the risk. Children become limited partners, with no control over assets and only limited risk. Such a structure effectively removes assets from the parent's estate, thereby reducing taxes.

All this sounds easy in theory, but in practice, an FLP can be a very complicated strategy to initiate. Most FLPs require extremely complicated legal and accounting arrangements. Those who choose to establish an FLP must pay close attention to attribution and other tax rules. To top it all off, an FLP often involves minority discounting – that is, the discounting of a minority position in a given business because it does not allow its owner full control over the business. Recently, such valuation techniques have come under increasing attack from tax authorities in many jurisdictions. My advice: be extremely cautious if you decide to establish a FLP, and make sure you receive sophisticated tax advice before finalizing any decisions.

## Case study: Putting it all together

Throughout this chapter, I've detailed various estate planning strategies in isolation. In most cases, however, estate planning involves several strategies working together. An estate plan that I constructed with the help of a close colleague of mine recently provides a good example of this general principle. Bob and Dorothy have owned and operated a medium-sized import/export business in the Vancouver area for almost 30 years. At the time they first saw me, their portfolio was substantial (well over $1-million), and it's grown since. But the bulk of their wealth has always resided in their business, which they built from scratch up to a present value of about $ 10-million. I remember Bob had just celebrated his 60th birthday when the couple scheduled an appointment to discuss their estate plan. I suppose seeing all those candles had made both Bob and Dorothy think a little about their future.

As it stood, Bob and Dorothy's son Dan was the primary heir to the couple's estate, including the family business. The couple had also earmarked assets for a few important charities. But beyond a very basic will, there wasn't much of an estate plan. As a result, they'd likely be passing along a huge tax bill to their son. In a worst-case scenario, most of the company's $10-million in value would be taxable. Assuming a capital gains rate of 50% and a marginal rate of about the same, the tax bill would amount to about $2.5-million. Dan may well have had to sell business assets (perhaps at a discount) or secure a large loan to raise the necessary cash. I realized the situation required a carefully co-ordinated estate planning strategy. I contacted my colleague – an estate planning specialist – to see if we could work something out for the family.

The solution to this challenge was twofold. First, we arranged for a reorganization of the share structure of the family business. Bob and Dorothy exchanged their common shares for voting preferred shares with a value of $10-million, and issued new common shares to Dan. This would essentially freeze the value of the estate, ensuring all future growth (and the taxes on that growth) would be attributed to Dan, while giving Bob and Dorothy the option of drawing dividend income from their company.

The second step involved the purchase of a joint last-to-die life insurance policy in which the company was the owner and beneficiary. The policy benefit was intended to be substantial ($5-million – we'll see why in a second) with annual premiums somewhere in the $50,000 range. A key part of the strategy was to set up a private foundation to fund a variety of ongoing charitable bequests. Upon the death of the last spouse, $5-million of the preferred shares would be donated to the foundation; that donation would generate a charitable receipt for about $2.5 million. The company would then use the proceeds of the life insurance policy to buy back those shares from the foundation, in effect allowing Dan to retain full control over the family business without having to pay a dime in taxes. What's more, the strategy would result in a $5-million capital dividend account credit, which could be used to pay out tax-free dividends in the future. And of course, Bob and Dorothy would be able to leave a continuing legacy to charities and causes they cared about.

This case study demonstrates how estate planning demands co-ordinated strategies. Particularly when it comes to reducing taxes, it's an absolute must to think about all pieces of the puzzle when formulating an effective solution. By coupling the needs of their business with their desire to make a charitable bequest, Bob and Dorothy were able to solve a number of estate planning challenges all at once.

## A final word on estate taxes

When considering estate taxes, U/HNWIs need to look at a variety of different elements all at the same time. That makes it a good idea to address the problem of taxes early in your estate planning process. That will give you time to investigate various combinations of strategies and provide you with maximum flexibility in implementing them.

## Key concepts: Chapter fifteen

- Taxes pose a significant threat to U/HNWI estates

- Estates in America are taxed on the total value of the assets held in the estate.

- In general, estates in Canada are taxed on any gains accrued to assets held within that estate.

- For those U/HNWIs who own assets in two or more jurisdictions, the rules are more complicated. Make sure to check with a qualified professional before finalizing your estate.

- Probate taxes are another important form of tax U/HNWIs need to deal with.

- There are a number of ways to minimize estate taxes; remember, not all of them may be suitable for your exact situation.

- Transfers or gifts can reduce the size of an estate, and therefore taxes. However, many jurisdictions place limits on what you can give away in any year. Income attribution rules also prescribe how income from gifts will be taxed.

- Life insurance is an extremely versatile tax-planning tool in U/HNWI estates.

- Joint ownership can be an effective method of reducing probate taxes. Be careful, however: not all assets can be jointly owned, and joint ownership doesn't make sense for all U/HNWIs.

- an estate freeze is a sophisticated estate planning technique that can help reduce taxes. It is ideal for U/HNWIs with business assets, but requires careful structuring and proper execution.

- A holding company can be another way to defer taxes owing on an estate. But recent changes to tax legislation have made them less attractive than before. The legislation overseeing holding companies can be complex, and may not allow for tax advantages in all situations.

## Resources

U/HNWIs will want to avoid the "do-it-yourself" will and estate planning kits that promise to teach you how to write a legal will in the comfort of your own home. They can be disastrous for a U/HNWI. Here are some better suggestions.

Sandra Foster's *You Can't Take it With You*

*The Canadian Guide to Will and Estate Planning* by John Budd and Douglas Gray

*Advanced Wealth Transfer Under New Tax Laws: Case Studies Simplify Sophisticated Strategies to Reduce Estate Taxe*s by Richard E. Haas

## Websites

National Network of Estate Planning Attorneys *www.netplanning.com* – loads of information from estate planning specialists

Estate tax calculator *www.banksite.com/calc/estate* estate – a useful tool for U.S. residents

# **All about** trusts

- *The mechanics of trusts; the advantages of trusts*
- *The disadvantages of trusts*
- *Types of trusts and how they're used*
- *Trusts in action*

*"I was born into [wealth] and there was nothing I could do about it. It was there, like air or food, or any other element. The only question with wealth is what you do with it."*

**John D. Rockefeller**

The subject of trusts is an estate planning topic that usually doesn't receive a lot of attention among the general population. Even among U/HNWIs, it's a subject that doesn't get the attention it deserves. And that's too bad. Because with the careful use of trusts, it's possible to achieve a number of important estate planning goals in a single tax-efficient structure.

This chapter will provide you with some of the basic information about trusts, and detail how U/HNWIs can utilize trusts to minimize taxes and ensure their estate planning intentions are followed. Just to be fair, I will also describe some of the drawbacks of trusts, and explain some circumstances where they might not be an appropriate estate planning choice. This chapter will then provide a quick summary of some of the most important types of trusts, along with their respective tax implications. Perhaps most importantly, this chapter will also give you some practical examples of how a trust works in real life, and how it can benefit a U/HNWI estate. By the end of this chapter, you'll know whether trusts are a suitable solution to your specific estate planning challenges, and what you need to do to establish one.

By their very nature, both the features and the advantages of various forms of trusts depend largely on the jurisdiction you live in. While I've tried to distinguish between the features and benefits of trusts in both U.S. and Canadian jurisdictions wherever possible, I've had to be general in my descriptions. For more specific details about some of the features of trusts in your jurisdiction, it's a good idea to consult an expert.

But before we get to features and advantages, we have to know what we're talking about – we have to understand exactly how a trust works. So here's a brief overview of the basic structure of a trust.

## The mechanics of trusts

The concept of a trust was recognized in Roman times, and trusts have been known in England since the eleventh century. Since then, trusts have evolved into complex legal arrangements sometimes involving several different people in several different countries. While the exact form (and advantages) of any trust can vary widely from jurisdiction to jurisdiction, the basic structure of a trust remains relatively simple. Every trust is a legal arrangement between at least three parties:

(a) **the settlor:** the person transferring ownership of property to the trust. In some jurisdictions, this person is called the "grantor."

(b) **the trustee:** the person or firm with legal ownership of trust assets. This person is responsible for managing trust assets, reporting trust taxes, and making periodic distributions of income.

(c) **the beneficiaries:** the persons (or an organization, as the case may be) who receives the benefit of assets held within the trust. In some cases, the beneficiaries may also receive ultimate control over those assets.

In some cases, a fourth party, the **protector**, acts as a liaison between the settlor and the trustee, assisting the trustee in managing and administering the trust in accordance with the wishes of the settlor.

Most jurisdictions require those establishing a trust to structure the trust in the same basic way. Usually, a settlor appoints a trustee (or a co-trustee) to make decisions regarding the property placed in trust. At the time of the trust's creation, the settlor also establishes the terms of the trust, which specify how the trustee will go about managing the trust – including how assets will be managed, how income will be distributed, what discretion the trustee has over the timing of those distributions, etc.

chart 16.1: **Basic trust structure**

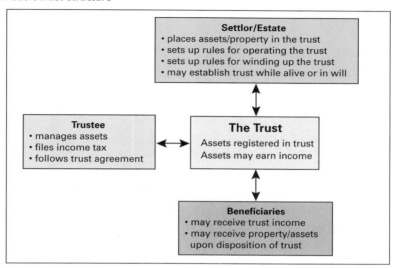

It's important to note that the trustee's job is to act in the best interest of the *beneficiaries* (something many jurisdictions require by law), not necessarily the settlor.

The pivotal role in any trust arrangement is the trustee. As the legal custodian of your assets, your trustee will have a tremendous impact on the effectiveness and the longevity of the trust (and by extension, the financial well-being of your beneficiaries). In theory, you can ask anyone to be a trustee. But think about what you're counting on this person (or persons) to do: to make timely, appropriate decisions regarding trust assets, including (in most cases) the allocation of trust assets into appropriate investments; to follow all necessary tax and reporting regulations to the letter (something very important with trusts); and, in the case of a discretionary trust, to act in a wise and prudent manner about which beneficiaries get what at what time. It should be clear that the complexity and the importance of the job eliminates all but the most capable lay person.

The level of "trust" (if you'll pardon the pun) required of trustees means U/HNWIs should consider only qualified professionals when it comes to managing their trust. Ideally, you'll want to seek out a competent trustee with years of experience managing the exact kind of trust you're looking for. Chances are your financial professional will be prohibited from working both as your wealth advisor and as your trustee (such is the case at my firm), but he or she will most likely be able to provide you with a list of reputable companies and/or individuals who specialize in this kind of work.

## My approach to trusts

I'll admit it: I'm a big fan of trusts. For most U/HNWIs, trusts are an extremely flexible, extremely efficient method of organizing U/HNWI estates. Here are four reasons why U/HNWIs need to investigate the possibility of using trusts in their estate plan:

(a) **Control over assets**. Trusts allow U/HNWIs an unprecedented level of control over how the assets in their estate are invested, who receives ongoing benefit from those assets, and who eventually will receive those assets. That makes a trust an ideal structure for U/HNWIs concerned about leaving a large inheritance to minor children, or for those U/HNWIs who want to ensure their money will only be used under certain circumstances.

(b) **Tax advantages.** Recent laws and regulations have made some trusts a less effective weapon in the fight against estate taxes. Even so, a properly structured trust can still offer tremendous tax advantages to U/HNWIs. Depending on the type of trust, a trust can help a U/HNWI initiate an estate freeze, avoid probate taxes, or split income with other members of the family (subject to attribution rules, of course). All these can help minimize the amount of estate lost to the taxman, and maximize the amount of estate left to heirs.

(c) **Protection of assets.** By transferring assets to a trust, U/HNWIs may be able to secure a degree of protection from potential creditors. Such protection can be immensely valuable for U/HNWIs who own their own businesses, for example, or are engaged in a professional practice (doctors, dentists, lawyers, or even accountants). In most cases, however, such transfers must take place long before any claim is made against such assets – otherwise it is possible for the trust to be declared invalid.

(d) **Confidentiality.** Another distinct advantage of a trust is its ability to offer a way to pass assets on to heirs privately. Because a trust technically exists outside the estate, assets transferred to the trust for eventual distribution to beneficiaries will not be a matter of public record. That makes trusts an ideal solution for those U/HNWIs concerned about the unwanted attention large bequests can sometimes attract.

These are all considerable benefits, to be sure. But as with any wealth management structure, trusts do have some drawbacks:

(a) **Set up fees, set-up time.** I'm not going to lie to you: it takes time and money to set up a trust. If you're serious about setting up a trust, you'll need to investigate a number of options, and determine what kind of trust you need, and where it should be domiciled. This will take some time. In most cases, the services of a number of financial professionals (including a lawyer) will be required. This will take some money. You'll also need time to find an appropriate trustee, and pay set-up fees when the trust is first established. That makes trusts inappropriate for those U/HNWIs looking to keep investments of either time or money in their estate plan to an absolute minimum.

(b) **Annual management and administration fees.** Trusts cost money to maintain. Such costs can vary widely according to the complexity of the trust, the value of the assets held within it, and the skills and/or reputation of the trustee. Many jurisdictions have guidelines as to what a trustee can legally charge for the administration and management of the trust, but even so, these fees can make a trust more trouble than it's really worth.

(c) **Hard to revoke.** Most trusts require permanent transfer of assets in order to take advantage of any preferential tax treatment arising from the trust structure. Under most circumstances, once you transfer those assets, it can be very difficult and very costly to get them back (assuming that's even possible). This feature makes trusts less than ideal for U/HNWIs whose financial circumstances or life circumstances might change frequently.

(d) **Taxes upon creation; ongoing taxes.** In most cases, the transfer of assets into a trust will be considered a deemed disposition of assets, attributable to the settlor. What's more, depending on the exact form of the trust, income produced from a trust can be subject to a high rate of tax – often the top marginal rate. Any potential tax benefit arising from a trust must be carefully balanced against the costs associated with creating it, as well as the trust's ongoing tax liability.

(e) **Deemed dispositions.** In certain jurisdictions, tax regulations require trust assets to be deemed disposed after a given period of time (in Canada, such dispositions happen every 21 years). That doesn't mean that a sale actually has to take place – it just means there will be a tax bill as if it had. If the settlor doesn't prepare for that tax bill, the trustee may be forced to sell portions of the trust's assets to fund such a tax bill, or elect to make special distributions to beneficiaries. Such requirements could be contrary to the settlor's wishes, or even force the premature dissolution of the trust.

Sure, some of these are significant drawbacks. But in my experience, the ability to offer U/HNWIs absolute control while maintaining tax efficiency makes the trust structure hard to beat. Simply put, trusts are a subject U/HNWIs absolutely need to investigate before finalizing their estate plans.

## Types of trusts

Depending on where you live, there may be many different types of trusts, all going by different names (in the U.S., for instance, there are literally dozens of different trusts, each named for a specific purpose). But at the end of the day, every trust has its birth in one of two events: the transfer of ownership of certain assets during the settlor's lifetime, or the transfer of assets upon the settlor's death. Let's take a look at each of them.

### Inter-vivos **trusts**

An inter-vivos trust can be created at any time during your life (*inter*="among"; *vivos*= "life"), and for a variety of purposes. Some of the more common uses of such a trust are to fund tuition and other costs of a post-secondary education for children or grandchildren, to provide ongoing gifts to charities, and to establish protection and privacy for certain assets. An inter-vivos trust can be revocable or irrevocable. While a revocable trust does provide for greater flexibility, in most jurisdictions, the tax advantages of an inter-vivos trust will only be available if it is irrevocable.

The tax implications of an inter-vivos trust can depend on a variety of factors. In Canada, when assets are first transferred to an inter-vivos trust, they are typically deemed disposed, and taxes must be paid by the settlor. On an ongoing basis, however, inter-vivos trusts have a number of attractive tax advantages. In the past, inter-vivos trusts were used by U/HNWIs to split income with family members: by transferring selected income-producing assets to a trust, some settlors were able to assign income to a family member who enjoyed a lower tax rate. Over the years, tax legislation in many jurisdictions has eliminated such advantages, making this strategy obsolete. In Canada, for instance, income from assets retained by an inter-vivos trust is taxed at the highest marginal rate, while income paid to beneficiaries is taxed at the beneficiary's rate. This is subject to a number of special attribution rules – these rules include a number of provisions that control the taxation of trust income for certain beneficiaries such as a spouse or minor child.

chart 16.2: **Diagram of inter-vivos trust**

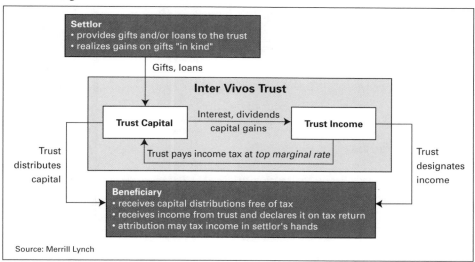

Source: Merrill Lynch

While these regulations have certainly limited the advantages of these trusts, many U/HNWIs will still find the inter-vivos trust an effective estate planning tool. An inter-vivos trust can be an excellent way to "freeze" the current value of investments or business shares (although the transfer itself may be declared a taxable disposition of assets). Like other estate freeze strategies, income from the assets is available for beneficiaries, but tax on future growth is deferred and passed on to the next generation.

Another significant advantage to an inter-vivos trust is privacy. Because an inter-vivos trust is created during your life, the income from that trust (and its eventual transfer to your beneficiaries) won't normally become a matter of public record, as it will with a testamentary trust.

Depending on where you live, there are a variety of specialized inter-vivos trust structures, any of which could prove useful to U/HNWIs. In Canada, for example, the alter-ego trust and the joint partner trust can be useful estate planning tools. While the tax advantages of such trusts are very limited, they do offer U/HNWIs an excellent way to avoid probate taxes and maintain privacy over estate assets. With both, the trust must be created after 1999, and the settlor must be at least 65 years old on the date of creation. The terms of such trusts are generally very strict: with an alter-ego trust, the settlor receives all income from the trust during the settlor's lifetime, and no one else may be entitled to any portion of the capital. With a joint partner trust, the situation is much the same, with the settlor's partner being able to enjoy rights to income or capital together with the settlor. With both types of trust, there is no deemed disposition on creation of the trust – only upon the death of the settlor (for alter-ego trusts) or the second partner (for joint partner trusts). Again, the purpose of such a trust is not so much to minimize taxes, but to limit the fees and other costs associated with having assets transfer through an estate, as well as the privacy concerns that may arise from that transfer.

## Testamentary **trusts**

A testamentary trust is born from your will. Your will names the trustee, the beneficiaries, the assets to be held in the trust, and provides guidance as to how those assets are to be managed and distributed. Because the assets are technically part of the estate before being transferred to the testamentary trust, the assets will still be subject to probate. And because a testamentary trust takes its power from your will, there must be specific provisions in the will to establish one – meaning your executor won't be able to set one up after you've gone.

The primary purpose of a testamentary trust is to minimize taxation. In Canada, a testamentary trust is taxed at the same graduated rates individuals are – which means tax will vary according to the amount of income realized in the trust in any one year, as well as the form of that income (note, however, that a testamentary trust cannot claim the same deductions available to individuals).

Depending on your jurisdiction, testamentary trusts can go by a variety of names. But by and large, there are two general classes of testamentary trust: spousal and family. As their name suggests, *spousal trusts* are created for the benefit of your spouse. They generally enjoy the same tax-deferral treatment as any other spousal transfer: assets may be transferred (or "rolled over") into a spousal trust without any deemed disposition.

chart 16.3: **Diagram of testamentary trust structure**

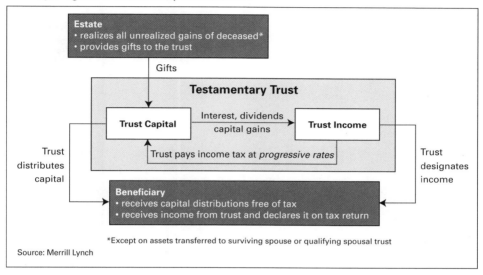

*Except on assets transferred to surviving spouse or qualifying spousal trust

Source: Merrill Lynch

In the past, spousal trusts were often used to provide professional financial care for widows who lacked the skills to manage their own finances. Today, they're more commonly used as an income-splitting tool after death: because income from a spousal trust will be taxed at its own rate (and not simply added to the income of the beneficiary), it's possible that a U/HNWI with a high income will enjoy significant tax advantages by receiving spousal assets through a testamentary trust.

Another common use of a spousal trust is to ensure children from a prior marriage receive something from your estate even if your new spouse remarries. By adding a provision to a spousal trust that stipulates *income* goes to your spouse, but *assets* pass to your children upon your spouse's death, you can provide for a surviving spouse while ensuring assets remain in the family. Such a strategy has the added benefit of avoiding a second probate tax. Because the distribution of trust assets is provided for in the original terms of the trust, there is no need for the assets to go through probate when the second spouse passes away. Understand, however, that in some jurisdictions, family law legislation does allow such a trust to be challenged by the second spouse, which makes proper legal wording of such a trust absolutely critical.

The second common form of testamentary trust is the *family trust*. The most common use of such a trust would be with children under the age of majority or children with disabilities. In such a situation, the trust holds assets and distributes them only after certain lawful conditions are met – when the child reaches a certain age, for example, or when the child enters university. Such a structure is a good idea with children who would otherwise receive a large lump sum inheritance at a young age, and might not yet be capable of managing such responsibility wisely. With older children, a family trust can be an effective way to provide children with a "protected" income. The basic concept: parents place assets in trust, and the child receives any income from trust assets. Because those assets technically belong to the trust, they should be protected (at least to a limited degree) from creditors or a divorce settlement. Again, the success of such an arrangement depends on the correct wording of such a trust, so professional advice is mandatory.

## Case study: making a good thing even better

As I mentioned, trusts are an extremely versatile tool for U/HNWIs looking to make their estates as tax-efficient as possible. In fact, structured properly, trusts can be so versatile and so tax efficient, they can often make a good estate plan even better. The case of a client "couple" of mine will provide a good example.

Throughout their marriage, the husband, a former executive for a large forestry company, had always managed the family finances, and had made most of the couple's investment decisions. Now that he was getting on in years, he was a little concerned about his estate plan. Before he became my client, the husband had purchased a life insurance policy with a $10-million death benefit to his wife. The husband calculated that $10-million invested in a balanced portfolio returning 7% would provide his wife with about $700,000 a year. At current tax rates, that would leave her with just over $400,000. Coupled with the income from other assets, that income would provide his wife with a comfortable living.

But as my client explained to me, it wasn't the money that was the real problem – or at least not the *amount*. Given his wife's lack of experience in managing the family portfolio, the husband was more worried about what may happen after the money was paid out. He had come to me to arrange for my continuing involvement in the family finances. With me overseeing the placement and management of the policy proceeds, the husband could rest a little easier, knowing he had done everything possible to ensure his wife's ongoing financial security.

I told him that he had certainly done his thinking, and constructed a reasonable estate plan. But as I told him at the time, it wasn't the best he could do. In fact, a trust might offer him the kind of security he was looking for – and more. If he were to include a stipulation in his will to establish a testamentary trust with the proceeds from his insurance policy, he would not only secure ongoing professional management for his wife's portfolio, he would also save her a lot of money in taxes. Because a testamentary trust is taxed at graduated rates, that annual income target of $700,000 wouldn't be taxed as heavily as it would be if it were combined with other income and taxed in the wife's name. Instead of taking home about $409,000 a year, his wife would enjoy $497,400. And by making the children the capital beneficiaries of the trust, he'd be ensuring trust assets would be kept within the family, regardless of whether his wife chose to remarry. Needless to say, I didn't have to work very hard to convince my client that a trust was the proper way to structure his estate.

I have to emphasize: it's not that there was anything *wrong* with my client's estate plan. He just wasn't getting the most for his money. By utilizing a rather simple testamentary trust structure, we were able to boost after-tax income from the policy, ensure an even better quality of life for the surviving spouse, and keep assets within the family.

## A final word on trusts

Trusts are complicated financial structures. And because they are most often irrevocable, there's often only one chance to get them right. If you're serious about setting up a trust, don't cut corners – seek out expert advice. When it comes time to file your tax return, you'll be glad you did.

# Key concepts: Chapter sixteen

- Trusts are one of the most flexible, most efficient estate planning tools available to U/HNWIs.
- The basic trust structure involves three parties

    (a) the settlor, who grants assets to the trust

    (b) the trustee, who manages those assets, and

    (c) the beneficiaries, who receive income and/or ultimate benefit from the assets within the trust.

- The role of the trustee is a vital one in any trust arrangement – make sure you select your trustee with utmost care.
- Trusts offer a number of substantial benefits to U/HNWIs. These are:

    (a) control over assets

    (b) tax advantages

    (c) protection for assets

    (d) privacy

- There are also a number of drawbacks to trusts. These are:

    (a) cost in time and money of establishing a trust

    (b) ongoing management and administration expenses

    (c) irrevocability

    (d) the high tax bracket some trust income is subject to

    (e) the deemed disposition of trust assets

- There are two general forms of trusts. Each have their own distinct advantages and disadvantages:

    (a) inter-vivos trusts are established during the settlor's life

    (b) testamentary trusts are established through a provision in the settlor's will. There are two main types of testamentary trusts: spousal trusts and family trusts

## Resources

There's no denying it: trusts are a complicated subject. As such, it's important to consider any books or reference materials you come across as general resources. Make sure to supplement any material you take from a book or a website with a detailed discussion with a qualified professional.

***The Complete Book of Trusts*** by Martin Shenkman

***Understanding Living Trusts: How You Can Avoid Probate, Save Taxes, and Enjoy Peace of Mind*** by Vickie and Jim Shumacher

## Websites

Duhaime and Company ***www.duhaime.org/ca-trus1.htm*** – an introduction to trust law in Canada

***www.estateplanninglinks.com*** – loads of links on estate planning

***www.taxprophet.com*** – aims to decipher U.S. tax law for residents and foreigners

# The *smart* way to give

chapter

# 17

*"The man who dies leaving behind him millions of available wealth, which was his to administer during his life, will pass away 'unwept, unhonoured and unsung' no matter to what uses he leaves the dross which he cannot take with him. Of such as these the public verdict will then be: 'the man who dies thus rich dies disgraced.' Such in my opinion, is the true gospel concerning wealth, obedience to which is destined some day to solve the problem of the rich and the poor, and to bring 'Peace on earth, among men Good Will.'"*

*Andrew Carnegie*

Throughout *True Wealth*, I've told you that on some level, wealth management is about *stewardship*. Simply put, U/HNWIs have an obligation to care for and nurture wealth for not only themselves, but for their families and their communities. I consider this to be one of the *moral* responsibilities of wealth.

For the most part, I've found U/HNWIs agree with me. Most of them have accepted this moral responsibility, and discovered that giving back can truly be a winning situation for everyone involved. For an individual, giving brings satisfaction and fulfillment, and a certain joy in knowing you're contributing to a higher purpose. For a charity, charitable giving means a source of stable funding – funding that doesn't require them to waste their time or resources on fund-raising initiatives. And for the community, charitable giving means it can offer services, programs and facilities that will ultimately improve the quality of life of its citizens. Those who leave the world a little better than it was when they came into it have done the greatest service anyone can do on this earth.

Despite all this, giving is still a financial transaction. Which means we must do it the smart way, with an eye to balancing our charitable goals against the financial implications of our gift. Giving you the knowledge to achieve this balance is the purpose of this chapter. The pages that follow will give you a basic understanding of the financial implications of charitable gifts, and a brief overview of the issues to keep in mind when deciding how to structure your charitable donation. After that, we'll review some of the more popular ways for U/HNWIs to structure their charitable donations, and discuss some of their benefits and drawbacks. By the end of the chapter, you'll have a clear picture of what form of charitable donation makes most sense for you.

## Trends in giving

If recent statistics are any indication, more and more U/HNWIs are making charitable giving a part of their financial plans. In its annual *Survey of the Affluent Americans*, U.S. Trust noted that 70% of survey respondents increased their charitable donations in response to the economic boom experienced in the 1990s. The survey estimates the average U/HNWI now gives 8% of their after-tax income to charity, or about $30,000 on an annual basis (this compares to 3% of after-tax income for the general population).

This general trend can be seen in Canada as well. The Canadian Centre for Philanthropy notes a gradual increase in the amount of charitable donations throughout the 1990s among the general population (specific statistics for U/HNWIs aren't available). In 1998, 5,396,000 Canadian taxpayers claimed more than $4.6-billion in charitable donations on their tax returns. That amounts to just over a quarter of the population. What's more, the Centre notes Canadians are giving with more than just money. In 1997, 7.5 million Canadians donated their time to some volunteer cause — that's just over 30% of Canada's population. These people spent a total of 1.1 billion hours volunteering over the year. That's the equivalent of 578,000 full-time jobs.

There are many reasons why U/HNWIs support charities. First among them is the genuine desire to support a worthwhile cause — 79% of respondents to the U.S. Trust survey cited this as an important reason for their philanthropy. But perhaps more important than this are the reasons that *didn't* make the list. Only 11% of U/HNWIs cited tax benefits as an important reason why they gave. What's more, 95% of U/HNWIs said they would still make donations even if such a donation weren't tax-deductible. While this may be surprising for some, it certainly comes as no surprise to those who work with U/HNWIs on a regular basis.

graph 17.1: **Why the affluent contribute to charities**

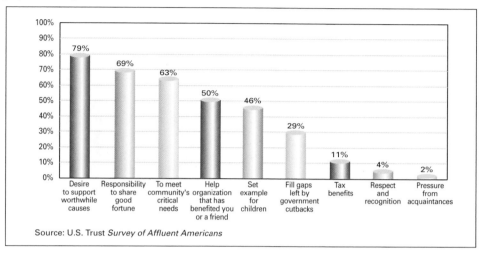

graph 17.1: **Why the affluent contribute to charities**

Source: U.S. Trust *Survey of Affluent Americans*

U/HNWIs support a wide range of charitable organizations. Principal among them are human services (88% of respondents noting frequent donations to such charities) and educational institutions (84%). These figures are a little different from the charities to which the affluent direct their *largest* donations, however. Religious organizations and educational institutions are the benefactors of the most sizable donations, with 30% and 22% respectively.

graph 17.2: **Organizations to which the affluent contribute most frequently**

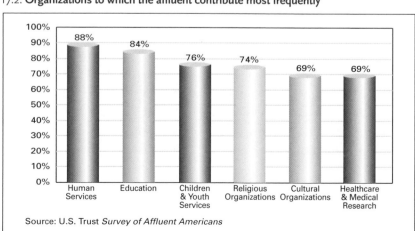

Source: U.S. Trust *Survey of Affluent Americans*

chart 17.3: **Organizations to which the affluent give their largest contributions**

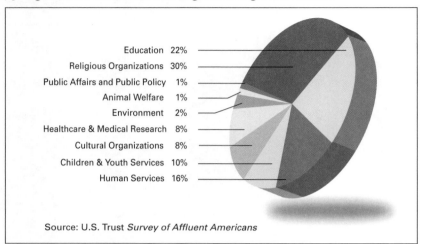

| | |
|---|---|
| Education | 22% |
| Religious Organizations | 30% |
| Public Affairs and Public Policy | 1% |
| Animal Welfare | 1% |
| Environment | 2% |
| Healthcare & Medical Research | 8% |
| Cultural Organizations | 8% |
| Children & Youth Services | 10% |
| Human Services | 16% |

Source: U.S. Trust *Survey of Affluent Americans*

## Philanthropy services: help for the charitable U/HNWI

One result of this increase in giving among the U/HNWI population has been the development of "philanthropic services" divisions within several of the leading financial firms. Such a service can help you refine your charitable vision and determine what you're looking to accomplish with your charitable dollars. It can provide a detailed survey of charities and causes in your area of interest, and help you finalize a short list of organizations you might consider supporting. In many cases, such groups can handle paperwork and other administrative duties as well as arrange for ongoing tax advice.

While these are all significant benefits, I'm not convinced every U/HNWI requires this kind of service. In my experience, most U/HNWIs have a very clear idea of why they're making a charitable gift, and already have a list of causes and organizations in mind. That said, it's nice to know such services exist. Personally, I can see these kinds of services growing in popularity over the next several years – if only for the administrative benefits they offer. Check with your wealth advisor to find out what services your firm offers, and whether they'd be of use to you.

# My approach to charitable giving

There's no denying that charitable giving can be one of the more complicated areas of wealth management. But no matter how complicated it gets, charitable giving starts with a simple idea. *Giving is about doing good for others.*

I realize this is really common sense, but in this day and age of conspicuous consumption, complicated tax rules, and burdensome regulations, I think it's a point that bears repeating. The purpose of your gift isn't to generate a tax receipt, or to show everyone how wealthy you are, or to get your name on the side of a building. No, it's to do good for others. When it comes time to decide on an appropriate structure for your charitable giving, by all means pay attention to the tax laws and other financial considerations. But when it comes right down to it, your choice should be based on one question: *how can I ensure my dollars do the maximum amount of good for the people I want to help?* Keeping this simple question at the top of your mind will help you navigate through some of the many options facing you, and make the charitable giving process much easier. Perhaps more importantly, it will help you sustain your charitable effort, without becoming frustrated about how complicated charitable giving can be.

# A (very) brief word on the tax rules

Most U/HNWIs know gifts to a registered charity result in a tax credit. What they don't always know, however, is the exact form that tax credit will take – and what limitations apply to it. I suppose that's understandable: the exact rules governing the tax treatment of charitable donations can be complicated and (as always) varies from jurisdiction to jurisdiction. Once again, what follows is only a general survey of some of the basic rules that guide the tax treatment of charitable gifts in the U.S. and Canada. Consult with a tax professional in your jurisdiction if you want the full story.

In most jurisdictions, a charitable gift results in a tax credit that donors then submit and claim against income on their tax return. The exact form of that tax credit will usually vary according to the kind of gift made, as well as the structure of that gift. In Canada, for example, a charitable gift usually results in anywhere from 40–45% of the gift value being returned in the form of a tax deduction, depending on the tax rate in the province of residence, and depending on whether the gift was made in the form of cash or appreciated securities. When the gift is made through a will, the receipt can offset taxes owing on death, making charitable giving an effective tax reduction strategy.

It is precisely for this reason that most jurisdictions place restrictions and limits on how much a taxpayer can give away and still claim a tax credit for. At the time of writing, gifts by American U/HNWIs to qualified charities can be claimed for up to 50% of the taxpayer's adjusted gross income in any year for cash gifts, and up to 30% for gifts of securities and many other assets. Generally, unused credits can be carried forward up to five years. If a gift is made through a will, it is generally fully deductible against the value of the estate, regardless of the amount of the gift.

The rules in Canada are similar. Charitable gifts can result in a tax credit of up to 75% of the donor's net income while the donor is alive, and 100% of the deceased's net income when the gift is structured through a will. Any unused tax credits can be used over the following five years if the gift was made while alive, or applied against tax owing in the previous year if the gift was made through a will, up to a maximum limit of 100% of the deceased's net income in that year. In both jurisdictions, however, there are a number of exceptions and qualifications of these rules. The more specialized and technical your giving is, the more important it is to carefully consider the tax rules, and seek quality tax advice before making any decisions.

Remember that to qualify for any tax receipt, gifts must be made to a charity or other organization *officially recognized* by the tax authorities in your jurisdiction. This won't be a problem for U/HNWIs looking to give to high-profile, nationally recognized causes. But for those who might be interested in supporting highly specialized or local charities, the issue is worth looking into. In most jurisdictions, checking up on a charity's status is relatively easy: most governments are in the habit of publishing lists of charities and other organizations they recognize, and there may be other groups who do the same. If you're ever in doubt as to the status of a group you might donate to, make sure to look into the status before you write the check.

## Charitable giving: things to consider

Self-knowledge and advance preparation are the keys to successful gift planning. Here are some of the things to think about before you decide on how to structure your gift.

### Financial **resources**

Before you give anything, it's important to understand how much you can afford to give. This may not seem like a problem to many U/HNWIs, but even the wealthiest should carefully consider whether the amount of an intended gift will affect their own quality of life, or the estate they plan to leave behind. This consideration will help determine an appropriate giving structure. Because some forms of giving require sizable donations (trusts and foundations), determining what you can give can help eliminate options, and streamline the planned giving process.

## What matters **to you?**

No matter how large your gift, if you want your gift to be truly fulfilling, you'll need to spend some time thinking about the exact purpose of your donation. Chances are you already have a general idea of some of the causes and issues that matter to you, but you'll want to be a little more focused before you actually make your donation. Think carefully about what *aspect* of a particular cause you'd like to donate to – a donation to a health related cause, for example, could be directed toward research, ongoing care, or new equipment. Once you've decided on a specific organization, you'll want to do some homework. Getting involved with a charity (either through fundraising or volunteering) is a good way to get a feel for what a charity does, and how it makes a difference in the community. Finally, you'll also want to think about whether the kind of support you'd like to give is immediate or ongoing. Obviously, your answer will have an impact on the structure of your gift. If you're committed to maintaining a lifetime involvement in the cause, then a foundation, trust, or endowment is a good decision. If it's an immediate concern you'd like to help, then a simple bequest of cash could be the perfect solution.

## Involvement **(and control)**

Different giving arrangements require different levels of involvement, so it makes sense to think about what kind of involvement you want before deciding on a gift structure. For those looking to maximize their involvement in a cause, it's best to select one of the giving structures that offers direct control over your donation dollars. In such a case, trusts, foundations, and other specialized structures would be the logical choice here. Structured properly, all of these can provide you with ongoing discretion as to exactly how your donation dollars are used.

## Recognition **or anonymity?**

Some U/HNWIs believe charitable giving should be largely left anonymous. For other U/HNWIs, attaching the family name to a cause is an important goal. Neither approach is any better than the other, but again, your choice will have a big difference on the exact form of your gift – some forms offer more privacy than others. Those seeking recognition should be aware that a substantial gift may attract fundraising solicitations from other charities, or even unrelated solicitations from telemarketers and other salespeople.

### "Bulletproof"

Another important consideration is whether you need to protect your gift from a potential challenge by your heirs. Probably the best way to prevent such a challenge is simply to communicate effectively with family members. By letting your family understand your intentions – and how important your cause is to you – well before the event, you're less likely to ruffle feathers when you actually make your donation. If it's clear family members will have a problem with charitable intentions, U/HNWIs should select giving structures that offer protection against such challenges, or better yet, make their gifts while still alive.

# Case study: U/HNWI creates his own charity

For some U/HNWIs, selecting a cause to support can be frustrating – with literally thousands of registered charities out there, it can be tough for them to determine the one cause they truly care about. For some U/HNWIs, however, the problem isn't the fact that there are too many charities, but rather, the fact that there are too few.

That was the position John Volken found himself in. As the owner of a successful chain of 150 discount furniture outlets in Western Canada and the U.S. Mr. Volken wanted to do something to help street youth in Vancouver's Downtown Eastside, historically one of Canada's poorest neighborhoods. There were existing organizations that worked in the area, but none of them offered the no-frills, straight-up approach that Mr. Volken advocates. His solution to the problem: create his own charity. The result was *Welcome Home*, a privately-run counseling and training center for needy kids in the area.

The exact structure of Mr. Volken's involvement will comprise a $6-million donation from his own charitable foundation (which he started six years ago). $2.6-million of that has gone to buy a site for *Welcome Home*, a location close to those who would need the facility. Mr. Volken has also pledged ongoing support for his charity: 2% of the proceeds from all furniture sold by his business will be donated to *Welcome Home*. To top it all off, Mr. Volken has taken it as his personal challenge to raise an additional $5-million in donations from both corporations and the community-at-large. If all goes well, these donations will only be the tip of the iceberg: Mr. Volken plans to ultimately take the *Welcome Home* concept throughout North America — and perhaps the world.

I'm offering this case study not so much to encourage U/HNWIs to found their own charities (don't get me wrong — that is a noble, and worthwhile cause), but rather to highlight the successful process that lay behind Mr. Volken's decision. It's obvious Mr. Volken cares very deeply about giving something back to his community. But before he started signing checks, he spent a good deal of time *thinking* about the kind of donation he wanted to make. He took the time to familiarize himself with existing organizations doing work in the area, and recognized there was a gap between what he wanted to do and what was being done. He took the time to carefully examine his own goals, and made an informed choice about the exact structure of his gift. He obviously consulted carefully with a number of professionals, and eventually decided on a giving structure that would provide maximum control over his money and maximum impact for his cause. Ultimately, this is the kind of self-knowledge and advance preparation that makes charitable giving meaningful and effective — both for the U/HNWI and the community at large.

## Giving in action: charitable giving strategies

There are many ways to structure a charitable donation; each of them has different implications for the giver. What follows is a brief review of some of the more popular methods U/HNWIs use to structure their charitable gifts. For a full briefing on all the charitable options available in your jurisdiction, it's best to consult with a qualified professional.

## Outright **gifts**

An outright gift is perhaps the easiest way to give. In such a scenario, the donor transfers ownership of an asset (cash, securities, real estate, tangible property, etc.) to a registered charity. In return, the charity issues a tax receipt entitling the donor to a tax credit. As mentioned above, the exact amount of that tax receipt will vary from jurisdiction to jurisdiction, and will probably depend on what you're giving (some jurisdictions offer special tax inclusion rates on gifts of appreciated securities, for example). But by and large, that's all there is to it.

Within the general category of outright gifts, there are a number of specialized giving options. For U/HNWIs looking to make a more personalized impact with an outright gift, the following may be worth considering.

**Endowments:** a donation given with the understanding that the charity spends only the income generated by the gift – not the principal. A good alternative for U/HNWIs looking to transform a single gift into several years of giving.

**Matching gifts:** a donation contingent upon the charity securing additional funding from other sources. This can be an excellent way to build community support for the charity and encourage others to help in the fundraising drive.

**Term gifts:** a series of gifts earmarked for a specific program or project. The charitable organization accepts the gifts with the understanding that at the end of the term, the charity must find alternate funding. Particularly useful for U/HNWIs looking to establish a limit to their charitable efforts.

There are a couple of big benefits to outright gifts. The first is their simplicity: you simply cut a check or transfer assets and your job is done. There are no hassles, no ongoing paperwork, and no follow-up required. The other benefit is the immediacy of an outright gift. An outright gift usually generates an immediate tax receipt, and your charity is able to use the money right away. On the other hand, outright giving is usually a rather inflexible giving strategy: once you give assets to a charity, chances are you won't be able to take them back.

## Life **insurance**

When most U/HNWIs think about charitable giving, they don't necessarily think about life insurance. But the fact of the matter is, life insurance can be an extremely flexible, extremely tax-efficient method for U/HNWIs to structure a charitable donation.

Depending on the exact form it takes, a charitable gift made from the proceeds of a life insurance policy can provide a number of benefits. Number one, it provides a way to boost charitable giving without diminishing the value of the estate – an important benefit for U/HNWIs who want to make a substantial gift, but remain concerned about leaving behind enough for their heirs. If privacy is an important consideration, an insurance-based gift is an excellent way to keep giving anonymous. Because a life insurance policy may be held outside a will, it doesn't have to become a matter of public record.

Giving with life insurance has one other advantage: it can be extremely tax-efficient. In many jurisdictions (Canada, for one), the exact nature of the tax benefits will depend largely on two factors, namely who owns the policy and who is its named beneficiary. The following outline applies to a Canadian context, but it should give U/HNWIs everywhere an idea of what's possible with insurance.

(a) **U/HNWI owns policy outside will, with charity as beneficiary.** Probably the easiest option. Such a gift would be eligible for a tax credit that could be applied to taxes owing on the terminal return. It would also avoid probate taxes, and provide confidentiality to the donor. It would also be difficult to challenge, since it lies outside the will.

(b) **U/HNWI owns policy; estate is beneficiary; charitable bequest in will.** In such a scenario, your estate receives policy proceeds, then uses them to make a donation. The estate will be able to claim a tax credit for the donation, which may be used to offset taxes owing on other assets. Passing policy proceeds through the will means there will be probate taxes owing, and the donation will become part of the public record. Such a gift could also be more vulnerable to challenge, so make sure any such gift is properly drafted if you decide to go with this route.

(c) **Charity as policy owner; charity as beneficiary.** In such a case, a charity is named not only as the beneficiary of an existing policy, but the owner of it as well. Signing over ownership in this way allows the U/HNWI to claim a charitable credit for the cash surrender value of the policy (if the policy has no cash surrender value, then there is no tax credit), but the death benefit cannot be claimed. If the policy requires ongoing premiums, those premiums can often be claimed as a charitable donation on a yearly basis. Keep in mind, though, that such a donation will usually be deemed a disposable event for tax purposes, and may result in a capital gain.

Whatever method you choose, you'll find insurance-based giving to be an extremely flexible, extremely efficient way of structuring a charitable donation. It should be seriously considered by all U/HNWIs looking to make a donation part of their estate plan.

## Charitable **gift funds**

An option for U.S. based U/HNWIs is the charitable gift fund (CGFs). For U/HNWIs looking to avoid the red tape and other administrative hassles of an independent foundation or making multiple donations, it can be an excellent tool that makes planned giving as easy as it is enjoyable.

In America, a number of prominent mutual fund companies have established sizable charitable gift funds (the largest of these, the *Fidelity Charitable Gift Fund*, currently has about $1.7-billion in assets). They all work in much the same way. Investors donate cash, mutual fund units, or other appreciated securities to the fund. While those funds are waiting for distribution, they can be placed in a portfolio (most CGFs offer several to choose from) that allows for further appreciation. When the time comes to make a donation, the investor directs the fund company to make the check out to the appropriate recipient and the company takes care of all the paperwork. Clean, simple, and effective.

In this way, CGFs are the ultimate low-hassle solution to charitable giving – a solution that offers the benefits of a private foundation without the hassles. CGFs offer U/HNWIs the same degree of control over bequests as a foundation does. CGFs also offer an opportunity for contributions to compound free of tax while waiting to be donated to an appropriate charity. But they're a lot less expensive than a foundation. With fees of about 1.7%, the Fidelity CGF, for example, offers U/HNWIs much lower expenses than a private foundation normally would. What's more, they usually require a much lower financial commitment than a foundation would (sometimes as low as $10,000). And, as mentioned, the fund company takes care of the paperwork – something that can make even the most committed philanthropist think twice about setting up a foundation.

CGFs are still a "hands–off" form of giving. With a CGF, your participation in the charitable activity will be mostly in the form of sending money. Those looking for a little more involvement might want to investigate another form of giving. Another drawback to CGFs is their focus on *recognized charities*. If there's a gap you're looking to fill, or a specialized cause you'd like to support that isn't technically a charity, chances are you won't be able to do it with a CGF.

## Gift **annuities**

Annuities have long been used to secure retirement income. They are becoming increasingly popular as a method of structuring a charitable gift. Very generally, an annuity is an "income contract" issued by an insurance company. In return for a large lump sum payment, you receive guaranteed payments of income and capital for the remainder of your life. Upon your death, the remainder of your lump sum payment transfers to the insurance company.

Gift annuities work in much the same way, but instead of assets transferring to an insurance company, they pass on to a charity. Many large, established charities issue their own annuity policies. Other charities have long-standing agreements with reputable insurance firms, and can direct you to one of them should you be interested in establishing an annuity. There may be a minimum gift required when structuring a gift annuity – you'll need to check with the charity in question to make sure.

Such a structure can be a highly tax-efficient way to make a charitable donation. In most cases, income from an annuity will be considered to include income (which is taxable) and return of principal (which is not). The end result is income that won't normally be taxed as heavily as regular income. The amount of that income can vary widely according to a number of factors (the terms of the annuity, your age, prevailing interest rates, special features you might request, etc.), so make sure to explore your options thoroughly before signing anything.

As for the tax credit resulting from a gift annuity, that can be a little complicated. If a donation made through an annuity is expected to be greater than the estimate of the lifetime annuity payments, it may be possible to receive a tax credit. Such a scenario depends largely on your age, as well as the actual terms of the annuity. Make sure to ask your charity (or the insurance company, as the case may be) for the details, and review them with your wealth advisor before making any decisions.

## Gifts of **residual interest**

Another gifting option is a gift of residual interest. With such a gift, you transfer ownership of a given asset to a charity, with the understanding that you are able to use the asset during your life. This is a great way to give real estate or other tangible assets (a vacation property, art, antiques, etc.) to charities while still enjoying those assets. In general, you'll receive a tax credit for your donation now, without having to make any significant change to your lifestyle. Your gift will not be subject to probate, and because it will be made outside the will, it will be completely private.

Despite these benefits, I tend to discourage gifts of residual interest. Because gifts of residual interest are irrevocable, U/HNWIs planning to make such gifts must be fully prepared financially and emotionally to relinquish control over the gifted asset. And quite frankly, that's not something everyone can do. I've seen it happen before: a U/HNWI decides to donate a vacation property or some other asset, a decision that may make a lot of sense on paper. Only after some time does the U/HNWI understand the *emotional* element of ownership, and appreciate that it means more than the financial value of the asset. For that reason, it's essential for U/HNWIs looking to give in this way to sit down with a qualified wealth advisor and think through the consequences before making any decisions.

## Charitable **Remainder Trusts**

Another effective method of charitable donation is to establish a charitable remainder trust (CRT). In such a scenario, the U/HNWI establishes a trust with income-generating assets. During the trust's lifetime, income from those assets flows to any number of beneficiaries. At the time of some pre-determined event (after a certain number of years, for example, or upon the death of last beneficiary), the trust is dissolved, and remaining assets transfer to a registered charity. Such trusts are very popular with U/HNWIs in the U.S., where they are used to minimize the effect of the estate tax by reducing the value of the donor's estate.

There are a number of benefits to a charitable remainder trust. First is its ability to allow you to make a charitable donation without having to readjust to a lower level of income. That makes CRTs a good way to preserve peace of mind. From a tax perspective, CRTs make a lot of sense: essentially, a CRT gives you the ability to receive a tax deduction now for a donation that will be made later. Depending on where you live, you may be able to spread that deduction over a number of years, making it even more valuable. In most cases, a CRT is an inter-vivos trust, meaning assets won't be subject to probate taxes upon your death. And of course, the gift will remain confidential: because the CRT isn't normally established through your will, it will not be on the public record.

As with any giving strategy, there are some drawbacks to CRTs. Generally, CRTs are irrevocable – that means you'll be giving up control of your assets for good if you set one up. As with any trust, there will be annual administration costs and trustee fees you'll have to account for. These fees can be significant, making CRTs inappropriate for smaller gifts (say, anything less than $250,000). And remember, even though the assets aren't yours anymore, the income from a CRT will be, meaning you'll still have to pay tax on it. All of which means that U/HNWIs looking to establish a CRT should consider their options carefully before making any decisions.

## Case study: Estate plan revolves around charitable trust

As I mentioned in the last chapter, trusts are an extremely flexible, extremely efficient way to structure a U/HNWI estate. When the main purpose of that trust is to fund charitable donations, that's even more the case. The settlement of the Onassis family estate is an excellent example. As could be expected, Jacqueline Kennedy Onassis left a large estate – one worth more than $200-million. In her will she made numerous bequests of properties, personal effects and historical documents to various individuals and organizations. But the central feature of her estate was a special charitable trust. Under the provisions of Jacqueline's will, the bulk of the Onassis fortune will go into a special Charitable Lead Annuity Trust, a variation of the Charitable Remainder Trust described above. Such a structure will maximize benefit to charity, minimize taxes, and ensure the Kennedy/Onassis legacy will live for a long time.

The structure of the trust is a classic case study in effective estate planning. With a pool of assets topping $170-million, the trust will aim to pay out 8% of its principal every year to prescribed charities. The trust will be administered by Mrs. Onassis' surviving child, Caroline, along with the estate attorney and a close family friend. At the end of 24 years, the trust will be dissolved and the balance (if any) will pass to Caroline's children. This is the exact opposite of a Charitable Remainder Trust: instead of the family receiving ongoing income and trust assets passing to a charity, the charity will receive income while the family will eventually inherit the assets.

While her will certainly proved her to be an extremely generous philanthropist, it's clear charitable giving wasn't the only thing on Mrs. Kennedy Onassis' mind when she formulated her estate plan. Her trust structure not only ensured substantial long-term funding for a variety of charitable causes, it also ensured there would be more money for her family. Estate planning experts estimate that there will only be an 11% reduction in the Onassis estate, compared to the 58% were the charitable trust not in place. The result: an estate plan that was truly a win–win–win situation: for Mrs. Onassis, for her family, and for everyone her foundation helps in the years to come.

## A final word on charitable giving

There are many options available to U/HNWIs looking to give. So be prepared to spend some time thinking about what form of support would make the best sense for you. That way, you can be sure both you and your charity get the most out of your donation.

## Key concepts: Chapter seventeen

- U/HNWIs have a responsibility to be responsible stewards of wealth for their families and their communities.

- Giving is a financial transaction. As such, it needs to be considered carefully, with thought to the financial consequences.

- The tax benefit of a charitable gift depends on the form of that gift.

- U/HNWIs need to consider the following things before making a donation:

    (a) financial resources – what they can reasonably afford to give

    (b) what matters – what kind of cause they want to support

    (c) involvement – how involved they want to be with their charity

    (d) recognition/anonymity – whether they want their gift to be made public

    (e) how to ensure their gift is safe from potential legal challenges

There are many ways to structure a charitable donation. Some of the most common among U/HNWIs are:

    (a) outright gifts – such gifts provide immediate tax relief and immediate benefit to the charity, but are often less tax efficient than other forms of giving

    (b) life insurance – an extremely flexible form of charitable giving. The exact tax benefit will vary according to ownership of the policy

    (c) charitable gift funds –an excellent option for U/HNWIs looking for a hassle-free form of giving

    (d) gift annuities – such gifts offer a way for U/HNWIs to receive tax-advantaged benefits from their assets while giving to charity

    (e) gifts of residual interest – a good solution for those completely comfortable with relinquishing control of an asset; for others, there are better solutions

    (f) charitable remainder trusts – an excellent option for those with significant amounts of assets to give

## Resources

Almost every book on estate planning covers the subject of charitable giving to some degree. For more detailed information, try the following.

***Don't Just Give it Away: How to Make the Most of Your Charitable Giving*** by Renata J. Rafferty

***The Gospel of Wealth*** by Andrew Carnegie

## Websites

***www.pnnonline.org***

Better Business Bureau Wise Giving Alliance ***give.org*** – reports and information on charitable organizations

The Canadian Centre for Philanthropy ***www.ccp.ca*** – news and information for those making charitable bequests

IRS tax-exempt status search engine ***www.irs.ustreas.gov/prod/search/eosearch.html*** – check to see if your charity has tax-exempt status before you donate

# Establishing your
## own foundation

- *Reasons for establishing a foundation*
- *Basic rules for foundations*
- *Things to consider before you establish a foundation*

*"I do not like to have anyone tell me what is my duty to give. There is just one man who is going to decide that question – who has the responsibility of deciding it – that is myself."*

**John D. Rockefeller**

Name some of the most famous U/HNWIs of all time. Carnegie. Ford. Rockefeller. Getty. These U/HNWIs are all from different backgrounds. They have all made their money in various ways, and at various times in North America's history. But they all have one thing in common: they have all established *foundations* to make their charitable bequests. Today, these U/HNWIs are known not only as some of the wealthiest people of all time, but as some of the most generous.

Many of today's billionaires are following in exactly the same footsteps. Gates. Moore. Allen. In the decades to come, theirs will be the names we will look back on and remember as some of the greatest philanthropists of all time. Why do so many U/HNWIs choose to give through a foundation? What makes a foundation such a valuable tool for U/HNWIs looking to give back to their communities?

This chapter will answer some of these questions. In the coming pages, I'll describe some of the of the benefits of the foundation structure, and review a list of basic rules and regulations governing the establishment of foundations. This chapter will also provide you with a list of considerations that will help you determine whether a foundation is a viable solution to your philanthropic needs. Even if establishing your own foundation isn't a viable option right now, reviewing the reasons why other U/HNWIs have established foundations will help you refine your own charitable goals, and will make you more knowledgeable about what criteria should determine your choice of giving arrangement.

# **The rise** of the foundation

By the looks of it, U/HNWIs are becoming a lot more interested in foundations. The Foundation Center, a non-profit organization founded in 1956 to support and encourage institutional philanthropy in the U.S., notes that between the years of 1985 and 1999, the number of active grantmaking foundations nearly doubled, from about 25,600 to over 50,200. The Center's survey of the largest of those foundations (some 19,500 of the total) found that more than a third of them had been established since 1990. In the past year, the Center estimates an 18.4% increase in giving by America's grantmaking foundations – that giving now totals over $23.3-billion. The assets controlled by those foundations rose by a similar pace, and now totals over $448.6-billion.

graph 18.1: **Growth in number of foundations 1980-1999**

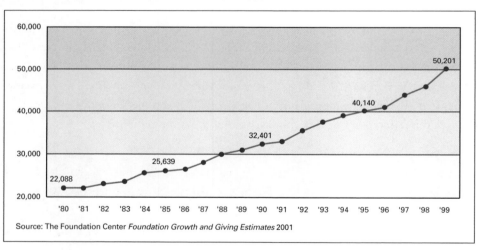

Source: The Foundation Center *Foundation Growth and Giving Estimates* 2001

Where is this money coming from? The Center points to a number of high-tech entrepreneurs as the leading source of foundation dollars. In 1999, the Bill and Melinda Gates Foundation became the biggest charitable foundation in the U.S., fueled by an $11.5-billion donation – the largest gift ever made to a U.S.-based foundation.

graph 18.2: **Growth in foundation giving 1990-2000**

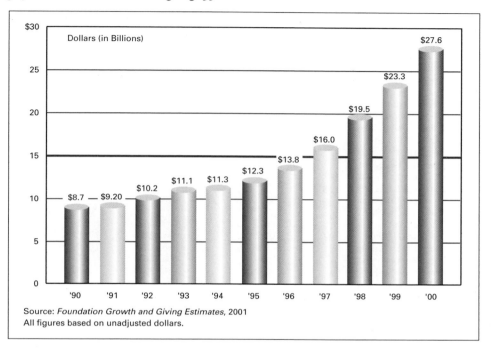

Source: *Foundation Growth and Giving Estimates*, 2001
All figures based on unadjusted dollars.

With assets topping $22-billion in 2000, the Bill and Melinda Gates Foundation now eclipses such venerable foundations such as the Rockefeller Foundation, the Pew Charitable Trusts, and the Ford Foundation. The newly created Moore Foundation (named after Gordon Moore, co-founder of Intel) is another example of high-tech philanthropy. Founded in November of 2000 with a donation of more than $5-billion worth of Intel stock, it is now one of the ten largest foundations in America. While these and other foundations have no doubt suffered from the recent downturn in the value of technology shares, they have the resources to become as well-known and as generous as the famous foundations of previous generations.

table 18.3: **Top foundations in the U.S.**

| | Foundation | Assets '98 | Assets '99 | % Change | Rank '98 |
|---|---|---|---|---|---|
| 1. | Bill & Melinda Gates Foundation | $ 5,368,694 | $ 15,515,455 | 189.0 | 7 |
| 2. | David & Lucile Packard Foundation | 9,577,894 | 13,144,242 | 37.2 | 3 |
| 3. | Ford Foundation | 9,675,452 | 11,960,280 | 23.6 | 2 |
| 4. | Lilly Endowment | 14,238,194 | 10,418,127 | -26.8 | 1 |
| 5. | J. Paul Getty Trust | 8,002,901 | 8,729,629 | 9.1 | 4 |
| 6. | Robert Wood Johnson Foundation | 7,867,785 | 8,640,408 | 9.8 | 5 |
| 7. | Pew Charitable Trusts | 4,734,122 | 4,894,418 | 3.4 | 8 |
| 8. | W.K. Kellogg Foundation | 6,387,841 | 4,853,384 | -24.0 | 6 |
| 9. | John D. & Catherine T. MacArthur Foundation | 4,168,673 | 4,629,519 | 11.1 | 9 |
| 10. | Andrew W. Mellon Foundation | 3,436,508 | 4,615,683 | 34.3 | 11 |
| 11. | Starr Foundation | 3,358,848 | 4,486,499 | 33.6 | 13 |
| 12. | California Endowment | 2,309,441 | 3,884,524 | 68.2 | 16 |
| 13. | Rockefeller Foundation | 3,308,891 | 3,837,542 | 16.0 | 14 |
| 14. | Annie E. Casey Foundation | 1,569,181 | 3,626,230 | 131.1 | 26 |
| 15. | Charles Stewart Mott Foundation | 2,348,342 | 3,229,256 | 37.5 | 15 |
| 16. | Robert W. Woodruff Foundation | 3,677,079 | 3,114,438 | -15.3 | 10 |
| 17. | Casey Family Program | 2,026,756 | 2,810,532 | 38.7 | 19 |
| 18. | Annenberg Foundation | 3,363,417 | 2,755,835 | -18.1 | 12 |
| 19. | William & Flora Hewlett Foundation | 1,937,376 | 2,738,945 | 41.4 | 21 |
| 20. | Kresge Foundation | 2,203,399 | 2,575,425 | 16.9 | 17 |
| 21. | Robert R. McCormick Tribune Foundation | 1,555,125 | 2,450,691 | 57.6 | 28 |
| 22. | Ewing Marion Kauffman Foundation | 1,767,089 | 2,443,456 | 38.3 | 23 |
| 23. | Duke Endowment | 2,108,042 | 2,335,496 | 10.8 | 18 |
| 24. | Harry & Jeanette Weinberg Foundation | 1,958,949 | 2,174,892 | 11.0 | 20 |
| 25. | McKnight Foundation | 1,891,340 | 2,020,878 | 6.8 | 22 |
| | **Total** | **$ 108,841,339** | **$ 131,885,784** | **21.2** | |

*(all numbers in 000's)*

Source: *Foundation Growth and Giving Estimates,* 2001.

# Reasons for establishing a foundation

U/HNWIs have a multitude of options available to them when it comes to charitable giving. So why would anyone want to go through the trouble of establishing a private foundation? I can think of several reasons.

- **Control over bequests.** Foundations allow U/HNWIs unprecedented control over ongoing donations. With a foundation, you retain control over how your bequests are distributed and when they are to be distributed. Such flexibility allows for a timely response to changing charitable interests, one that could theoretically continue even after your death.

- **Control over assets.** Many forms of giving require the U/HNWI to relinquish control over gifted assets. Not so with a foundation. Even though a foundation requires you to relinquish ownership of assets, it allows you to retain control over how those assets should be managed on an ongoing basis. This allows for greater flexibility and the potential to increase the size of foundation assets far beyond the original bequest.

- **Privacy.** For those U/HNWIs looking to retain privacy regarding their charitable intentions, a foundation offers a level of anonymity that's hard to beat. Unlike a testamentary trust or other bequest made in a will, the creation of a foundation does not become a matter of public record.

- **Publicity.** Alternatively, if a U/HNWI is looking to raise stature in the community, a foundation is an excellent way to do it. The establishment of a named foundation is one way to ensure your family's generosity will be known for many years.

- **Ability to target specific organizations.** A foundation allows U/HNWI to target specific charities and causes, including smaller, more local organizations that might have otherwise been unnoticed by larger philanthropic efforts. That's not always possible with other forms of giving.

- **Longevity.** Managed properly, a foundation gives U/HNWIs the opportunity to extend their giving well beyond the span of their own lives. Some of the largest and best-known foundations in America are well over fifty years old.

- **Family participation.** A foundation is an excellent way to foster a culture of giving in your family. Children and grandchildren can easily participate in foundation activities, and may even be able to help decide what causes to support.

- **Tax efficiency.** In addition to the benefits of making a charitable donation, foundations allow for the tax-free compounding of investments within them. This makes for an extremely tax-efficient method of giving, one that maximizes the benefit of your charitable dollars over time.

## Case study: A foundation makes a difference at the local level

A primary reason for establishing a foundation is the power to shape positive change on the level of the individual community. That seems to be the impetus behind the J.A. and Kathryn Albertson Foundation based in Boise, Idaho. The Albertsons made their wealth by operating a large chain of supermarkets throughout several western states. So when the time came to give back, the Albertsons naturally thought of helping those who have helped them. The solution: a private foundation, with assets of almost $665-million that specifically targets causes based in Idaho, where the Albertson family has its roots.

The focus of the Albertson foundation is to fund educational efforts throughout the state. As such, it fills a distinct need: Idaho currently ranks 46th in the nation in per-pupil spending. At last count, the foundation had made over $100-million in grants over the past three years or so, and had made a dramatic improvement to the lives of many state residents. The town of Bovill (population 301) is a prime example. With a poverty rate of 63% and only a few paved roads, it's a community that has very limited resources to spend on the education of its youth. But with a $661,000 grant from the Albertson Foundation, the town was able to build a childhood learning and health program – something the community would never have been able to afford otherwise.

As I mentioned, the ability to provide this kind of local-level assistance is a big reason why more and more U/HNWIs are structuring their giving through foundations. The Albertson foundation has a very narrow focus – the improvement of educational institutions in a single state. But this fits in perfectly with the purpose of the family's charitable giving. By establishing a foundation, the Albertsons have an opportunity to make a *real* difference, and the opportunity to see the benefits of their efforts on a first-hand basis. By allowing donors to be intensely involved in the selection of a charitable cause – and discerning in the application of charitable dollars to that cause – foundations offer the ability to be responsive to specific challenges facing even the smallest of communities. The result: dramatic improvements where they're needed most.

## Foundations: basic regulations

Foundations are complex charitable entities, bound by a number of government regulations that dictate the form and the scope of their donations. These regulations give rise to a number of important considerations any U/HNWI must consider before establishing a foundation.

## The size of a **foundation**

In most jurisdictions, there is no official rule that says foundations must be of a certain size. That said, there are a number of administration fees and other costs associated with foundations that suggest a practical minimum. It's hard to come up with a bottom-line number on this, but here's my general rule: if you're not intending to donate at *least* $1-million, it's probably best to consider another method of giving. And even at that level, the costs of running a foundation might not be worth the time and effort required.

That's not to say a foundation can't be constructed with less than that level of funding. I've seen foundations established with less than that, but special considerations almost certainly have to be made (provisions for more donations, special arrangements with professional managers, etc.), and those considerations may make a foundation more trouble than it's worth. What I tell my U/HNWI clients is if they are set on establishing a foundation with less than $1-million, they should be prepared to have the foundation exhaust its assets during your lifetime. Either that, or have the clear intention of making additional donations during life or through a will.

## Foundation **distributions**

Most jurisdictions have pre-established rules that require foundations to adhere to a strict code of conduct in order to retain their status as charitable organizations. Generally, a private foundation will have its status revoked if it conducts any business, or if it doesn't distribute a minimum amount of funds every year on charitable causes or programs. The exact formulation of these rules will vary from jurisdiction to jurisdiction, but the general concept behind them will be similar to the ones I've listed below. To retain its status as a registered charity, a Canadian foundation must spend at least the sum of:

(a) 80% of the prior year's receipted donations other than bequests;
(b) 10-year gifts and gifts from registered charities;
(c) 80% of previously excluded gifts;
(d) the total of gifts from other charities in the preceding year, excluding specified gifts;

(e) 4.5% of the average value of investment assets over the previous 24 months that were not used directly in charitable activities or in administration. The amount also does not include those amounts listed in (a), (b), or (c) above.

The above rules are pretty complicated, but for practical purposes, it's the last one that matters most. Essentially, it states that a Canadian foundation's assets must generate at *least* a 4.5% annual return – otherwise it will be in danger of exhausting its supply of capital. Obviously, this has important implications for the allocation of foundation assets, as we'll discuss below.

## The cost of a **foundation**

A foundation can be expensive to manage. Annual fees for the ongoing maintenance of a foundation will of course vary according to the firm managing the foundation, but many run about 2-3% of the total value of the foundation. In addition, many jurisdictions (the U.S., for example) impose an *excise tax* on foundation assets – this can amount to between 1% and 2% a year. These fees are *on top* of the minimum disbursements many jurisdictions require of foundations. All told, an American foundation could be looking at an annual reduction of about 9%-10% of the total value of the foundation.

Dealing with such a drain is the key to any foundation's long-term survival. Careful planning (including proper drafting of the foundation's structure) and top-level asset management is critical for managing this outflow. U/HNWIs must be committed to securing such management *before* setting up their foundation.

## Foundations **and taxes**

In most jurisdictions, contributions to a private foundation are treated much like other donations to charities. In the U.S., for example, contributions to private foundations made through a will are 100% deductible for estate tax purposes.

That said, there are often limits on the size and form of those contributions. In many jurisdictions, U/HNWIs are limited on the total amount they may contribute to a foundation in any year – at least if they still want to claim a tax deduction. In the U.S., for instance, founders may donate up to 30% of adjusted gross income on cash donations to a private foundation (compared to 50% on direct gifts to public charities), although any unused portion of the deduction may be carried forward for up to five years. For gifts of appreciated stock, the amount is even less – 20% of adjusted gross income. In Canada, contributions of publicly-traded shares to a private foundation are not eligible for special capital gains tax treatment. Bottom line: if you're only in the giving mood for the tax write-off, there are probably better ways to give.

# **Personal** considerations

By now, it should be obvious a foundation isn't something you just throw together. Beyond the rules listed above, there are a number of important personal issues U/HNWIs must consider before they establish a foundation.

## Foundation **mission**

Successful foundations can support a wide variety of charities or causes, but most have a single, clearly defined mission. Such focus allows for maximum benefit from foundation dollars. Obviously, it makes sense to sort this mission out *before* the foundation is established: without a clear vision of the foundation's purpose, founders are likely to become more frustrated than fulfilled by their charitable effort.

If you're interested in establishing a foundation, you first need to develop a clear vision of why you want to give, and why it should be done through a foundation. Some questions to ask yourself include what causes you'd like to support, where you want to make an impact (on a local, a national, or an international level), and what causes you're interested in supporting. Of course, these should be questions you should ask before making any kind of charitable donation, but they are absolutely crucial before establishing a foundation.

## Family **involvement**

One of the main benefits of a foundation is its ability to encourage family involvement. But unless clearly defined, that involvement can lead to problems – particularly when the philanthropic goals of the founder are in conflict with those of subsequent generations.

If your goal is to involve your family in your foundation, it's probably best to solicit involvement right from the start. Sit down with family members and discuss the purpose of your foundation as a *group*. You'll want to talk about board membership, and whether family members will be responsible for administration and paperwork. Establishing a clear donation policy as well as potential causes to support is also an important task, and can eliminate conflicts before they begin. Whatever answers your family comes up with, it's a good idea for founders to give other family members a full opportunity to speak their minds, and come to their own conclusions about foundation priorities. If you're not prepared to do that, then it's probably a good idea to look at other giving options.

## Foundation **lifespan**

A foundation can extend charitable giving far beyond the lifespan of its founder. There's no rule that says it *has* to, of course, but because the projected lifespan of your foundation will have such a big impact on the way your foundation is run, it makes sense to spend some time thinking about the issue before setting one up.

The longevity of your foundation will depend largely on your charitable goals. If it's important for you to see the benefit of your gifts, a one-time contribution to a short-lived foundation can make sense (although it's probably more costly than other charitable giving options). In such a case, you'll most likely want to establish a policy of generous contributions, and manage foundation assets with liquidity (rather than growth) in mind. On the other hand, if your goal is to extend giving beyond your lifetime, you'll probably want to keep donations close to the government-prescribed minimum, and invest a good portion of foundation assets for long-term growth. Whatever you decide, it's important to have an idea of the lifespan *before* you discuss management and donation policy.

## Annual **bequests**

As mentioned above, most jurisdictions require foundations to disperse a minimum amount of their assets every year. But depending on your own charitable goals, you may want to pursue a more aggressive bequest schedule.

Foundations can support different levels of bequests. Most are established with the intention of maintaining a minimum bequest, but many others are established with the intention of donating 6% to 8% of their assets every year. If the founder wants the foundation to exhaust its resources while he or she is still alive, that number may well be higher. And of course, there's always the possibility of a one-time large bequest to a special cause or temporary emergency. Probably the most sensible solution is to establish an ideal bequest target, along with minimum and maximum bequest levels. The decision on how much to give in any year will fall to foundation directors, so you'll need to determine some bequest guidelines when you establish your foundation. This is particularly important if you plan for your foundation to outlive you.

## Bequest **procedure**

After deciding on your foundation's bequest targets, you'll want to establish set procedures and policies for making those bequests. A big part of those procedures will be administrative (filing documents, writing checks, accounting, etc.), but you'll also want to establish research guidelines for potential donation recipients. These guidelines can be as simple or as detailed as you like, but you'll want to consider your directors here. Unless you're willing to set aside funds to hire professional staff, many of your directors will no doubt have other responsibilities (including full-time jobs). For that reason, it makes sense to make the bequest procedure as simple as possible. Pre-selecting a range of donation targets can be a big help, as can setting clear guidelines for what kinds of funding requests a foundation will accept. Resolving these issues will make it easier for everyone involved with in your foundation to share in the joy of giving.

## Investment policy **and allocation**

Another topic to consider is the investment policy of your foundation. As assets within the foundation grow, those assets will need to be managed. Formulating an appropriate investment policy and asset allocation plan will make it easier for directors to ensure a foundation meets its bequest targets.

There is no one way to manage a foundation's assets – an appropriate management strategy really depends on the goals of the individual foundation. Most experts agree that much like individuals, foundations require between one and two years worth of liquid assets. Such a pool would allow the foundation to survive an extended market downturn without reining in its gift-giving activities. Beyond that, a conservative, balanced investment approach usually makes the most sense, although aggressive holdings like venture capital or hedge funds may be appropriate for larger foundations.

For the vast majority of foundations, it's a good idea to involve a professional when it comes to asset management decisions. There are many capable investment managers who specialize in managing foundation assets. These people can construct customized portfolios according to a foundation's charitable goals, and can create an asset allocation policy that will help foundation assets grow. Perhaps more importantly, delegating investment management to professionals will mean one less thing for foundation directors to worry about. Just remember, a foundation requires more attention than other types of charitable giving. A professional manager will still require guidance from the foundation founder, particularly if the founder intends to supply additional funds to the foundation.

### Monitoring and **refinement**

Unlike some other forms of giving, a foundation isn't a one-time charitable event. Whether you plan on making a one-time gift or a series of ongoing donations to your foundation, you'll need to remain involved in it. At the very least, that will mean taking a leadership role on the foundation's board of directors. Ideally, however, it will mean more than that. Revisiting foundation bequests is an essential part of establishing a foundation. By conducting periodic checkups on recipients, foundation directors can ensure donated funds are actually being used for their expressed purpose, and whether the money could have been better used elsewhere. This ongoing monitoring will allow you to refine your foundation's bequest policy, and can help ensure your foundation continues to make a difference.

## **A final word** on foundations

No doubt about it, establishing a foundation is a more complicated way of structuring your charitable gift. But don't let that discourage you. For U/HNWIs with significant assets to give, foundations are an extremely flexible giving tool, offering a chance for U/HNWIs to give long after they pass into the great beyond.

# Key concepts: Chapter eighteen

- There are many reasons for establishing a foundation. Some of these are:

    (a) control over bequests - foundations offer control over who gets what

    (b) control over assets – foundations offer control over how assets are managed

    (c) privacy – a foundation can ensure gift-giving remains anonymous

    (d) publicity – a foundation is a good way for U/HNWIs to raise their stature in the community

    (e) ability to target small organizations – a foundation makes donating to small, community-based organizations easier

    (f) longevity – a foundation can extend giving well beyond a single lifetime

    (g) family participation – a foundation can foster a culture of family giving

    (h) tax efficiency – foundations allow for tax-free compounding of assets

- Foundations are best suited to larger, more substantial donations. $1-million would probably be a reasonable minimum, due to the costs to set up and maintain a foundation.

- In order to maintain its status as a charitable entity, foundations must adhere to strict rules of conduct and disperse a minimum percentage of assets every year.

- Foundations can be expensive. With fees and necessary disbursements factored in, it's possible for an American foundation to suffer a 10% drain every year.

- Most jurisdictions allow a tax receipt for donations to private foundations. But there is often a limit to the size of such contributions in any given year.

- U/HNWIs looking to establish a foundation need to consider a number of things:

    (a) foundation mission – what is the purpose of the foundation?

    (b) family involvement – what role will the family play in managing the foundation?

    (c) lifespan – how long is the foundation intended to survive?

    (d) annual bequests – what is the target distribution rate for the foundation?

    (e) bequest procedure – what is the procedure for making bequests?

    (f) investment policy – in what does the foundation invest, and in what amount?

    (g) monitoring– how will directors ensure bequests are used appropriately?

## Resources

The material on foundations can become pretty complicated pretty quickly. Those U/HNWIs who need to know more can look into the following.

***Private Foundations*** by Bruce R. Hopkins and Jody Blazek

***Foundation News and Commentary*** (magazine/newsletter)

## Websites

The Foundation Center ***www.fdncenter.org*** – loads of statistics and other resources on U.S. foundations

Council on Foundations ***www.cof.org*** – news and other information on foundation giving

# section 4

## Living wealth

Wealth is about more than just money —
it's about *life*. The emotional challenges
of wealth are every bit as complicated
as the financial challenges. And they're
not something you can ignore.

# **Your** changing life

- *How wealth changes life*
- *Common changes wealth brings*
- *How to manage those changes*

*"Riches are not an end of life, but an instrument of life."*

*Henry Ward Beecher*

As I've said throughout *True Wealth*, with wealth comes change. Sometimes this change will be positive. Other times, it will be negative. Preparing for these changes – in both one's finances and in one's lifestyle – is the central challenge facing all U/HNWIs.

That challenge wouldn't be so acute if U/HNWIs had resources to help them navigate through it. But that hasn't been the case. There have been many volumes that propose to tell investors how to accumulate wealth. There are far fewer that offer advice about how to handle that wealth once you have it. And there are fewer still that warn you about the kinds of changes you'll most likely have to face in your life once you have it.

I think it's time for that to change. This chapter will provide an overview of some of the most important life changes you'll face as a U/HNWI. If you've recently experienced a wealth event that has made you a U/HNWI, this chapter should be of immense value to you – it will make you more prepared for the changes you'll likely experience in the near future.

Even if you've been wealthy for some time, this chapter will serve as a confirmation of your own experiences, and will help you determine whether your wealth continues to affect your life. It's strange, but even after many years of having wealth, many U/HNWIs continue to lack an understanding of how wealth has affected their lives.

As I've often explained to my U/HNWI clients, wealth tends to *amplify* a personality – and that amplification can take place over a number of years. A kind-hearted, generous individual will tend to become more so after attaining wealth. A difficult, aggressive individual will do the same, becoming more so after wealth. Understanding these changes from a new perspective should help U/HNWIs understand themselves better. That understanding should help them live more fulfilling lives.

Keep in mind, however, that like life itself, wealth is an intensely personal experience, meaning no two U/HNWIs will experience it in quite the same way. That makes it difficult to come up with any hard and fast rules about the life changes wealth can bring. Instead of attempting to build an exhaustive catalogue of all the possible changes a U/HNWI could possibly face, I've selected some of the most dramatic. These are the changes I've most often seen in the U/HNWIs I work with. To my mind, they are the changes that have the potential for the greatest impact on the life of a U/HNWI, and serve to distinguish U/HNWIs from the rest of the population.

## My approach to a truly wealthy life

There's more to wealth than *money* – much, much more. Once you achieve a certain level, wealth starts to become demanding. Sometimes it will feel as if your wealth is calling the shots in your life. Even if you've built your wealth over several years, dealing with wealth means dealing with a lot of different challenges all at the same time – financial and life issues you have to confront *now*, not later. That's why I believe it critical for U/HNWIs to maintain a degree of *balance* in their lives. I understand balance is a rather vague concept, but in this context, what I mean is the understanding that wealth isn't an end in itself. Rather, it is a means by which you can *enrich your quality of life*. Wealth that brings happiness, fulfillment, and a range of new and exciting experiences – that's what I call *true wealth*. Wealth that brings hassles, anxiety, stress, and a shallow, empty life – well, that's the worst form of bankruptcy there is.

Given this general definition, it makes sense to structure one's life to emphasize that balance. Most of the U/HNWIs I've met understand this. They practice "stealth wealth." They don't obsess about their money. They don't feel the need to brag, demonstrate, or remind others of how rich they are. They take no pleasure from making other people envious of their lives. When they do feel like spending, they spend because whatever they're buying genuinely gives them pleasure, not because they're looking to climb up a couple of rungs on the social ladder. While they don't like giving handouts, they are always willing to help those genuinely in need. This is what I consider a healthy attitude to wealth, one in which the U/HNWI uses wealth to *enrich* his or her life (and the lives of loved ones) rather than as a yardstick by which to measure success.

Of course, there will always be some U/HNWIs who see things a little differently – those who conform more closely to stereotypes of the wealthy you might see on TV, those whose purpose in accumulating wealth is simply to accumulate wealth. I'll be honest with you: I don't tend to work with many of these people. When push comes to shove, our values are just too different. Those unable to see wealth management as a strategy for building a better life are really beyond the help of a wealth advisor who is focused on making financial decisions based on that one goal. It's difficult for me to derive any enjoyment (a crucial element in any business relationship) in helping a U/HNWI who is only looking for *more* – I want to work with someone looking for *better*. And, if it comes down to it – and sometimes it does – the decision not to work with that kind of U/HNWI is a decision I'm perfectly comfortable with.

## Life changes; life challenges

We've discussed many of the financial challenges U/HNWIs face in other chapters. Now, it's time to address some of the more pressing *life* challenges that face you as you become (and stay!) wealthy.

### Getting comfortable **with your wealth**

Those who achieve wealth over a number of years have the benefit of *easing* into their lifestyle. Through the course of time, they often become comfortable with many of the lifestyle changes their wealth can bring. For those who achieve their wealth suddenly, however, the transition isn't likely to be quite so smooth.

If you're new to wealth, you should be prepared for a period of adjustment as you get used to the idea of being a U/HNWI. This period of adjustment can manifest itself in many areas of your life. One obvious example is in how you spend your wealth. It would be surprising for non-U/HNWIs to hear this, but many of the wealthy find it difficult to spend money on a grand scale. Many of them became rich through careful money management, and they continue to feel a twinge of anxiety when they pull out their checkbook for a luxury item. I remember having a conversation with one U/HNWI about whether he could afford an extended vacation, even though his net worth was over ten million dollars. He is an older entrepreneur who had started a construction company from scratch, and had managed to survive in a very cyclical industry by being extremely cautious with money. Even though he's a millionaire many times over, he remains a very down-to-earth kind of guy, still showing up at the office at 7:00am most mornings, and still driving a company pickup. To be blunt, this was a man who didn't *think* of himself as a millionaire, and still managed his money (at least his spending) as if he weren't a millionaire. His mindset is typical of many entrepreneurial U/HNWIs I've met, particularly those who grew up during the Depression. With these people, frugality is "bred in the bone," making it tough for them to spend on the kinds of material goods that are commonly associated with millionaires.

To my mind, it's important for U/HNWIs not to "fake" their way through wealth. Rather than go to extravagant lengths to hide wealth from family and friends, or keep on living as if they had little or no money, I believe it's important for U/HNWIs to be who they are, and live life the way they want to. A big part of that is not feeling guilty about wealth: that is, not feeling fearful of using wealth to accomplish life goals. So get used to spending a little on that car you've had your eye on. Go ahead and ask for a first-class ticket. Sure, use your status as a U/HNWI to gain access to first-class events and services. *Feel free to use your wealth to enrich your life.* Yes, you may ruffle a few feathers with some people. But to me, that's ultimately a better option than a lifetime of anxiety and guilt when it comes to money.

Don't get me wrong here: I'm not suggesting that U/HNWIs start living like they were on *Lifestyles of the Rich and Famous.* All I'm saying is that it's a bad idea to try to be something you're not. Instead trying to deny the fact that you're a U/HNWI, embrace your new identity and live according to your own rules.

## Money **amplifies personality**

Maybe money won't change you – but chances are it will change some of your friends and family. Whether you notice it right away or it happens over time, more than likely you will notice your wealth will transform your relationships with those you care about.

Very rarely do these transformations result in a 180-degree personality change. As I explained above, money doesn't *change* a personality – it *amplifies* it. I've seen it many times before: minor problems and petty disagreements between an individual and a family member or friend suddenly become major issues once wealth arrives. Or perhaps a friend who had been drifting away from a U/HNWI drops out of sight altogether once the news of wealth becomes common knowledge. Or maybe it's just the opposite: an otherwise casual acquaintance hears of the U/HNWI coming into money, and suddenly becomes a long-lost "friend." These events can be hard to deal with for some U/HNWIs, and can lead some to question the sincerity of all relationships. In extreme cases, it can lead the U/HNWI to question whether wealth is really worth all the trouble.

Such feelings can hit any U/HNWI, but I've noticed these kinds of problems affect the newly wealthy in particular. That should come as no surprise – those who have received their wealth through a sudden, unexpected event are often shocked by the changes that wealth brings about in relationships they've taken for granted. Personality is usually much less of a problem with U/HNWIs who have become wealthy over time, or earned their wealth by building their own businesses or working long hours in the executive boardroom. More often than not, these U/HNWIs still remember the hard work they've had to do over the years (even if the actual reward for that work comes about suddenly), and are more likely to feel they *deserve* what they have.

I've always encouraged U/HNWIs to take a laid-back approach to this particular challenge. Everything changes in time – that's true of relationships as much as anything in this world. By all means, do everything you can to keep up with relationships and maintain old ties, and don't use your wealth to drive a wedge between you and people you associate with. But if things change, don't necessarily blame yourself. After all, any relationship is 50% beyond your control anyway.

## Maintaining **your privacy**

Often one of the first changes U/HNWIs notice in their lives is how privacy is suddenly a thing of the past. Sometimes this erosion is subtle: an otherwise anonymous inheritor suddenly feels all the telemarketers in the world have his phone number. Sometimes it is extreme: a high-profile entertainer has to hire a private security company to prevent intruders and trespassers from sneaking quick photos for the tabloids. Whatever effects you experience, chances are there will be little you can do to prevent these invasions – at least not completely. Like it or not, the lack of privacy is often one of the disadvantages of wealth.

Again, the potential impact of this change will largely depend on how quickly wealth was achieved. For those who took many years to become wealthy, lack of privacy is something that happens gradually, and is something that almost seems natural given enough time. For those who attained wealth suddenly (athletes and entertainers for example), it's a completely different story. The instant notoriety and public profile wealth can bring in such situations can be a considerable challenge – even more so if such wealth comes when the individual is very young.

No matter how long you've had to get used to your wealth, however, intrusions can be difficult to deal with when friends and family are doing the invading. Many times the grapevine will hear one of its own has "struck it rich" (this despite the fact that your wealth might be the result of years of hard work). A slew of "instant friendships" can be the result, as long-lost acquaintances or a horde of second and third "cousins" interrupt your professional and personal life. Even when these people aren't looking for any financial gain, their sudden attention can be unsettling.

As I said, unless you're willing to go to extraordinary lengths, you'll most likely have to get used to giving up some privacy. But you can limit the erosion by maintaining control over any information regarding your wealth. Absolute secrecy probably isn't required (and is more than likely impossible anyway), but it's a good idea to be cautious about sharing information, particularly when it comes to figures. If someone asks you about your wealth, speak in general terms. You don't need to provide details about it, explain how you got it, or apologize for it – all this will simply be fuel for those who would belittle your achievements or criticize your life. And don't feel you have to treat your family any differently on this one. At the end of the day, there are only a handful of people who need to have a detailed knowledge of your financial affairs: you, your spouse, your wealth advisor, and the team of professionals working with that advisor (i.e., your accountant, your lawyer, etc.). With everyone else, you can be as open or as private as you'd like.

## Pressure **to give**

In some cases, wealth transforms personal relationships into financial ones. At one time or another, most U/HNWIs I've met have received a phone call from a friend or family member asking for money. Such requests can sour both new and long-standing relationships, and lead U/HNWIs to question whether others perceive them as people or as bank accounts.

These requests for financial assistance can take different forms. Some drop subtle hints or off-hand comments about their financial difficulties, while others prefer a more direct approach. Still others will express a sentiment of entitlement, pressuring the U/HNWI to "pay back" those who offered emotional or financial support through the years. In some cases, such pressure comes not from outside, but from *within* the U/HNWI. I've known many cases where new U/HNWIs feel obligated to share or dispose of their wealth in such a way that enriches those around them. On the surface, that sounds like a noble goal, but I remember a meeting with one young U/HNWI where I got the distinct impression that the desire to give back didn't come through a sense of charity, but rather from a need to purge mixed feelings about wealth.

I'll be honest with you: there's no easy way to handle this pressure to give. Over time, it becomes more natural to "just say no." Many of the U/HNWIs who have experienced their wealth for some time have grown accustomed to saying no directly (yet politely), and aren't terribly bothered by sour looks anymore. Others have simply developed an uncanny ability to change the subject smoothly and subtly. To my mind, the best way to deal with these uncomfortable situations is to be honest with the person asking. Tell the person you're unclear as to whether such a gift or loan would be a wise decision right now. Before you make any financial commitment, you have to discuss the matter thoroughly with your financial professional or accountant, and that will take time.

I strongly suggest you make this statement a truthful one. If giving or lending is something you feel you'd like to do, consult with a financial professional to see exactly how much you can afford to give – the number requested from your "friend" can be very different than the number presented by a financial professional. Chances are a small loan or gift won't be a problem for most U/HNWIs, but that's not really the point. By acting on someone's request for money, you may well be establishing a precedent, and set yourself up for further requests. If you absolutely must give a gift, probably the best thing to do is to make it perfectly clear it is a one-time event. Gently, of course, but firmly.

It's not my place to tell you to whom you should give money – it's your money, so you get to make the decisions. But make no mistake: giving or lending money to friends or family is often more trouble than it's worth. If something unforeseen happens and your friend or family member is unable to pay you back, there will be consequences. At best, there will be an awkward distance between the two of you. At worst, you may have to sacrifice your own quality of life to make up for the lost money. Which is why I usually recommend U/HNWIs keep personal and professional relationships in two distinct categories.

## People **like you**

There are times in life when you need to talk to someone – someone with whom you can see eye-to-eye. For U/HNWIs, finding a person that fits the bill can be difficult. Particularly if your wealth has pushed you beyond the status of many of your friends and family members, it can be difficult to find someone who can empathize with your life circumstances.

Which is why I encourage my U/HNWI clients to seek additional friendships with other U/HNWIs. To me, the benefits of such relationships are clear. With another U/HNWI, you can seek financial or life advice from peers who are going or have gone through the same thing you have, and can contribute to any discussion on an equal level. With another U/HNWI, you can discuss financial matters without the fear of discomfort – there's less likelihood for resentment or unfair assumptions based on one's financial position when there is less discrepancy between the two parties. And of course, other U/HNWIs will actually understand you when you discuss just how much of a challenge wealth truly is: it can be difficult for non-U/HNWIs to believe wealth brings any challenge whatsoever.

Again, please don't take my suggestions the wrong way. I'm not telling U/HNWIs to dump their old friends and start associating with the *crème de la crème* of the community. I'm pleased to say that very few of the U/HNWIs I've ever known have picked their friends in order to climb the social ladder. Rather, they establish new friendships with U/HNWIs because other U/HNWIs offer them something that's hard to find in the rest of the population: *understanding*. If you find your non-U/HNWI friends capable of such understanding after you attain wealth, so much the better. If they're not, then there's nothing wrong with actively seeking out people who are.

For most people, finding other U/HNWIs will come naturally: they move to a more upscale part of town and meet people of comparable financial status; their growing business brings them in contact with other U/HNWI business owners; or a new lifestyle direction introduces them to a new circle of friends. With those who have gained their wealth rapidly, the transition will most likely be a little more jarring. If you find yourself in such a situation, there are a number of established groups dedicated to helping U/HNWIs find balance in their lives. Not only can these organizations provide contacts and potential friendships for U/HNWIs, they can also be an excellent place to search for professional referrals. All in all, it's worthwhile looking them up.

## Case study: A Canadian billionaire lives large

Mention the name Jimmy Pattison to anyone living in Western Canada and they will instantly know the name. Just in case you haven't heard of him, Jimmy Pattison is the sole owner of a Vancouver-based business empire that's involved in everything from car sales to amusement centers. As one of North America's wealthiest individuals, Mr. Pattison is a prime example of a U/HNWI whose wealth could easily create problems.

By all accounts, business has been good to Mr. Pattison. How good? At last ranking, *Fortune* magazine ranks him at number 251 in its annual survey of the wealthiest 500 people in the world, with a net worth hovering around the $1.9-billion range. Among the various businesses he owns: a number of car dealerships, a large supermarket chain, an outdoor advertising agency, and a string of Ripley's Believe It Or Not! museums. He is an active member of the Vancouver business community, and the former head manager of the 1986 Vancouver World's Fair (a position that gained him considerable fame, but a salary of only $1). In the Vancouver area, Mr. Pattison is known not only as an astute businessman, but as someone who appreciates the finer things too. He owns a large, ocean-going yacht (complete with a crew of seven). A few years ago he purchased Frank Sinatra's former Palm Springs estate, which he uses to entertain business clients.

As I said, business has been good to Mr. Pattison. But more importantly, *life* has been good, too. At 72 years old, Mr. Pattison still loves his work – he routinely puts in a 70-hour work week – and shows no signs of retiring. He likes the way his business has developed and grown over the years, and isn't looking to take his creation public or change the way it works simply to satisfy someone else's whims. Perhaps most importantly, he's using his wealth in ways that make him feel good, and he's not trying to be someone he's not. He enjoys music (he owns several pianos and plays the trumpet) and entertaining. He has strong opinions, and he isn't afraid to share them with anyone who will listen – but by no means does he force them upon anyone. He has spent money generously, both on luxury goods and on causes that matter to him. And while he loves his family, he's made it clear to his children they should not count on him to make them fabulously rich when he passes away.

I'm not going to lie to you – I admire Mr. Pattison. But not because he's a billionaire. Rather, I admire him because he has achieved success *on his own terms*. From what I know of him, Mr. Pattison is a prime example of what I'm talking about when I say wealth is a means to an end, not an end in itself. Mr. Pattison lives life the way he wants to, and isn't afraid to spend or save as he sees fit. He is a well-balanced U/HNWI who is completely comfortable with who and what he is. Simply put, that's something to which every U/HNWI can aspire.

## A **final word** on your changing life

Despite the changes I've listed here, wealth isn't something to be scared of. While the changes may be difficult to deal with at times, most of the U/HNWIs I have met have overcome them with flying colors. And there's no doubt that you will too.

## **Key concepts:** Chapter nineteen

- Wealth brings change. Dealing with that change is one of the central challenges of wealth.

- U/HNWIs should aim for balance in their lives. More than anything else, this means understanding that money is a means of enriching one's life – it is not an end in itself. Most U/HNWIs I've met have understood this.

- There are many changes brought about by wealth. Some of the most common (and most important) are:

  (a) Getting comfortable with wealth – U/HNWIs need to understand how their life has changed, and accept their position as wealthy individuals.

  (b) Money amplifies personality – U/HNWIs need to be prepared for changes in their relationships with family and friends.

  (c) Maintaining privacy –U/HNWIs should prepare for an erosion of privacy and be cautious about sharing financial information with anyone other than their spouses and wealth advisor.

  (d) Pressure to give –unwanted solicitations for financial assistance from family, friends, and charitable organizations can make existing relationships for U/HNWIs awkward – and potentially destroy them.

  (e) People like you – U/HNWIs can find it difficult to identify with or find empathy from non-U/HNWIs.

## Resources

Of all the subjects in this book, the subject of how wealth changes one's life is perhaps the most personal. The books below have influenced my view of wealth, and have led me to a deeper understanding of what it means to live a wealthy life.

***Business as a Calling: Work and the Examined Life*** by Michael Novak

***9 steps to Financial Freedom: Practical and Spiritual Steps So You Can Stop Worrying*** by Suse Orman

***The Seven Stages of Money Maturity*** by George Kinder

# Affluenza, and how to cure it

- *The problem of affluenza*
- *Why U/HNWIs are worried about it*
- *Practical tips on preventing it*

*"It is poor encouragement to toil through life to amass a fortune to ruin your children. In nine cases out of ten, a large fortune is the greatest curse which could be bequeathed to the young and inexperienced."*

**Jean de la Bruyère**

According to U.S. Trust, the next 15-20 years will see the largest transfer of wealth in American history. Over $5-*trillion* is scheduled to be handed down to younger generations over this time frame.

For some U/HNWIs, such thoughts are the cause of considerable happiness. For others, they are the cause of considerable anxiety. Because while most of us are reasonably confident of our spouse's ability to carry on financially after we're gone, we are often much less sure of our child's or grandchild's ability to do the same. The younger generation often doesn't share our sensibilities when it comes to managing money. Without careful tutelage, a large inheritance can easily be squandered by a youngster too immature to know how to handle that wealth. Or so we think.

Even if our children are capable of managing their inheritances, we worry whether wealth will change them — or whether it has already. While most of us want our children to have everything they would ever want in life, we don't want them to grow up with everything handed to them on a silver platter. That would be a disaster: a selfish, spoiled brat who expects the luxuries of wealth but lacks the will or the desire to create it for him or herself. Hardly the kind of legacy most U/HNWIs want to leave behind. The question then becomes: is a multi-million dollar inheritance really in the best interests of our children?

## Concerns about affluenza

These kinds of questions are on the minds of more and more U/HNWIs. So much so that professionals have coined a name for the subject: *affluenza — lack of ambition or aspiration, brought on by a life of wealth and privilege.* And by all accounts, it's a subject that's gaining increasing attention. The 1996 edition of the U.S. Trust annual *Survey of Affluent Americans* contained a detailed study on the subject of affluenza. And speaking from the perspective of someone who works with the wealthy, the results are hardly surprising. When asked what their primary concern was regarding their children and wealth, 68% of U/HNWI respondents answered they were concerned their children would place too much emphasis on material possessions. 60% were concerned their children would end up less well-off than Mom and Dad, and 50% were concerned that the material advantages enjoyed in childhood would dampen their children's initiative and independence.

table 20.1: **Concerns of affluent parents**

| Concern for Children | Cited by |
|---|---|
| They will place too much emphasis on material possessions | 68% |
| They will be naive about the value of money and how hard it is to earn | 64% |
| They will not do as well financially as parents have | 60% |
| They will not do as well financially as parents would like | 58% |
| They will have limited exposure to people with different socio-economic backgrounds | 55% |
| They will spend beyond their means | 55% |
| They will have their initiative and independence undermined by having material advantages | 50% |

Source: U.S. Trust *Survey of Affluent Americans*

These concerns seem to have shaped respondents' attitudes toward estate planning. In regard to the inheritance they plan to pass on to their children, 58% of U/HNWIs surveyed believed it was better to set a precise age for a child's inheritance, rather than simply pass the money on to the child immediately after the death of the parent. The majority of U/HNWIs in the survey chose 28 as the preferred age an individual should be before receiving a significant inheritance. The average respondent cited 23 as the *minimum* age. The average respondent believed $5.5-million would be the maximum an individual could inherit without it impacting the individual's values or attitudes.

Let me put some of these fears to rest. There is little evidence to suggest that a large inheritance *automatically* predisposes a child to a life of laziness. At the same time, common sense should tell us that the danger is a real one. Which is why I feel it necessary to discuss ways to overcome it. This chapter will detail some of the common challenges U/HNWIs face when trying to decide how their children will inherit wealth. It will discuss some of the techniques other U/HNWIs have employed to teach children the value of thrift and hard work – even though the wealth they left behind would require neither. This chapter will offer practical tips on how parents can ensure their children grow up with a healthy, responsible attitude toward wealth, without feeling guilty or excessively proud. And finally, it will outline some of the steps parents can take to shape their inheritances so as to minimize the chances of affluenza poisoning their children. Taken together, these tips should help parents feel more comfortable that they're raising their children right – that wealth is a beneficial influence rather than a corrupting influence in their children's lives.

## My approach to passing on wealth to children

At the core of this issue is the question of how best to pass on wealth to children. I've found most U/HNWIs already have strong opinions on the subject, but if a client asks for my opinion, I usually tell them to aim for a balanced solution. To my mind, that means leaving children in a position that offers ample security, yet provides ample motivation for them to earn their own living and achieve success on their own terms. So how does one achieve such balance in the real world? By considering two important questions:

## Question #1: **When should children receive wealth?**

Some U/HNWIs believe children should gain control of their parents' wealth when parents pass away. That's the easiest solution, to be sure, but it does fail to address a couple of important issues surrounding inheritance. If parents leave children with little wealth until late in life, parents will be denying themselves the opportunity to actually see the benefits of their gifts while still alive. Even worse, such behavior may generate considerable resentment: from the perspective of children struggling to establish themselves, a lack of generosity may well seem like miserliness rather than prudence. On the other hand, if parents dole out money too early, they risk training their children to expect ongoing allowances as their rightful due. It should be easy to see how such actions could lead to a lifetime of financial dependence and foolhardy behavior.

Unfortunately, there's no one-size-fits-all solution to this problem – it ultimately depends on the maturity of the people involved. In general though, I usually recommend a large inheritance be kept in trust until the child has reached adulthood. And I mean *full* adulthood – a couple of years out of college doesn't count. In most cases, that means age 30 or 35. By that age, parents should have a good understanding of the kind of person their child is, and should be in a position to evaluate whether or not that child can handle being a U/HNWI. Keeping such money in trust until then gives you as a parent the opportunity to formulate alternative strategies for passing on your wealth should it become clear your child will be irresponsible with anything you leave behind.

If the U/HNWI is concerned with giving while alive, then once again I recommend moderation. Personally, I'm of the mind that infrequent gifts of less than $10,000 don't pose much of a risk of warping a child's personality or turning a child into a spendthrift. If such gifts are made regularly, or if they are made for frivolous, luxury items, then it's quite a different story. As I said before, it comes down to common sense.

One solution I like to suggest is an *incremental inheritance*. Here's how it works. A large lump sum is set aside in trust for the child (either during the child's lifetime or upon the parents' passing), with the stipulation that the child receive it in three or four portions, with the largest portion saved for the final installment. Upon the creation of the trust, Mom and Dad establish certain dates upon which their child receives each portion of the money: the first could be when the child reaches the age of majority, for example, the second could be when junior finishes a post-secondary degree, the third when he lands his first "real" job, etc. Such a structure limits a child's access to wealth, thereby limiting the temptations big money can present to a young mind. At the same time, by giving the child *some* wealth, parents will be giving the child the opportunity to develop responsibility for his or her own wealth – an important lesson for future U/HNWIs to learn. Parents can easily put such a structure in place while still alive, giving them the opportunity to see the benefits of their gift, and provide financial guidance too. All in all, an excellent solution to the problem of timing an inheritance.

## Question #2: How much **is too much?**

An equally important question facing U/HNWI parents is the question of *how much* to pass on to their children. Once again, Mom and Dad find themselves in a dilemma. On one hand, they want to leave behind enough to allow the kids to enjoy a higher quality of life (after all, what else is wealth for?). On the other hand, they are worried that the amount they leave behind will be so much that the children will drop out of school, forget about finding a job, and make unhealthy lifestyle decisions.

Sorry, but there is no cut-and-dried answer to this question either. Once again, it comes down to the child's ability to manage wealth responsibly and make good decisions for his or her own life. A lot of times this can depend on a child's age. Personally, I wouldn't worry too much about giving a 55-year old son or daughter a substantial inheritance – they've had an opportunity to develop their own responsibilities. I would, however, think twice about giving a kid just out of university the same amount.

As a general rule, I caution parents about leaving behind the kind of wealth that can warp a child's self esteem – the kind of wealth that makes it difficult for children to feel that they are doing anything but living off Mom and Dad's money. In practical terms, that means leaving an inheritance big enough to make a practical difference to the child's life, but small enough that the child still has to get up in the morning and go to work. Call me old-fashioned, but I see work as the source of more than just income: it's where kids learns to be proud of their own success. A big inheritance can take that away from a child, making it difficult for the child to find a way in which to define an achievement. Far from doing their children a favor, parents who leave behind that kind of money are depriving them of what matters most in the world: the ability to earn their way in the world, and take ownership of their own financial success.

## Preventing affluenza

So beyond these general guidelines, what can a U/HNWI parent can do to prevent affluenza from becoming a problem? I like to group my suggestions into two general categories: personality solutions (what parents can do to develop a well-rounded personality immune to affluenza), and financial solutions (financial structures that reduce the possibility of affluenza infecting a child). Let's take a look at each.

### Personality **solutions**

### Teach achievement **and self-reliance**

Most U/HNWIs I talk to tell me their drive to achieve was a vital part of their financial success. Instilling a similar drive in your children can help prevent affluenza. How can you make that happen? By providing tangible motivation for making special efforts and accomplishing specific goals. One common method is to offer some form of reward for scholastic, athletic, or personal achievement. The point of such a system isn't to "bribe" your child into a scholarship, but to clearly illustrate the cause-and-effect relationship between hard work and rewards.

Another important step in the development of motivation is to clearly outline your expectations for your children. I'm of the mind that every U/HNWI needs to tell their children openly and honestly that the handouts will end some day. In other words, that you expect them to work and support themselves. Don't get me wrong here: I'm not suggesting Mom and Dad launch into the standard "get up off the couch" type of speech. Rather, parents should be encouraging children to seek their own opportunities. This is *not* a bad thing. By letting your children know there will be a limit to parental assistance, you'll be encouraging them to make their own way in the world, and ultimately giving them the right to take credit for their own achievements.

### Don't be **a control freak**

Parents need to teach their children to make wise financial decisions. But there's a point where such instruction goes too far. Some U/HNWIs think they're doing their children a favor by making money decisions for them, or by withholding rewards if a child makes bad lifestyle decisions. But such control is ultimately self-defeating. By stripping away a child's responsibility, you'll be condemning that child to a lifetime of insecurity and financial dependence. And you may just be condemning yourself to a lifetime of resentment from your child.

Yes, children need guidance. Yes, they need assistance. But if you want to raise strong, independent children who have the drive to succeed, *you must allow them the opportunity to make their own financial and lifestyle decisions.* Let your kids accept either the benefits or the consequences of those decisions freely. At the end of the day, accountability will do more to prevent affluenza than a heavy-handed approach ever will.

## Encourage curiosity **and learning**

U/HNWI parents need to bring children up in an environment that encourages curiosity and a desire for new experiences. Such traits will encourage a lifetime of activity rather than a lifetime of laziness. In practical terms, such education might involve encouraging the child to learn new skills – even better if those skills might one day be of use on the job. A family vacation can also be an educational experience, teaching a child there's a whole world out there that's just waiting to be experienced. Giving education-oriented gifts can often be a good idea, too. While a computer may be a source of entertainment, it may also give your child working knowledge they may find useful in their careers. Whatever you decide to do, the point is to instill a sense of curiosity – a desire to explore boundaries, investigate new ideas and discover what life has to offer. That will help form a personality that's naturally focused on getting ahead.

## Teach humility **about wealth**

Wealth is an immense privilege, as well as an immense responsibility. There's no reason why children of U/HNWIs shouldn't know this. By teaching children to be respectful of that privilege, and mindful of that responsibility, parents will help instill a healthy sense of humility when it comes to wealth. Such humility will make children less inclined to spend wealth on expensive status symbols and material possessions. It will also help prevent the destructive behaviors that often lead to squandered inheritances.

Parents can help foster such humility in a number of ways. Teaching children to respect other people's money and property is a common sense place to start, as is insisting that they respect those who aren't as fortunate. Another good way to teach respect is to involve children in charitable activities, and tell them why giving back is an important activity. But there's a fine balance here: you don't want your children to feel *guilty* about the wealth they will someday enjoy. Constant reminders of how "lucky" the family is will most likely weigh children down with emotional baggage, and may well cripple their motivation to make their own wealth.

## Financial **solutions**

### Financial **education**

This one should be common sense. U/HNWI parents need to teach their children to value the wealth they will one day inherit. They also need to instruct their children on how to manage that wealth. I'm pleased to say most U/HNWI parents are doing that already. In fact, the 1996 U.S. Trust *Survey of Affluent Americans* identified a number of steps U/HNWIs have taken to teach their children about wealth. Fully 89% of respondents noted they have established savings accounts for their children, and 66% have assisted them in developing a budget for personal expenses. Slightly more than half (51%) have set up a brokerage account. These are all effective methods to build a child's sense of responsibility about money, and combat the effects of affluenza.

table 20.2: **Remedies for affluenza**

| Step taken | Cited by |
|---|---|
| Setting up a savings account for them | 89% |
| Giving their children an allowance | 89% |
| Helping them develop a budget for personal expenditures | 66% |
| Setting up a checking account for them | 52% |
| Setting up a brokerage account for them | 51% |

Source: U.S. Trust *Survey of Affluent Americans*

## Encourage the kids **to find jobs**

I'm going to be direct on this one: if you ever want your children to respect money, they need to work. Even if your children will someday inherit so much that they will never have to get off the couch again, the experience of an honest day's work will give them a sense of respect for wealth and lead them away from unwise decisions.

As to what kind of job they need – well, that's a matter open to some debate. Personally, I believe U/HNWIs should encourage their children to find their own opportunities. A summer job at the family business isn't quite as educational (or as satisfying) as a job they have to land themselves. Perhaps I'm being a little harsh – a job at the family business can certainly be educational, but it has to be the *right* job. If the position in question is an entry-level or labor-oriented one, it can teach children to respect the workers they may eventually manage, and make children understand that there's a lot of sweat that went into Mom and Dad's money.

Whatever job your kid eventually finds, remember that the lesson here has nothing to do with money. Rather, it's the idea that work can be fulfilling, satisfying, and a source of pride. Ideally, these lessons should start well before junior actually goes to work. By taking your child into the office and exposing them to what you do, your children will know there's more to life than simply lounging around all day. In the long run, that's the kind of attitude that will do the most to prevent affluenza.

## Be cautious about allowances **and other financial aid**

Allowances can be an excellent way for a child to gain practical financial experience, establish financial discipline, and encourage saving habits. How much should a parent give? That's really up to the individual. My only advice is to be cautious before you give the kids big handouts. Extremely generous allowances, large unearned gifts, and other freebies may all contribute to affluenza.

Far more important than the issue of how much to give is when that allowance should stop. When an allowance continues through adulthood, it can quickly become a problem. I'm pleased to say most U/HNWIs seem to be aware of this. According to the 1996 U.S. Trust survey mentioned above, most U/HNWIs have an idea of when they plan to stop supporting their adult children – typically that age is 23. That said, many of these U/HNWIs are willing to maintain financial assistance for adult children in certain circumstances. Personally, I think that's a balance that makes sense.

I emphasize the word *balance* here. There's nothing wrong with wanting to help your children out – after all, what else is wealth for but to enrich the lives of those you care about? But there comes a point at which assistance robs children of their ability to become self sufficient.

table 20.3: **Expenditures U/HNWIs are willing to pay for their children**

| Expenditure | Cited by |
|---|---|
| Vacations they take with their parents | 88% |
| Medical expenses | 86% |
| Buying a home | 76% |
| Expenses related to starting a business | 67% |
| Private school or college for a grandchild | 67% |
| Lessons or summer camp for a grandchild | 64% |
| Furniture | 46% |
| Rent | 34% |
| Car purchase or lease | 30% |
| Clothing | 15% |
| Vacation they take without their parents | 14% |

Source: U.S. Trust *Survey of Affluent Americans*

My general rule is that when gifts become large, frequent, and more life*style*-oriented (a new car, for instance) than life*skills*-oriented (an education), that point has been reached. Better to take a cautious approach to gifts and allowances, and make it clear to children that there is a limit to Mom and Dad's financial graces.

## Case study: a billionaire's thoughts on affluenza

For many in the financial world, Warren Buffett is the wisest investor who's ever lived. In the thirty-five years or so he's been the head of Berkshire Hathaway, Mr. Buffett has built his business from about $100,000 to a market value of $100-billion. At last count, Mr. Buffett is personally worth somewhere in the neighborhood of $33-billion. With a net worth like that, you'd think his children stand to become billionaires someday too.

You'd be wrong. As he has explained in a number of published statements, Mr. Buffett intends to leave the bulk of his wealth to charities (including a private foundation), not his children. Why? It's simple, really: he wants his children to pursue their own success in the world. Buffett sincerely believes leaving too much money can sap a child's drive or desire to achieve. As he famously advised in an interview for *Forbes* magazine back in 1986, parents should leave "enough money to your kids so they can do anything, but not enough so they can do nothing."

That seems like wise enough advice. But in the years since this statement was published, there have been many commentators who have passed judgement on Buffett for his miserly qualities in regard to his children. In fact, some writers have gone so far as to suggest Buffett's estate plan is evidence of a mean–spirited, selfish man. Myself, I don't see it that way – but I have to admit, I can see where such comments come from. There can be little doubt that the inheritance of several billion dollars would have a disruptive effect on the Buffett children. On the other hand, the knowledge that you were disinherited from one of the largest estates in history could be disruptive too.

If his annual reports and other writings are any indication, Mr. Buffett is anything but an ignorant man. I wouldn't be surprised if Mr. Buffett has realized the potential damage a *complete* disinheritance could create, and instead achieved some kind of balance that leaves his children a more significant sum without necessarily warping their personalities or stealing their right to achieve their own success. I suppose we'll find out eventually, although if Mr. Buffett's pronouncements about his good health are to be believed, we're going to have to wait quite some time before we do.

## Structure your **estate properly**

The organization of your estate can have a dramatic impact on your children's relationship with wealth. I've listed only a few of the many innovative estate structures that can help parents prevent affluenza from afflicting their children.

## Incentive **trusts**

As I've mentioned before, one of the primary benefits of a trust is the control it offers over an inheritance. Exercised properly, such control can do much to prevent affluenza. Understand, however, that there is a point at which a trust becomes damaging, and limits a child's ability to take responsibility for their own financial decisions. Any trust that attempts to control a child's decisions in life about career, or a choice of spouse, will ultimately have a detrimental effect on the child's development, fostering dependency and lack of self-esteem. Bottom line: if you're thinking about establishing an incentive trust as part of your estate plan, make sure to have a frank discussion with your financial professional about how far to go with it. Chances are your professionals will have seen good trusts and bad (I know I have) and can steer you in the right direction when it comes time to create one for the next generation.

## Tangible **gifts**

Another effective remedy for affluenza is to leave heirs illiquid or tangible assets. Such gifts improve your children's quality of life, yet provide less of a temptation to become a spendthrift. The possibilities for such gifts are limited only by your imagination: fine art, antiques, or even season tickets for a local sports team are all examples I've seen in my dealings with U/HNWIs.

## Communal **bequests**

Communal bequests can help prevent affluenza. In such a scenario, an asset is left in trust, with the understanding it would be used by multiple heirs. Such a structure works well with family real estate (a vacation property is a typical example) and ensures a single heir is never given the ability to cash in a large asset and run away with a sack full of money. That said, parents looking at communal bequests need to be aware of the potential conflicts such gifts can generate. When multiple heirs can't agree on the ongoing management of a communal gift, bitter arguments and strained relationships can be the result.

## The family bank or **emergency fund**

One innovative way to prevent affluenza is through a general inheritance pool – a family "bank" as it were. In such a scenario, Mom and Dad transfer a significant sum to a special trust, and instruct a professional trustee to distribute cash for qualified uses. These uses would be established by the terms of the trust, while giving the trustee considerable discretion over situations that aren't necessarily covered. Heirs would have to "apply" for trust funds, and would be restricted as to how they could use any money received. As a result, parents can have a degree of assurance that money would be put to good use rather than spent frivolously. An additional benefit would be that funds could be utilized by a number of beneficiaries over a number of years.

Such a fund could have a variety of uses. A parent could establish such a trust to supply low-interest rate mortgages to heirs. Entrepreneurs could establish such a trust to provide "venture capital" for heirs looking to start a business. I know of one U/HNWI family who established a collective trust as a kind of "disaster fund." Trust funds were to be used in cases where an unforeseen emergency might inflict a grave financial burden on the children; the question of what constituted a "disaster" was largely left up to the trustee.

Whatever the exact terms of such a trust, the end goal is to provide *assistance* to heirs – not necessarily to give them a house on easy street. That's an attractive proposition to many U/HNWIs. Personally, I can see such a structure best used in tandem with a basic level of direct inheritance. That way, heirs wouldn't end up resenting either the parent or the trustee, but would still be protected from the emotional and psychic disruption a large inheritance can inflict on a person.

## A final word on affluenza

Don't feel guilty because you're not giving your children everything they're asking for. At the end of the day, your children don't need wealth – they need *you*. Teach your children respect. Pay attention to them. And show them you care not only about their financial well-being, but about them as people. That's the best way to cure affluenza.

# Key concepts: Chapter twenty

- Affluenza is the syndrome experienced by many of the children and grandchildren of U/HNWIs. In its worst form, the privileges of wealth lifestyle can lead a child to be lazy, and grow up without ambition.

- While it's unclear whether a large inheritance *automatically* predisposes a child to laziness, many U/HNWIs are concerned about affluenza. Many of these have taken practical steps to ensure their children don't fall victim to it.

- U/HNWI parents need to consider two issues when planning their estates:

  (a) when should children receive wealth? In most cases, large inheritances should be left in trust until the child reaches the age of 30 or 35. An incremental inheritance can be a good solution.

  (b) how much is too much? Parents should be cautious about leaving children enough money that would secure an independent income without ever working.

- There are two main areas by which parents can prevent affluenza:

  (a) by carefully shaping their children's personality, and

  (b) by structuring inheritance in such a way to limit the possibility of affluenza.

Personality issues:

- Parents should teach their children to achieve and to be self-reliant

- Parents should be cautious about controlling the lives of their children.

- Parents should encourage education and learning – both financial and otherwise.

- Parents should teach humility about wealth – but not guilt.

Financial issues

- Parents should allow their children to work.

- Parents should be cautious about providing allowances or financial aid.

- Parents need to structure their estate properly. Incentive trusts, tangible gifts, and a "family bank" are all structures that will help prevent affluenza.

## Resources

There are many resources for parents looking to teach their kids to deal with money the right way. Here are a few of my favorites.

*Kids and Money* by Jayne A. Pearl

*Rich Dad, Poor Dad: What the Rich Teach Their Kids About Money — That the Poor and Middle Class Do Not!* by Robert T. Kiyosaki

*Quest for the Pillars of Wealth* by J.J. Pritchard

*Wimpy Parents: From Toddler to Teen: How not to Raise a Brat* by Kenneth N. Condrell and Linda Lee Small

## Websites

*www.kidsmoneystore.com* — books, games, and other products to teach your kids about money

*www.affluenza-and-wealth.com* — a small site, but some interesting resources

# **Your** health

- *The impending health care crisis*
- *Effective strategies for dealing with health care costs*
- *Dealing with aging parents: a special report*

*"Money, to some extent, sometimes lets you be in more interesting environments. But it can't change how many people love you or how healthy you are."*

**Warren Buffett**

What good is wealth if you aren't healthy enough to enjoy it?

It's an important question – a question a lot of U/HNWIs will be facing soon. Over the next two decades, many of us will have to confront the issue of health care, either through our own experiences or through those of our extended family, and determine exactly what kind of value we place on good health.

I'm pleased to say most of the U/HNWIs I've met have understood this. Securing quality health care remains a top concern among the wealthy. As of yet, that concern isn't really about the cost of that care – most U/HNWIs can afford the best care available. Rather, the health care concerns of most U/HNWIs I've dealt with surround the issue of *access*. U/HNWIs (like the rest of the population) want access to top-quality care when they need it. They don't relish the thought of having to wait in line for a life-saving procedure sometime in the future.

Dealing with this issue will be the central topic of this chapter. This chapter will give you a good grasp of some of the challenges that will likely face our health care system in the future, and will explain how you can prepare for those challenges now. Even if you're young and in good health, you'll find this chapter to be of value. Eventually, there will come a day when we'll have to confront the subject of health care, either with ourselves, with parents, or with other members of our family. U/HNWIs who are unprepared could be putting their wealth – and indeed, their very lives – at risk.

## Good news, bad news

You're a U/HNWI – I have some good news for you. All other things being equal, you'll most likely live longer than the rest of the population. It's true. In a landmark study of British civil servants published back in 1994, researchers at University College London found that those with higher incomes typically lived longer, even after accounting for lifestyle-related factors such as smoking and exercise. This despite the fact these civil servants all had access to state-sponsored health care, and enjoyed relatively hazard-free jobs. Researchers have offered many hypotheses to explain this phenomenon (most believe it has more to do with the social status enjoyed by higher-ranking individuals rather than their actual wealth), but they have yet to come up with anything definitive. Whatever the reason, I'm sure this will come as a pleasant bit of news to most U/HNWIs.

Here's the bad part: just because U/HNWIs live *longer* doesn't necessarily mean they're living *better*. As we grow older, there is an increased probability of serious injury and a growing likelihood of contracting a debilitating disease. As they live beyond the average life expectancy, U/HNWIs may find themselves having to rely upon long-term care and other health care options more than the rest of the population. That could make U/HNWIs more vulnerable than the rest of the population in any health care crisis. Ironic, but true.

## Health care crisis: an overview

That phrase "health care crisis" is one you've no doubt heard before. Over the past 25 years, there have been a number of developments – most of them positive in their own right – that have put immense pressure on health care systems around the world. New drugs along with preventative vaccinations and greater access to medical treatments have resulted in a dramatic increase in the average life expectancy. According to the World Health Organization's *World Health Report* of 1998, world life expectancy in 1955 was 48 years. In 1998, it was 68 years. By the year 2025, it will be 73 years. Remember too, these are life expectancies *from birth*. Once an individual reaches the age of 60 (as most of the population in the affluent nations of the world will), there's a good chance of living well beyond the average.

All this is good news, to be sure. But such trends are not without their consequences. Simply put, there are more elderly living in the world today than ever before. In 1997, there were 390 million people over the age of 65 (about 6.6% of the world's population). By 2025, there will be 800 million (about 10%), and two-thirds of these will be in developing nations. In some areas of the world (Latin America and South-East Asia), the number of older people is expected to increase by up to 300%, while China alone will be the home of over 274 million elderly – close to the current population of the United States. This ratio between youth and age will be the highest the world has ever seen. That means there will be more demand for treatments and drugs that enhance quality of life for the aged than the world has ever seen.

Let me be blunt: it's going to be difficult for the world to take care of all of these people. The World Health Organization recognizes this shift as one of the most profound economic and social challenges the world will have to face in the next quarter century. In most nations, the elderly simply don't have the means to pay for their ongoing care. Even in the developed nations, governments are beginning to admit they don't have the resources to ensure their population over the age of 75 maintains a dignified quality of life.

To top it all off, North America has an additional problem to worry about. The population bulge known as the baby boomers, (those born between 1947 and 1966), constitutes some 100 million people on the continent, and they're just beginning to enter that time in life when health care becomes a pressing concern. A year 2000 study by Consumers Union entitled "The Health Care Divide" found that 50% of American households headed by someone over 65 are spending 10% or more of family income on health care. The National Institute for Health Care Management Foundation (a Washington, D.C. based nonprofit group) noted spending on drugs rose some 40% between 1998 and 2000 alone, accounting for 44% of the overall increase in health care spending. Sure, there's an argument to be made that spending more on drugs ultimately results in a cost savings to society (drugs and other preventative treatments are usually cheaper than surgery and hospital stays). Even so, the rising cost of drugs is expected to result in higher health insurance premiums and added strain on government funding.

You don't need a crystal ball to determine what all this will mean to our health care system. As the huge block of boomers ages, there will be increasing demand for health care services. While all of this is happening, the number of people actually supporting the health care system (through their income taxes) will actually decrease. The result: the possibility of a severe funding crunch.

## **My approach to** health and health care

Only time will tell whether our governments can solve this crisis before the system collapses. One thing is for sure: I don't think U/HNWIs should bet their health on whether they can or not. A two-tiered health care system already exists in the U.S., and in my opinion, will be further developed in countries like Canada in the years to come (in fact, many Canadians are currently crossing the border to visit a variety of private health care clinics in the U.S.). Like it or not, private health care is becoming less of a matter of choice and more a matter of necessity. Given such an environment, it seems to me that it's high time for health care planning to take its rightful place as an essential element in every U/HNWI's overall wealth management strategy.

In the years ahead of us, health care planning will very likely become one of the most important financial goals in life – as important as retirement planning or estate planning is today. Which is why U/HNWIs need to familiarize themselves with some of the central issues surrounding health care, and review some of the strategies necessary for securing personal funding for health care expenses should the need for it arise.

### Health coverage **and the need for insurance**

The first step in any health care strategy is to understand your health care coverage. At the very least, this means familiarizing yourself with your health care policy and/or your state or company-sponsored plan, and making sure you know what kinds of ailments and conditions you're covered for. Even after several years serving U/HNWI clients, I still find it surprising to meet U/HNWIs – people for whom funding health insurance is usually not a problem – who can provide me with reams of data on almost any stock they hold, but can't give me even the most rudimentary overview of their health care plan.

Going through the ins and outs of health insurance would easily fill this entire book, so I'll provide only the most basic suggestions here. For most U/HNWIs, the main question to ask won't be whether to have health insurance or not. Rather, it will be a question of *how much* to have. Of course, the answer to that question is a very personal one, and will depend on your personal health history, the health history of your family, your individual financial situation, and ultimately your tolerance for risk. For that reason, it's hard to tell you what constitutes a "good" policy – that will be different for every U/HNWI. But as a general rule, you'll want a policy that is comprehensive and has a high claim limit. While most U/HNWIs can afford routine procedures, extraordinary claims of $500,000 or even $1-million are not uncommon. These kinds of numbers can pose a significant threat to your wealth, even if you have several million to fall back on. Last but not least, remember to review your coverage on a fairly regular basis (at least annually) and make any modifications that your age and ongoing health require. Keeping on top of these things will ensure you're covered when you actually need it.

## Health insurance **for business owners**

For U/HNWIs who own their own businesses, the subject of health insurance is an especially important one. It's easy to see how a catastrophic illness or an extended hospital stay can drain a hard-working consultant or professional of their personal assets, and cripple an otherwise solid business.

When it comes to health insurance, U/HNWI business owners generally have two options: individual coverage, or group coverage through a professional association or community group (a trade group, for instance, or perhaps the local chamber of commerce, etc.). The latter option is generally a cheaper one, and often doesn't require a medical exam. That said, individual coverage is often the only form of health insurance available to the self-employed. In either case, you will probably be able to deduct at least a portion of your health insurance premiums as business expenses. The rules will of course vary according to where you live, so make sure to consult a qualified tax advisor and an insurance professional before making any deductions.

Another option for business owners in the U.S. is to establish a *medical savings account* (MSA). These are tax-advantaged savings plans that allow investors to save for future health care expenses. Not everyone is eligible for such plans – usually you have to have a "high premium" insurance plan. This is a relatively new solution to the problem of health care coverage, so insurance providers in your area may not yet be set up to offer high premium plans and/or products with a savings component. In some states, they may not even be able to, as state law may prohibit the high premium plans MSAs require. Bottom line: check with your financial professional to make sure an MSA is even an option before you start investigating.

## Insurability

A central element in all insurance planning is *insurability* – whether an insurance company will agree to underwrite a policy on a given individual. In my experience, it's an issue many take for granted. Don't fool yourself: insurance companies are in the business of making money, and most won't hesitate to deny coverage if they think you're too unhealthy. Even if you do meet the basic requirements of insurability, insurance companies can attempt to offset their risk through prohibitively high premiums. All in all, good reason to learn a little more about insurability, and whether it's an issue you'll have to confront.

By far the best way to stay insurable is to buy insurance *before* you actually need it. Preferably *well* before. Not only will this guarantee insurability, it will help keep premiums low. But there comes a point at which the coverage offered isn't really worth the high premium. In such a situation, it's probably better to carefully consider your insurance options rather than blindly rush in to a policy that does you more harm than good. Keep in mind, however, there are very few people who are absolutely "uninsurable." Often, rejection simply means you have to shop around a little harder.

If you're denied coverage, there's usually no need to panic. Insurance companies look at several factors to determine your eligibility for insurance, and some of these are in your power to control or change. Insurance companies tend to look favorably on good diet and exercise. Eliminating stress, making positive lifestyle changes (quitting smoking, for instance) will also help. Such changes will produce immediate benefits that may help you secure coverage, or if you're already eligible, may help to lower premiums.

## Health **tourism**

One health care trend more and more U/HNWIs are looking at is "health tourism" – travelling to a foreign locale to receive health care services. Seeking care overseas is by no means a new idea. For Canadians, for instance, a quick trip over the border can provide access to some of the best health care in the world (albeit at premium prices). But recently, the horizons of health tourism have expanded. Now, U/HNWIs from all over the world are travelling to developing nations such as India, Costa Rica, Cuba, and South Africa. These and other countries are marketing health-care services to U/HNWIs in countries with big health care line-ups. It's a win–win situation: U/HNWIs receive on–demand health care (coupled with a vacation in a warm part of the world), while cash-strapped hospitals receive much needed hard currency, and a chance to keep highly qualified staff within the country.

There are a lot of things going for health tourism. Obviously, one of the big benefits is the cost. Even after including the price of a plane ticket, a procedure that could cost tens of thousands of dollars back home might cost a fraction of that overseas. Perhaps more importantly, health tourism can offer quick solutions to health care problems that could otherwise take months to solve in one's home country. For routine, non-life-threatening surgeries and procedures (cataract surgery, cosmetic dentistry, varicose vein removal are some typical examples), health tourism gives U/HNWIs the opportunity to bypass waiting lines and improve their quality of life.

As of right now, health tourism is more of a novel topic than it is a viable alternative to traditional health care. To be honest, I'm not convinced if it will ever replace quality health care in one's home country – the potential hassles and uncertainty are probably too great for that. But there's little doubt U/HNWIs will be hearing more about it in the future.

## Disability **and long-term care insurance**

Ironically, death is *not* the worst thing that could befall us – at least not from a financial perspective. Rather, it is a crippling disability, one that requires an ongoing stay in a professional care facility. Maybe that sounds unattractive, but as we grow older, it's more and more of a possibility. Citing data that goes back to 1995, Milbank Memorial Fund noted a steady increase in the number of us requiring long-term care. Depending on where you live, such care can easily run over $60,000 or more per year. Add in costs for drugs and ongoing treatments and procedures and you could be facing a bill of $75,000 to $150,000 a year. To top it all off, our aging population is sure to create more of a demand for long-term care in the years to come. Translation: prices are most likely going up. Given these circumstances, it's easy to see how even a U/HNWI could be concerned.

In my experience, long-term care isn't something U/HNWIs generally think of until they need it. For obvious reasons, that's a less than ideal situation. So allow me to provide a basic summary of the key issues surrounding long-term care. There are four general levels of ongoing health care, each with different financial implications:

- **The first, *in-home care,*** is usually temporary, with the purpose of recuperating from a major illness or short-term disability. It is typically conducted in your own home by skilled professionals, and is usually not covered by health insurance policies.

- **The second type of ongoing care is *custodial care*.** It involves either a health care professional or other caregiver coming to your home and assisting you with the ADLs (Activities of Daily Living): walking about the house, cooking, bathing, dressing, etc. By definition, it is not medically necessary, but many elderly people would be unable to function without it. The vast majority of ongoing care situations are custodial (upwards of 95% in the U.S.), but most insurance policies don't cover it.

- ***Skilled care* involves round-the-clock care** and assistance provided by licensed professionals (nurses and doctors). Skilled care is generally covered by insurance plans, and is recuperative in nature.

- ***Intermediate care* is likewise medically necessary,** but can be provided by either licensed or unlicensed health care providers.

chart 21.1: **Prevalence of functional limitations among elderly and non-elderly populations**

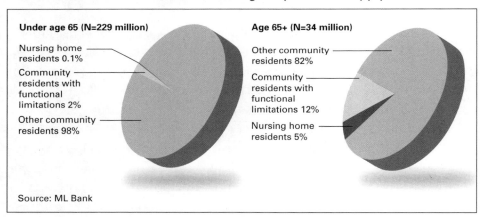

**Under age 65 (N=229 million)**

Nursing home residents 0.1%

Community residents with functional limitations 2%

Other community residents 98%

**Age 65+ (N=34 million)**

Other community residents 82%

Community residents with functional limitations 12%

Nursing home residents 5%

Source: ML Bank

What do these levels of care cost? You'll have to do some research to find out. Both the level and the quality of care offered can vary widely depending on where you live. Calling around to nursing homes in your area is a good place to start, but you'll want to follow up with a conversation with your family physician and perhaps a senior's organization in your community too.

graph 21.2: **Prevalence of long-term care need among elderly**

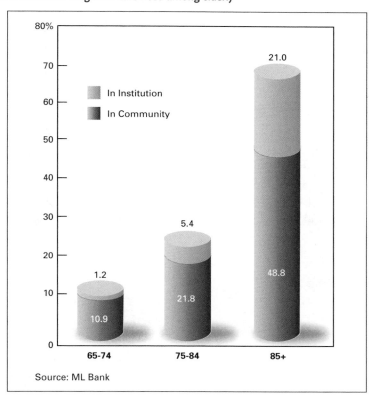

Source: ML Bank

As for funding such care, there are a variety of options. The costs of most long–term care facilities are well within the reach of most U/HNWIs. Even so, those who like to plan ahead will want to investigate long–term care insurance. Depending on who you ask, industry experts will tell you long–term care insurance is targeted at those people with a net worth of anywhere from $500,000 and $5–million: anything more and the person will most likely be able to cover the cost of long–term care alone; anything less and the person most likely can't afford the premiums. Personally, I think that's a conservative estimate. Premiums for long–term care insurance can be extremely high, and a good many U/HNWIs will find it makes more sense to pay for long–term care out of their own pockets if the need arises. My general rule: if your investment portfolio generates more than $150,000 a year, you can be fairly confident you'll be able to pay for long–term care for yourself without too much trouble. If income is something less than that, buy only what it takes to make up the difference.

If you are interested in long-term care insurance, you'll want to keep a couple of issues at the top of your mind. Foremost of these will be your insurability. The American Association for Long-Term Care Insurance notes that anywhere between 10% and 25% of those between 60 and 75 are denied coverage for medical reasons, so if you think you'll need coverage, make sure to get it early. Secondly, you'll want to carefully investigate policy options before signing on the dotted line. In many cases, the "perfect" policy – one that combines lifetime coverage, a high monthly benefit, and a low premium – doesn't exist. If you have to make a compromise, I recommend you place greater emphasis on lifetime coverage than a high monthly benefit – U/HNWIs can usually cover the difference. Thirdly, you'll want to insist on a policy that covers custodial care (some policies don't), and doesn't require prior hospitalization or doctor approval before benefits are paid. Last but not least, you should only buy a policy with a guaranteed renewable premium. If you don't, you could be risking having the policy cancelled or your premiums raised sometime down the road.

## Preparing **for incapacity**

It's sad, but true: in some cases, declining health will not only rob us of our quality of life, but of the ability to make appropriate financial and lifestyle decisions. Which is why preparing for incapacity should be a vital part of everyone's health care strategy.

Of course, the decisions regarding incapacity are among the most personal of all financial planning decisions (indeed, of all life decisions). So the first step is understanding what you want. Whatever decisions you come up with, it makes sense to clarify your wishes with your loved ones well in advance. That way, you'll be sure you'll be in charge of your own life, in the event you can't make those decisions yourself one day.

Beyond understanding your personal wishes, the key to incapacity planning is the power of attorney or living will document. This is the document that communicates your wishes to your chosen representative, and gives that representative the legal power to act upon those wishes. Depending on where you live, such instructions go by a variety of names and encompass a variety of powers. In most jurisdictions, the power of attorney document is able to give your representative the ability to manage your finances and make a wide variety of decisions regarding your investments, your business, and your day-to-day financial matters. In addition, more and more jurisdictions are allowing your power of attorney to make decisions regarding your health – whether to discontinue life support, for instance. That range of power may or may not be what you feel comfortable with, so make sure to discuss your options and set appropriate limits on your power of attorney when you write your document. No matter what arrangement you decide on, it should be obvious that your choice of representative is of the utmost importance. That person could one day have tremendous power over nearly every aspect of your life, so it's critical to choose someone who understands your values, your needs, and your intentions.

A power of attorney document isn't complicated. But it does have to be constructed with care. Because so much rides on the exact wording, you'll want to consult with a professional who has a good deal of experience drafting them for U/HNWIs – in other words, don't just settle for someone you find in the yellow pages. And don't think incapacity is something you prepare for once: be prepared to review and update your power of attorney every three years or so. As with your will, financial and life circumstances can make some of its provisions obsolete.

## Special report: health care planning for parents

A generation ago, my discussion of health care planning would have ended right there. Today, however, health care planning means not only planning around your own health, but the health of your parents as well. As life expectancies increase, more and more U/HNWIs will find themselves members of the "sandwich" generation, taking care of not only their children, but of their elderly parents too. For most U/HNWIs, funding such care won't be a problem. Funding it *wisely* – well, that's another story. Which is why I think it's a good idea for all U/HNWIs to take a closer look at health care planning for their parents.

### Communication **is key**

If you think you might have to support your parents someday, I have two words of advice: *prepare now*. Schedule a time for a frank discussion with your parents. Talk to them about the issue of long–term care, and ask about their ability to pay for it if needed. Ideally, such a conversation should take the form of a "family meeting," and should involve anyone who will be called upon to offer assistance (financial or otherwise) to your parents when the time comes. Understand, however, that the subject may be a difficult one – particularly if parents aren't normally in the habit of discussing money matters with their children. My advice: broach the matter slowly, and don't expect to solve anything in one sitting.

## Funding **options**

There are many ways to fund parental care. If substantial assets are available, it might make sense to set aside appropriate funds for long-term care expenses. A living trust would be an ideal choice here. Another option is long-term medical or "nursing home" insurance. Many insurance companies now offer policies tailor-made for children looking to insure themselves against the costs of parental care. If you decide on this option, you'll definitely want to discuss the matter with your siblings. By sharing the costs of policy premiums, insurance can be more affordable.

Whatever you decide on, make sure to assess the time it will take to establish your parental care plan. Again, this won't be a problem for many U/HNWIs, but if the bulk of your wealth is tied up in illiquid assets (as it is with many business owners) or if the need for funds is immediate, it makes sense to boost life insurance coverage until you can raise appropriate funds. Such a strategy will ensure you don't pass on any burden to heirs.

## Tax **considerations**

Parental care can bring up a number of tax implications. Those implications can vary from jurisdiction to jurisdiction, so it's a good idea to consult with a qualified tax professional where you live before starting any parental care plan. Make sure to get the facts straight before you commit to anything.

## Power **of attorney**

Just like your own health care plan, any parental care plan should include an enduring power of attorney and/or health care instructions. Preparing the proper legalized instructions well before any such event happens will enable your family to avoid the legal and personal problems incapacity can bring.

## Emotional **considerations**

Perhaps the most important advice I can give on the subject of parental care is to be aware of the emotional considerations as well as the financial. When a parent needs care or support, a child needs to be there – you can't just write a check for the time and the emotions involved. Part of your planning process should be preparation for these complex emotions, and an understanding that care is indeed a long-term commitment.

# **A final word** on health care

Financially, U/HNWIs may not be as vulnerable to the health care crises than other segments of the population. But they won't be immune. The rising costs of health care will affect everyone, and for those U/HNWIs who do become sick, those costs could be financially devastating. That's a risk I think every U/HNWI should look to minimize.

## Key concepts: Chapter twenty-one

- Wealth is worth very little if you're not healthy enough to enjoy it.

- Securing quality health care will be a growing concern for U/HNWIs in the decades to come.

- As they live longer, U/HNWIs may come to rely on long-term care and other health care services even more than the rest of the population.

- The first step in any health plan is to investigate your health coverage. Don't assume your coverage is comprehensive.

- Business owners need to be cautious with their health insurance, and determine whether group coverage, individual coverage or other options make most sense.

- As we grow older, insurability will become a more pressing concern. It may be wise to secure insurability by purchasing appropriate health coverage well before you actually need it.

- Every U/HNWI needs to consider their disability and long-term care insurance.

- There are four general levels of long-term health care:

    (a) in-home care

    (b) custodial care

    (c) skilled care

    (d) intermediate care. finding how much each kind costs is an important part of health care planning.

- Every health plan should also include provisions for incapacity.

- Increasingly, U/HNWIs will be responsible for supporting their parents. Such obligations require special planning.

- Communication is the first step in that planning. Talk to your parents about their wishes, and investigate your options. A living trust, additional health coverage, or long-term care insurance are all possibilities.

## Resources

As the growing health care crunch garners more attention, I expect we'll see more books and websites on the subject. In the meantime, we'll have to do with the following:

***Boom Bust and Echo*** by David K. Foot and Daniel Stoffman

***Long-Term Care Insurance Made Simple*** by Les Abromovitz

***Be Prepared*** by David S. Landay

# **Dealing** with divorce

c h a p t e r

**22**

- *How a divorce can impact a U/HNWI*
- *Alternatives to litigation and conflict*
- *Common financial challenges faced by divorcees*
- *Multiple families*

*"[Marriage is] like signing a 356-page contract without knowing what's in it."*

**Kenneth Hartly Blanchard**

A generation ago, divorce was a cataclysmic event – an emotionally and financially devastating occurrence that usually became the talk of the town. That's no longer the case. With over 40% of marriages meeting an untimely end, divorce is a subject many U/HNWIs are familiar with – or will be some day. Some say this is clear indication of the decaying moral fiber of our times. Others say it is an inevitable result of shifting values and more hectic lives.

Whatever you think of its social ramifications, there can be little doubt divorce can be one of the most significant financial events in a U/HNWI's life. Depending on the laws in your jurisdiction, a divorce may entitle your spouse to 50% or more of everything you own, leaving your net worth well below the U/HNWI threshold. Any event with the potential for that kind of impact deserves some serious thinking.

A divorce typically covers an entire spectrum of financial challenges – everything from one's income to one's estate plan can be affected by a divorce. And that, in a nutshell, is why I've included a chapter on the subject in this book. If you are currently going through a divorce settlement, the information in this chapter will help you avoid the kind of financial devastation that can make a U/HNWI divorce front page news. It will also help you navigate through some of the important financial issues you'll be facing immediately after your divorce, and find effective solutions to some of the ongoing concerns you'll confront as you reorganize your finances. It will give you practical advice on what you should be doing to get your financial house in order in the wake of a divorce, and offer guidance on how best to manage your new financial obligations – either as the spouse who transfers wealth or the spouse who receives it. Even if you're not going through a divorce, you should find some sections of this chapter valuable. For those U/HNWIs not yet married, the discussion of pre-nuptial agreements will give you a primer on this useful piece of financial protection. Those in long-standing, stable relationships will find value in the section on *post*-nuptial agreements, or the sections on how a divorce among your children may affect the wealth you pass on to heirs.

Despite this wide range, there are subjects this chapter will not cover. This chapter will *not* provide you with legal advice, nor will it provide any guidance as to what constitutes a "fair" financial settlement. It will not tell you how to hide assets so as to avoid their inclusion in a settlement. It will not tell you how to extract a punitive financial settlement from your spouse. In other words, it will not serve to make the already volatile divorce process any worse. Rather, it will concentrate on *healing* – financial healing – and give you suggestions and tips on how you can make smart money decisions at a very difficult time in your life. Quite frankly, that's the kind of positive, clear-thinking approach that is long overdue on the subject.

## My approach to divorce planning

Let me be clear: divorce planning is complicated, emotional and messy. It's not a part of my job that gives me any pleasure – quite frankly, it's something I dread. But it happens. Over the years I've been working with U/HNWIs, I've had a number of clients go through divorces. And if there's one thing I've taken away from helping clients through such experiences, is that *anger benefits nobody*. The more spouses try to "get back" at the other through the divorce settlement, the more destructive and costly the divorce will be. Not only in terms of one's financial position, but in terms of one's life.

To that end, the first step in any divorce should be to ensure anger and bitterness are kept as far away from the negotiations as possible. You can do that by entering into *alternative dispute resolution*. This is the general name for a variety of settlement processes that steer splitting spouses away from bitter (and expensive) legal battles. Many people don't know this, but in most jurisdictions you *don't have to go to court* to settle a divorce – at least, not to settle the disposition of communal property. Instead, you can enter into a *negotiated settlement*, where you and your ex-spouse work out a deal privately. If it's not possible to do that civilly, a *mediated settlement* might be the answer. In such a situation, a professional mediator is brought in to assist in negotiations and act as a liaison between the two parties. If that doesn't work, then an *arbitrated settlement* is another possible solution. Arbitration is a formal legal process that is usually as binding as any trial decision, but is less costly and more private than a lengthy battle in court.

There are a number of clear benefits to these alternative resolution processes. First and foremost, alternative dispute resolution is usually much cheaper than any formal legal procedure. It's also quicker than a court-sanctioned divorce. Besides the emotional strain it can inflict, a lengthy divorce can put assets in financial limbo, a situation that's of little benefit to anyone. Alternative dispute resolution is also a private process. That can be a big benefit to U/HNWIs who want to keep their finances out of the public record. Perhaps most importantly, it can be a lot less adversarial. Mediators and arbitrators are hired to reach a settlement, not to "stick it" to the other side. In the long run, that's in everyone's best interest.

## Before **a divorce**

Nobody plans for a divorce. But there are steps U/HNWIs can take well before any break up that can make the divorce process a lot smoother if and when it happens.

### Prenuptial agreements

Many people are wary of prenuptial agreements. Such people would argue prenuptials project a level of distrust and cynicism about the sanctity of marriage. I've even heard some people go so far as to say a prenuptial agreement is a self-fulfilling prophecy, and actually *predisposes* a marriage to a less than happy ending. I don't share these opinions. To me, a prenuptial agreement is simply another form of protection, one that deserves to be considered with an objective mind, free from superstition.

The benefits of a prenuptial should be easy to understand. For U/HNWIs, prenuptial agreements can offer protection (albeit limited protection) in a marriage where there is a large discrepancy in assets. For U/HNWIs entering a marriage on a more equal footing, a prenuptial can help distinguish assets brought into a marriage, making it easier to protect assets destined for one's heirs.

Prenuptials are extremely flexible. Anything and everything can be included in a prenuptial (within the boundaries of the law, of course), making it easy to customize one to your exact needs. That said, it's a good idea for every prenuptial to address both the *assets* and the *income* of the respective spouses. As many U/HNWIs have discovered, one can grow faster than the other, and if the agreement offers sketchy details about either, it can be the source of future problems. Prenuptial agreements may be revocable or irrevocable, but in most cases, a changeable agreement will allow both partners to avoid being trapped in an agreement that is out-of-sync with current financial circumstances. And of course, if the passage of time takes away the threat of a premature divorce, there's nothing to say the two spouses can't throw the agreement into the trash can.

Before you sign a prenuptial, you'll need to be aware of a few important issues. Number one, a prenuptial agreement needs to be drawn up properly – preferably by a qualified lawyer who's constructed one for U/HNWIs before. Number two, keep in mind that prenuptial agreements are by no means "bulletproof": in many jurisdictions, courts are under no obligation to accept a prenuptial agreement as a binding contract. Should a judge find a discrepancy between the prenuptial and the real-life circumstances of either partner, he or she won't hesitate to ignore it.

### Inheritance protection: prenuptials for your children

For some U/HNWIs, prenuptial agreements aren't so much a tool to protect their own assets, but rather a tool to protect assets intended for their children. A prenuptial helps ensure an inheritance will find its way to a child (or grandchild, as the case may be), rather than to that child's estranged spouse.

It's easy to imagine how forcing such a prenuptial on a child can be an incredibly offensive way of controlling a child's life or passing judgement on a potential spouse. But in other cases, it can be a good idea. I know of one case where a U/HNWI couple wanted their daughter to secure a prenuptial covering that portion of the family construction business the daughter was to inherit. The exact circumstances of the family finances were very complicated, involving an estate freeze that was initiated many years ago, but the key to it all was the family's 51% control of their business, the ownership of which had been transferred in trust to the couple's four children. If even a small portion of that ownership stake was brought into dispute through a divorce, the family could have lost control of the entire business. The subject was indeed a delicate one, but the father (to his credit) decided to broach the topic with his daughter. I'm pleased to say that the discussion went well: Dad was able to help the daughter and her soon-to-be spouse work out an agreement that was fair to everyone.

### Inheritance protection: trusts

More often than not, however, a parent's mention of a prenuptial will cause shock and anger. Which is why I usually recommend a trust structure for parents looking to protect a child's inheritance. That way, a child can receive income, but because assets are technically owned by the trust, they won't normally be considered part of the child's assets for the purposes of a divorce settlement. Be aware, though, that such a solution is by no means airtight. Those who live in a jurisdiction with communal property laws may well have trust property deemed communal – this is a real danger if trust income was co-mingled with other income, or if trust income purchased assets that were used jointly. Remember too, that nearly all jurisdictions require trust assets to be disposed of at some point. When they do, they may well become part of the child's property anyway.

As always, parents need to exercise caution when it comes to establishing trusts. To you, a trust may be simply a way to protect your children. To your children, it could constitute a mean-spirited judgement on their marriages, and a domineering "control from beyond the grave" approach to the family finances. I'm sure some U/HNWIs would say such opinions are a small price to pay for the protection of one's legacy. Myself, I'm not so sure. Bottom line: think carefully about the message you might be sending your children before deciding on this kind of structure.

## During **the divorce**

Those who have gone through a divorce know how difficult it can be to juggle the complicated legal and financial issues at the same time. What follows is a brief list of some of the more common "problem areas" encountered during the typical divorce process, along with some suggested ways to overcome them.

### The emotions of divorce

Divorcees usually find themselves in the middle of an emotional whirlwind. Often the first thing to be carried away by that whirlwind is financial judgement. A divorce forces both spouses to make difficult financial decisions at a time when they are most vulnerable. U/HNWIs need to be aware of these emotions, and how those emotions may affect their financial decisions.

Of course, no two people will experience divorce in quite the same way. But there are some common emotions many divorcees experience, and each of these has potential financial implications. One of them is a sense of despair – a lack of hope or caring about one's future. Such feelings can prevent a divorcee from making timely decisions about their wealth. In other cases, a feeling of low self-esteem or lack of confidence can result in an endless deferral of financial decisions – even a complete paralysis. Some divorcees do exactly the opposite: the intensity of the divorce process can force them into snap judgements simply because they want to "get it over with." Sometimes, divorcees are overwhelmed by a desire to "get even" with their ex-spouse. In such cases, the divorcee can make bad financial decisions just to spite their former partner.

Each of the above emotions can be incredibly destructive – both financially and otherwise. At the same time, they are perfectly natural responses to the trauma of divorce. Probably the best advice I have to help divorcees through such emotions is to work closely with a professional – a *financial or legal* professional to make sure financial decisions are made for the right reasons, and an *emotional* professional (that is, a counselor, psychologist, therapist, etc.) to keep these emotions from being a problem in the first place. While it's naive to assume a divorce can happen without *some* kind of emotion, it's my belief a dispassionate settlement should be the goal, at least as far as the finances are concerned.

## Alimony and maintenance

Probably the primary financial goal of any divorce settlement is to provide a secure and stable lifestyle for the divorcing spouses. In many cases, this will take the form of ongoing alimony or maintenance payments. Deciding on an appropriate schedule and structure for such payments will be a major focus of most divorce settlements.

There are many different options for structuring support payments; many of them have unique tax advantages. In many jurisdictions, maintenance or alimony may be tax deductible (certain conditions most likely must be met). Another advantage to alimony and maintenance is that most jurisdictions count them as earned income as far as retirement plans are concerned. Despite these advantages, there are situations where declaring support payments as alimony may not make sense. Check with a qualified tax advisor to find out what kind of structure would work best for you, and try to approach any discussion on the topic with an open mind in the settlement proceedings.

In many cases, alimony and maintenance payments constitute the only source of income a divorcee can rely upon. Unfortunately, they are often less than dependable. I can think of one example where a divorced U/HNWI had arranged for mortgage payments to be made from ongoing support payments. When her ex-spouse died unexpectedly, she was suddenly left scrambling to make the payments. It's easy to imagine a similar situation arising if for some reason an ex-spouse withholds payments – either out of financial need or out of spite. Because of this inherent uncertainty divorcees should treat income payments with caution, and be conservative when it comes to making long-range financial assumptions based upon the income those payments provide.

### Divorce and your business

One of the most challenging areas of divorce planning revolves around the disposition of a closely-held business. For most U/HNWIs, the sheer size of business assets virtually guarantees their inclusion in divorce proceedings. The illiquidity of those assets, however, brings up an acute problem. In extreme cases, the inability for ex-spouses to come to mutually agreeable terms regarding business assets can force an otherwise healthy enterprise to collapse.

I can't stress this enough: dispute resolution is absolutely vital when it comes to the disposition of business assets. With a mediated or arbitrated settlement, there's a good chance of ex-spouses reaching some form of compromise. If your divorce goes through the courts, the chances are much lower. In some jurisdictions, courts are infamous for taking a straightforward and brutal approach to the division of business assets. I've seen some settlements that forced an outright liquidation of a long-standing business – at rock-bottom prices, no less – simply because the two parties couldn't come to a compromise.

In addition to a negotiated settlement, there are things a business owner can do to protect a business before a divorce. A prenuptial agreement is an obvious solution. I would go so far as to call a prenuptial a requirement of U/HNWIs bringing business assets into a marriage. Beyond that, it might make sense to explore specialized financial structures that distance business assets from family assets. I'm thinking primarily of trusts and partnership agreements here: structured properly, both can be used to ensure a business survives a divorce settlement. Just make sure to investigate these options through a qualified professional. They need to be structured properly to be effective.

## Divorce and options

As options become standard compensation for executives and senior employees, they have naturally become a more standard part of divorce proceedings. But the very nature of options brings up a number of questions when it comes to divorce. Should unvested options be considered communal property? Should a spouse be forced into a premature exercise of options to satisfy the terms of a divorce settlement? What about taxes? Which spouse is liable for tax on options that are technically in that spouse's name, but are transferred to the other as part of a divorce settlement? Or how about the big one: what kind of firm value can you realistically put on options that fluctuate daily with the value of the underlying stock? These questions are not easy to answer. Yet the answers can have a tremendous impact on any divorce settlement.

There are two central issues concerning the treatment of options in divorce proceedings. The first issue is whether the options are in fact considered marital assets. In general, unvested options granted as a reward for *past* performance, or as part of general compensation for *current* performance, are regarded as part of the marital estate. Options granted as incentive for *future* performance are not. Determining what category your options fall into will be a major concern for either the courts or your mediator/arbitrator. The second issue revolves around how options are actually going to be distributed to the other spouse. There are two common methods. The first is to defer distribution until exercise, usually through a trust structure to formally separate them from the individual's property. The other form is to provide cash or cash-equivalent compensation for the present value of the options. This last alternative can be particularly challenging, often requiring a "best guess" estimate of the future market value of the underlying stock.

Understand that while options have been used as compensation for some time, they are somewhat of a new issue in the divorce courts. As more and more divorces involve options, I suspect the treatment of options in many jurisdictions will become more standardized, and the tax laws regarding transfer of options will become more clear. The only way to make sure you receive a fair settlement is to consult with a skilled professional well-versed on the subject.

## Children

Securing the well-being of children is an important goal of any divorce settlement. For most U/HNWIs, child support won't be a financial burden. But it can still cause conflict. In some cases, it's possible for payments to be so high they cause further feuds between the parents, and resentment toward the children. In such a case, everybody loses – most of all the child. This is the most important reason why parents should do everything possible to reach a support settlement with a minimum of animosity.

Beyond the issue of ongoing support, the most pressing financial issue involving children is their education. In most of the cases I've seen, the willingness to fund a child's education is rarely an issue, at least in principle. When it comes time to put a dollar figure on that commitment, however, things can change. Tuition fees have been rising rapidly throughout the past decade, and a four-year undergraduate degree can easily top $100,000 (and that's not including living expenses, books, and other costs). And if private school is something you believe in, you'll want to factor in at least another $20,000 per year of school. All told, you could be looking at an education bill of a million or more for a family of four children. Even for a U/HNWI, such a sum is a major financial commitment – a commitment that can make a divorce even more complicated.

There are many options available to parents looking to fund a child's education (some of them are even tax-advantaged). But for divorced U/HNWIs, a well-constructed trust is probably the best answer. A trust offers flexibility and control, and the best possible guarantee that assets assigned for the use of the child will actually be used for the child's benefit. A trust can allow for more flexibility than other forms of education savings – if the child decides not to go to school for instance, assets can be directed toward something else. And of course, trusts also allow for a measure of protection against immature children receiving large lump sums.

## After **the divorce**

After the divorce, the focus of financial planning shifts from settlement to reconstruction. Chances are one or even both spouses will have to spend some time rebuilding the pillars of their financial house. Here are some of the major issues involved with such an effort.

### Estate planning

As I've mentioned throughout *True Wealth*, an estate plan is an essential element of overall financial health. Ironically, it's often the one element that's completely ignored in a divorce settlement. Which is why reviewing your estate plan should be an *immediate* priority after your settlement is finalized.

Even the best estate plan will be a disorganized mess after a divorce. The first step toward reconstructing it is to conduct a thorough review of your assets and your bequests. Obviously, you'll want to change some of your beneficiary designations. My advice is to do this as soon as possible. I still remember coming across one longstanding U/HNWI will that named a previous spouse as the primary beneficiary of the individual's estate, while leaving new family obligations completely ignored. Such a situation would have been an unthinkable tragedy if it weren't changed (I'm glad to say it was, and quickly!). Beyond your will, you'll also want to pay particular attention to the *title* of your assets. Assets that are yours under terms of the settlement may still be held in title by your former spouse well after the settlement. Leaving titles unchanged makes it very hard for your heirs to claim assets that are titled under another name.

### Insurance: life, disability, and health

Another crucial element of every estate plan is insurance coverage. In a divorce, both the need for and the structure of an insurance policy can change dramatically. Ideally, securing an appropriate level of insurance should be part of your divorce settlement; if that's not possible, make sure to bring up the matter when you discuss your new financial situation with your wealth advisor.

For those divorcees who already had insurance at the time of the divorce, you'll need to review ownership of your policy, and change the beneficiary designation if required. This sounds like common sense, but I hear of at least one or two stories from my colleagues every year about unfortunate U/HNWIs who didn't change their beneficiaries after a divorce or other significant life change. This is a big problem: with the increasing use of life insurance in U/HNWI estates, insurance proceeds can represent a good portion of a decedent's estate, and it can wind up going to your ex-spouse if you don't change it.

Health insurance should be another important concern. In some jurisdictions health coverage will survive the dissolution of a marriage. But even in such jurisdictions, your ex-spouse's plan may offer significant benefits that may not be available to you after a divorce. Make sure to check what you're eligible for after your papers are filed.

# Multiple or "blended" families – a true challenge

One result of the rising divorce rate is the "blended family" – a family brought together by one or more previously married spouses. Despite what we might see on *The Brady Bunch*, the challenges of such a situation are usually far from humorous. Here is a brief review of some of the unique challenges facing blended families, along with some suggested solutions.

## Income and obligations

With many previously married spouses, financial obligations extend to both the new family and the old. In some cases, court-sanctioned divorce settlements can put a real drain on a blended family's finances, and stunt the ability of one or both spouses to build a financial future together. There is no quick and easy way to solve such problems. The best (and only) suggestion I have is to have a frank discussion about each other's financial obligations *before* tying the knot. If conducted in an honest, respectful fashion, such a discussion will provide a framework for the family's future financial planning. Ideally, such a conversation should include a discussion of how each partner will treat assets brought into the new family, and how each plans to contribute to the new family's ongoing expenses. Such discussion may lead to immediate solutions (a prenuptial agreement), but even if it doesn't, it should minimize conflict and provide a starting-point for an eventual solution.

## Adoption

Sooner or later, all blended families have to confront the issue of adoption. For many couples, the decision to adopt is the final consummation of their marriage commitment, and an emotional and spiritual joining of two separate families. However pure the sentiment, however, adoption is also a *financial* decision. In most jurisdictions, signing adoption papers means accepting financial responsibility for the child until that child reaches the age of majority – and sometimes beyond. My advice: if adoption is something you're considering, make sure you understand what you're getting into. Financial considerations may pale in comparison with the emotional and spiritual value of adoption, but at the very least, U/HNWIs should be aware of their new liability before they adopt.

### Estate planning

Estate planning can be an immensely difficult challenge for a blended family. In some cases, ex-spouses and previous children will be entitled to special consideration in your estate plan, despite your new family circumstances. In other cases, spouses will want to give previous children (and sometimes even ex-spouses) such consideration. Either way, it makes sense to review each other's responsibilities before constructing a new estate plan. Depending on the circumstances, it may be possible to construct a single estate plan for the new family (this is often the case when the remarried couple is young). But in my experience, it's usually a better idea to construct separate estate plans. Separate plans make it easier to balance prior obligations with current needs. Trusts are tailor-made for such situations. Their versatility gives U/HNWIs the opportunity to provide for both old and new families in a variety of ways, while offering a degree of protection against legal challenge – an immensely important benefit in some situations.

## A final word on divorce

A divorce can be emotionally devastating. But there is no reason why it must also be financially devastating. Make sure to consult thoroughly with a qualified financial professional (and not just a *legal* professional) throughout the proceedings. A financial specialist can make sure your wealth survives your divorce, even if your emotions still need time to heal.

# Key concepts: Chapter twenty-two

- Divorce can have devastating financial consequences for U/HNWIs. Any event that poses such a threat deserves to be considered before it happens.

- Divorce is emotional and messy. Ex-spouses can make it less so by opting for alternative dispute resolution, settle differences through negotiation, mediation, or arbitration. Such a process is usually cheaper, less antagonistic, and more private than a court-sanctioned settlement.

Before the divorce

- Prenuptial agreements offer a limited form of protection for U/HNWIs entering a marriage with a large discrepancy in assets.

- The exact terms of a prenuptial agreement are up to the individuals; in general, it's a good idea for the agreement to cover both assets and income.

- Prenuptial agreements may offer a way for parents to ensure wealth goes to an adult child, rather than an estranged spouse.

During the divorce

- Divorcees typically experience a range of emotions while going through a divorce. While natural, these emotions can be financially destructive.

- Securing a means of income is the primary financial goal of most divorce settlements. There are many ways of structuring such income; check with a financial professional to find out what payment structure works best for you.

- Regardless of how such payments are structured, income payments should be treated with caution. They need to be carefully guarded against potential risks.

- When a divorce involves a business, special caution is warranted. Alternative dispute resolution should be a top priority. Specialized trust or partnership arrangements can help keep a business outside of divorce proceedings.

- Divorce proceedings that involve options can be complicated. In general, courts will determine the reason why the options were granted before making any decision about their disposition.

- The ongoing support of children is another major priority of any divorce settlement. The structure of such payments can often cause animosity between parents, and is better left in the hands of a trusted mediator or arbitrator.

- Funding a child's education is another important goal of divorce settlements. For U/HNWI divorcees, a trust is probably the best solution to such challenges.

After the divorce

- Reconstructing one's estate plan should be a top priority for divorcees.

- Securing appropriate insurance (life, disability, and health insurance) is a big part of that effort.

Multiple or "blended" families

- Multiple families face a variety of unique financial challenges. The best solution to such challenges is to have a frank and open discussion before tying the knot.

- Adoption is another financial challenge facing multiple families. Those couples who decide to adopt should be aware of the financial liabilities they're accepting.

- Estate planning can be exceptionally difficult for multiple families. U/HNWIs should be cautious about constructing joint estate plans after a divorce.

## Resources

There is no lack of resources that will help you with the emotional and financial consequences of divorce. Just be aware, however, that information offered in many books and/or websites may not be applicable in your jurisdiction.

*The Divorce Mediation Answer Book* by Dolores Dean Walker and Carol A. Butler

*Getting Divorced Without Ruining Your Life* by Sam Margulies

## Websites

*www.divorcesource.com* – all sorts of resources for divorcees

*www.divorcenet.com* – professional listings, bulletin boards, and more

# Working with a wealth advisor

- *What U/HNWIs look for in a wealth advisor*
- *The person you're looking for: tangible qualities, intangible qualities*
- *The firm you're looking for: specialized focus, special services*
- *Making a change for the right reasons*

*"The best advice is only as good as the use we make of it."*

**Anonymous**

t's hard to go it alone in this world. And in the world of personal finance, it's nearly impossible. That's particularly true for U/HNWIs.

One of the refrains you've heard throughout this book is the need for U/HNWIs to seek professional help. That might sound a little biased coming from someone who works with U/HNWIs himself, but I think it's common sense. *The reason why U/HNWIs need to work with a professional is because they have too much to lose.* Once the investment portfolio reaches a certain size, you have a unique opportunity to secure freedom – a kind of freedom very few people ever experience. Such an opportunity should be valued highly, and should not be squandered by ill-conceived and poorly-executed financial decisions. The stakes involved suggest that it only makes sense to hire a specialist to handle your wealth for you.

With wealth comes a number of challenges – and these challenges aren't the same as those experienced by investors of more modest means. The challenges of wealth demand careful attention and more complicated solutions. Try to navigate through these challenges alone, and you could end up costing yourself your fortune. An experienced, capable professional can alert you to these challenges before they affect you, and highlight the specific opportunities that you may not have been aware of. Add to that the complicated and intricate details of other elements of wealth management – taxation, estate planning issues, business succession – and I'm sure you'll agree that even if you had all the time in the world, it would simply be too much for one person to handle. Most of the wealthy people I've met have better things to do with their time.

But not just anyone will do. The complexities of the U/HNWI portfolio demands a professional of the highest calibre. That's a rare breed. Which means U/HNWIs need to know what they're looking for when they look for a professional. This appendix will show you. By the end of this appendix, you'll know more about some of the specific qualities that U/HNWIs need in a wealth advisor. You'll be better able to fairly assess the quality of the product your prospective choice is offering, and you'll be able to determine how his or her personal qualities (i.e., drive, ambition, etc.) may fit with your objectives. This section will also tell you what to look for in the firm for which your prospect works, and help you determine whether that firm is committed to satisfying the unique needs of the wealthy. All of which will help you ensure you get the specialized service and customized advice your wealth demands.

## The search for advice

By and large, U/HNWIs have a good idea of what they're looking for when they look for a wealth advisor. In a survey conducted by consulting firm Arthur Anderson in 2000/2001, U/HNWIs from around the world were asked a variety of questions about how they prefer to receive service from the professionals who manage their wealth. Their findings are intriguing, with wide-ranging implications for those who work in the financial industry, and for those U/HNWIs who are looking for an advisor.

## The personal touch

In an age of internet trading and hand-held communications, most U/HNWIs still value one-on-one contact when it comes to managing their wealth. 55% of survey respondents to the Arthur Anderson survey are looking for a contact-driven relationship with a financial professional they can trust, rather than an online relationship with a computer database. What's more, most respondents stated a strong preference for a well-developed personal relationship compared to a "hired gun" system involving a rotating list of specialists.

## Products and research? Or advice?

When shopping for a financial professional, most U/HNWIs aren't looking for a financial secretary – someone who fetches research, executes orders, and never questions the U/HNWI's decisions – but rather a strategic partner. When asked what features of the relationship were important to them, most U/HNWIs placed relatively little importance on issues like access to research, up-to-date market data, and other functions that do-it-yourselfers crave.

## Service and expertise

In terms of service, U/HNWIs are discriminating buyers. Like other investors, most U/HNWIs look for regular meetings with their financial professionals, along with detailed, regular reporting. They're also looking for a professional who can provide "open architecture" financial solutions – that is, a wide range of financial options and alternatives, rather than pre-packaged, exclusive products offered by a single firm. By and large, U/HNWIs are looking for top talent when they go shopping for a financial professional. When asked to rank the factors that determine how they choose an investment professional, U/HNWIs ranked product capability a 70 out of 100. Obviously, the capability of the individual to understand and present a wide variety of financial options was an important part of that score. 57% of U/HNWI respondents cited the ability to provide venture capital opportunities was an important factor in their decision to work with a given professional. A further 53% said the ability to provide access to alternative investments (such as hedge funds) was important.

## Performance matters

Given the relative importance U/HNWIs place on these highly sophisticated investments, it should come as no surprise that performance matters to U/HNWIs. Asked to rank the performance of certain factors when considering working with a financial professional, the average U/HNWI ranked historical performance a score of 80 out of 100 – higher than any other factor. Many U/HNWIs expressed a willingness to engage in performance-based compensation for quality advice. Fully 45% of those surveyed responded they would prefer minimum flat fees to be coupled with some form of performance-based compensation. 25% more noted they would prefer performance based fees that incorporate a profit-sharing structure. Such responses may help to explain the shift to fee-based service by more and more wealth advisors who serve the U/HNWI population.

I was pleased when I read these findings. For the most part, they back up my own observation that most U/HNWIs find professional financial advice of considerable value.

But what about those who don't yet have a wealth advisor? What can they do to ensure they have access to quality investment advice and top-flight service? Here is a brief summary of how a U/HNWI like you can find a trusted, independent wealth advisor.

## Selecting a wealth advisor: what you're looking for

Shopping for professional advice is like shopping for anything else: the process works better if you know what you're looking for. A good place to start is to break down the search into two areas: the skills and qualities of the individual person, and the abilities and reputation of the firm for which that person works.

### The person **you're looking for**

While you'll most likely be drawing on the services of an entire team of financial professionals, the most important of these will be your wealth advisor. This is the person who will have first-hand knowledge of your personal finances, and co-ordinate strategies with the various specialists you'll be using. In this way, you can think of this person as your "personal CFO."

Ideally, your choice will have a wide range of experience, and a deep, probing knowledge of complicated financial subjects. He or she should have a well-developed sense of judgement, and an ability to understand and explain not only your individual life circumstances, but what's going on in the markets too. That's a lot to be looking for, so let's examine some of these qualities one by one. I've divided them into two general qualities: tangible and intangible.

## Tangibles: experience and education

Obviously, the education and experience of your prospective choice should factor largely in your decision. As far as experience goes, you're looking for an individual who has a number of U/HNWIs already in their client base. Personally, I'm of the mind that a wide range of experience is probably better than a narrow specialization: the typical U/HNWI needs someone skillful with retirement planning, business succession and divestiture planning, charitable giving strategies, insurance, as well as elite-level portfolio construction and management. As a general rule, I would eliminate anyone with less than a decade of experience serving U/HNWI clients – but again, this is a general rule. Probably more important than the sheer number of years is the *kind* of experience the person has had. You'll want your choice to have worked on the *client* side of the business. Even years of experience on the institutional side of the industry can't really prepare you for sitting down with real people and solving real life challenges. Unfortunately, turnover at some firms can be very high, forcing people into client-side positions before they're really ready for it.

In terms of education, there are a wide variety of degrees, designations, and diplomas a financial professional can achieve. Unfortunately, there is no international body co-ordinating these designations, so make sure to investigate just what the initials mean before you become too impressed by them. Here is a brief run-down of some of the most common credentials you should be aware of:

### Bachelor of Arts, Commerce, Science (BA, B Comm, B.Sc.); Master of Business Administration (MBA); Bachelor of Law (LLB) (worldwide)

Standard university degrees that are recognized in most countries. Program lengths and composition will vary depending on the country in which the degree was granted; a four-year program is typical for most bachelor degrees, while two years is standard for graduate education or professional degrees.

### Certified Financial Planner (CFP); Registered Financial Planner (RFP) (North America)

An advisor who has completed ongoing educational requirements and examinations specific to the construction and organization of personalized financial plans.

### Chartered Life Underwriter (CLU) (North America)

An advisor in the USA or Canada who has completed advanced training in life and health insurance, as well as employee benefits – an essential designation to look for if it's estate planning services or insurance products you need.

**Chartered Accountant (CA) (worldwide); Certified General Accountant (CGA), Certified Management Accountant (CMA) (Canada)**

An advisor who has detailed and specific knowledge of taxation and accounting issues. Requirements vary according to the particular designation. CAs must usually complete a university degree, two years of further education, and successfully pass a comprehensive examination.

**Chartered Financial Analyst (CFA) (North America)**

An advisor who has completed comprehensive financial education requirements, supervised by the U.S.–based Association for Investment Management and Research. A common designation among stock analysts and professional money managers.

**Certified Investment Manager (CIM) (Canada)**

An advisor who has completed specialized training and education, with a focus on portfolio and wealth management. Supervised by the Canadian Securities Institute.

**Fellow of the Canadian Securities Institute (FCSI) (Canada)**

An advisor who has completed extensive education requirements (including completion of lower-level courses and training), and has at least five years' experience in the industry. The designation also requires the completion of an ethics module.

This is by no means an exhaustive list, but rather some of the initials you'll come across most frequently. Of course, what looks good on paper doesn't necessarily look good in the cold, clear light of day. Just because your prospective choices are *qualified* to do what they do, doesn't mean they're actually *good* at it.

**Tangibles: performance, portfolios, and people**

After you've taken a look at the *person*, you'll want to take a look at the *product*. That means taking a close look at the hard data: the investment policy statement, the portfolio composition, and the corresponding performance figures for real-life portfolios constructed for U/HNWI clients like you.

Most established professionals are willing to provide this information relatively easily. But you need to understand what you're looking at before you begin to assess quality. Usually, this means looking at an "investment policy statement." The IPS is a detailed, client-specific statement of principle that lays down the "rules" by which the investment portfolio will be managed. Take a quick glance at the one that's been provided – there should be clear, tangible goals and a strong sense of purpose. If it's too general, too vague, or simply unclear, you should ask yourself why.

Next, you'll want to look at the sample portfolios. You shouldn't spend too much time comparing these to your own situation – remember, everyone's different, and your portfolio probably will be too. But at the very least, it should be clear how the portfolio composition relates to the policy statement you read. At this point, it's not important that you discuss why specific recommendations were made – what you're trying to evaluate is the approach. Does it look like this person is selling one particular product, or products from one particular firm? If so, ask why. Does it look like the portfolio is built to solve specific challenges, or is it a real "dog's breakfast," with a little bit of everything thrown in? In an ideal case, you should look at the portfolio and come away with a strong sense of the person's ability to match a variety of investment products to specific client needs.

Finally, you'll want to take a look at the performance figures. This requires some caution and perspective. Performance numbers viewed in isolation are relatively useless; you need to juxtapose them against those of the general market to gain any true insight into how a professional adds value to a portfolio. Keep in mind, however, that the point of looking at performance numbers isn't really to see if a given professional can match a certain number, but rather if the professional can match a portfolio with a person's *risk tolerance*. And make sure you understand whether the figures represent after-tax returns. Obviously, such considerations can dramatically affect your assessment of the performance figures in front of you.

In my experience, most U/HNWIs understand that long-term performance is more important than short-term. But long term performance isn't the same thing as long-term investor *experience*. That's why you need to take a look at quarter-over-quarter performance – and year-over-year, and hopefully even longer than that too. What you're looking for are the swings – the volatility your professional will expose you to. A lot of things can happen in the space of twelve months when it comes to performance. A year that starts off with a dramatic boom can crash dramatically, only to break even by the end of the year. A year like that ends up looking fine on paper, but it doesn't really speak to the experience of the individual investor. By understanding what happens to portfolios on a quarterly or yearly basis, you'll be better able to see if the kind of performance your prospective choice can provide is the kind of performance your stomach can handle.

In addition to an examination of investment portfolios, you'll want to ask your prospective choice to provide a reference or two – again, something most established professionals are happy to provide. Make sure to call these people, and ask them some general questions about the plans and the portfolios your prospective choice has provided for them. Again, you're not really trying to figure out if the professional can satisfy your need for performance, but rather if the professional runs the kind of business where the client is respected, cared for, and even catered to – the kind of business that generates trust and loyalty from satisfied clients.

### Tangibles: fees and all that

Finally, you'll want to discuss fees. Most professionals will be frank and open about what they charge. You should be wary of those who aren't.

Very generally, there are two forms of fee structure in the financial services industry. The first, commission-based planning, is probably the more well-known. With such a structure, you pay nothing for planning and general advice (at least, not directly), but pay commissions on any investment products you buy. In recent years, this form of compensation has come under a lot of criticism, and for good reason: it gives less-than-scrupulous salespeople plenty of motivation to make inappropriate recommendations. Among professionals serving U/HNWIs, a flat-fee management structure is by far more common. In such a structure, the professional charges a flat fee based on assets under management, usually on a graduated scale depending on the size of the portfolio. Depending on the professional, additional charges may apply for specialized services (such as estate planning), and of course, there may be some fees that are built into managed products like mutual funds. The advantages of such a structure should be clear: a flat fee ensures commissions play no part in the advice given. It's also provides an excellent incentive for superior performance over the longer term. With a flat-fee structure, portfolio growth is in everyone's interests.

Make sure to examine the fee structure thoroughly before signing up with any wealth advisor. Pay particular attention to what services are covered under the fees, and what services aren't – you may be paying more for specialized services such as business succession planning, for instance, or for legal services like the drafting of a will. Above all else, remember that the old saying about getting what you pay for is especially true in the financial services industry. Most professionals who deal with U/HNWIs provide elite-level advice and superior service. Most of us think our fees are very reasonable given the value-added service we provide. Anyone daring to call themselves a professional should be able to look you in the eye with a straight face and say the same.

## Intangibles

Like it or not, the selection of a financial professional concerns more than objective, measurable qualities – ultimately, it comes down to "fit." After all, you and your family will hopefully be working with this person closely over many years, and potentially even over many generations. Things tend to go more smoothly if you can get along. While the exact qualities you'll be looking for will depend on your own personality, there are a couple of key qualities to keep an eye out for.

## Intangibles: approach

Let me be very clear about one point: U/HNWIs shouldn't be looking for a stock picker. Rather, you're looking for someone who can oversee your finances and co-ordinate effective strategies for your personal financial challenges – a personal CFO, in other words. This person will select qualified investment managers, and will help allocate and rebalance your assets to provide optimum diversification. This person will assess all your financial planning needs, from estate planning to tax planning to succession planning to everything else. When circumstances require, this person will seek out and retain the very best specialists who can execute your plan. All this is a lot different from someone who sits at a desk and reviews research reports. So have the professional in question talk to you about what he or she does for clients, and why. If you hear a lot of talk about performance, about market events, and about sophisticated, complex financial "theories," your guard should be up. If on the other hand the person talks about goals, lifestyle, and security, then you might have a real candidate on your hands.

## Intangibles: drive and passion

In any business, the enthusiasm of the personnel often determines the success of the enterprise. This is true of financial professionals too. U/HNWIs need a passionate, enthusiastic professional working with them – someone who exhibits an unusual excitement for what they do. You don't necessarily want someone who's chained to a desk, but you do want someone who still enjoys their job – someone who finds the financial world both an interesting and challenging place, someone who has no problem coming to the office in the morning, someone who's not thinking about the golf course when the clock strikes 3:00pm.

I might be ruffling some feathers here, but I think it's perfectly OK if the primary reason for that enthusiasm is remuneration. (I remember the immortal words of Gordon Gecko in the movie *Wall Street*, "greed is good." He may have had a point . . .) Let me qualify: I'm not talking about someone who exhibits a mean, miserly approach by charging outrageous fees, or someone who demonstrates a certain thrill in being able to con a grandmother out of her gold teeth. Rather, I'm talking about an intensity, an energy, a drive to make money both personally and for clients. In my experience, this kind of incentive is a good way U/HNWIs can end up getting what they pay for. After all, the best heart surgeons, hockey players, or CEOs tend to be the *best paid* heart surgeons, hockey players, or CEOs. It really is that simple.

Call me biased, but personally, I think the best wealth advisors are "real" people, not *sales*people. They are enthusiastic, professional, and committed to doing their jobs in the best way they are able. They understand the responsibility their clients have entrusted them with, and they treat client needs with respect. They are skilled listeners, but they have a backbone too: they aren't afraid of talking about what the client *needs,* not just what the client *wants.* But more than anything, they are *real* people. They have families, they care about the people around them, they care about their communities. They have their feet on the ground rather than their heads in the sky. They care less about the material benefits of wealth than they do about what difference they can make to their clients' lives. Again, that's not to say they don't appreciate what wealth can bring, and aren't driven to acquire more. But at the end of the day, such people understand that wealth is about more than just money. It's about *life.* They're in the business of changing people's lives for the better. That's what they offer you, and they're not afraid to tell you that. I like to think I'm that kind of professional. I've certainly worked very hard to be.

## The firm **you're looking for**

Simply put, the choice of investment firm is a more important one for U/HNWIs than it is for the general population. While there are many investment firms (both large and small) fully capable of handling the needs of the average investor, the needs of the U/HNWI – in terms of investment products and in terms of service – demand more attention. Which is why you want to know a little about the firm that's backing up your wealth advisor.

## Specialized focus

You'll need a firm experienced in dealing with the particular needs of U/HNWIs – and ideally, a firm that *specializes* in them. The company in question should be recognized as a leader in providing quality advice to U/HNWI clients, and should be able to explain how they do it. Large firms are probably the ideal choice here, but there are plenty of excellent boutique firms servicing the U/HNWI market. This is especially true in well-developed markets such as the USA.

As far as products go, look for "open architecture," not just proprietary products. To U/HNWIs, access to a wide variety of investment opportunities, wherever they may be in the world, regardless of what firm is underwriting them, is far more important than access to exclusive in-house products or programs. You'll also want to pay attention to the firm's access to top-quality alternative investment opportunities and research. You're looking for a company that can act as your gatekeeper to the opportunities open to people of substantial net worth. Not every firm fits the bill, so make sure to ask.

## Specialized services

Beyond products and opportunities, the firm should have specialized services available specifically for its U/HNWI clients. This can include a whole range of special frills – VIP and concierge services, or special considerations like at-home computer stations and access to portfolio managers and company executives. Depending on your own specific needs and lifestyle, these services may be very useful or completely irrelevant.

Some firms offer highly specialized investment services to the wealthy. You'll definitely want to ask any prospective choice about *family wealth* or *home office* services – specialized products and services offered to help meet the financial needs of your entire family. Integrated services like investment counselling for young adults, trust services, and intergenerational planning can make it easier to deal with some of the specific challenges of wealth. You'll also want to ask about a *rapid response team*. That's what we call it in my own practice – a team of financial specialists who can tackle complicated financial challenges that erupt in a short period of time. That kind of service can be a financial and psychological lifesaver if you're a U/HNWI whose financial position can change rapidly. An *exclusive business sales and divestitures group* is another specialized service my firm offers. If you're a business owner, these people can put you in contact with other buyers, and help secure the best price for your business, with a minimum of hassles. And, as I mentioned earlier, you'll also want to check to see if the firm has trained specialists in place to help you with hedging or divesting a large stock position. Not all firms have the resources to handle that kind of transaction, so ask.

## Time to move on: **making a change for the *right* reasons**

It happens. Despite the care and attention you've given to the selection process, there may well come a time when you realize you've hired the wrong person. When the problem is a clash of personalities, the decision is easy to make. The same can be said for those rare cases of out-and-out ineptitude. And there are times when high staff turnover or the loss of a significant team member makes it necessary to leave a given company. But most of the time it's not like that. Most of the time it's difficult to put your finger on the source of your dissatisfaction.

I'm going to be honest with you: sometimes, the decision to switch wealth advisors is made for the *wrong* reason. Namely, the reason of short-term performance. Quite simply, most investors have too short a mindset to judge performance fairly and objectively. It's easy for an investment manager to go through periods of underperformance (this is especially true when the manager is first allocating funds, or with those whose investment styles aren't in vogue). But that's not the way some U/HNWIs feel about it. They want consistently spectacular performance. And they want it every year.

This is an unrealistic expectation. Even the best money managers can suffer through periods of difficulty when they underperform their peers. But at the same time, underperformance is not what you're paying for. There must be some compromise. My general rule is this: if the person is a skilled professional experienced with U/HNWIs, with appropriate credentials and a team of specialists with whom to consult, give the advisor the benefit of the doubt for at least two to three years. Then take a look at your relationship with that person. Take a look at what that person has done for you, and compare your performance to a given benchmark – an index, other financial professionals or investment managers, etc. At the end of this examination, you should ask yourself a simple question: if you could do it over again, and sign a contract to "lock in" the performance you've realized over the past two or three years, would you? If you hesitate even a little, then your decision is made.

This isn't a hard-and-fast rule. There will be exceptions, when it's evident very early on that there is no sign of excellence. But most of the time, it will be an "on the line" type of situation. Speaking from my own experience, I've met with U/HNWIs who have come in for a second opinion on the state of their holdings. Frequently, there are things I can do to improve their position. But it's rare that I uncover a situation of complete incompetence — for the most part, the industry has developed beyond that (at least in the U/HNWI market). Bottom line: the ideal situation for the U/HNWI is to stick with one professional, rather than jump ship every few years. Unless your choice consistently fails to meet what you consider to be fair and objective expectations, I think you should take a long-term view and ride out the rough patches.

## A final word on professional help

When it works properly, the relationship between a wealth advisor and a U/HNWI is one of interested, active partnership. Both parties respect each other, and understand they must work together to achieve common goals. The financial professional respects the individual needs of the client, and listens to their concerns rather than simply dictating policy. On the client side, the U/HNWI trusts the financial professional, and respects both the professional's time and recommendations. These are the relationships I strive to develop in my own practice. They are the ones I most value.

## Summary: appendix

### Key **concepts:**

- There are many reasons why U/HNWIs need to work with a wealth advisor. The most important of these reasons: U/HNWIs have too much to lose.

- U/HNWIs typically look for a variety of things in their financial professional. Among the most important is the one-on-one, personal relationships and the ability to provide a wide array of investment opportunities.

- U/HNWIs need to think carefully about the firm they work with. Ideally, that firm should have extensive experience in dealing with U/HNWI clients, and should offer access to elite-level opportunities and financial solutions.

- As far as the person goes, the qualities can be separated into two sections:

- Tangible qualities

  experience and education: U/HNWIs need to work with a professional who is experienced in handling sizable portfolios. U/HNWIs should familiarize themselves with the variety of financial designations.

  performance and portfolios: while an evaluation of performance is an important part of the selection process, U/HNWIs need to understand how performance figures (both good and bad) can be misleading.

  fees: there are two general forms of fees for managing U/HNWI accounts. Generally, flat-fee management is the more appropriate of these.

- Intangibles:

  approach: you're looking for someone who understands that the business of managing wealth is ultimately more about lifestyle than performance.

  drive and passion: you're looking for someone who's enthusiastic about managing wealth and helping you overcome wealth challenges.

- There are times when you may have to "fire" your professional and seek new help. Such a decision should be considered very carefully, and based upon sound reasons. Short-term performance doesn't fall into that category.

# About the authors: **Thane Stenner**

Thane Stenner is First Vice-President and Senior Investment Advisor with CIBC Wood Gundy in the Vancouver area. Thane formerly worked as a Director with the International Private Wealth Services Group of Merrill Lynch.

An honors graduate in Investment Analysis and Portfolio Management from Arizona State University, Thane specializes in elite-level portfolio construction and wealth management for a select group of high-net-worth and ultra-high-net-worth clients. Thane also provides investment advice and financial consulting services for a number of charitable foundations. In December of 2000, *Business in Vancouver* magazine formally recognized Thane for his expertise in dealing with high-net-worth individuals by naming him "Advisor to the Wealthy."

Within his firm, Thane and his team work closely with a group of highly-skilled financial specialists, a group that provides tailor-made financial strategies to some of the wealthiest people in North America and the world. CIBC Wood Gundy is the full-service retail investment division of CIBC World Markets Inc. CIBC World Markets is one of North America's premiere wealth management firms, with 1.5 million clients and $156-billion in assets under administration.

Thane's commitment to top-quality client service has won him a number of industry accolades, including being one of only 23 Canadian financial advisors to receive the client-driven Dalbar Seal in the year 2000. He has been awarded "Ace Advisor" status by U.S.-based *Ticker* magazine, and was also recently given the prestigious "Top 40 Under 40" award by *Business in Vancouver* magazine.

Thane is a well-known authority on investment and other financial matters. He is often canvassed by the media for his opinions and observations on the wealthy and the way they invest. His reputation for clear, confident financial communication has led him to the advisory boards of both *Advisor's Edge* and *IE: Money* magazines.

Thane believes strongly in being an active professional citizen. He is currently on the Board of Directors for the Greater Vancouver YMCA. He is also the past chairperson for the FSCI ethics committee. He has been a hard-working fundraiser for a number of local and national charities, including the Canadian Cancer Society, the Peace Arch Hospital Foundation, the CKNW Orphan's Fund, and the Surrey Food Bank. More recently, he and his wife Darci were appointed co-chairs of the fundraising committee for the new Surrey Family YMCA. To date, the committee has raised over $5,000,000 for the new centre, a figure that includes a significant personal contribution from the Stenners themselves.

When Thane's not busy helping clients, you'll usually find him spending time with his family. A big believer in the value of personal fitness, Thane is involved in a number of sports, including indoor rock climbing, weightlifting, and ice hockey (his personal favourite). He and his wife Darci enjoy travelling, and look forward to their journeys as an opportunity to learn new things from the many cultures of the world.

Questions for Thane may be directed by e-mail message to thane.stenner@cibc.ca . For more information about *True Wealth*, visit *www.truewealth.ca* .

# About the authors: James Dolan

James Dolan is a writer and creative professional who has written extensively on a wide range of personal finance topics. He holds an honors BA from the University of British Columbia and an MA from Queen's University in Kingston, Ontario. For the past five years, James has worked with The Newsletter Factory, a marketing and communications firm serving the financial services industry. He has written articles for many of the major financial companies in Canada, including Merrill Lynch, Fidelity Investments, RBC Dominion Securities, BMO Nesbitt Burns, and TD Evergreen. His writing has appeared in a variety of newspapers, magazines, and investment newsletters.

James currently lives and works in Vancouver. He is looking forward to becoming a U/HNWI himself one day.

# Rave reviews from fellow industry professionals

*"You won't 'get' this book unless you've already got real wealth. For those who do, the book offers something I've never seen from any guide to money: enduring perspective. Thane knows what you're going through. His perspective is enhanced by the years of work he's done with families that have real wealth. This fabulous book is the one important read you need this year. Share it with your family and friends."*

**Duff Young, CFA** – CEO, FundMonitor.com Corp., BESTSELLING AUTHOR AND COLUMNIST, *The Globe And Mail*

*"True Wealth should find a large and receptive audience as the number of individuals with over $1 Million of investable financial assets grew rapidly throughout the 1990's and is expected to continue to grow at a rapid pace in the coming decade. Good advice is a very valuable commodity and this book provides lots of sound advice and insight for the increasing number of people fortunate enough to have achieved the 'magic million' status."*

**Colin Deane** – PRINCIPAL, Global Financial Services Cap Gemini Ernst & Young, Toronto

*"High-net-worth clients unfamiliar with the techniques advisors must use to protect their clients' wealth will find this book an excellent education, as will advisors who aspire to this market. From collars and calls to estate taxes and charitable giving, True Wealth will guide those adept at making a fortune through the processes used to keep and maintain it. Explanations of complex subjects are lucid and liberally illustrated with examples that high-net-worth clients will take to heart."*

**Marlene Y. Satter** – SENIOR EDITOR, *Investment Advisor* magazine

*"Thane Stenner is a highly regarded private wealth advisor. His book,* True Wealth, *offers practical solutions to the unique challenges faced by the wealthy and the super-wealthy: how to protect and continue to grow their wealth amid uncertain markets, how to deal with the tax man, how to maximize the effectiveness of charitable giving, and how to simplify their financial affairs.* True Wealth *provides common sense and uncommon insight on these issues and more, backed by solid research and by case studies drawn from Thane's extensive experience. Whether you have $1-Million, $10-Million or $100-Million or more – or whether you simply aspire to be wealthy – you should benefit from reading* True Wealth *and applying some of its practical advice to your own financial affairs."*

**Bill Sterling, PhD** – CHIEF INVESTMENT OFFICER, CI Global Advisors, FORMER GLOBAL CHIEF ECONOMIST, Merrill Lynch and BESTSELLING CO-AUTHOR, *Boomernomics*

*"Here it is at last. A book that is long overdue! Few individuals need as much guidance in their financial affairs as the wealthy, and even fewer advisors understand the plight of the wealthy as Thane Stenner does. If you're a high-net-worth individual, or expect to be one day, you need to read this book!"*

**Tim Cestnick, CA, CFP, TRUST AND ESTATE PRACTITIONER (TEP)** – AUTHOR, *Winning the Tax Game* and *Winning the Estate Planning Game*, MANAGING DIRECTOR, National Tax Services, AIC Group of Funds

*"Essential reading for investors with substantial wealth.* True Wealth *explores the broad financial issues that wealthy investors need to understand and translates them into specific guidance and advice. Of critical importance, it goes beyond generalities and gets into the specifics required to make informed decisions – and does so in an engaging fashion which is easy to read and understand."*

**Dan Richards** – PRESIDENT, Richards Buitenhuis Associates

"Busy executives in fast growing companies (private or publicly traded) have little or no time to spend on managing their personal financial affairs. Very few financial advisors understand the many challenges and risks that face today's business owner and corporate executive as well as Thane Stenner does. Thane understands the value of time and his new book offers many insights and recommendations that will help "wired" executives regain their family balance, control their financial futures and reduce the risks of having all their eggs in one business basket. The sections on selling businesses and dealing with concentration risk are worth the cost of entry alone. True Wealth is a blueprint for showing busy executives how to protect their hard earned assets and enjoy life by knowing that they have secured their wealth."

**Christopher Hanna, PhD** – PRESIDENT AND CEO, TeraMEDICA Inc., Milwaukee, WI, USA

"Taking on the life and financial challenges of the wealthy is a uniquely courageous thing, especially in a country that likes to skewer its rich and famous. Stenner, no stranger to this world, offers up an immensely readable abundance of personal and technical wisdom...the kind those with serious cash should not even remotely consider living without."

**Joanne Thomas Yaccato** – FOUNDER AND PRESIDENT, Women and Money Inc., Educating Women About Money, Educating Companies About Women, AUTHOR, *Balancing Act*

"Having known Thane on both a personal and a professional level for over ten years, I'm in a unique position to judge his talent. And I can say without hesitation that no one else I know is more capable of either talking about or solving the unique challenges facing wealthy people today. What makes Thane stand out is his understanding of not only the financial challenges of wealth, but the personal challenges – Thane understands the mindset of the high-net-worth investor as much as he does the financial strategies. Quite simply, True Wealth is a world-class resource written by an exceptional and trusted financial professional who works for a top-notch firm. A great addition to the library of every wealthy investor."

**Bill Holland** – PRESIDENT AND CEO, CI Group

"A must read for those who have accumulated wealth and for those who aspire to do so. It will provide you with a fascinating insight into how to maintain and grow your wealth for your own benefit. But just as importantly, it will also show you ways in which to steward your wealth for your loved ones and society at large as you define it. True Wealth will clearly help you define your 'True Self' when it comes to principled wealth accumulation."

**David R. Temple, TEP** – Insurance & Estate Planning Specialist

"As a lawyer with 15 years of experience in assisting with the purchase and sale of entrepreneur-owned businesses, I've acted for many business owners who, having sold their business, suddenly realize they have a serious new responsibility – how to preserve their new-found wealth. Thane Stenner's book True Wealth answers this need. I strongly recommend that all business owners read this book – but especially business owners who are thinking of selling their business. True Wealth goes a long way to helping these new multi-millionaires preserve their hard earned fortune!"

**Don C. Sihota** – BUSINESS LAW PARTNER, Clark, Wilson, Lawyers, Vancouver, Canada

"True Wealth is a must read for high-net-worth individuals and their advisors. Wealth accumulation, wealth utilization and wealth preservation are discussed with an insight never before put to paper. High-net-worth individuals will use True Wealth as a confirmation, or challenge, of their tax minimization strategies, balanced with the advancement of family, community and charitable objectives."

**Tom R. Kirstein, CA** – Kirstein, Neidig & Vance Chartered Accountants

"Stenner's book on wealth management is one of the most comprehensive books produced to date on the topic in North America. A powerful reference tool for the high-net-worth individual. An essential educational tool for the high-net-worth financial advisor."

**Kurt Rosentreter,** CA, CFP, CIMA, TEP — BESTSELLING AUTHOR AND RENOWNED WEALTH MANAGEMENT STRATEGIST, VICE-PRESIDENT, Private Client Services, AIC Limited

"Thane Stenner has created a blueprint for keeping, building, and managing wealth. More importantly, this book addresses broader wealth management issues including taxes, estate planning, trusts and foundations. True Wealth is a comprehensive and cogent analysis of the key issues facing the wealthy and those who advise them."

**Robert Parnell** — PRESIDENT, Tremont Investment Management, Inc. (WELL-KNOWN AND RESPECTED HEDGE FUND MANAGER)

"This is a unique book for anyone interested in the subject of wealth. It focuses on the financial challenges, problems and opportunities of the wealthy. The author shares his extensive experience in helping high-net-worth individuals deal with their assets. The parts of the book describing how the wealthy think about their wealth — and the common mistakes made by their respective personality types — makes for particularly interesting reading since it holds a mirror up to us all. The book's scope is wide and comprehensive with sections on topics such as business divestiture, stock options, and how to make charitable donations for the best effect. A fascinating and penetrating study."

**J. Mark Mobius,** PhD — MANAGING DIRECTOR, Franklin-Templeton Asset Management Ltd., PORTFOLIO MANAGER, Franklin-Templeton Emerging Markets Fund

"My experience in discussing wealth management with more than 50,000 investors over the past ten years has me convinced that Thane has hit the nail on the head — the thing that wealthy people fear most is not being wealthy. This is one of the most encompassing and compelling treatments of the subject of managing money for high-net-worth individuals that I have ever seen — and from someone who knows whereof they speak."

**George Hartman** — BESTSELLING AUTHOR, Risk is STILL a Four Letter Word, COLUMNIST, Investment Executive

"Believe it or not, the simple thing is making money...most everybody with a bit of entrepreneurial spirit has that chance once or even several times in their working life. The tough part is keeping it and making it grow...Thane's book is a simple guide that gives you the building blocks to keep and grow your fortune. A great and easy read."

**Michael Levy** — FINANCIAL ANALYST, CKNW Radio, Vancouver Canada, SENIOR EXECUTIVE VICE-PRESIDENT, Custom House Currency Exchange

"So you want to know how the wealthy think and invest? Then read the book written by the man who has been dealing with high-net-worth investors since the days they were just called rich people! Thane Stenner examines the many unique problems, opportunities and needs of this growing group of investors, drawing on a wealth of experience spanning more than a decade."

**Rob Bell** — VICE-PRESIDENT, Morningstar

"Thane's track record speaks for itself. His expert insights on all aspects of wealth management will help make the road travelled by high-net-worth Investors smooth and profitable."

**Donald F. Reed** — PRESIDENT & CHIEF EXECUTIVE OFFICER, Franklin-Templeton Investments Corp.

"I have known Thane Stenner personally for over eight years and have watched him invest more time and resources into making his advisory practice one of the top in Canada, and become an expert on the high-net-worth investor. You do not achieve that without hard work and satisfied clients. Certainly wealthy people (and those aspiring to wealth) can benefit from reading this book. More importantly, serious financial advisors MUST read AND follow this book. Why? Because, those high-net-worth clients will become increasing dependent on your advice — advice that is best done with a true understanding of their life situation and the complex needs of the wealthy."

**Stephen J. Kangas, CA, CFA** — MANAGING EDITOR, Fundlibrary.com

"While conventional wisdom says that wealth makes life easy, experience shows that achieving high-net-worth status actually creates many new challenges. But, as Thane Stenner shows in True Wealth, dependable wealth management solutions are at hand for anyone prepared to follow his logical and truly co-ordinated approach. Highly recommended!"

**Phil Cunningham** — PRESIDENT, Mackenzie Financial Services Inc.

"Becoming a millionaire is just the first step. It's keeping your money and enjoying it that's the real challenge. Thane Stenner reveals the secrets of everlasting wealth in this highly readable and immensely useful book. A must-read for anyone who has achieved financial success."

**Gordon Pape** — BESTSELLING AUTHOR, 6 Steps to $1-Million and Buyers Guide to Mutual Funds

"True Wealth articulately addresses and provides solutions to the issues topical in the mind of the ultra-high-net-worth individual. It is an excellent educational and reference tool for advisors and their clients. Congratulations Thane, you certainly nailed it."

**Michael A. Lee-Chin** — CHAIRMAN AND CHIEF EXECUTIVE OFFICER, AIC Group of Funds

"Thane's experience gives him a unique insight into the challenges facing the wealthy. His thoughts and ideals concerning the responsibilities of the wealthy are especially important. This is a "must-read" book for everyone, but especially for the wealthy for "...to whom much is given, from him much will be required." (Luke 12:48)"

**Tim Collings** — PROFESSOR, Tech BC, V-Chip Inventor